I love brandy, but I can't stand chocolates with brandy in them. If you ate a ton of them, could you really end up drunk? (My current weight...70 kg!! That's right, one kilo at a time is great! I'm doing fantastic!!)

--Mitsutoshi Shimabukuro, 2016

Mitsutoshi Shimabukuro made his debut in **Weekly Shonen Jump** in 1996. He is best known for **Seikimatsu Leader Den Takeshi!**, for which he won the 46th Shogakukan Manga Award for children's manga in 2001. His current series, **Toriko**, began serialization in Japan in 2008.

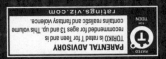

www.viz.com

TORIKO VOL. 38
SHONEN JUMP Manga Edition

STORY AND ART BY MITSUTOSHI SHIMABUKURO

Translation/Christine Dashiell
Weekly Shonen Jump Lettering/Erika Terriquez
Graphic Novel Touch-Up Art & Lettering/Pado Gattone & Chiara Antonelli
Design/Veronica Casson
Editor/Marlene First

TORIKO © 2008 by Mitsutoshi Shimabukuro
All rights reserved. First published in Japan in 2008 by SHUEISHA Inc., Tokyo.
English translation rights arranged by SHUEISHA Inc.

The stories, characters and incidents mentioned in
this publication are entirely fictional.

Printed in the U.S.A.

Published by VIZ Media, LLC
P.O. Box 77010
San Francisco, CA 94107

10 9 8 7 6 5 4 3 2 1
First printing, May 2017

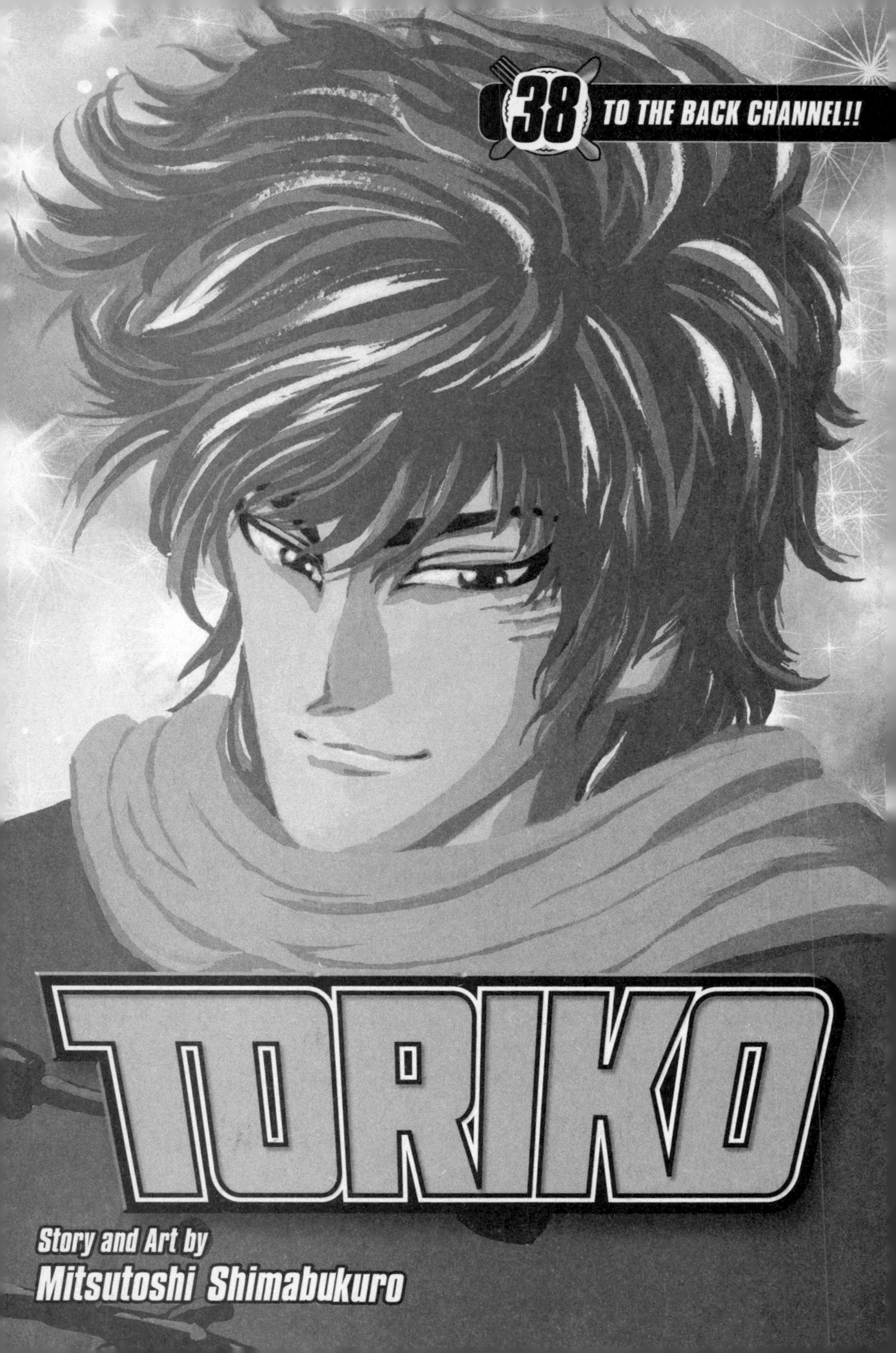

38 TO THE BACK CHANNEL!!

TORIKO

Story and Art by
Mitsutoshi Shimabukuro

TORIKO

THE ULTIMATE GOURMET HUNTER WHO'S ON A NEVER-ENDING QUEST TO FIND AND SCARF UP THE RAREST FOODS ON EARTH! HE FIGHTS WITH A KNIFE (HIS FIST), A FORK (HIS FIST), AND SPIKED PUNCH (ALSO HIS FISTS).

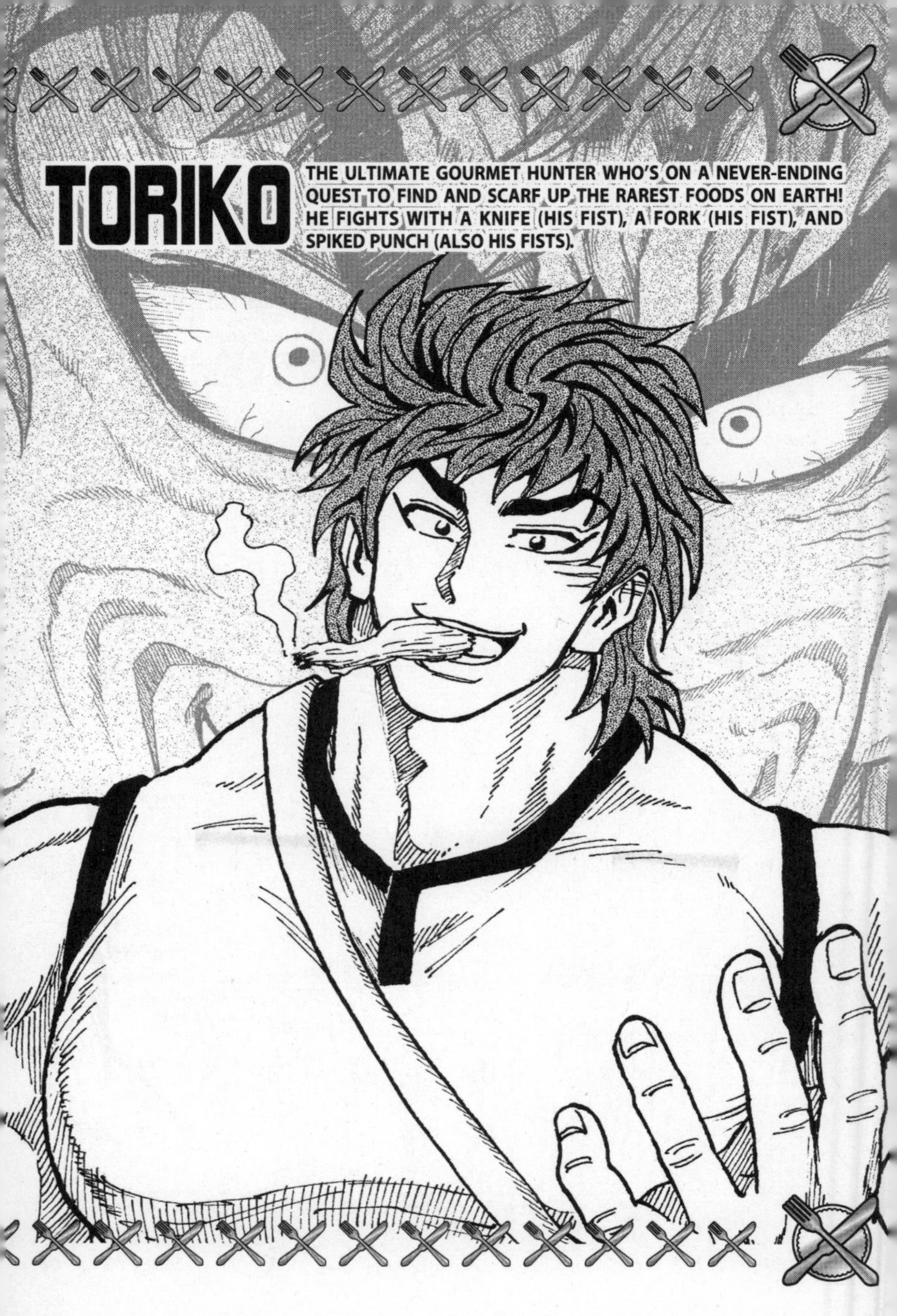

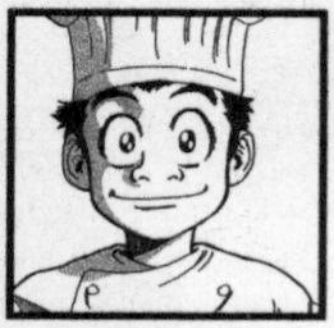

● KOMATSU
TALENTED IGO HOTEL CHEF AND TORIKO'S #1 FAN.

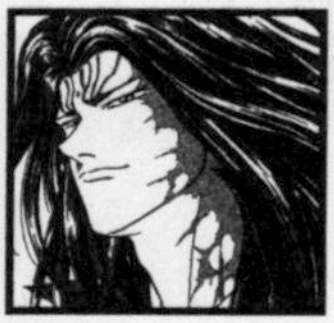

● STARJUN
ONE OF GOURMET CORP'S THREE VICE CHEFS. HE HAS NOW JOINED FORCES WITH TORIKO AND THE GANG.

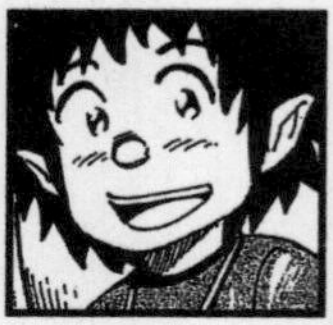

● CHACO
A BOY FROM BLUE GRILL WHO RANDOMLY MEETS KOMATSU. HIS MOTHER IS PARTICIPATING IN THE PROJECT, SO HE LIVES ALONE.

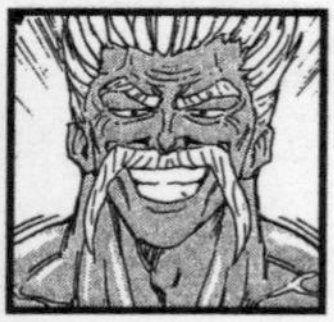

● ICHIRYU
THE FORMER IGO PRESIDENT AND DISCIPLE OF THE LATE GOURMET GOD ACACIA. HE DIES WHILE FIGHTING MIDORA.

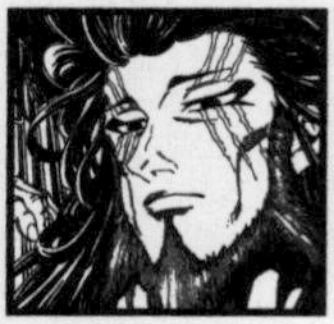

● MIDORA
THE BOSS OF GOURMET CORP. HE'S ACACIA'S PUPIL, LIKE ICHIRYU. HE'S AFTER THE PHANTOM INGREDIENT, GOD.

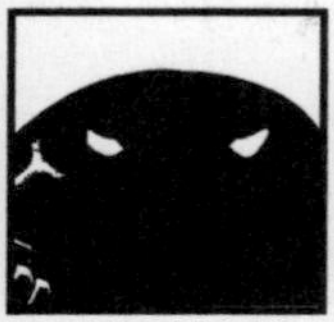

● DON SLIME
THE KING OF BLUE GRILL. HE'S A FOOD SPIRIT SHROUDED IN MYSTERY WHO HAS JOINED FORCES WITH KOMATSU AND THE GANG ON THEIR MISSION.

WHAT'S FOR DINNER

THE AGE OF GOURMET IS DECLARED OVER. IN ORDER TO GET KOMATSU BACK FROM GOURMET CORP., TORIKO VENTURES INTO THE GOURMET WORLD ON HIS OWN. EIGHTEEN MONTHS LATER, THE PAIR RETURNS HOME ALONG WITH A MASSIVE AMOUNT OF PROVISIONS TO FEED THE HUMAN WORLD. UPON THEIR RETURN, THE TWO ARE COMMISSIONED BY THE NEW IGO PRESIDENT, MANSOM, TO SEARCH FOR THE REMAINDER OF ICHIRYU'S FULL COURSE MEAL. JOINING FORCES WITH THE OTHER FOUR KINGS, COCO, SUNNY AND ZEBRA, THEY SUCCEED IN RETRIEVING THE MIRACLE INGREDIENT THAT WILL SAVE HUMANITY FROM STARVATION: THE BILLION BIRD. IN ORDER TO REVIVE THE AGE OF GOURMET, THE FIVE OF THEM TAKE AN ENORMOUS ORDER. THEY MUST TRAVEL TO THE GOURMET WORLD AND FIND ACACIA'S FULL-COURSE MEAL. ARMED WITH THE INFORMATION AND THE OCTOMELON CAMPER MONSTER GIVEN TO THEM ICHIRYU'S MYSTERIOUS FRIEND CHICHI, THE FIVE MEN SET THEIR SIGHTS ON THE GOURMET WORLD.

TEPPEI, WHO HAD DEFECTED TO NEO, ATTACKS KOMATSU. WHAT BRINGS KOMATSU BACK FROM THE BRINK OF DEATH IS ACACIA'S SOUP, "PAIR." KOMATSU MAKES A FULL RECOVERY AND PREPARES PAIR, BRINGING TOGETHER THE WORLD OF THE LIVING, AND THE WORLD OF THE DEAD—THE BACK CHANNEL. THAT IS WHERE TORIKO AND THE GANG LEARN THE TRUTH HIDDEN WITHIN ACACIA'S FULL-COURSE MEAL. KAKA, THEIR GUIDE, INFORMS THEM THAT THE BLUE NITRO'S PLAN TO RESURRECT A MONSTER. UPON THE START OF THE GOURMET ECLIPSE, THE EARTH WILL SUCCUMB TO RUIN. IN ORDER TO AVOID THIS CRISIS, TORIKO AND THE GANG SPLIT UP TO FIND THE REMAINING PARTS.

KOMATSU IS LEFT IN CHARGE OF ACACIA'S FISH DISH "ANOTHER" AND ARRIVES AT THE DEEP SEA GOURMET CITY OF BLUE GRILL IN AREA 6 ALONG WITH THE OTHER CHEFS. ONCE THERE, THE SUDDEN DISAPPEARANCE OF A LITTLE BOY NAMED CHACO LEADS HIM ON A PATH TO DISCOVERING A SINISTER PROJECT BEING CONDUCTED IN THE UNDERSEA CIVILIZATION.

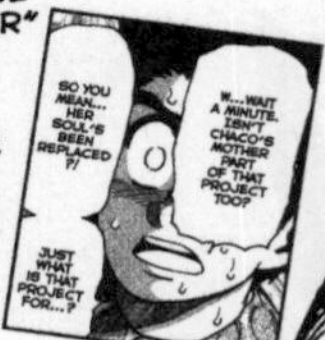
W...WAIT A MINUTE. ISN'T CHACO'S MOTHER PART OF THAT PROJECT TOO?
SO YOU MEAN... HER SOUL'S BEEN REPLACED?!
JUST WHAT IS THAT PROJECT FOR...?

MEANWHILE, THE BOSS OF THE GOURMET CORP., MIDORA, MAKES A PROMISE WITH TORIKO AND HEADS TO CONFRONT HIS FATED RIVAL: JOIE! THE BLUE NITRO ARE MAKING PROGRESS WITH THEIR OWN PLANS TO COMPLETELY REVIVE THE GOURMET CELL DEMON KNOWN AS NEO, AND TIME IS OF THE ESSENCE.

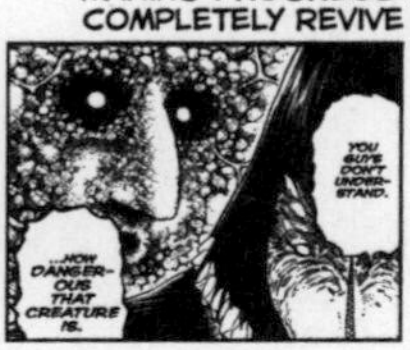
YOU GUYS DON'T UNDER-STAND.
...HOW DANGER-OUS THAT CREATURE IS.

Contents

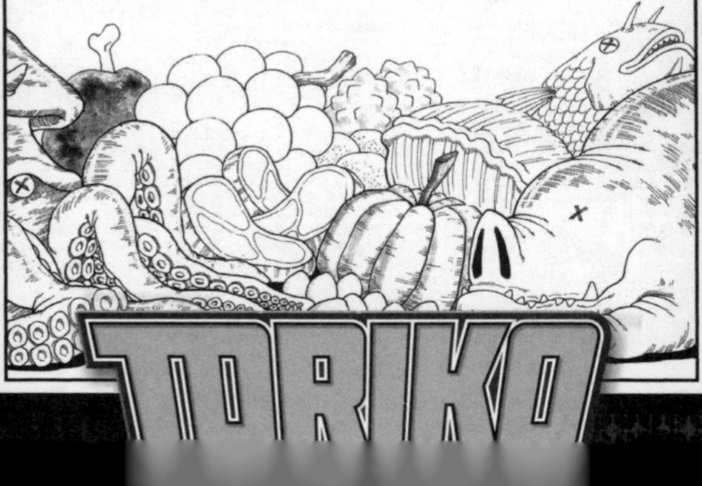
TORIKO

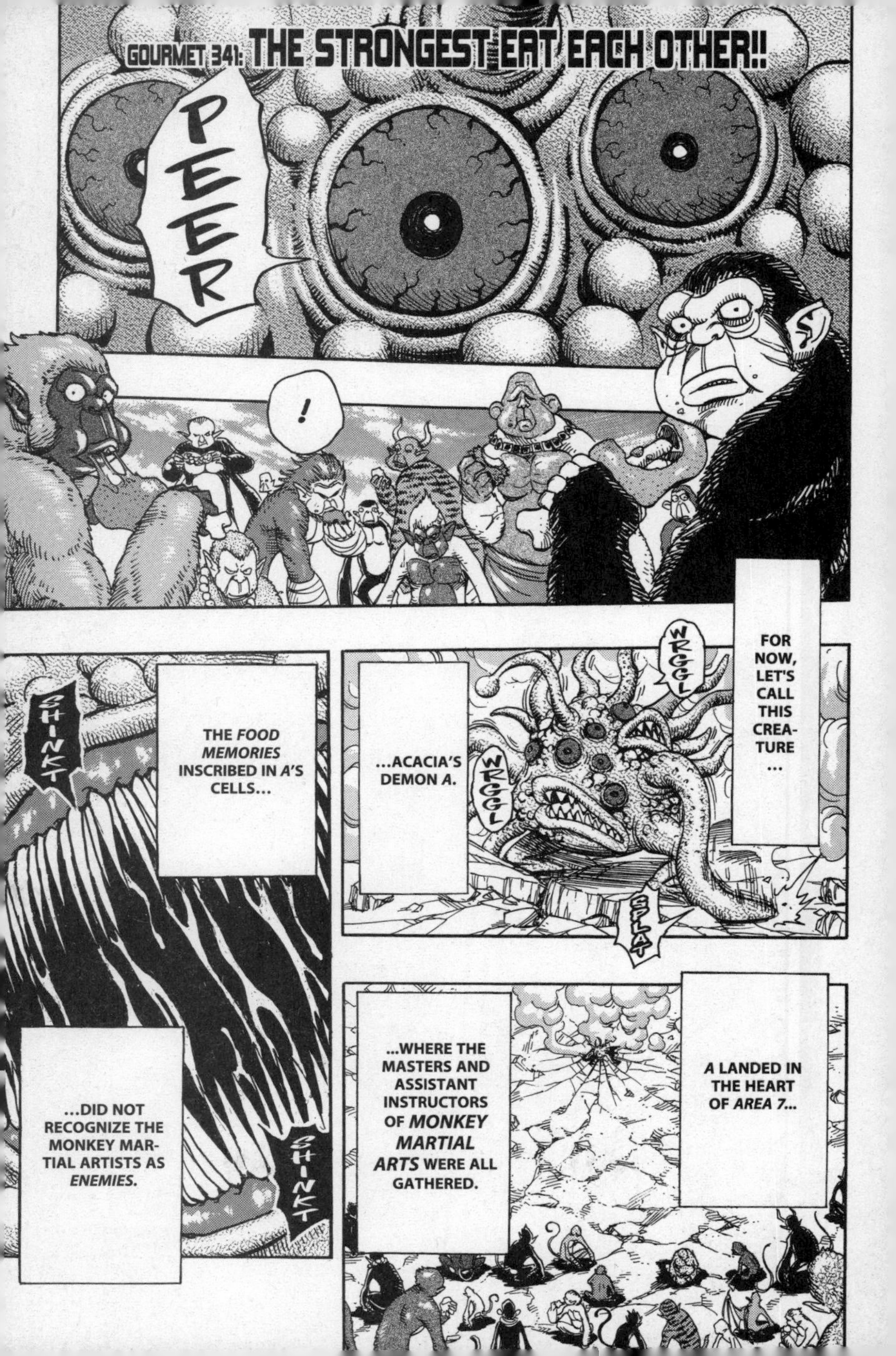
GOURMET 341: THE STRONGEST EAT EACH OTHER!!
PEER
!
FOR NOW, LET'S CALL THIS CREA-TURE...
WRGGL
WRGGL
...ACACIA'S DEMON *A*.
SPLAT
A LANDED IN THE HEART OF *AREA 7*...
...WHERE THE MASTERS AND ASSISTANT INSTRUCTORS OF *MONKEY MARTIAL ARTS* WERE ALL GATHERED.
THE *FOOD MEMORIES* INSCRIBED IN *A*'S CELLS...
SHINKT
...DID NOT RECOGNIZE THE MONKEY MAR-TIAL ARTISTS AS *ENEMIES*.
SHINKT

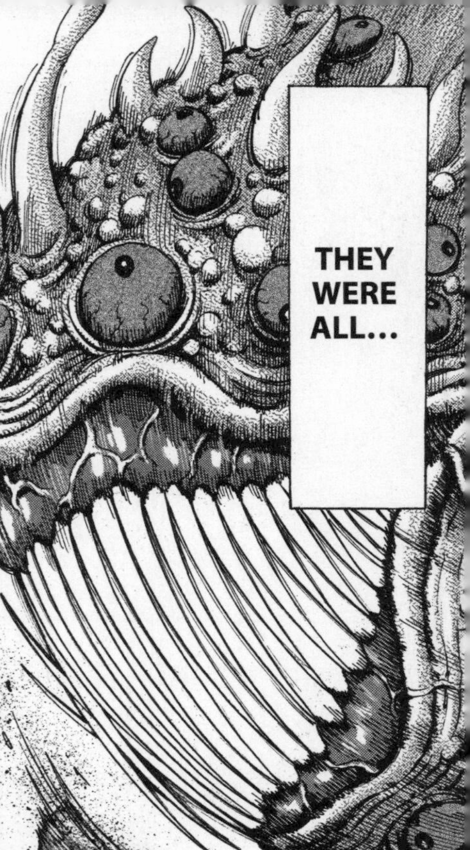
THEY WERE ALL...

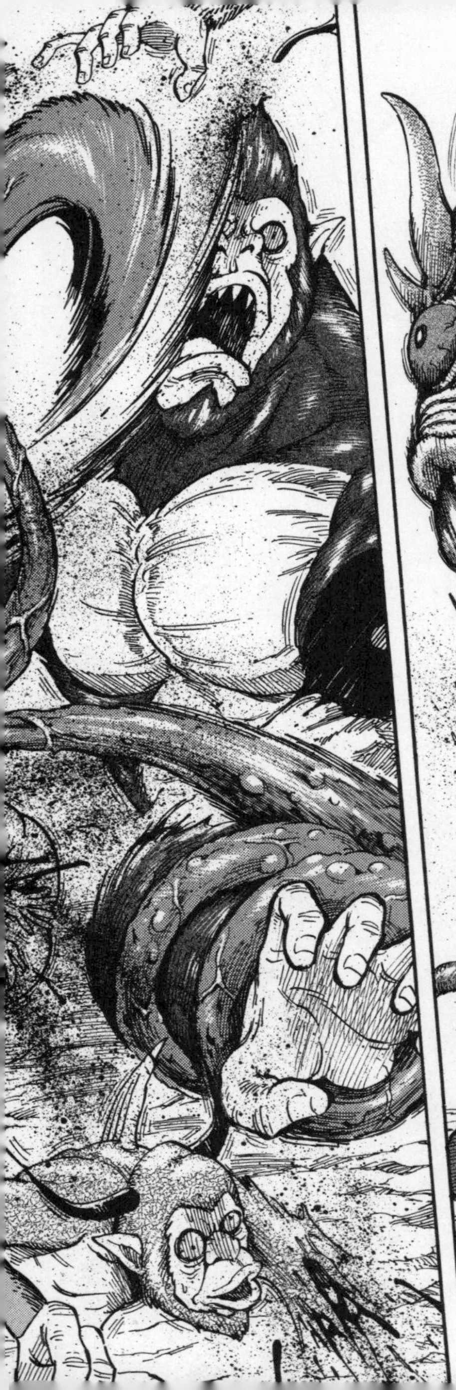

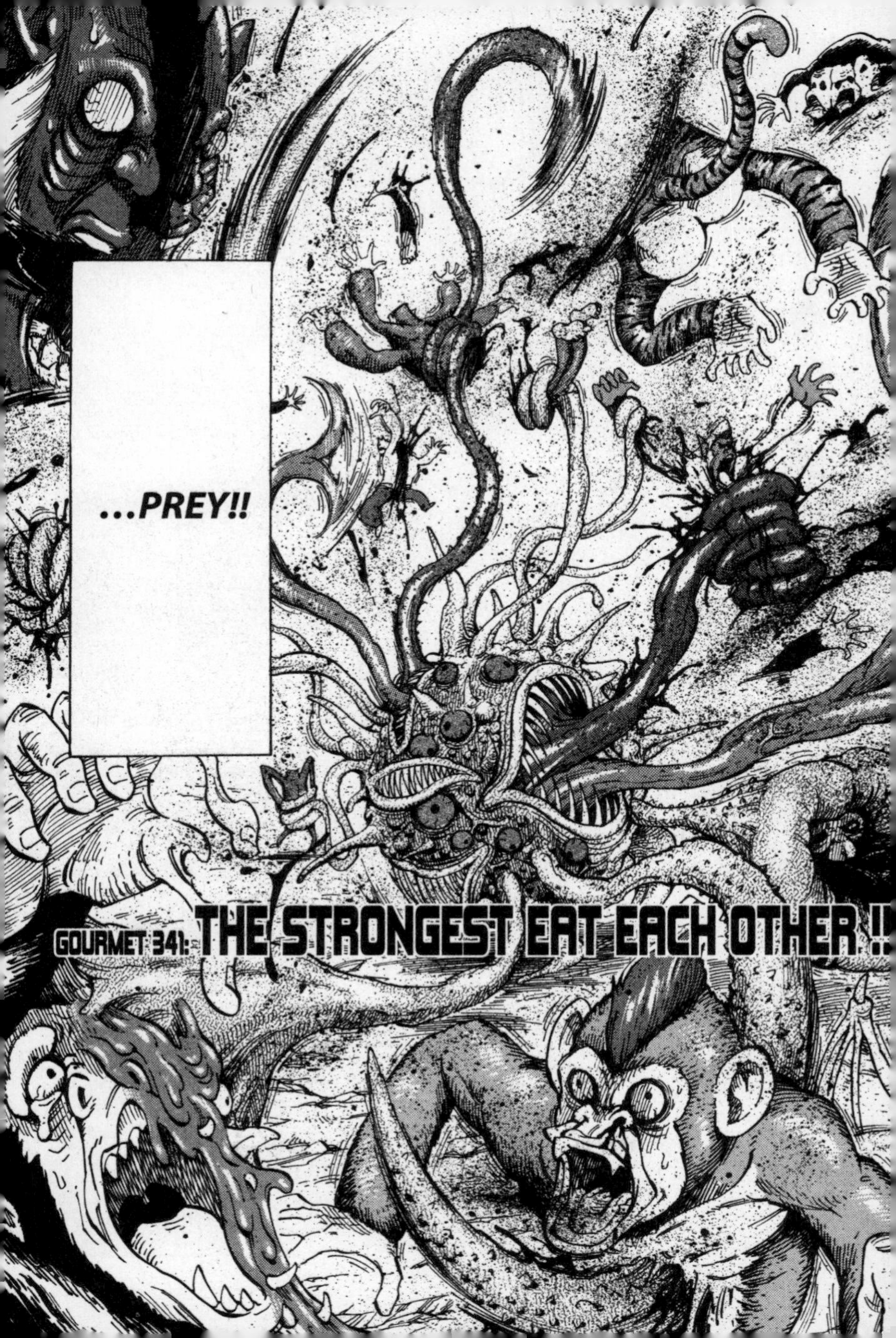
...PREY!!
GOURMET 341: THE STRONGEST EAT EACH OTHER!!

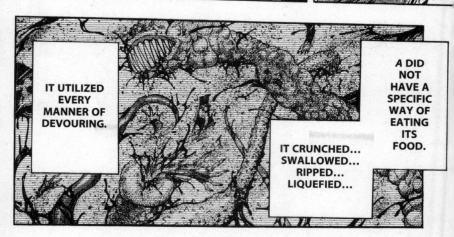

A DID NOT HAVE A SPECIFIC WAY OF EATING ITS FOOD.
IT CRUNCHED... SWALLOWED... RIPPED... LIQUEFIED...
IT UTILIZED EVERY MANNER OF DEVOURING.
BUT THERE WAS ONE...
...WAY OF EATING...
...THAT *A* CLEARLY PREFERRED.

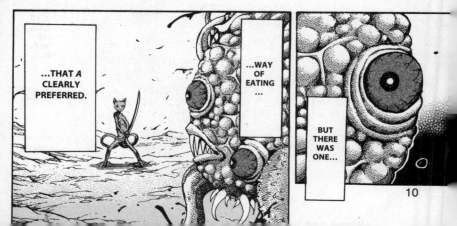

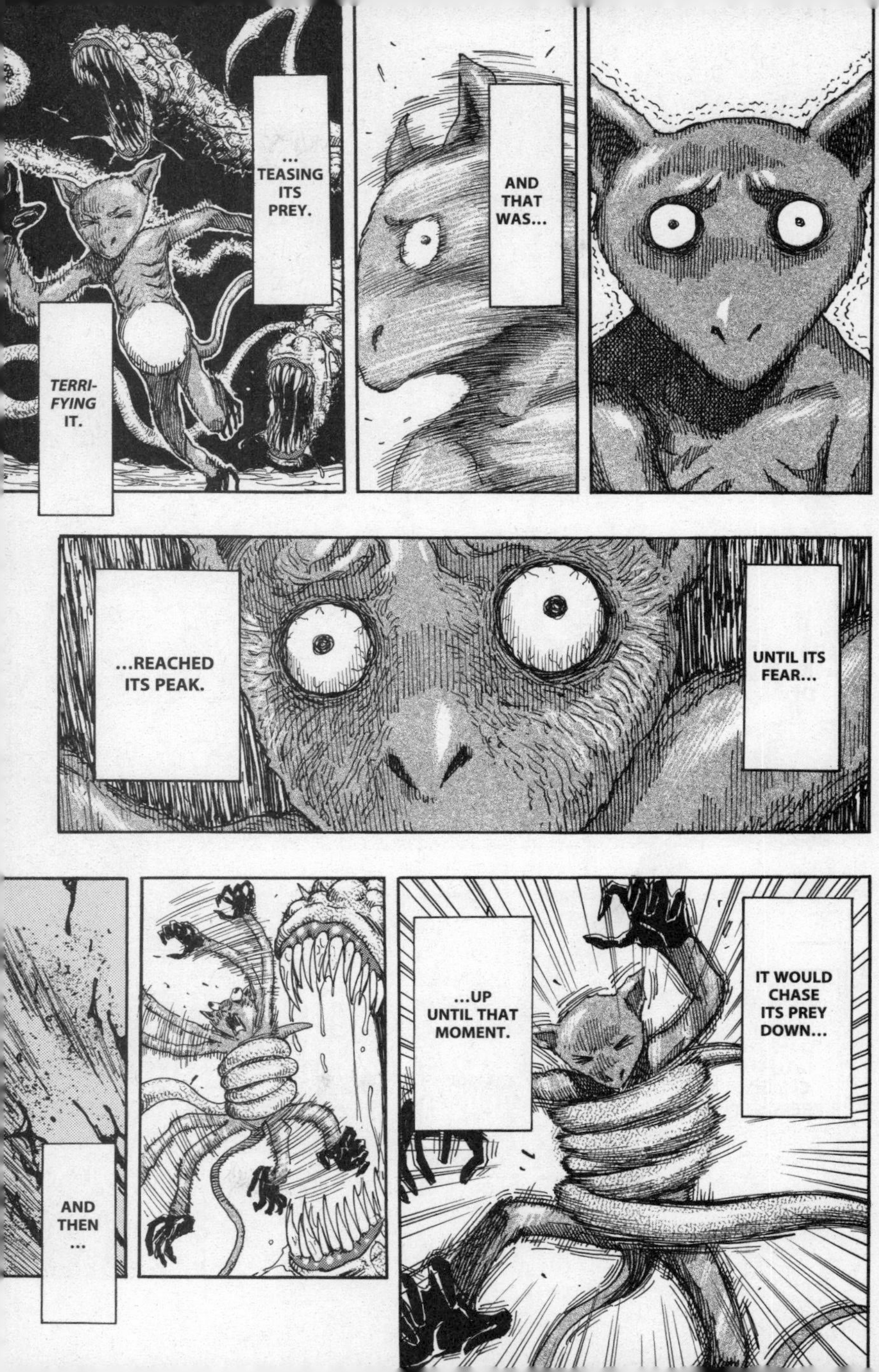
AND THAT WAS...
...TEASING ITS PREY.
TERRI-FYING IT.
UNTIL ITS FEAR...
...REACHED ITS PEAK.
IT WOULD CHASE ITS PREY DOWN...
...UP UNTIL THAT MOMENT.
AND THEN ...

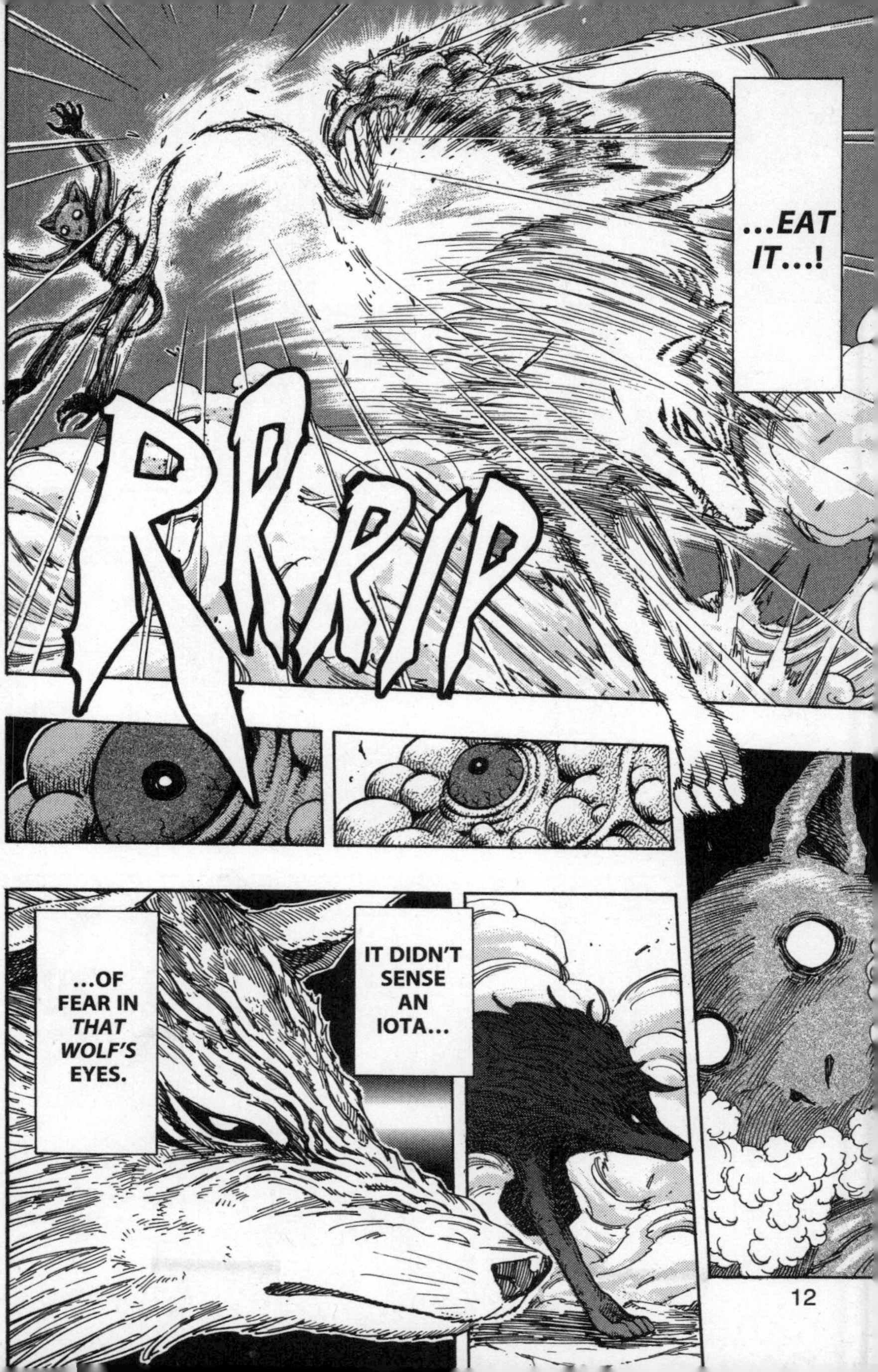
...EAT IT...!
RRRIP
IT DIDN'T SENSE AN IOTA...
...OF FEAR IN THAT WOLF'S EYES.

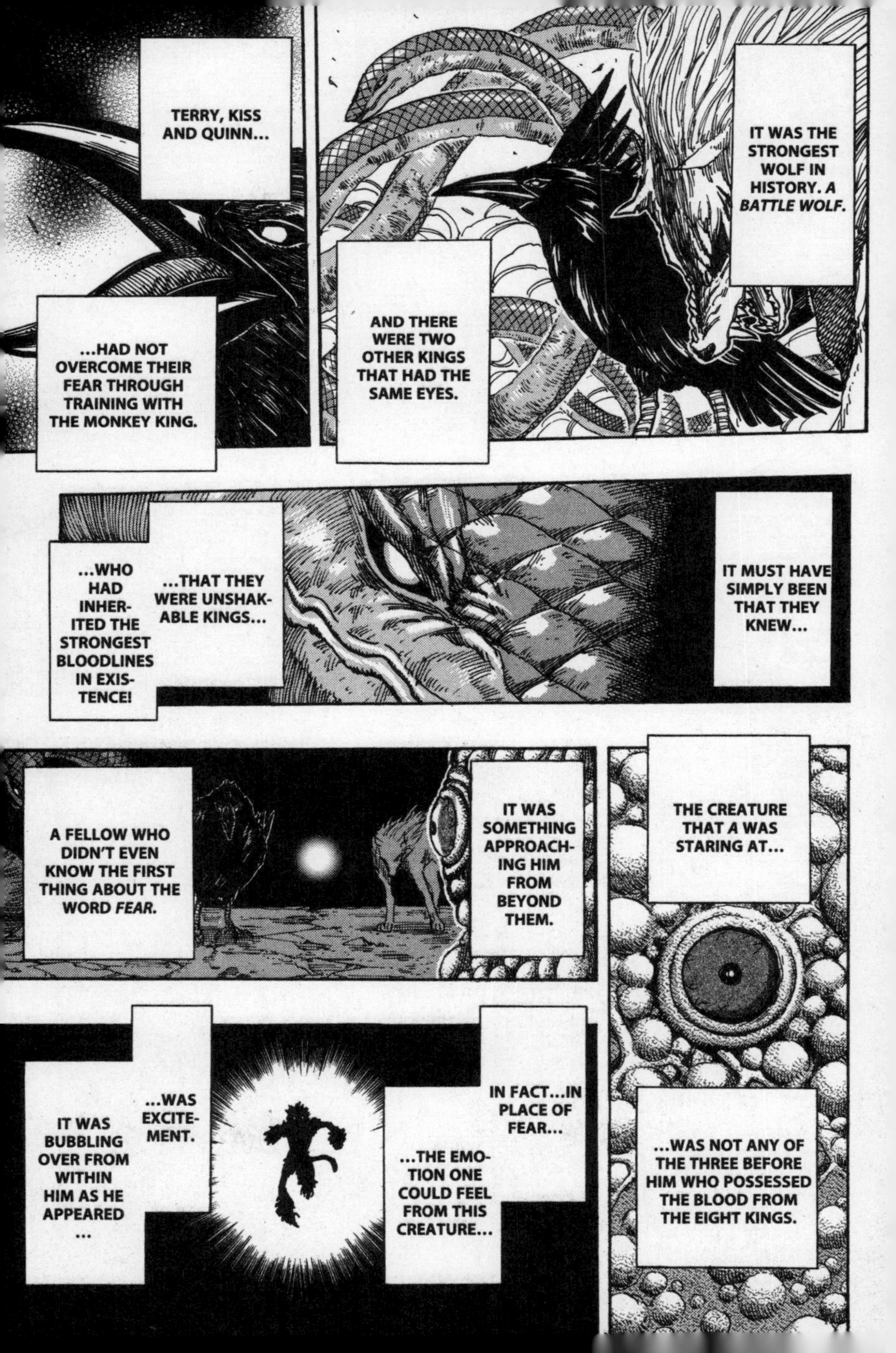
IT WAS THE STRONGEST WOLF IN HISTORY. *A BATTLE WOLF.*
AND THERE WERE TWO OTHER KINGS THAT HAD THE SAME EYES.
TERRY, KISS AND QUINN...
...HAD NOT OVERCOME THEIR FEAR THROUGH TRAINING WITH THE MONKEY KING.
IT MUST HAVE SIMPLY BEEN THAT THEY KNEW...
...THAT THEY WERE UNSHAKABLE KINGS...
...WHO HAD INHERITED THE STRONGEST BLOODLINES IN EXISTENCE!
THE CREATURE THAT *A* WAS STARING AT...
...WAS NOT ANY OF THE THREE BEFORE HIM WHO POSSESSED THE BLOOD FROM THE EIGHT KINGS.
IT WAS SOMETHING APPROACHING HIM FROM BEYOND THEM.
A FELLOW WHO DIDN'T EVEN KNOW THE FIRST THING ABOUT THE WORD *FEAR.*
IN FACT...IN PLACE OF FEAR...
...THE EMOTION ONE COULD FEEL FROM THIS CREATURE...
...WAS EXCITEMENT.
IT WAS BUBBLING OVER FROM WITHIN HIM AS HE APPEARED...

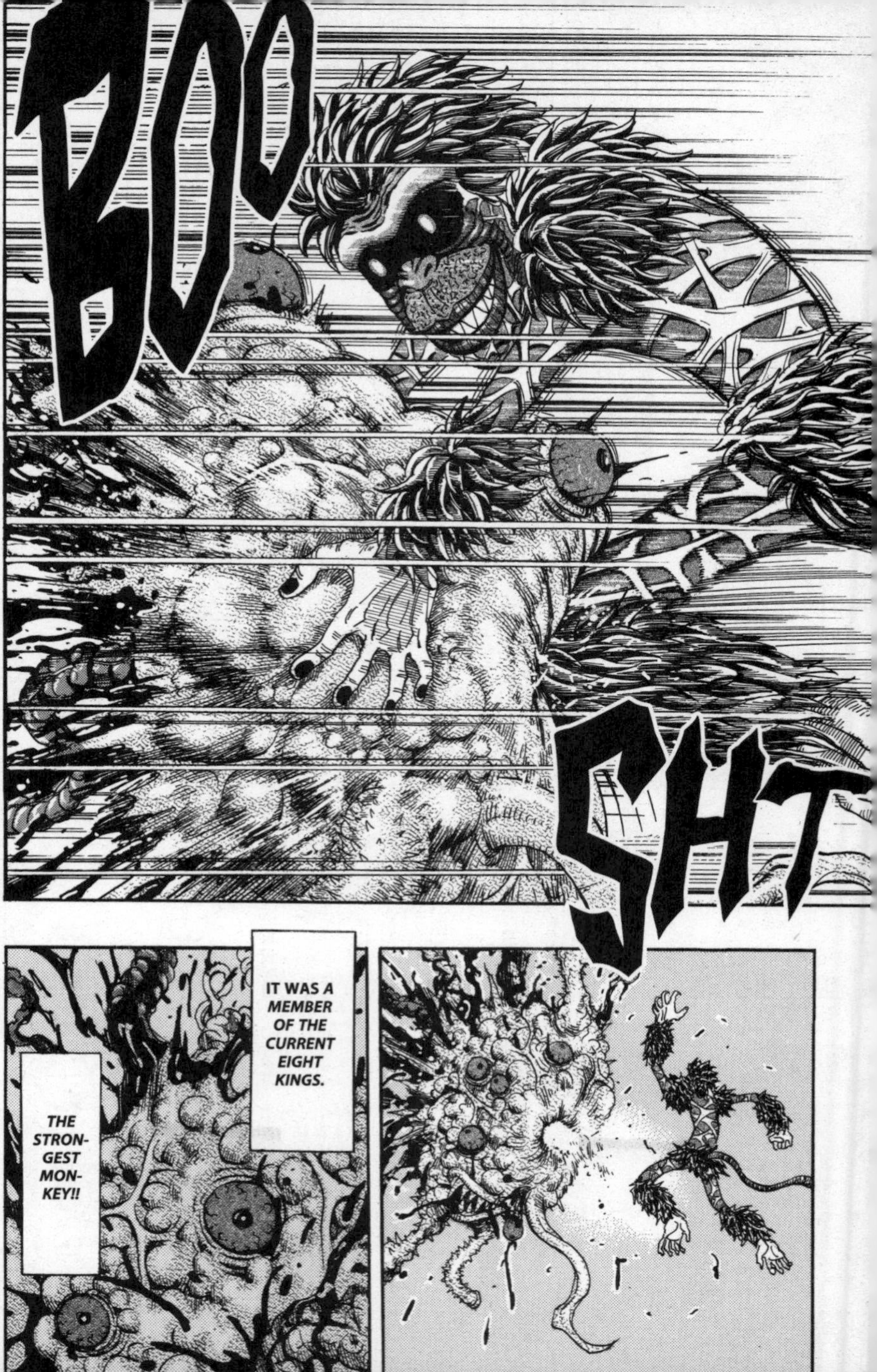
BOO
SHT
IT WAS A MEMBER OF THE CURRENT EIGHT KINGS.
THE STRON-GEST MON-KEY!!

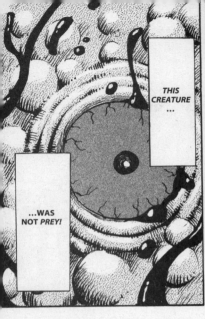

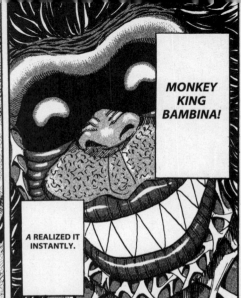

MONKEY KING BAMBINA!
A REALIZED IT INSTANTLY.
THIS CREATURE ...
...WAS NOT PREY!
IT WAS AN ENEMY!
MEAN-WHILE, IN AREA 8.
NIGHT-MARE HILL.
THE CREATURE THAT LANDED HERE INCREASED ITS SIZE.
BULGE
...BECAUSE THE BODY OF ITS ENEMY WAS SO MASSIVE.
BULGE

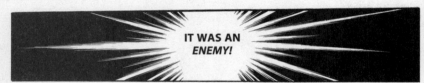

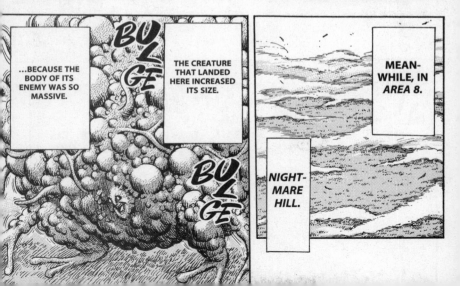

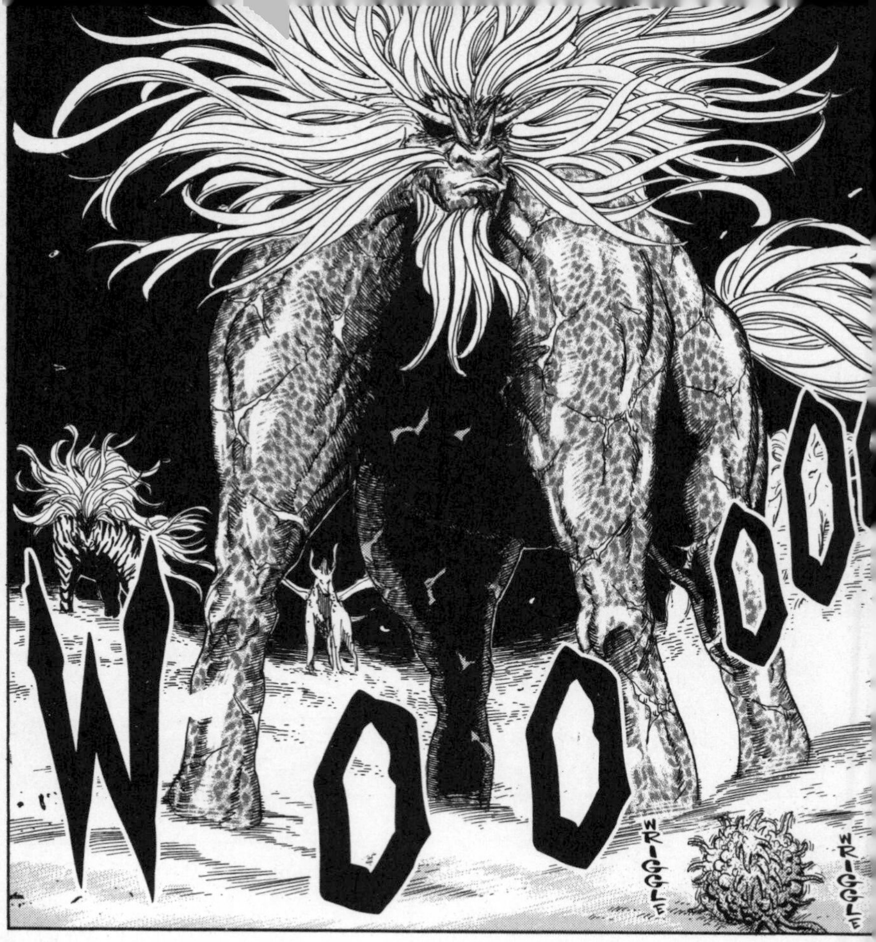
WOOOOO
WRIGGLE
WRIGGLE
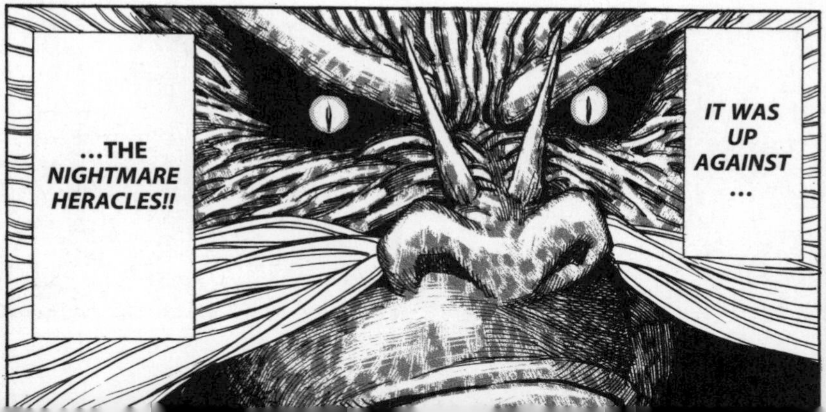
IT WAS UP AGAINST ...
...THE NIGHTMARE HERACLES!!

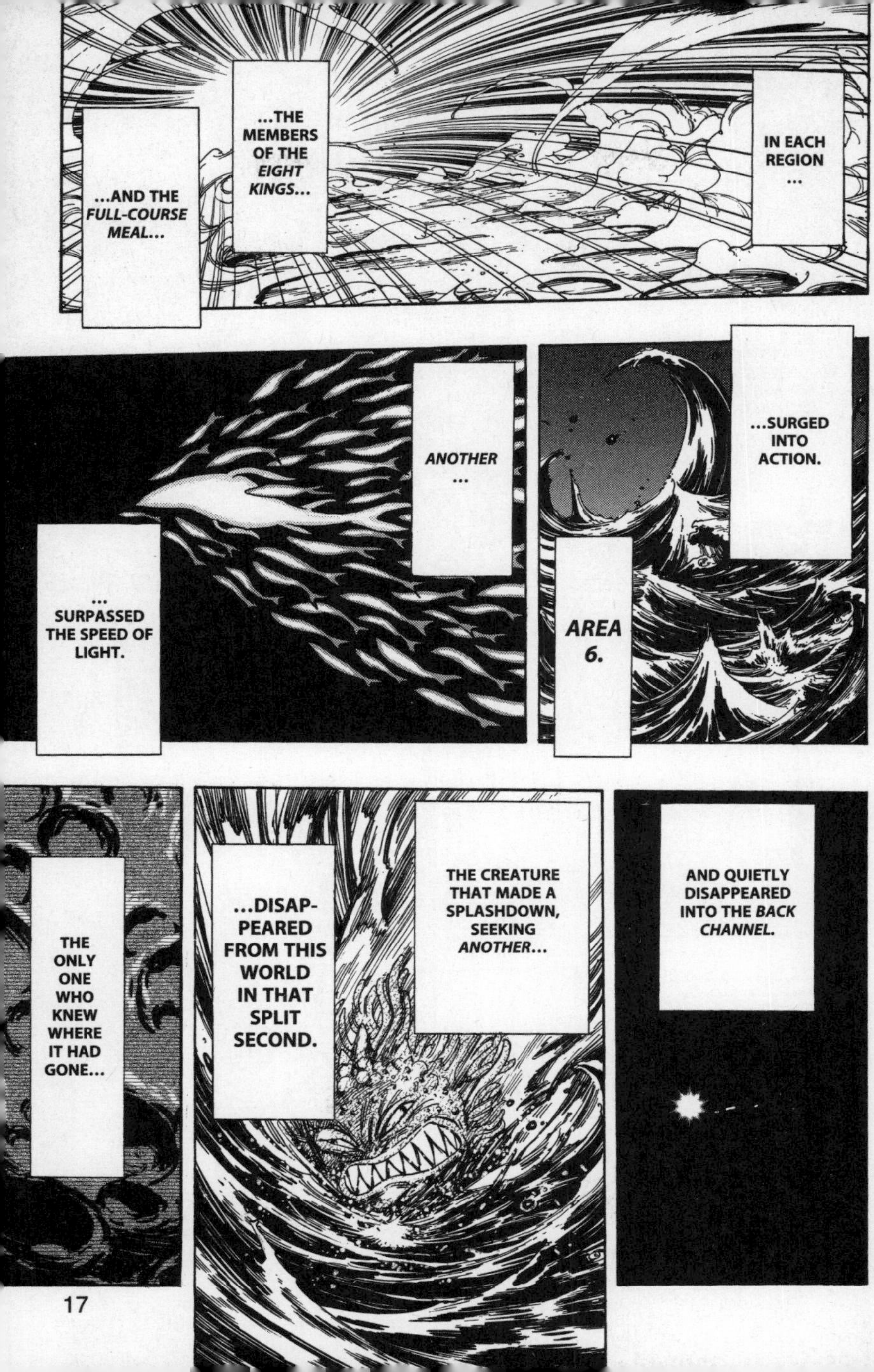
IN EACH REGION ...
...THE MEMBERS OF THE *EIGHT KINGS*...
...AND THE *FULL-COURSE MEAL*...
...SURGED INTO ACTION.
AREA 6.
ANOTHER ...
... SURPASSED THE SPEED OF LIGHT.
AND QUIETLY DISAPPEARED INTO THE *BACK CHANNEL*.
THE CREATURE THAT MADE A SPLASHDOWN, SEEKING *ANOTHER*...
...DISAP-PEARED FROM THIS WORLD IN THAT SPLIT SECOND.
THE ONLY ONE WHO KNEW WHERE IT HAD GONE...

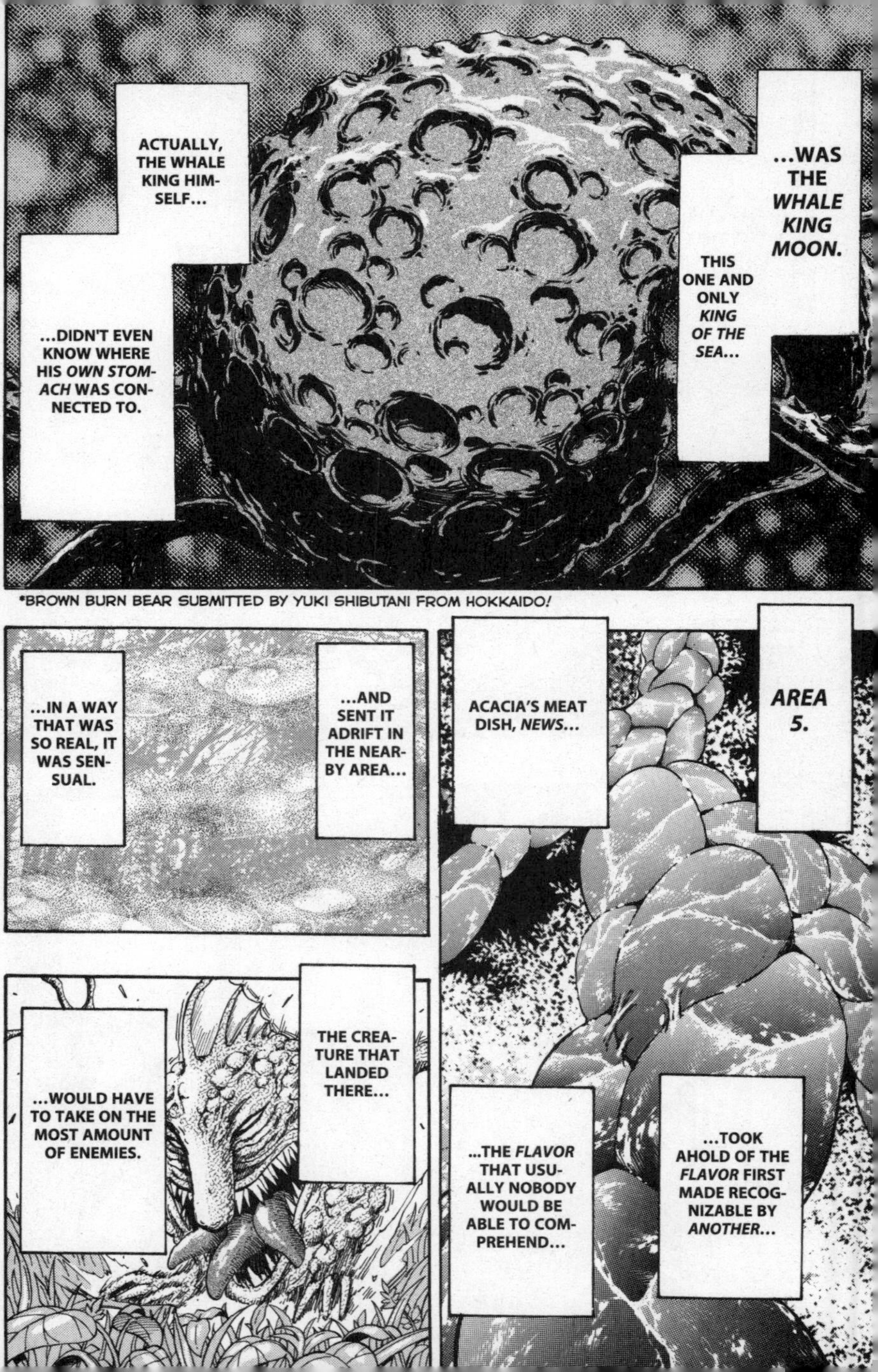
...WAS THE WHALE KING MOON.
THIS ONE AND ONLY KING OF THE SEA...
ACTUALLY, THE WHALE KING HIMSELF...
...DIDN'T EVEN KNOW WHERE HIS OWN STOMACH WAS CONNECTED TO.
*BROWN BURN BEAR SUBMITTED BY YUKI SHIBUTANI FROM HOKKAIDO!
AREA 5.
ACACIA'S MEAT DISH, NEWS...
...TOOK AHOLD OF THE FLAVOR FIRST MADE RECOGNIZABLE BY ANOTHER...
...THE FLAVOR THAT USUALLY NOBODY WOULD BE ABLE TO COMPREHEND...
...AND SENT IT ADRIFT IN THE NEARBY AREA...
...IN A WAY THAT WAS SO REAL, IT WAS SENSUAL.
THE CREATURE THAT LANDED THERE...
...WOULD HAVE TO TAKE ON THE MOST AMOUNT OF ENEMIES.

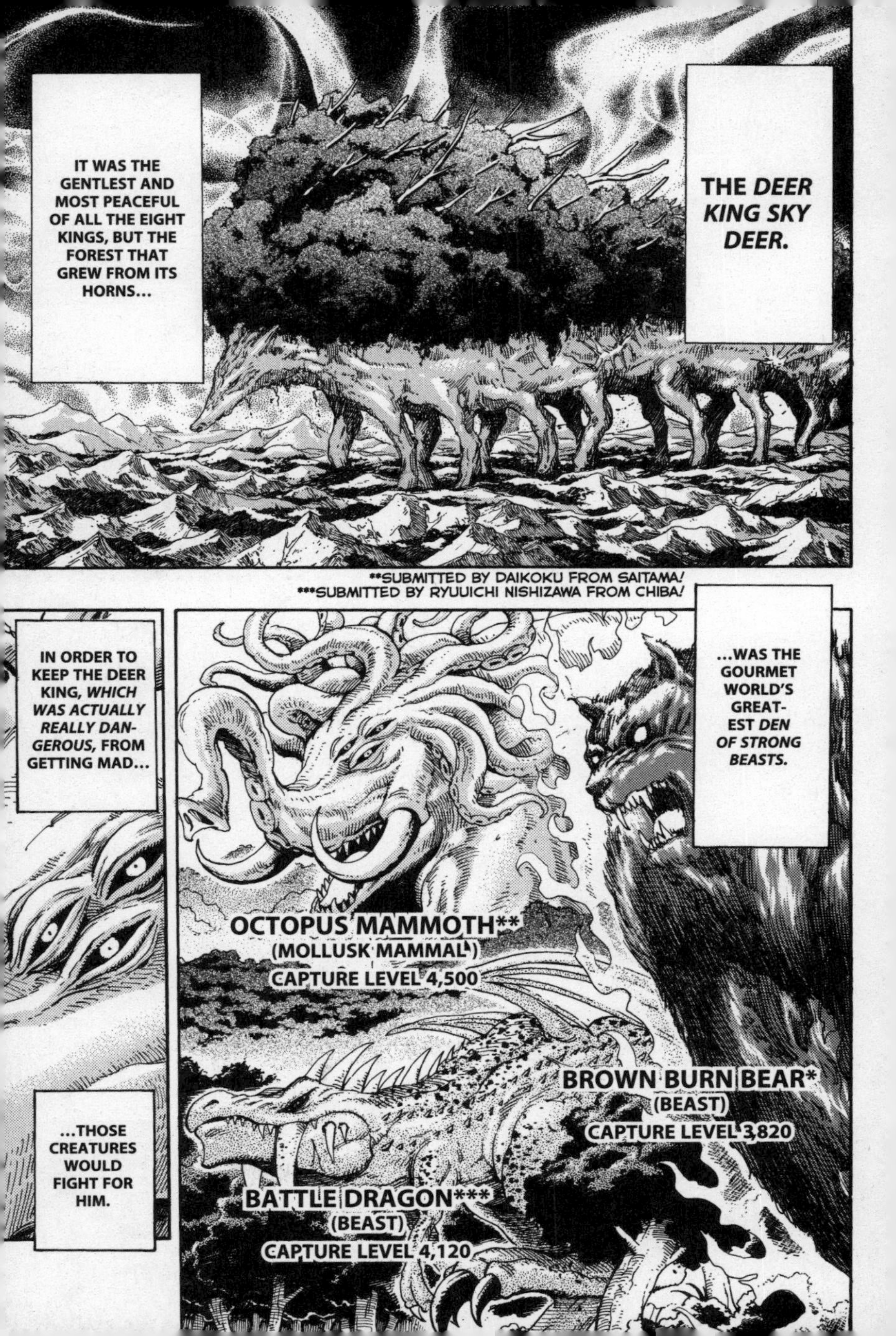
THE DEER KING SKY DEER.
IT WAS THE GENTLEST AND MOST PEACEFUL OF ALL THE EIGHT KINGS, BUT THE FOREST THAT GREW FROM ITS HORNS...
**SUBMITTED BY DAIKOKU FROM SAITAMA!
***SUBMITTED BY RYUUICHI NISHIZAWA FROM CHIBA!
...WAS THE GOURMET WORLD'S GREATEST DEN OF STRONG BEASTS.
OCTOPUS MAMMOTH** (MOLLUSK MAMMAL) CAPTURE LEVEL 4,500
BROWN BURN BEAR* (BEAST) CAPTURE LEVEL 3,820
BATTLE DRAGON*** (BEAST) CAPTURE LEVEL 4,120
IN ORDER TO KEEP THE DEER KING, WHICH WAS ACTUALLY REALLY DANGEROUS, FROM GETTING MAD...
...THOSE CREATURES WOULD FIGHT FOR HIM.

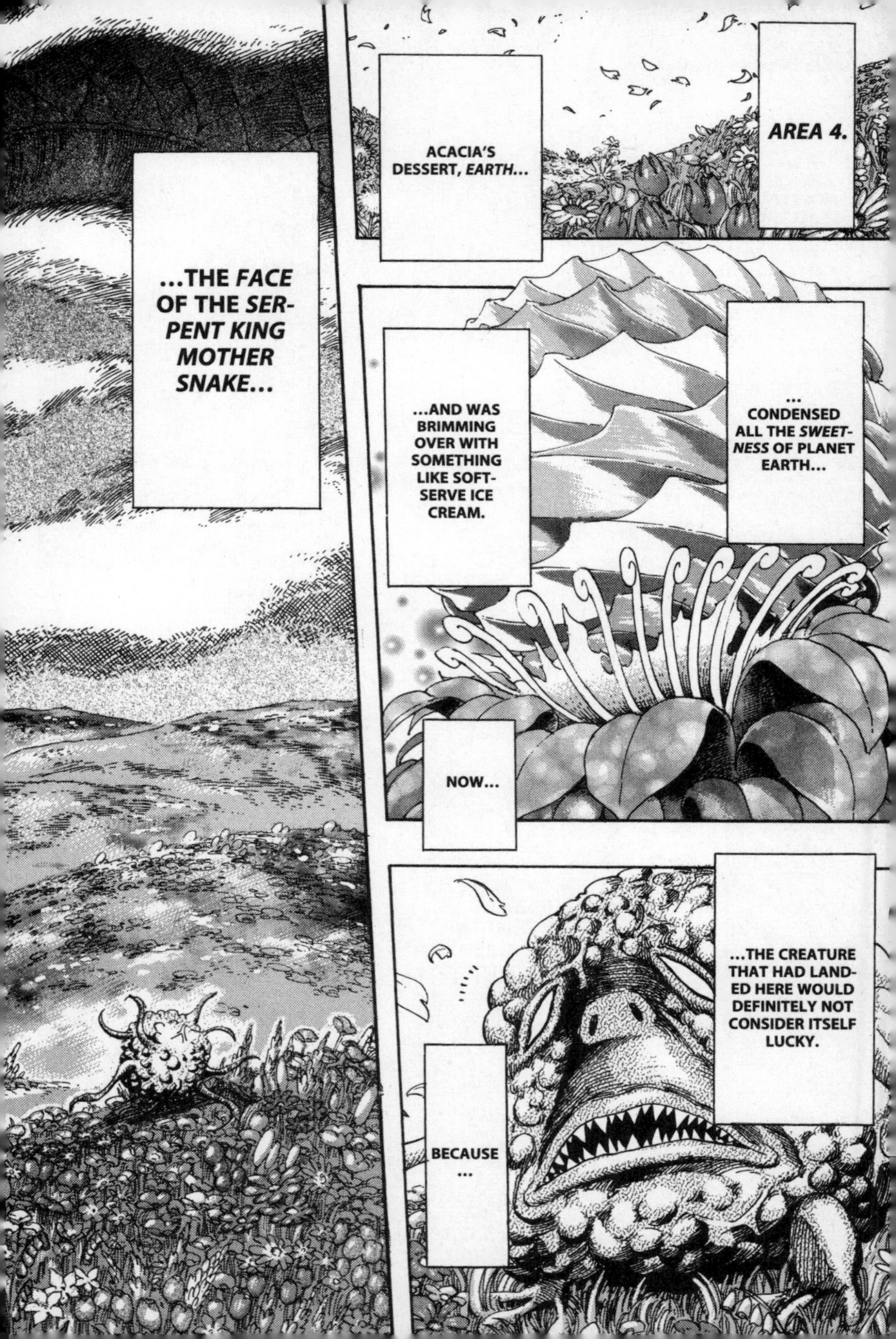

AREA 4.
ACACIA'S DESSERT, *EARTH*...
... CONDENSED ALL THE *SWEETNESS* OF PLANET EARTH...
...AND WAS BRIMMING OVER WITH SOMETHING LIKE SOFT-SERVE ICE CREAM.
NOW...
...THE CREATURE THAT HAD LANDED HERE WOULD DEFINITELY NOT CONSIDER ITSELF LUCKY.
BECAUSE ...
...THE *FACE* OF THE *SERPENT KING MOTHER SNAKE*...

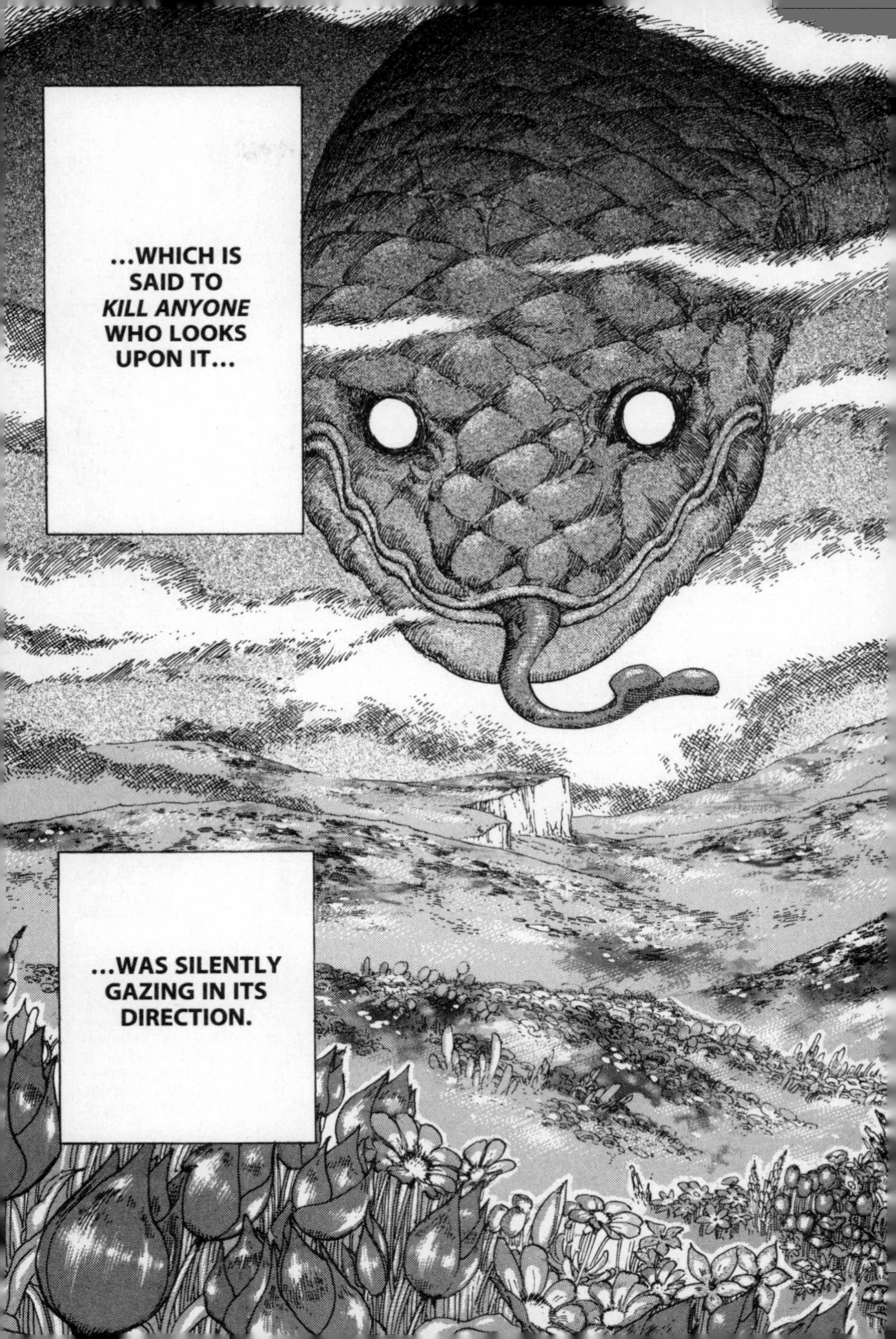
...WHICH IS SAID TO *KILL ANYONE* WHO LOOKS UPON IT...
...WAS SILENTLY GAZING IN ITS DIRECTION.

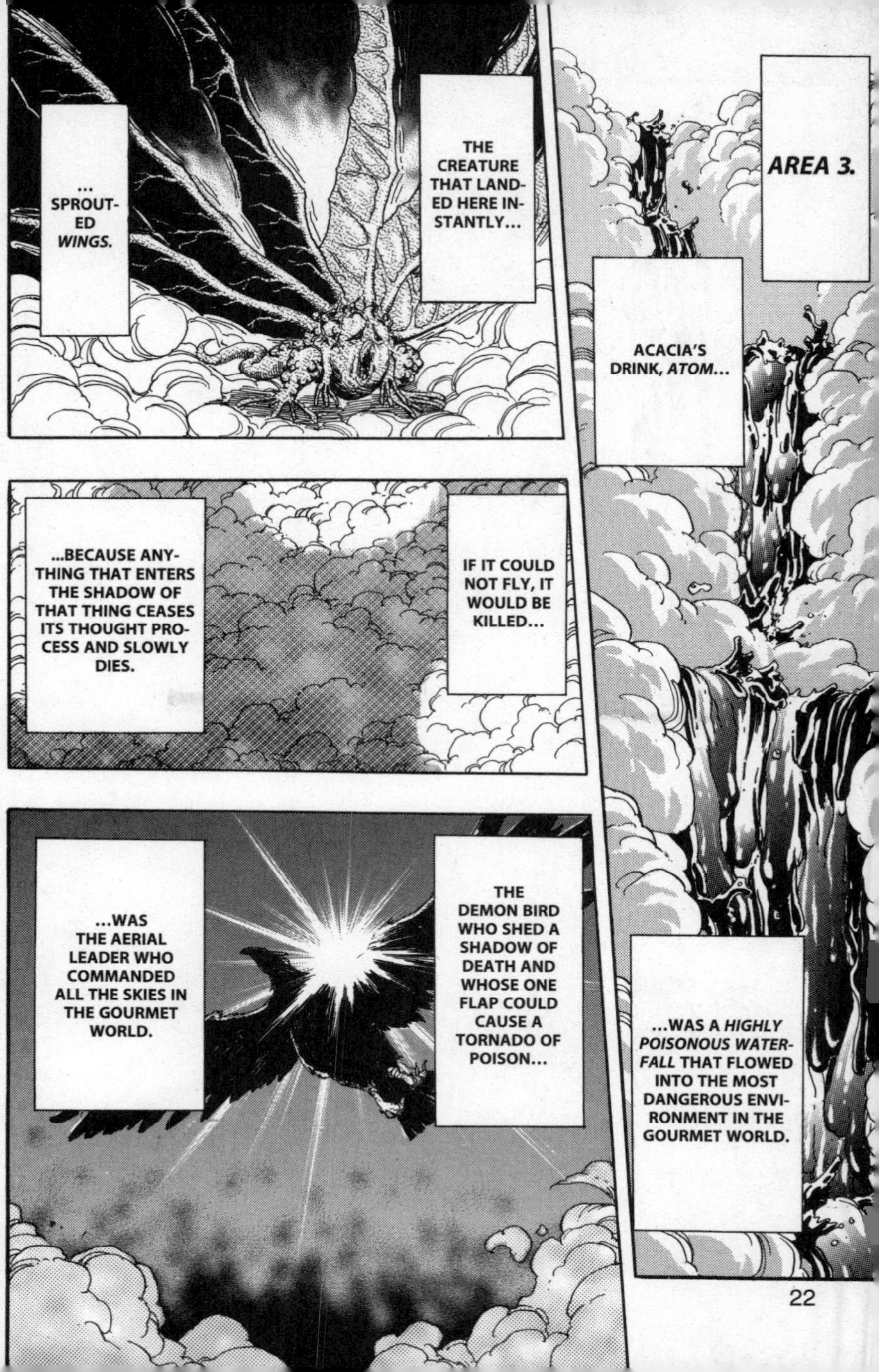
AREA 3.
ACACIA'S DRINK, ATOM...
...WAS A HIGHLY POISONOUS WATERFALL THAT FLOWED INTO THE MOST DANGEROUS ENVIRONMENT IN THE GOURMET WORLD.
THE CREATURE THAT LANDED HERE INSTANTLY...
...SPROUTED WINGS.
IF IT COULD NOT FLY, IT WOULD BE KILLED...
...BECAUSE ANYTHING THAT ENTERS THE SHADOW OF THAT THING CEASES ITS THOUGHT PROCESS AND SLOWLY DIES.
THE DEMON BIRD WHO SHED A SHADOW OF DEATH AND WHOSE ONE FLAP COULD CAUSE A TORNADO OF POISON...
...WAS THE AERIAL LEADER WHO COMMANDED ALL THE SKIES IN THE GOURMET WORLD.

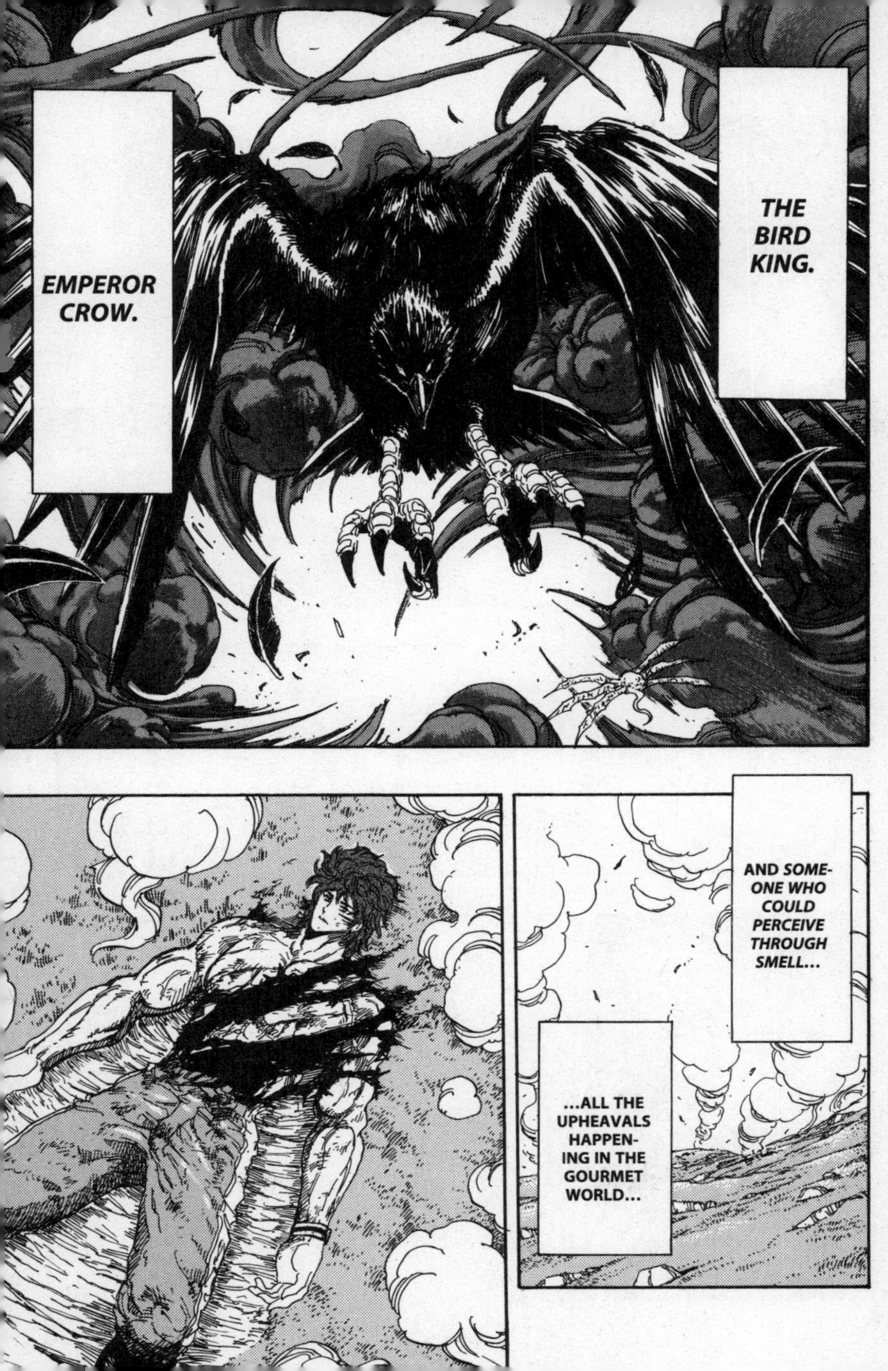
THE BIRD KING.
EMPEROR CROW.
AND SOME-ONE WHO COULD PERCEIVE THROUGH SMELL...
...ALL THE UPHEAVALS HAPPEN-ING IN THE GOURMET WORLD...

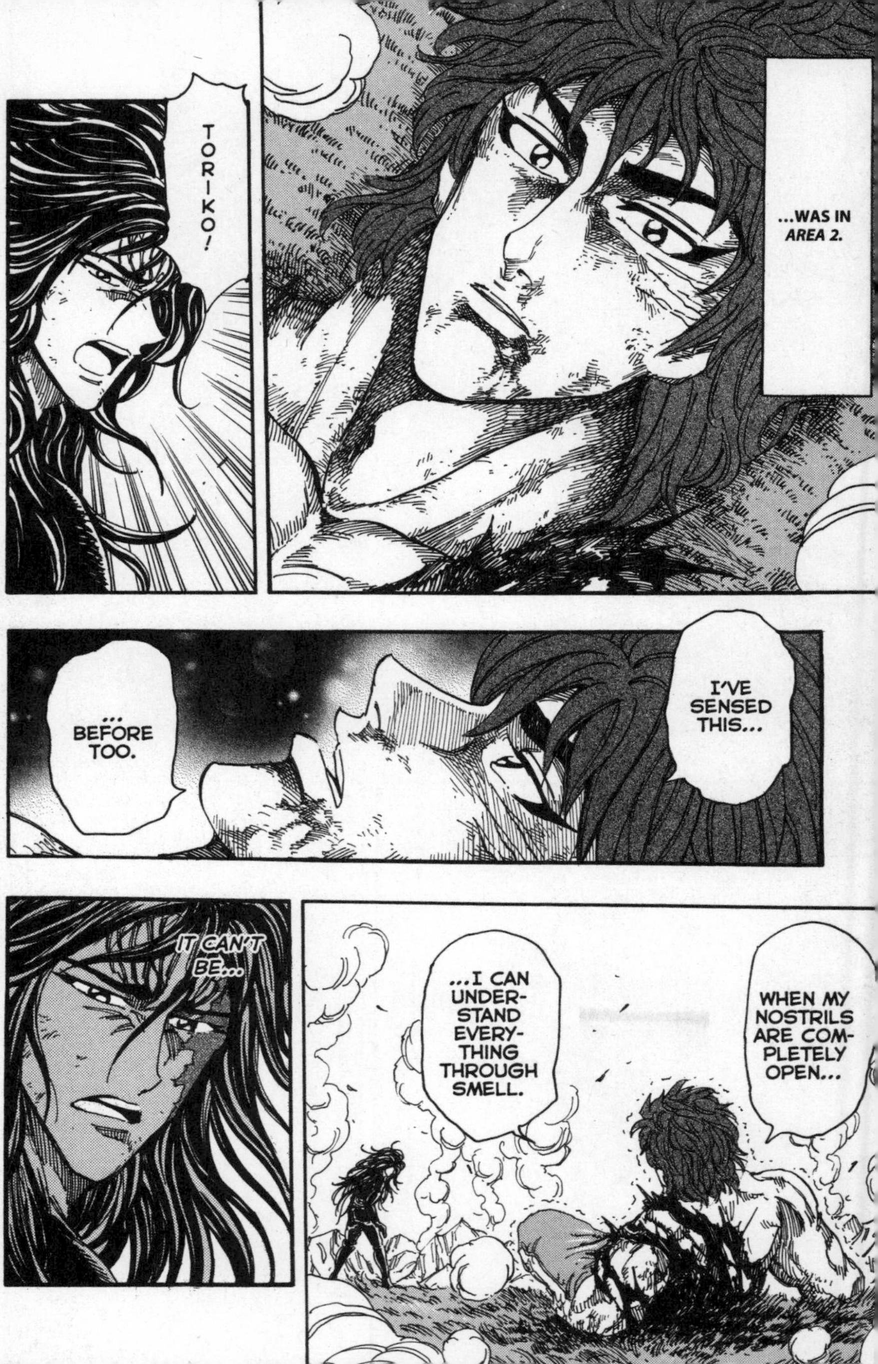
...WAS IN AREA 2.
TORIKO!
I'VE SENSED THIS...
... BEFORE TOO.
WHEN MY NOSTRILS ARE COMPLETELY OPEN...
...I CAN UNDERSTAND EVERYTHING THROUGH SMELL.
IT CAN'T BE...

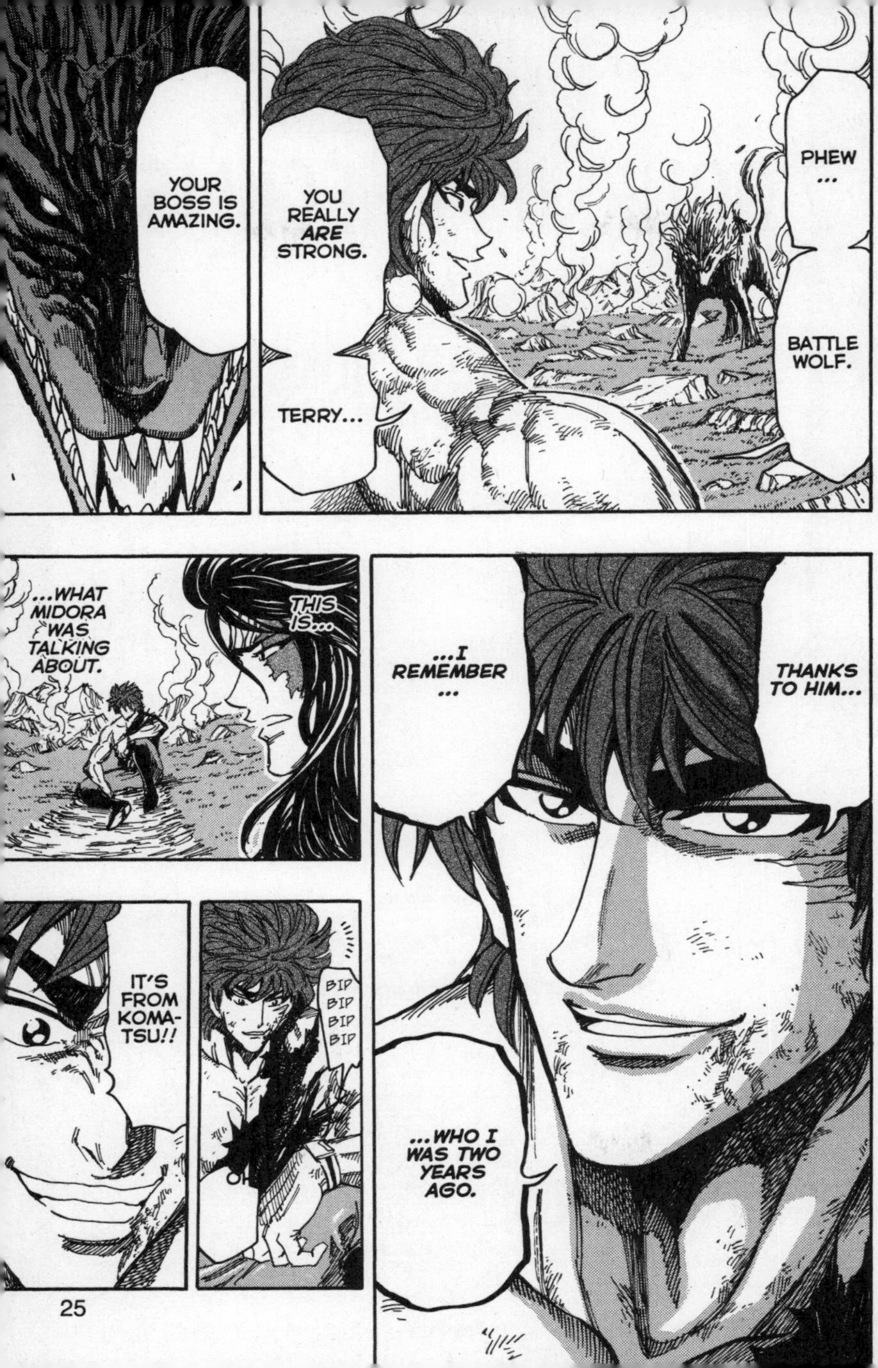
PHEW ...
BATTLE WOLF.
YOU REALLY *ARE* STRONG.
TERRY...
YOUR BOSS IS AMAZING.
THANKS TO HIM...
...I REMEMBER ...
...WHO I WAS TWO YEARS AGO.
THIS IS...
...WHAT MIDORA WAS TALKING ABOUT.
BIP BIP BIP BIP
IT'S FROM KOMATSU!!

TORIKO

GOURMET CHECKLIST

Vol. 371

CHOO CHOO CHOMPER
(CRUSTACEAN)

CAPTURE LEVEL: 605
HABITAT: GOURMET WORLD'S AREA 8
SIZE: 2 KM
HEIGHT: 3.8 M
WEIGHT: 350 TONS
PRICE: ONLY ITS FINS ARE EDIBLE AND THEY GO FOR 50,000 YEN EACH

NOW'S THE TIME!
SPOOT
ZOOOM

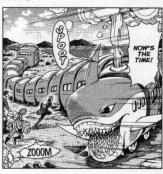

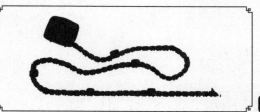

SCALE

THIS IS THE CAMPING MONSTER THAT TEAM TORIKO RODE IN TO GET TO THE GOURMET WORLD'S AREA 7. ITS BODY IS ABOUT 2 KILOMETERS LONG AND ITS HEAD IS THE STRONGEST PART OF THE SAFE ZONE. ELECTRICITY RUNS THROUGH ITS WHEELS, AND IT EMITS ONE MILLION VOLTS OF HIGH-TENSION CURRENTS FROM ITS WINDOWS. IT'S NATURALLY VIOLENT, BUT IT'S A BETTER SAFE ZONE THAN THE OCTOMELON—MAKING IT THE IDEAL CAMPING MONSTER FOR SNEAKING INTO AREA 7.

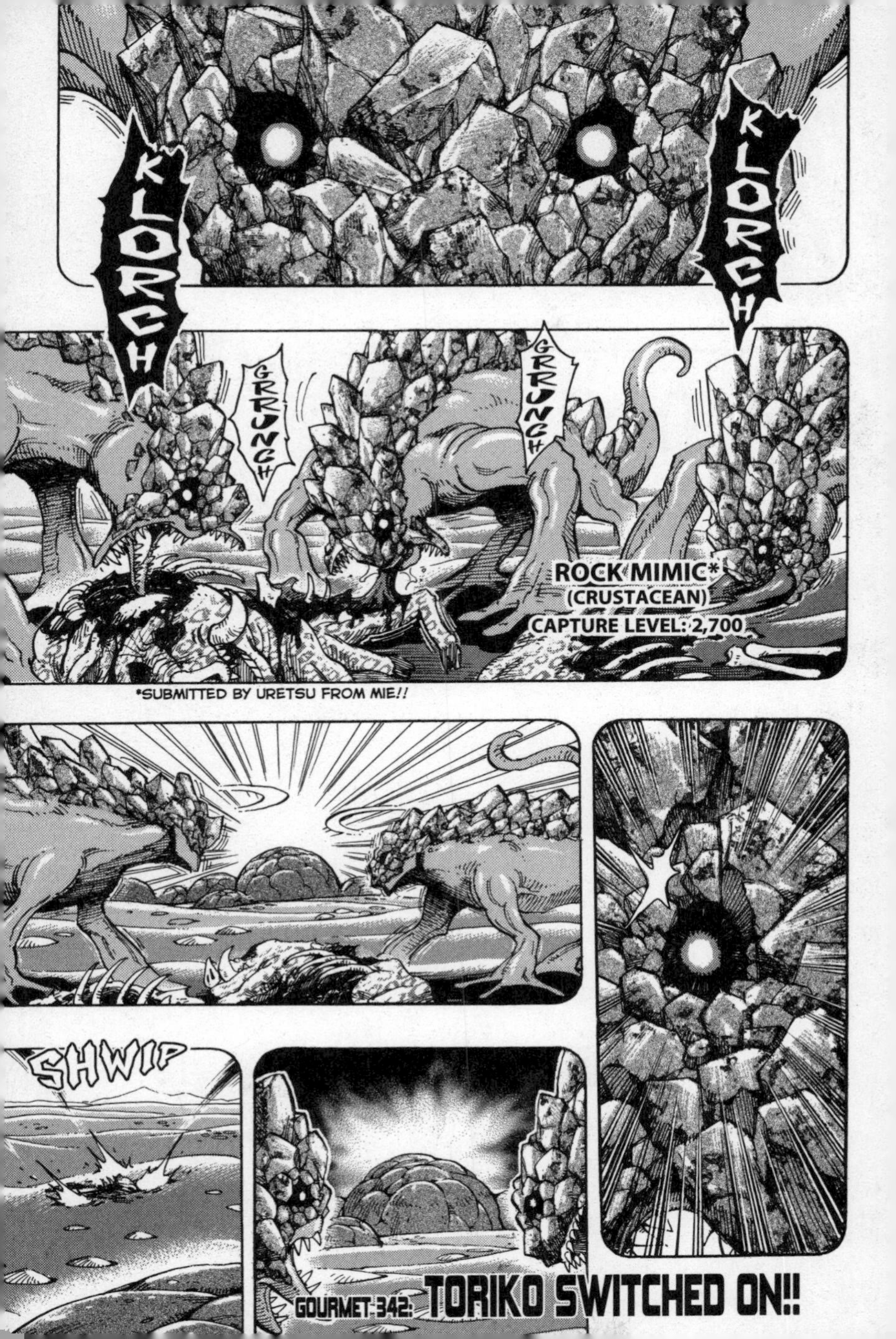
KLORCH
KLORCH
GRRUNCH
GRRUNCH
ROCK MIMIC*
(CRUSTACEAN)
CAPTURE LEVEL: 2,700
*SUBMITTED BY URETSU FROM MIE!!
GOURMET 342: TORIKO SWITCHED ON!!
SHWIP

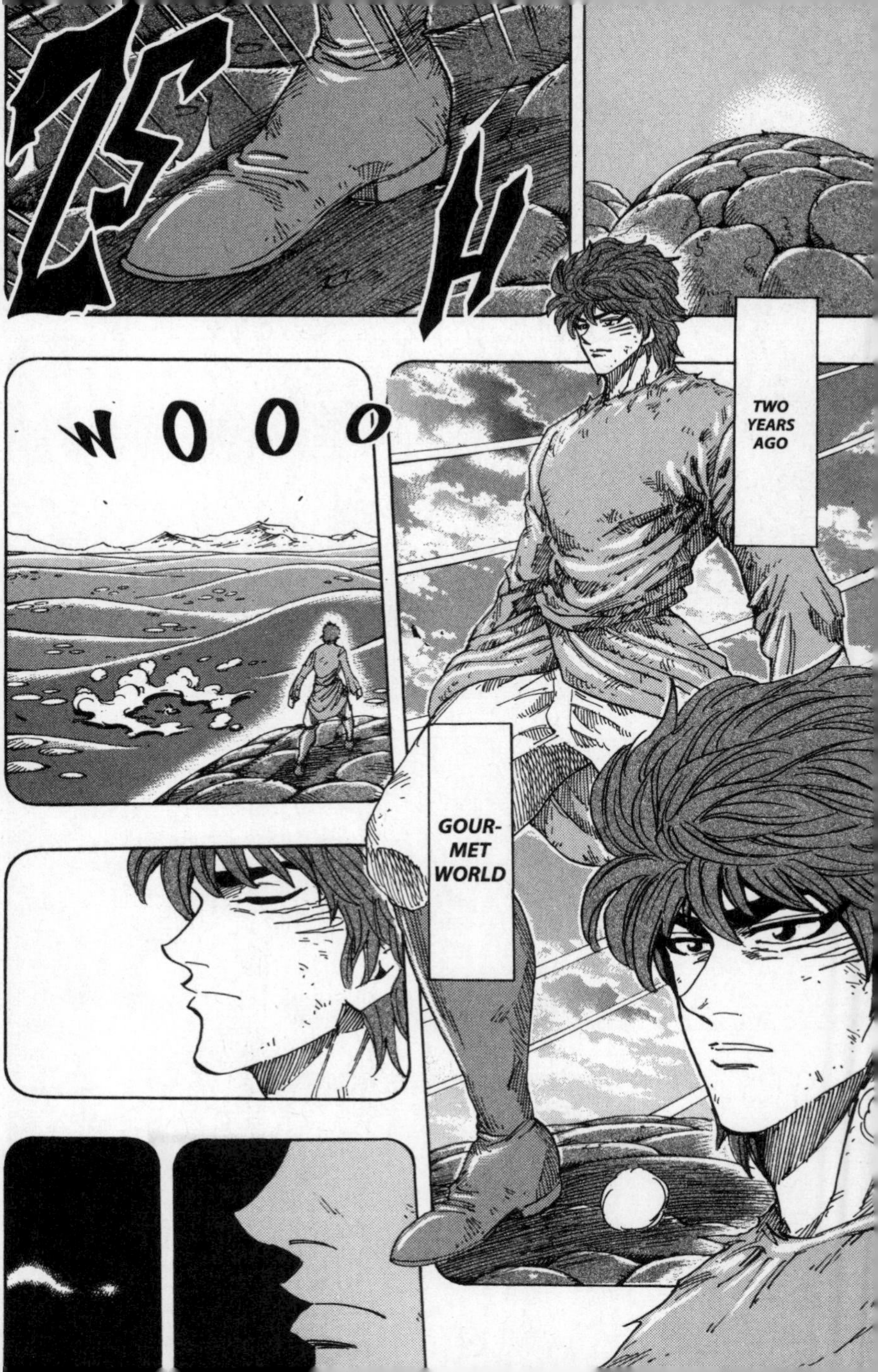
ZSH
TWO YEARS AGO
GOUR-MET WORLD
WOOO

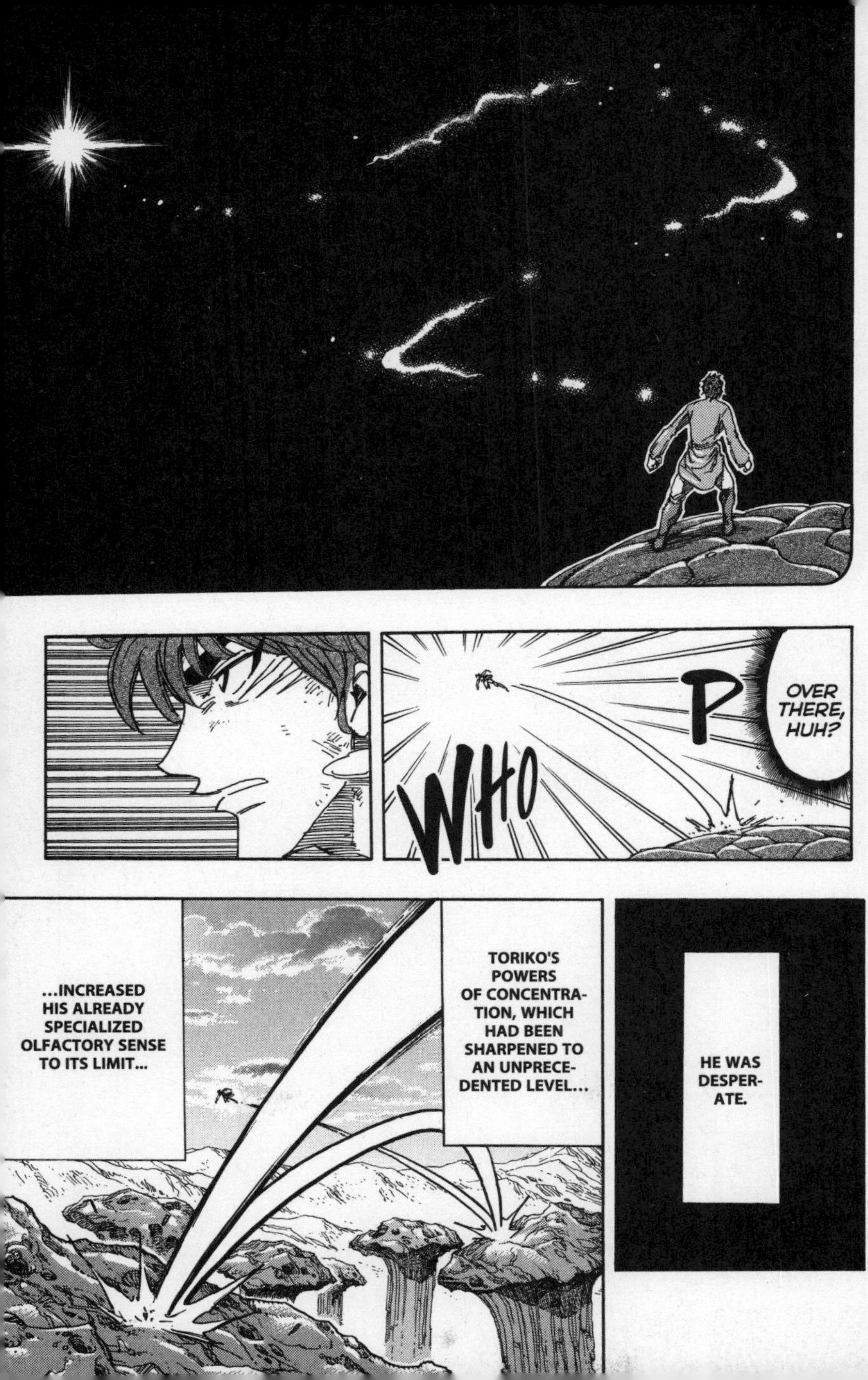
OVER THERE, HUH?
WHOP
HE WAS DESPERATE.
TORIKO'S POWERS OF CONCENTRATION, WHICH HAD BEEN SHARPENED TO AN UNPRECEDENTED LEVEL...
...INCREASED HIS ALREADY SPECIALIZED OLFACTORY SENSE TO ITS LIMIT...

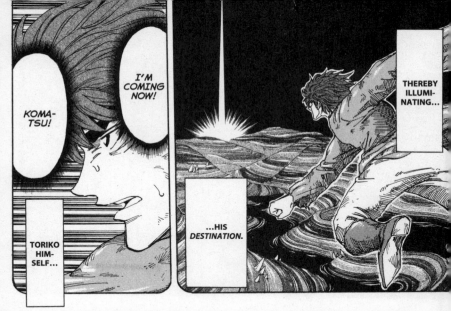

THEREBY ILLUMINATING...
...HIS DESTINATION.
I'M COMING NOW!
KOMATSU!
TORIKO HIMSELF...
...MUST NOT HAVE EVEN REALIZED IT.
FOR THAT YEAR AND A HALF ...
...AFTER LEAVING THE HUMAN WORLD AND BEFORE BRINGING KOMATSU BACK...

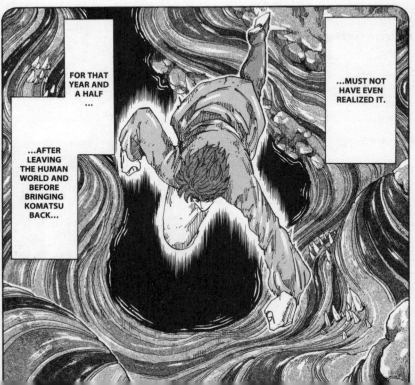

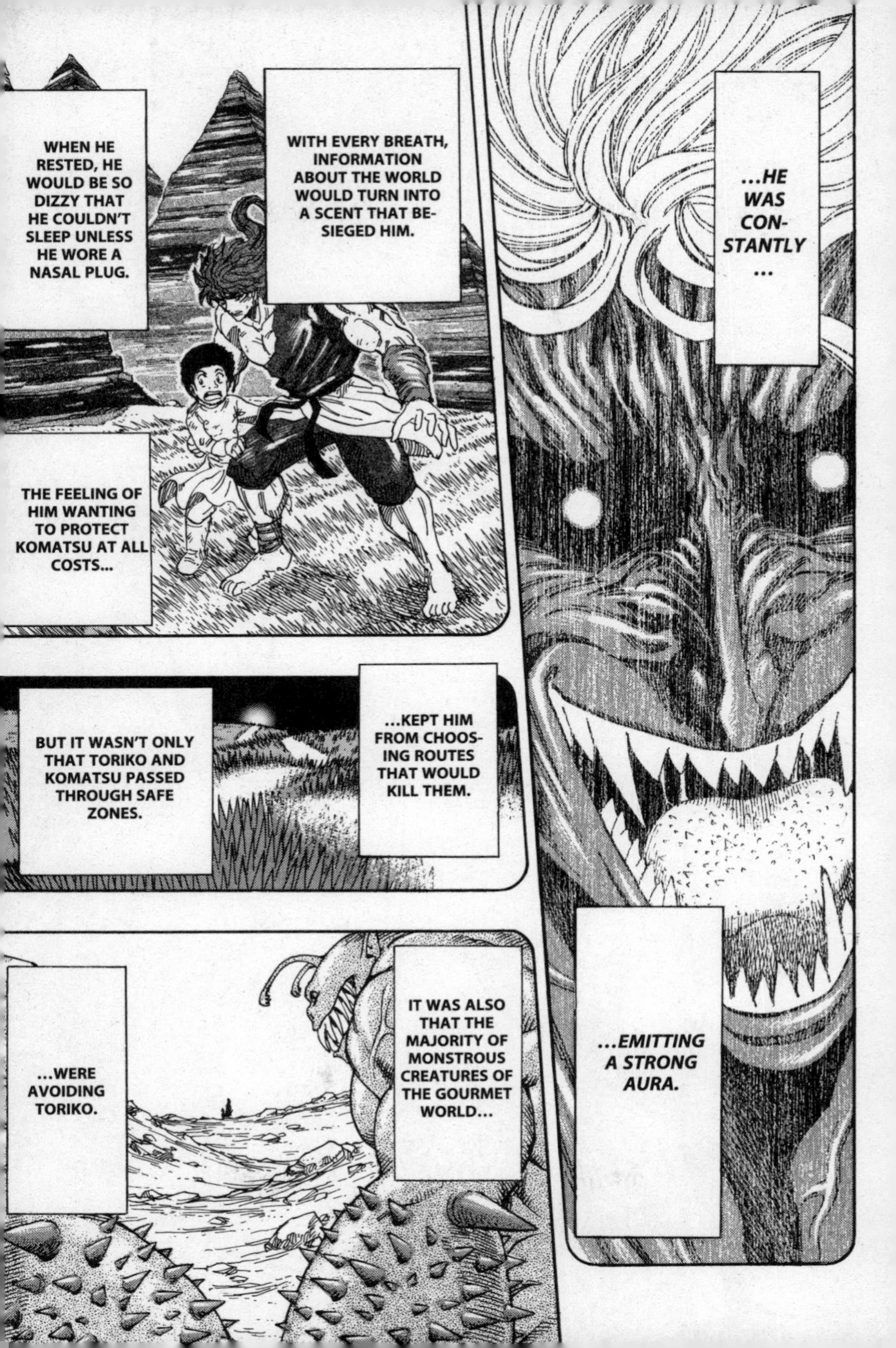

WITH EVERY BREATH, INFORMATION ABOUT THE WORLD WOULD TURN INTO A SCENT THAT BE-SIEGED HIM.
WHEN HE RESTED, HE WOULD BE SO DIZZY THAT HE COULDN'T SLEEP UNLESS HE WORE A NASAL PLUG.
THE FEELING OF HIM WANTING TO PROTECT KOMATSU AT ALL COSTS...
...KEPT HIM FROM CHOOS-ING ROUTES THAT WOULD KILL THEM.
BUT IT WASN'T ONLY THAT TORIKO AND KOMATSU PASSED THROUGH SAFE ZONES.
IT WAS ALSO THAT THE MAJORITY OF MONSTROUS CREATURES OF THE GOURMET WORLD...
...WERE AVOIDING TORIKO.
...HE WAS CON-STANTLY ...
...EMITTING A STRONG AURA.

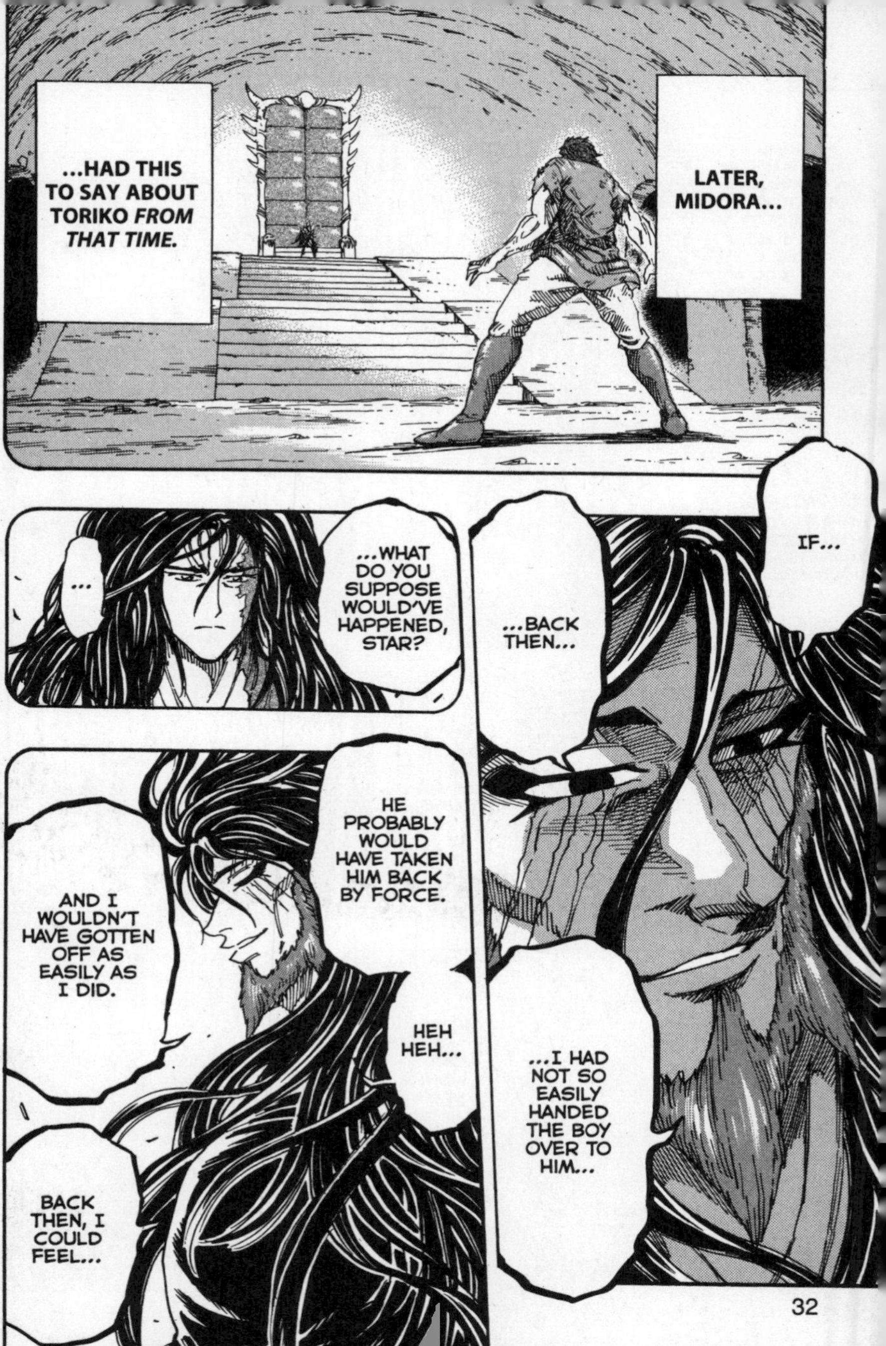
LATER, MIDORA...
...HAD THIS TO SAY ABOUT TORIKO *FROM THAT TIME.*
IF...
...BACK THEN...
...I HAD NOT SO EASILY HANDED THE BOY OVER TO HIM...
...WHAT DO YOU SUPPOSE WOULD'VE HAPPENED, STAR?
...
HE PROBABLY WOULD HAVE TAKEN HIM BACK BY FORCE.
AND I WOULDN'T HAVE GOTTEN OFF AS EASILY AS I DID.
HEH HEH...
BACK THEN, I COULD FEEL...

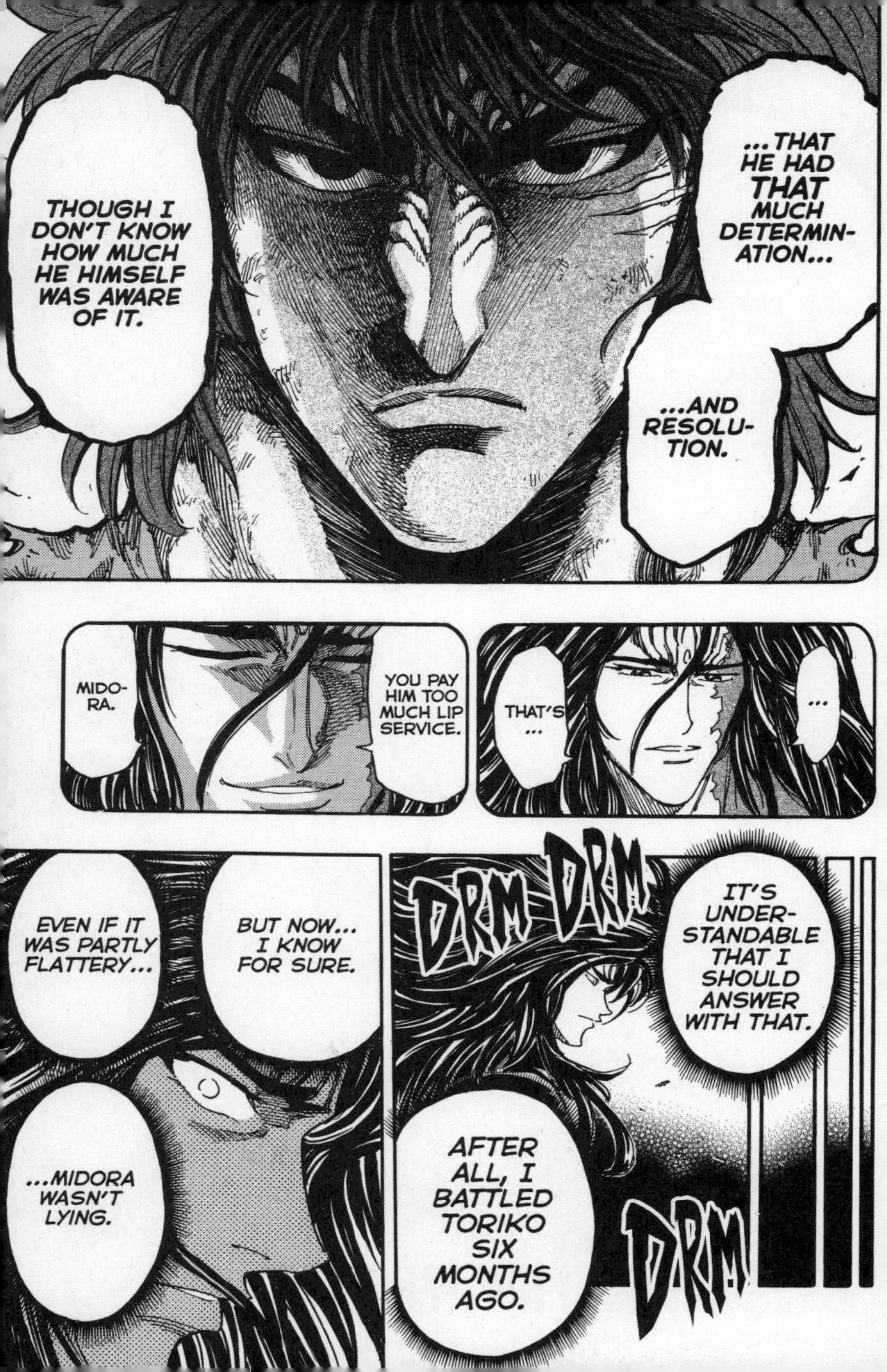
THOUGH I DON'T KNOW HOW MUCH HE HIMSELF WAS AWARE OF IT.
...THAT HE HAD THAT MUCH DETERMINATION...
...AND RESOLUTION.
...
THAT'S ...
YOU PAY HIM TOO MUCH LIP SERVICE.
MIDO-RA.
DRM DRM
IT'S UNDERSTANDABLE THAT I SHOULD ANSWER WITH THAT.
AFTER ALL, I BATTLED TORIKO SIX MONTHS AGO.
DRM
BUT NOW... I KNOW FOR SURE.
EVEN IF IT WAS PARTLY FLATTERY...
...MIDORA WASN'T LYING.

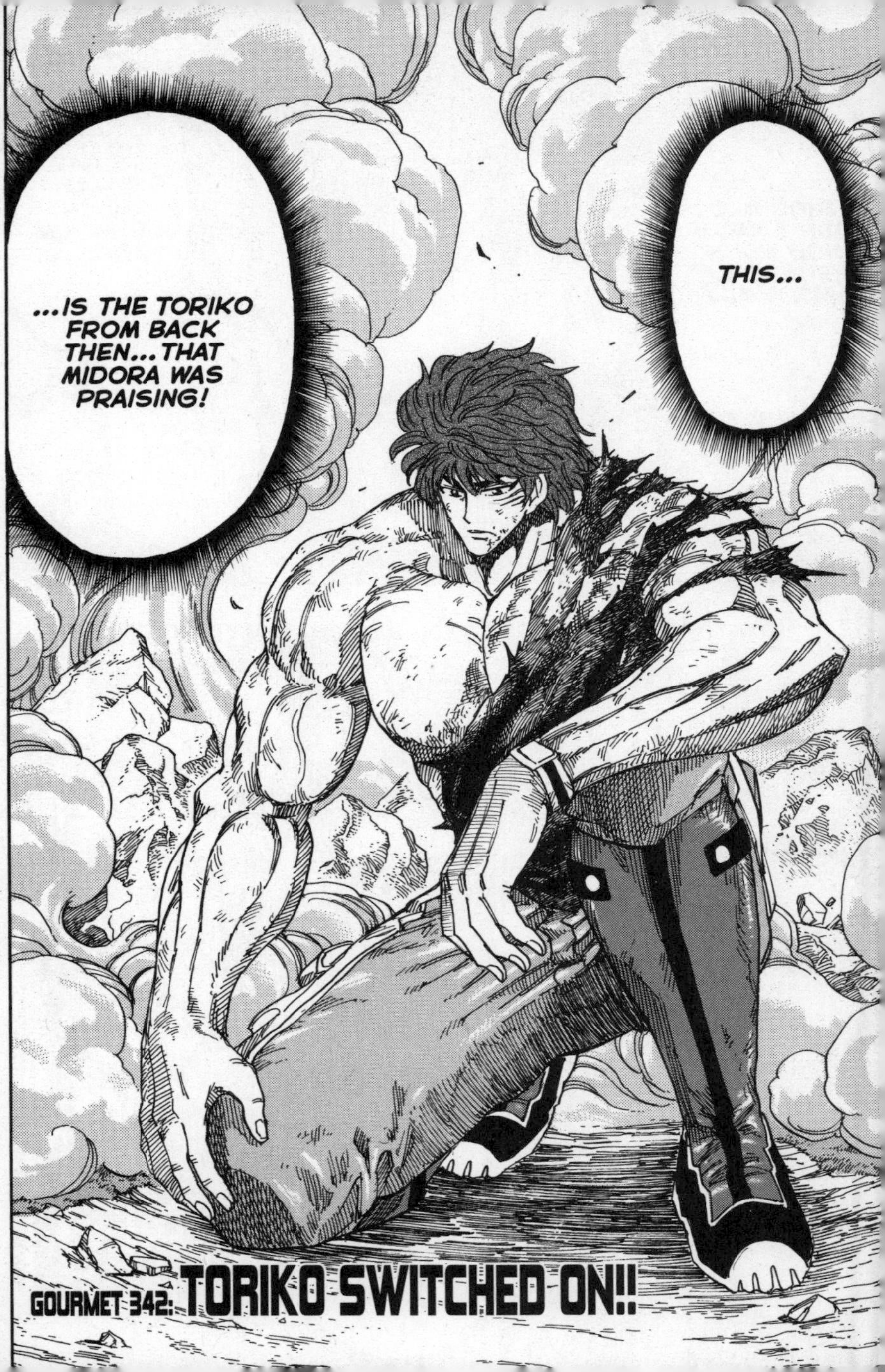
THIS...
...IS THE TORIKO FROM BACK THEN...THAT MIDORA WAS PRAISING!
GOURMET 342: TORIKO SWITCHED ON!!

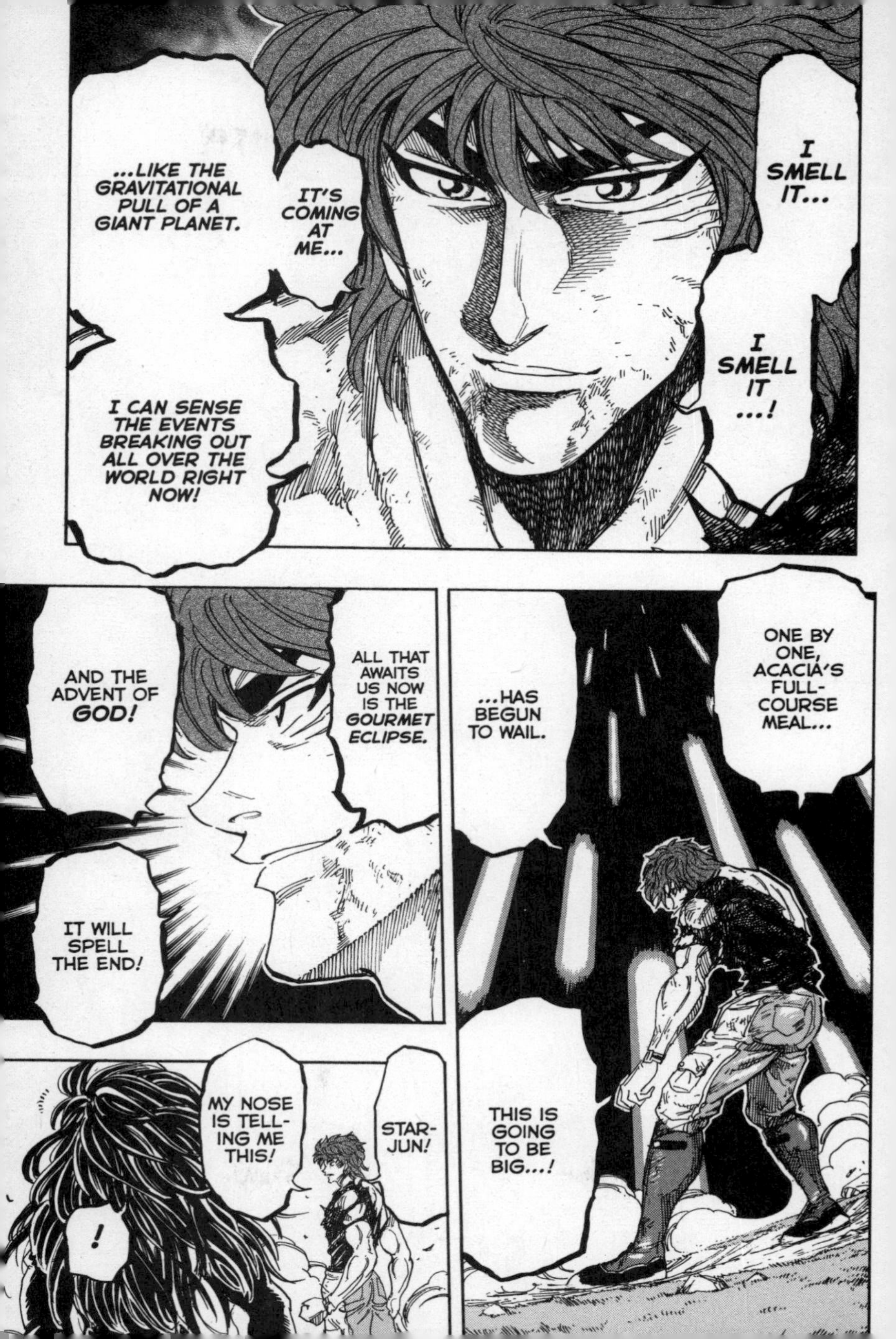
I SMELL IT...
I SMELL IT ...!
IT'S COMING AT ME...
...LIKE THE GRAVITATIONAL PULL OF A GIANT PLANET.
I CAN SENSE THE EVENTS BREAKING OUT ALL OVER THE WORLD RIGHT NOW!
ONE BY ONE, ACACIA'S FULL-COURSE MEAL...
...HAS BEGUN TO WAIL.
THIS IS GOING TO BE BIG...!
ALL THAT AWAITS US NOW IS THE GOURMET ECLIPSE.
AND THE ADVENT OF GOD!
IT WILL SPELL THE END!
STAR-JUN!
MY NOSE IS TELLING ME THIS!
!

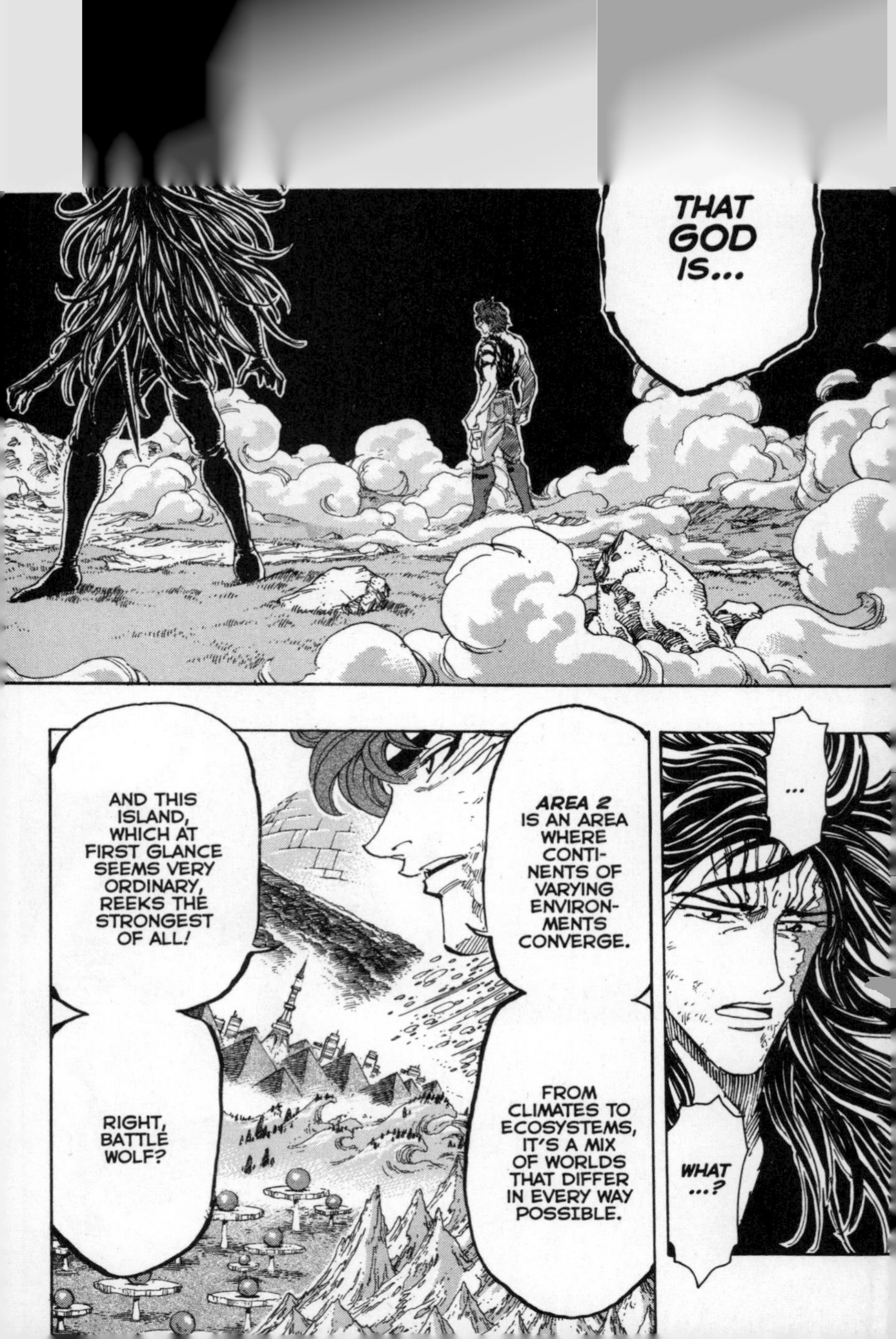
THAT GOD IS...
...
WHAT ...?
AREA 2 IS AN AREA WHERE CONTI-NENTS OF VARYING ENVIRON-MENTS CONVERGE.
FROM CLIMATES TO ECOSYSTEMS, IT'S A MIX OF WORLDS THAT DIFFER IN EVERY WAY POSSIBLE.
AND THIS ISLAND, WHICH AT FIRST GLANCE SEEMS VERY ORDINARY, REEKS THE STRONGEST OF ALL!
RIGHT, BATTLE WOLF?

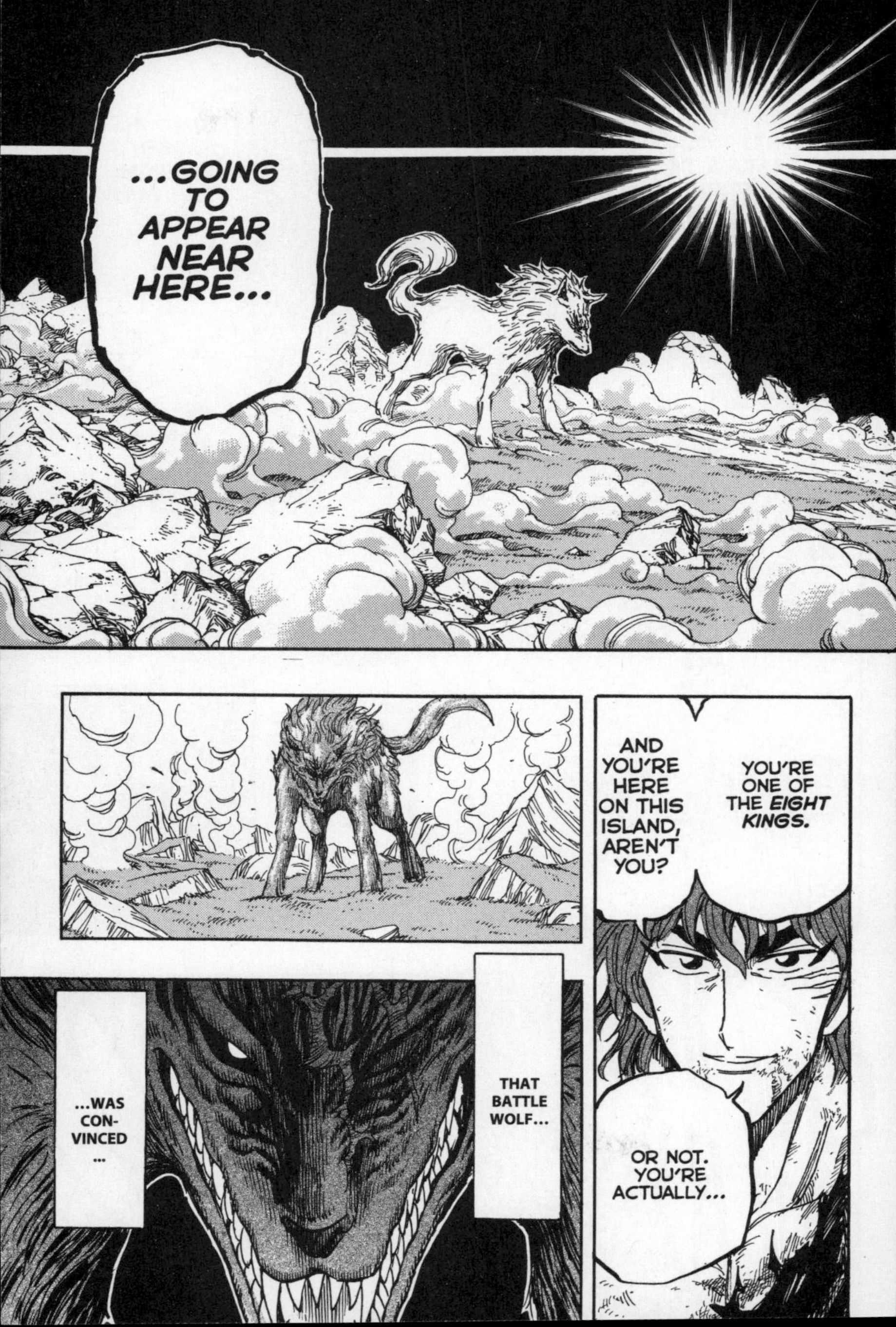
...GOING TO APPEAR NEAR HERE...
YOU'RE ONE OF THE *EIGHT KINGS.*
AND YOU'RE HERE ON THIS ISLAND, AREN'T YOU?
OR NOT. YOU'RE ACTUALLY...
THAT BATTLE WOLF...
...WAS CON-VINCED...

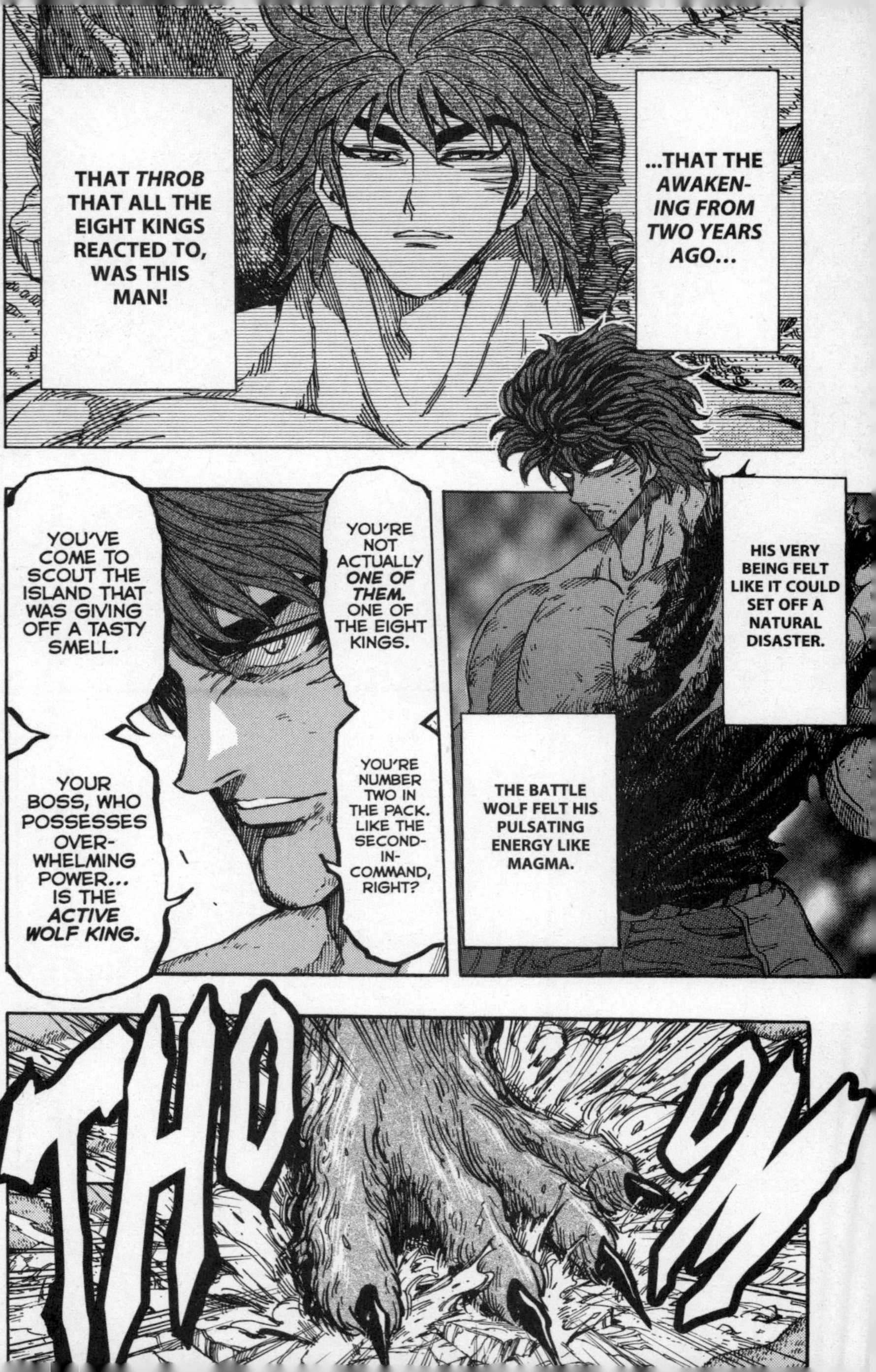
...THAT THE AWAKENING FROM TWO YEARS AGO...
THAT THROB THAT ALL THE EIGHT KINGS REACTED TO, WAS THIS MAN!
HIS VERY BEING FELT LIKE IT COULD SET OFF A NATURAL DISASTER.
THE BATTLE WOLF FELT HIS PULSATING ENERGY LIKE MAGMA.
YOU'RE NOT ACTUALLY ONE OF THEM. ONE OF THE EIGHT KINGS.
YOU'RE NUMBER TWO IN THE PACK. LIKE THE SECOND-IN-COMMAND, RIGHT?
YOU'VE COME TO SCOUT THE ISLAND THAT WAS GIVING OFF A TASTY SMELL.
YOUR BOSS, WHO POSSESSES OVERWHELMING POWER... IS THE ACTIVE WOLF KING.
THOOM

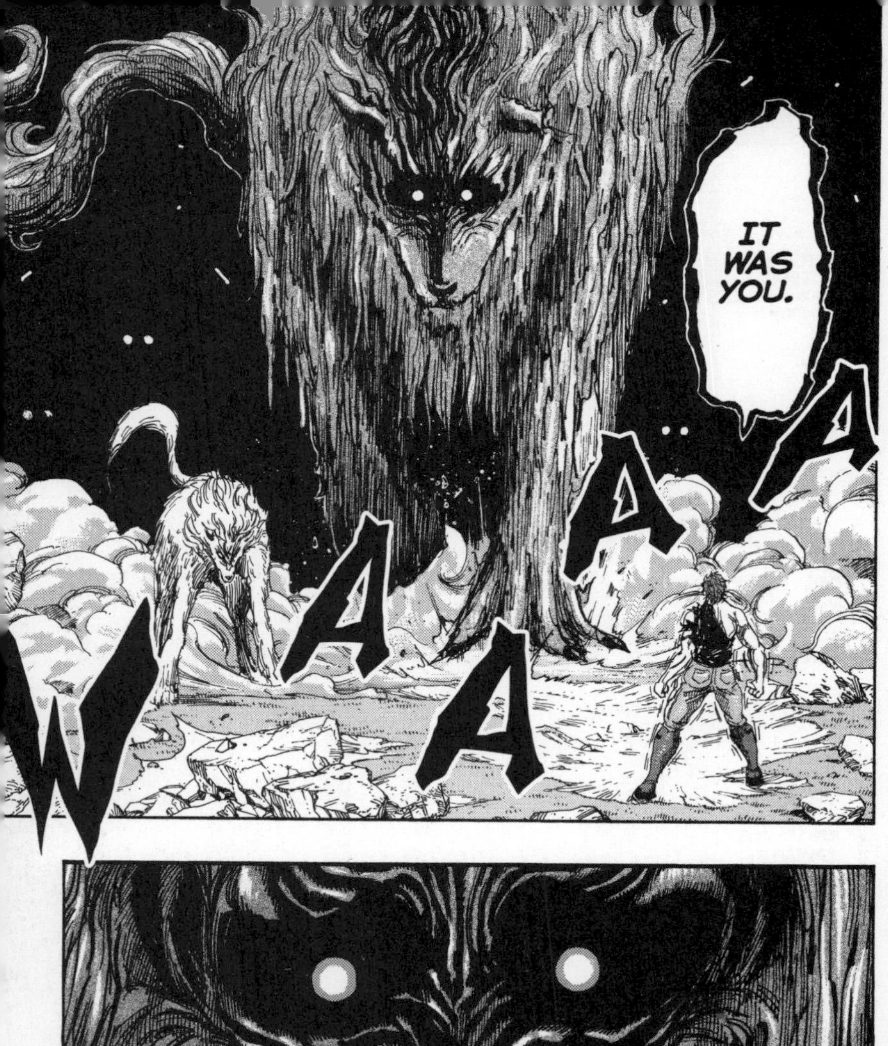
IT WAS YOU.
WAAAAA

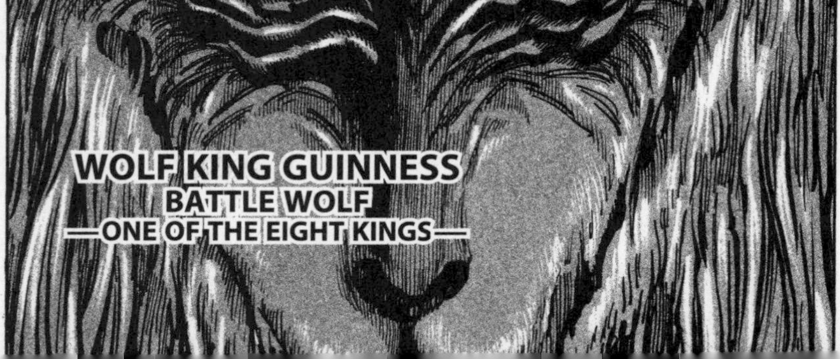
WOLF KING GUINNESS
BATTLE WOLF
—ONE OF THE EIGHT KINGS—

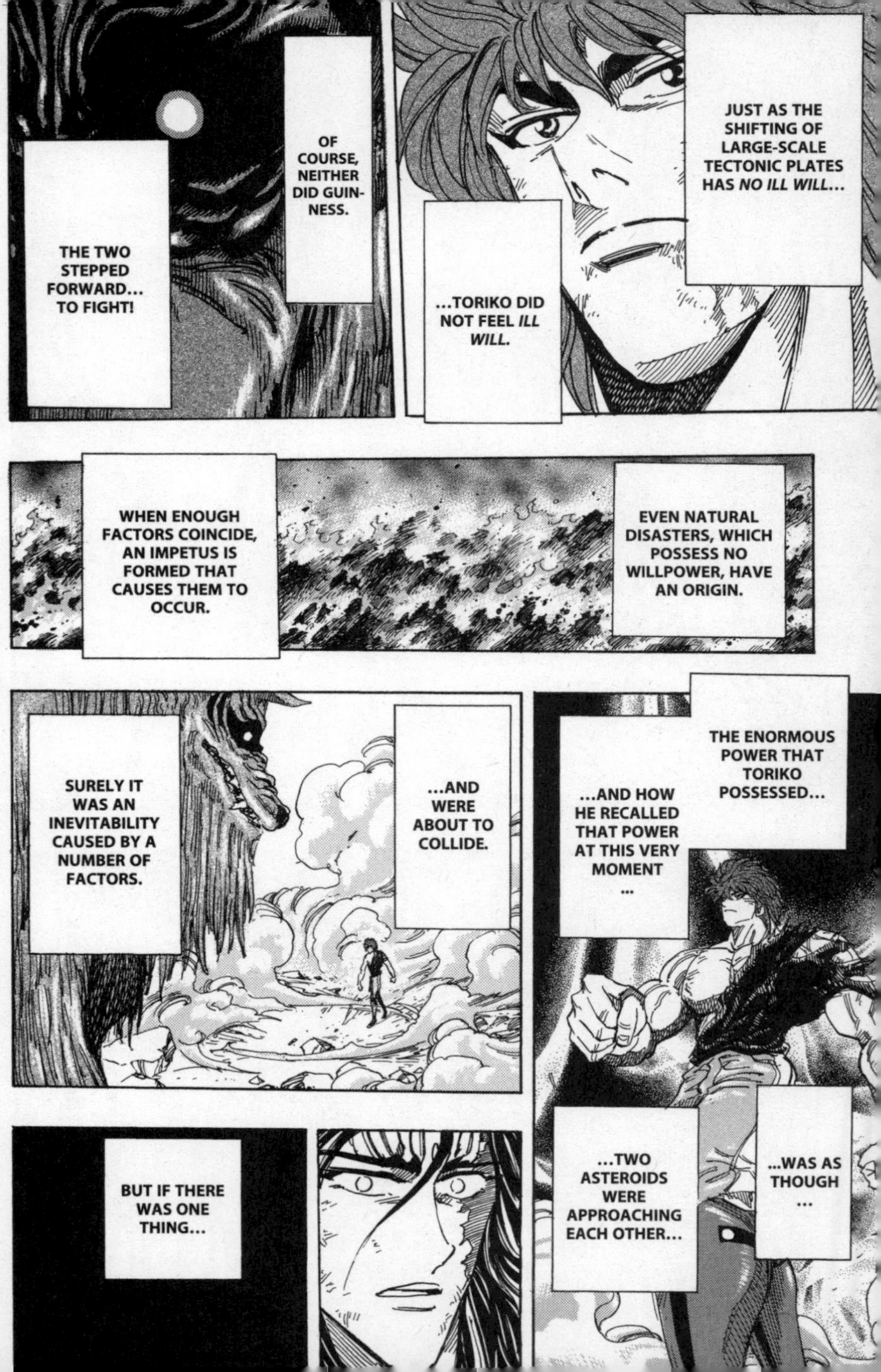
JUST AS THE SHIFTING OF LARGE-SCALE TECTONIC PLATES HAS *NO ILL WILL*...
...TORIKO DID NOT FEEL *ILL WILL.*
OF COURSE, NEITHER DID GUIN-NESS.
THE TWO STEPPED FORWARD... TO FIGHT!
EVEN NATURAL DISASTERS, WHICH POSSESS NO WILLPOWER, HAVE AN ORIGIN.
WHEN ENOUGH FACTORS COINCIDE, AN IMPETUS IS FORMED THAT CAUSES THEM TO OCCUR.
THE ENORMOUS POWER THAT TORIKO POSSESSED...
...AND HOW HE RECALLED THAT POWER AT THIS VERY MOMENT ...
...WAS AS THOUGH ...
...TWO ASTEROIDS WERE APPROACHING EACH OTHER...
...AND WERE ABOUT TO COLLIDE.
SURELY IT WAS AN INEVITABILITY CAUSED BY A NUMBER OF FACTORS.
BUT IF THERE WAS ONE THING...

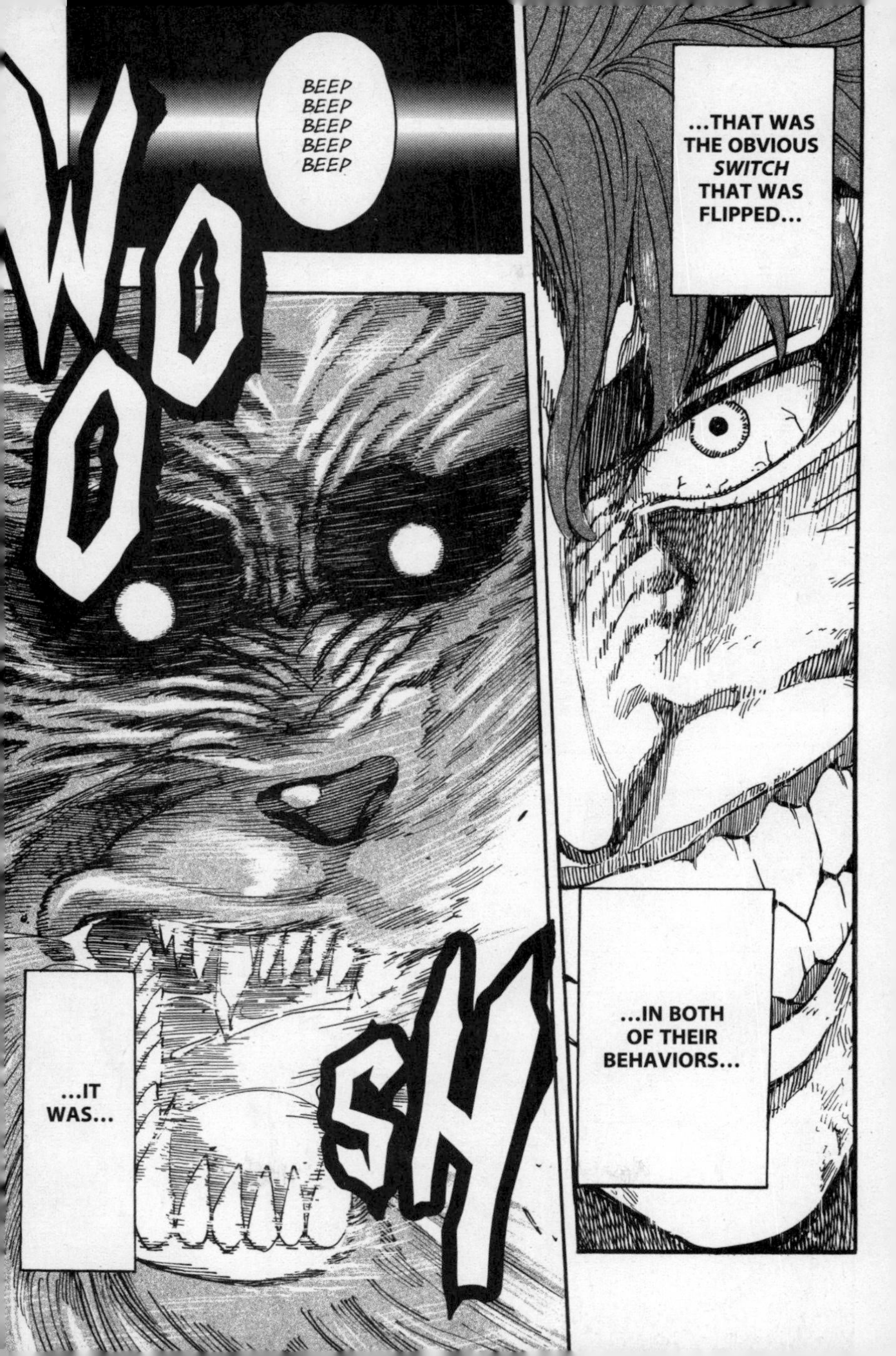

...THAT WAS THE OBVIOUS *SWITCH* THAT WAS FLIPPED...
...IN BOTH OF THEIR BEHAVIORS...
BEEP BEEP BEEP BEEP BEEP
W.O.O.
...IT WAS...
SH

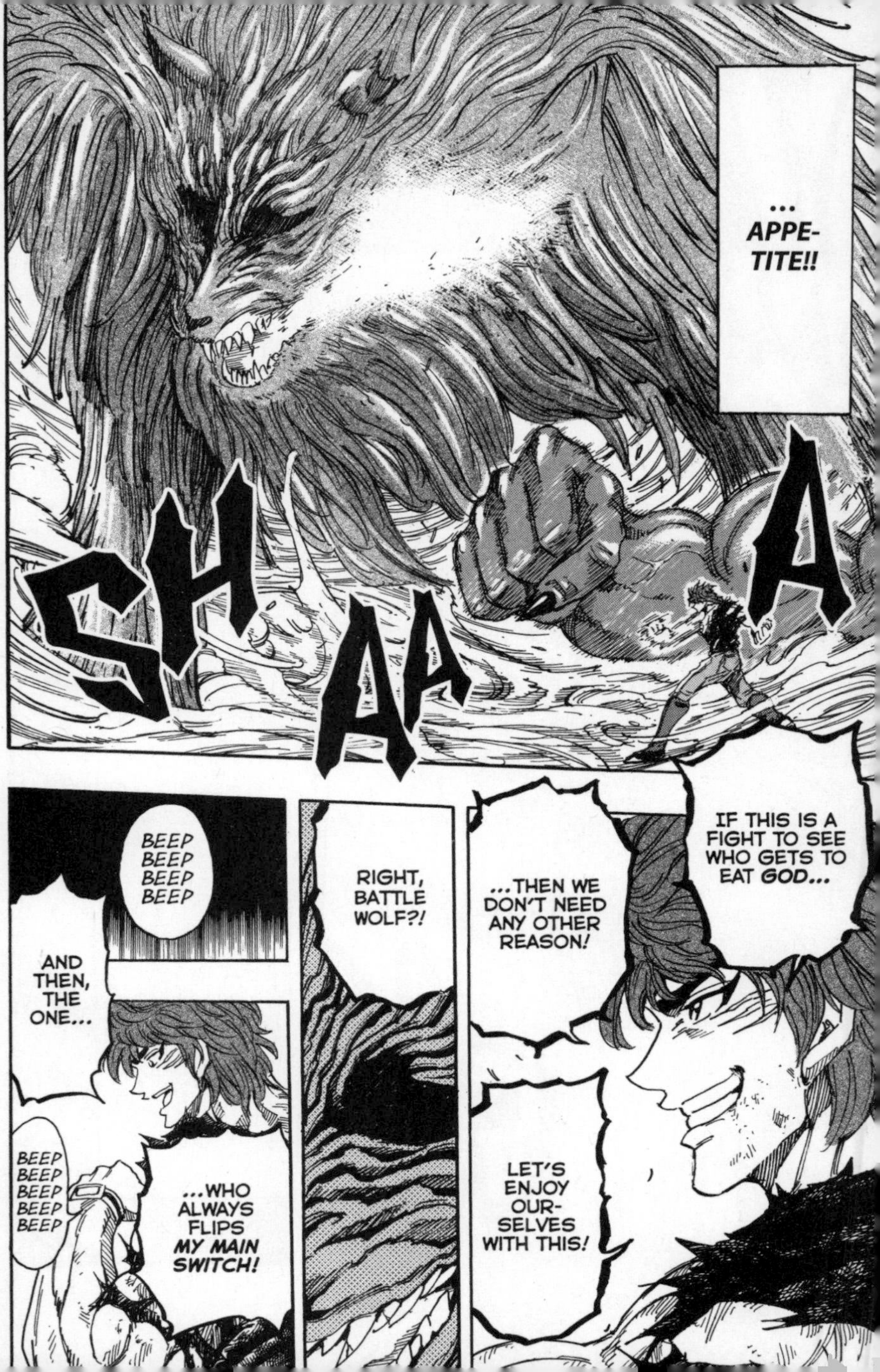
...APPE-TITE!!
SHAAA
IF THIS IS A FIGHT TO SEE WHO GETS TO EAT *GOD*...
...THEN WE DON'T NEED ANY OTHER REASON*!*
LET'S ENJOY OUR-SELVES WITH THIS*!*
RIGHT, BATTLE WOLF?!
BEEP BEEP BEEP BEEP
AND THEN, THE ONE...
...WHO ALWAYS FLIPS *MY MAIN* SWITCH*!*
BEEP BEEP BEEP BEEP BEEP

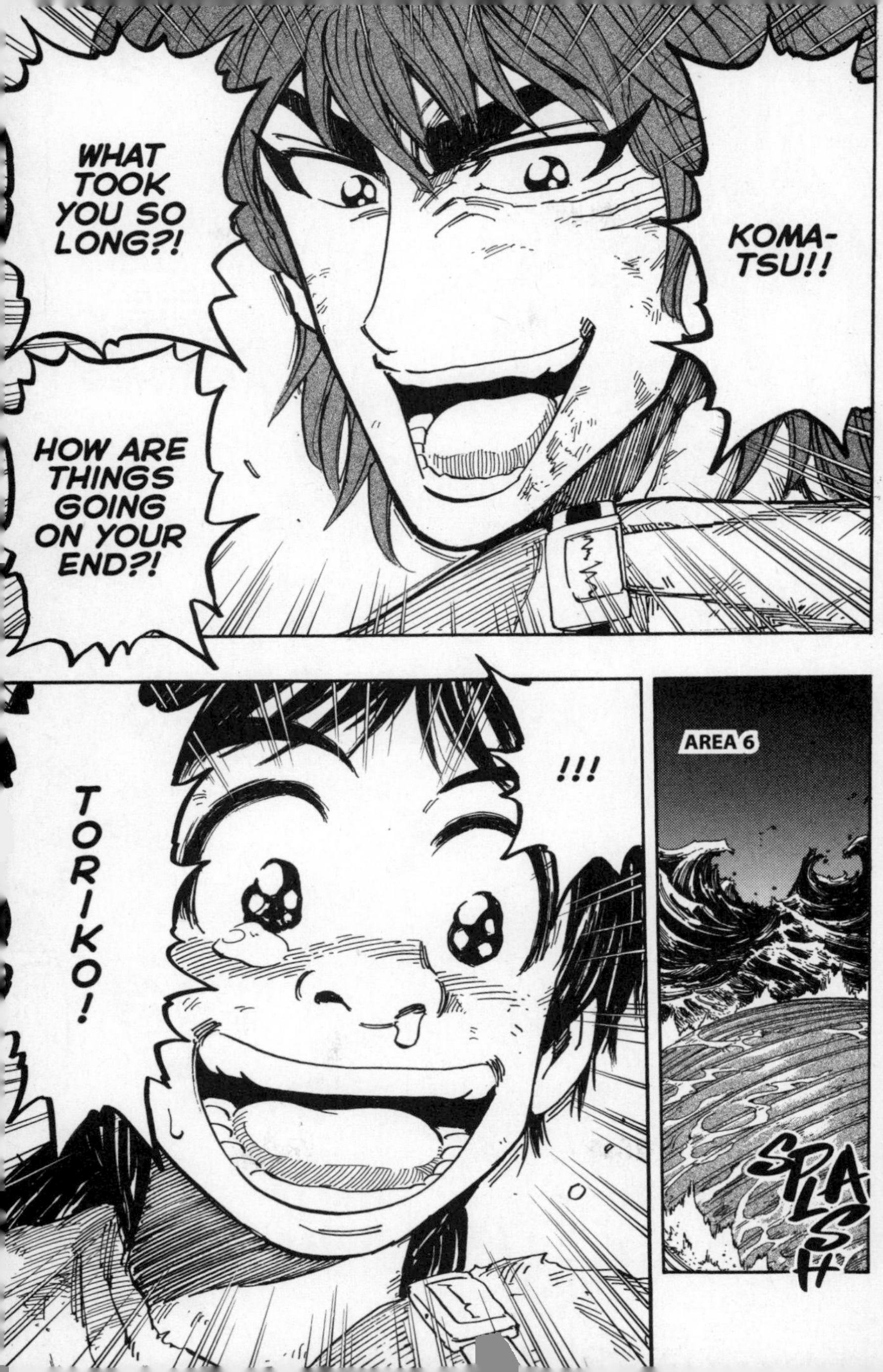
KOMA-
TSU!!
WHAT TOOK YOU SO LONG?!
HOW ARE THINGS GOING ON YOUR END?!
AREA 6
SPLASH
!!!
TORIKO!

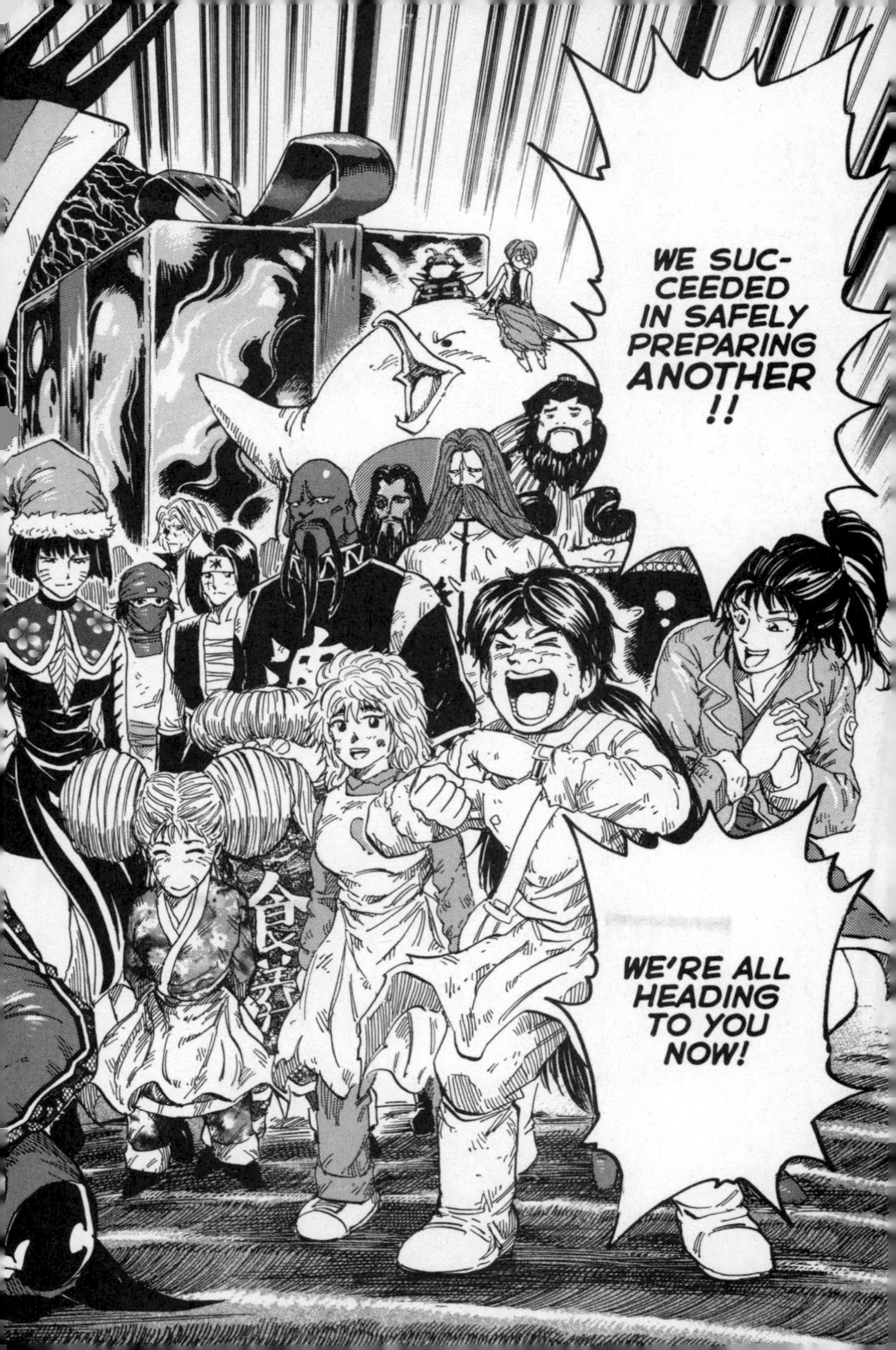
WE SUC-CEEDED IN SAFELY PREPARING ANOTHER !!
WE'RE ALL HEADING TO YOU NOW!

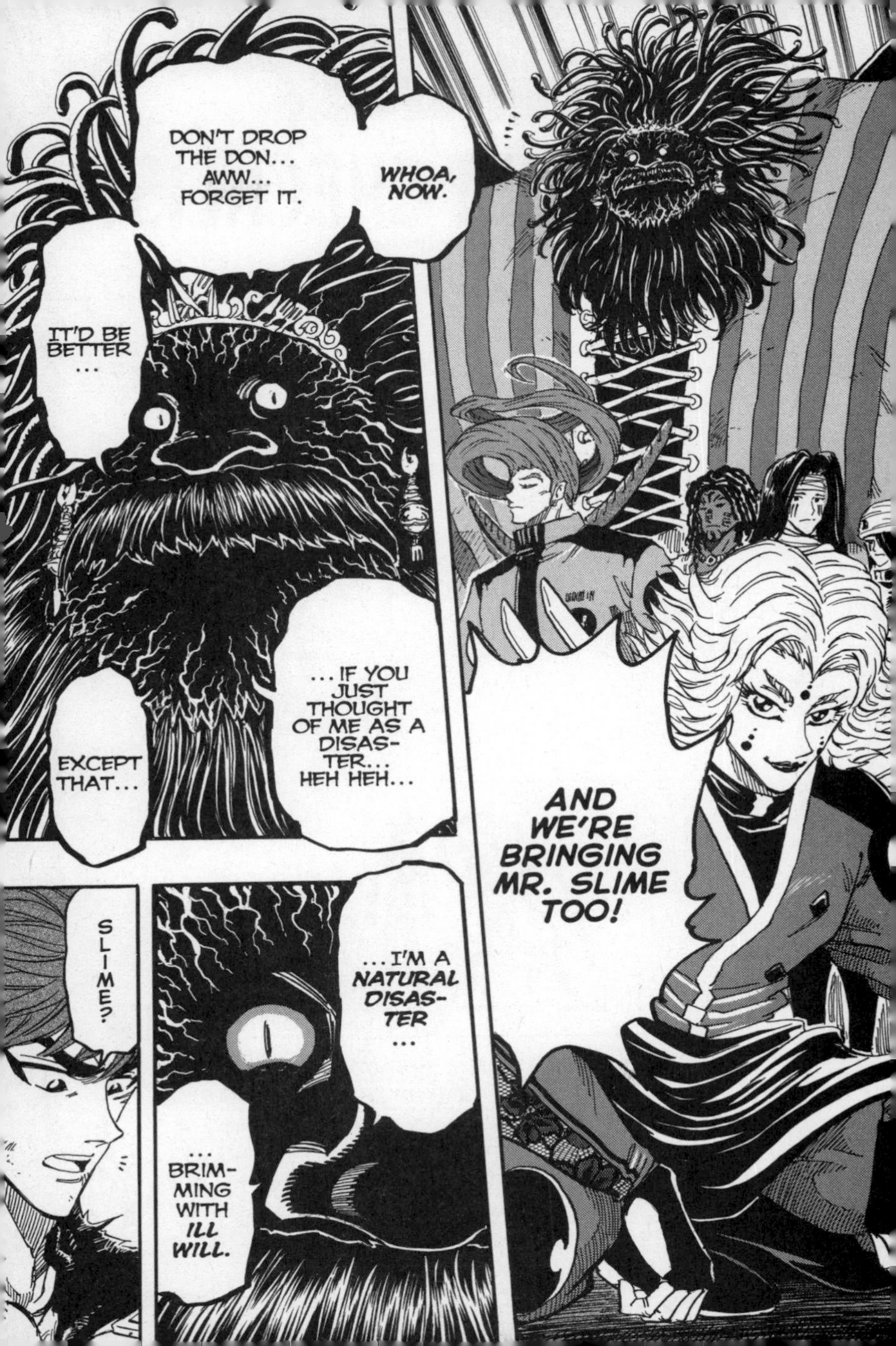
AND WE'RE BRINGING MR. SLIME TOO!
WHOA, NOW.
DON'T DROP THE DON... AWW... FORGET IT.
IT'D BE BETTER...
...IF YOU JUST THOUGHT OF ME AS A DISASTER... HEH HEH...
EXCEPT THAT...
...I'M A NATURAL DISASTER...
...BRIMMING WITH ILL WILL.
SLIME?

TORIKO

GOURMET CHECKLIST

Vol. 372

IAI-AYE
(MAMMAL)

CAPTURE LEVEL: 622
HABITAT: NORTHERN MOUNTAIN, IN AREA 7
SIZE: 150 CM
HEIGHT: ---
WEIGHT: 50 KG
PRICE: NOT EDIBLE

OOK! EEK!

IAI-AYE*
(MAMMAL)
CAPTURE LEVEL 622

SCALE

A MAMMAL THAT LIVES IN "MONKEY RESTAURANT," A PLACE WHERE ANIMALS ARE NOT ALLOWED TO INDISCRIMINATELY PREY ON EACH OTHER. THE IAI-AYE IS RANKED LOWEST AT MONKEY MARTIAL ARTS, BUT HAS A GOOD COMMAND OF THE BASICS AND WILL ALSO USE THE KATANA AT THE TIP OF ITS TAIL TO ATTACK. IT'S A FORMIDABLE OPPONENT. ONCE IT SENSES NEARBY DANGER, IT WILL POSITION ITSELF A SUITABLE DISTANCE AWAY FROM IT AND QUICKLY DRAW ITS SWORD TO SLICE ITS PREY IN TWO! IT REALLY DOES HAVE IMPRESSIVE SWORDSMANSHIP.

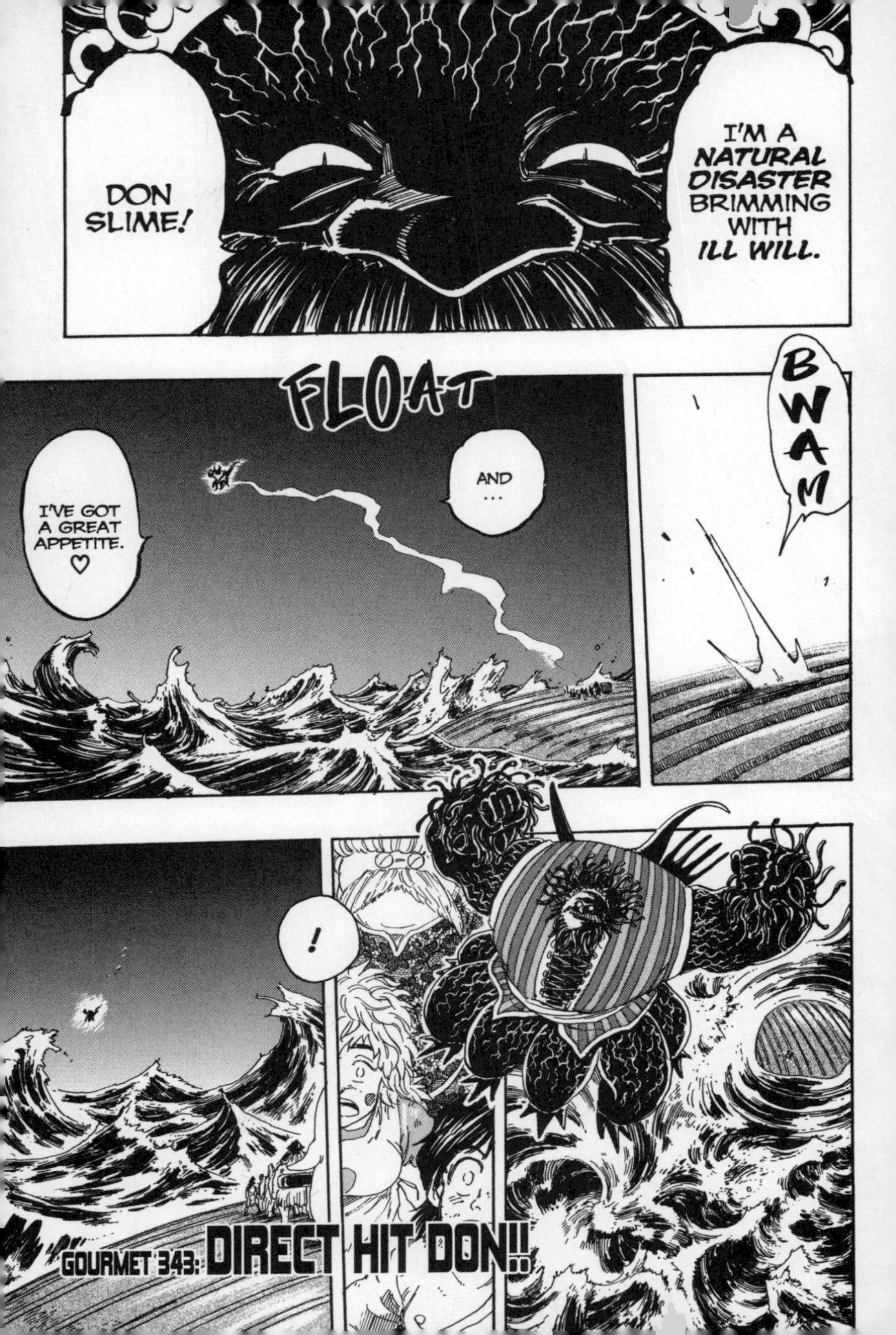
I'M A NATURAL DISASTER BRIMMING WITH ILL WILL.
DON SLIME!
BWAM
FLOAT
AND ...
I'VE GOT A GREAT APPETITE. ♡
!
GOURMET 343: DIRECT HIT DON!!

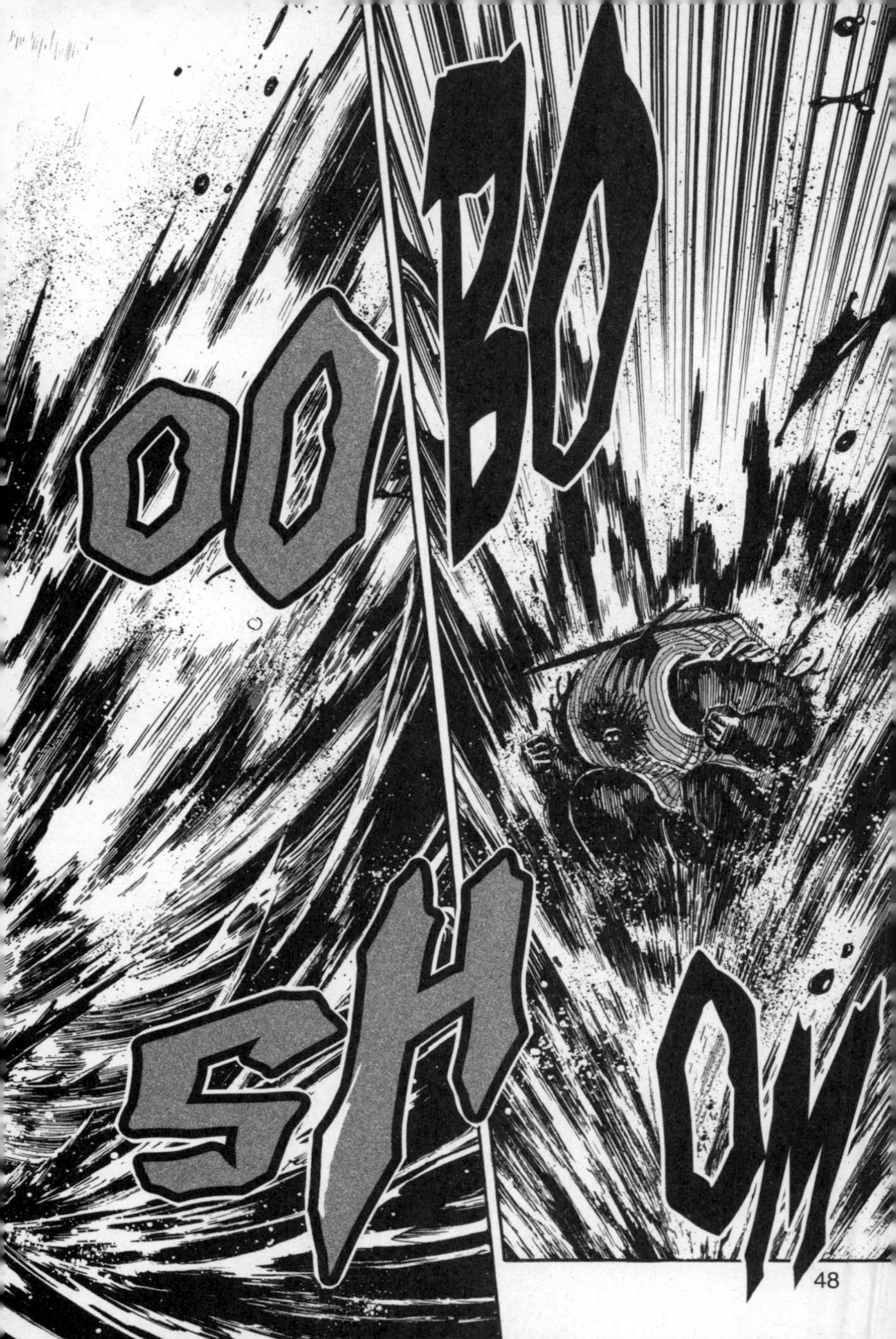
BOOOSHOM

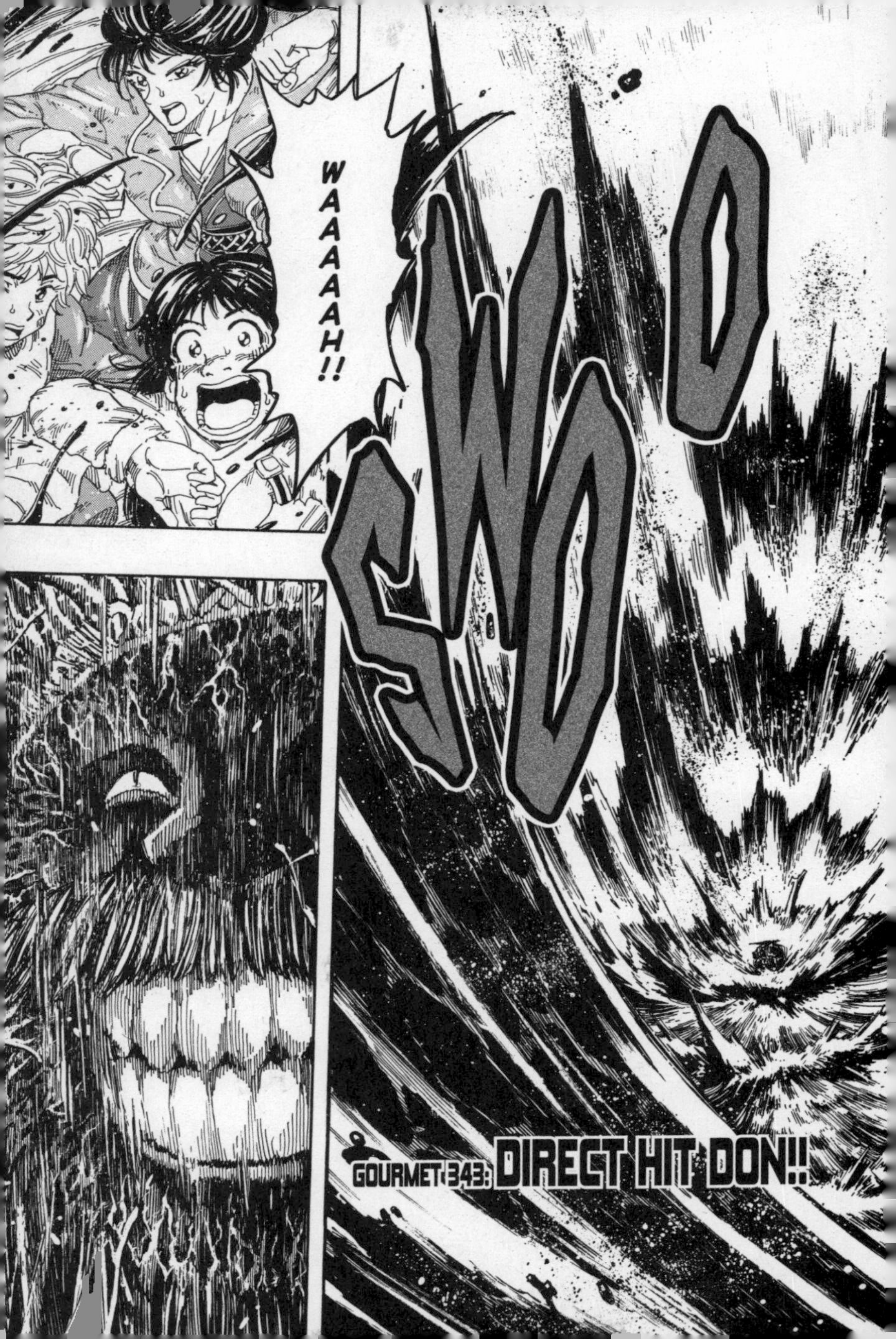

SWOOD
WAAAAAAAH!!
GOURMET 343: DIRECT HIT DON!!

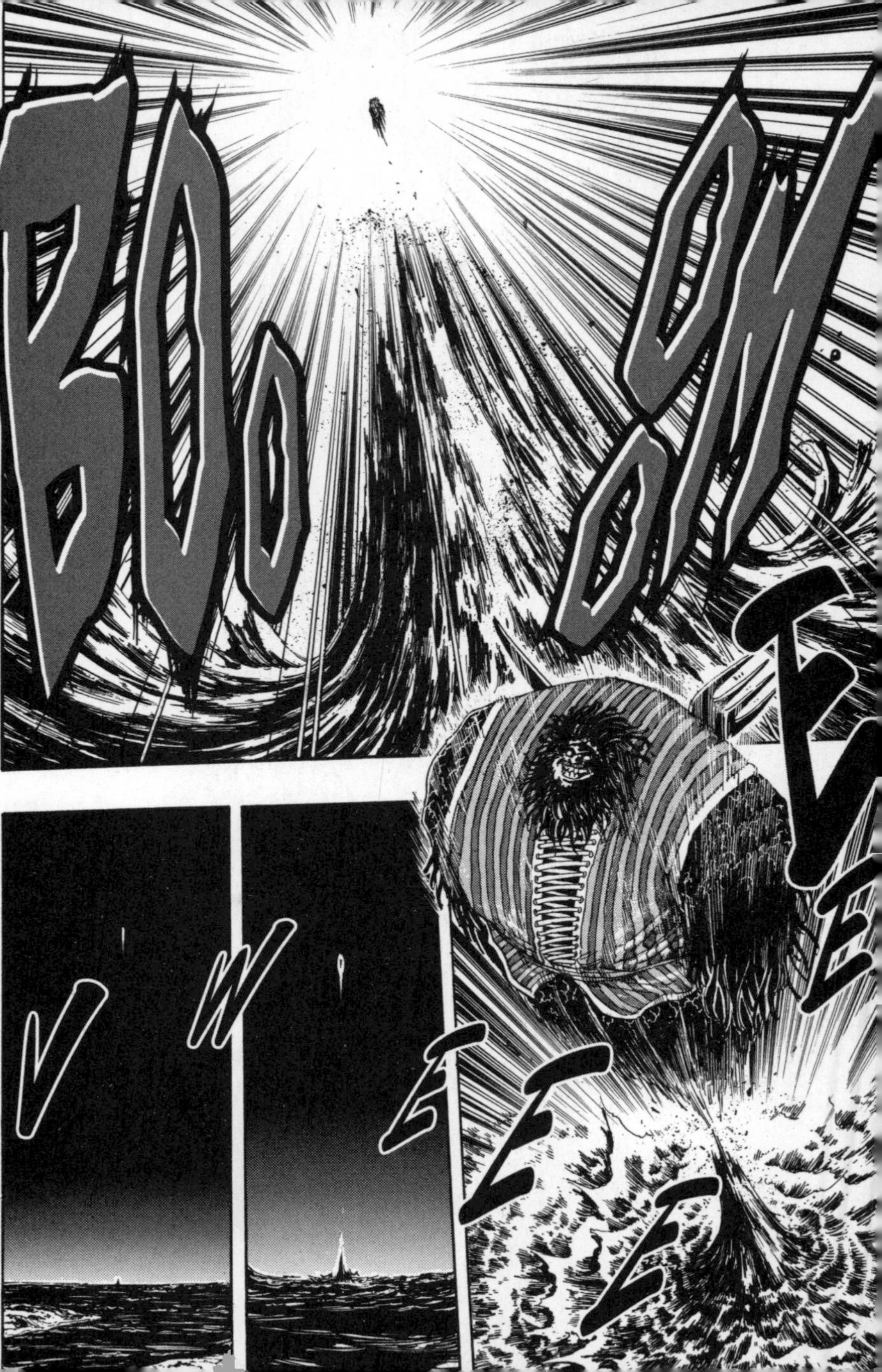
BOOOSH
VWEEEE

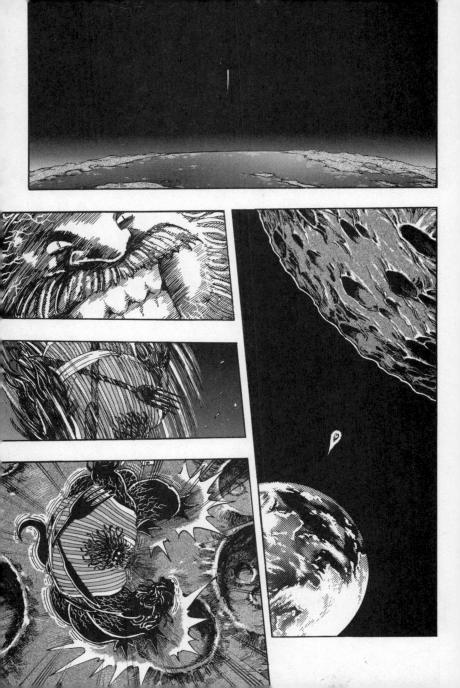

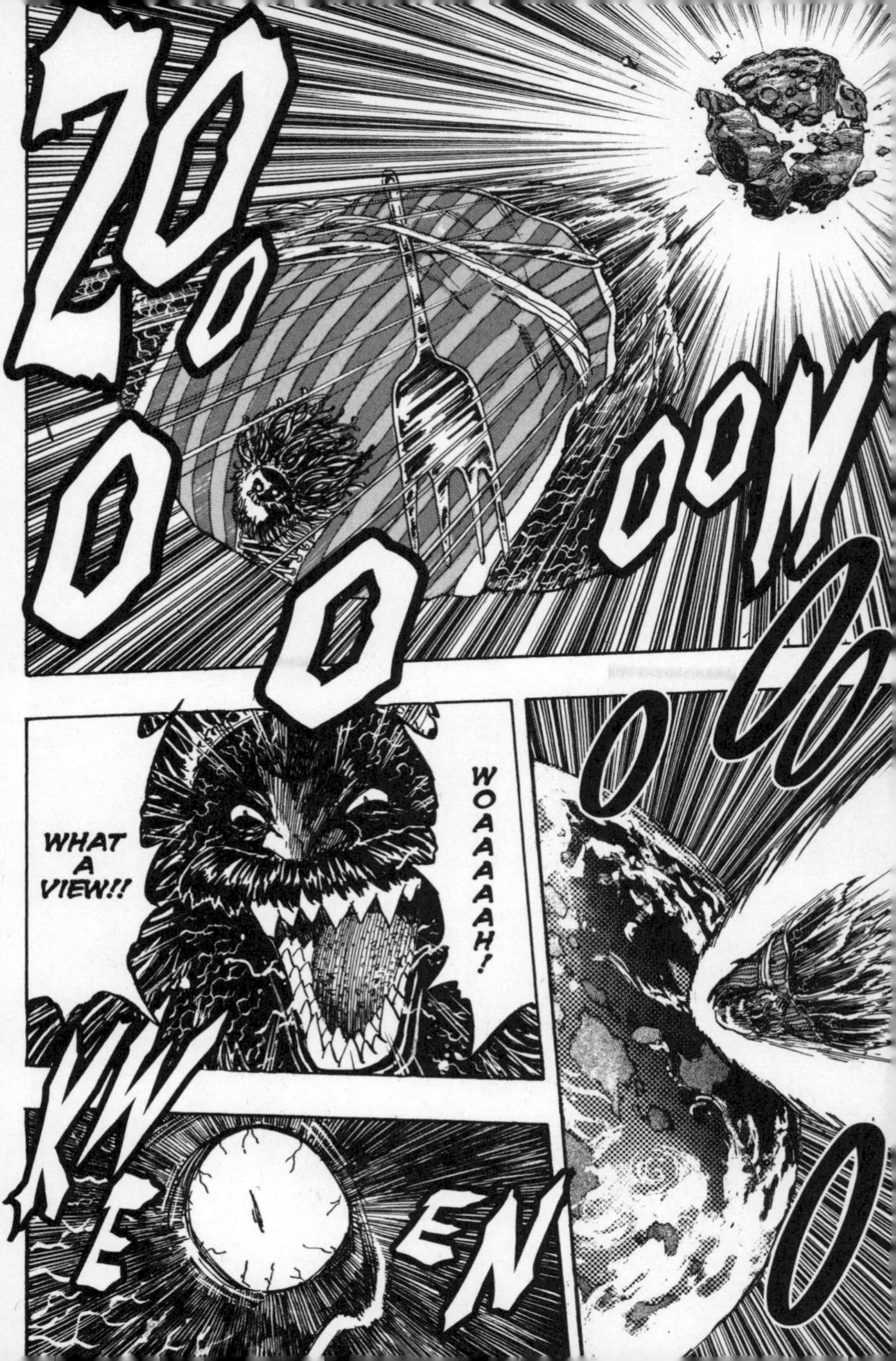
WOAAAAAH!
WHAT A VIEW!!

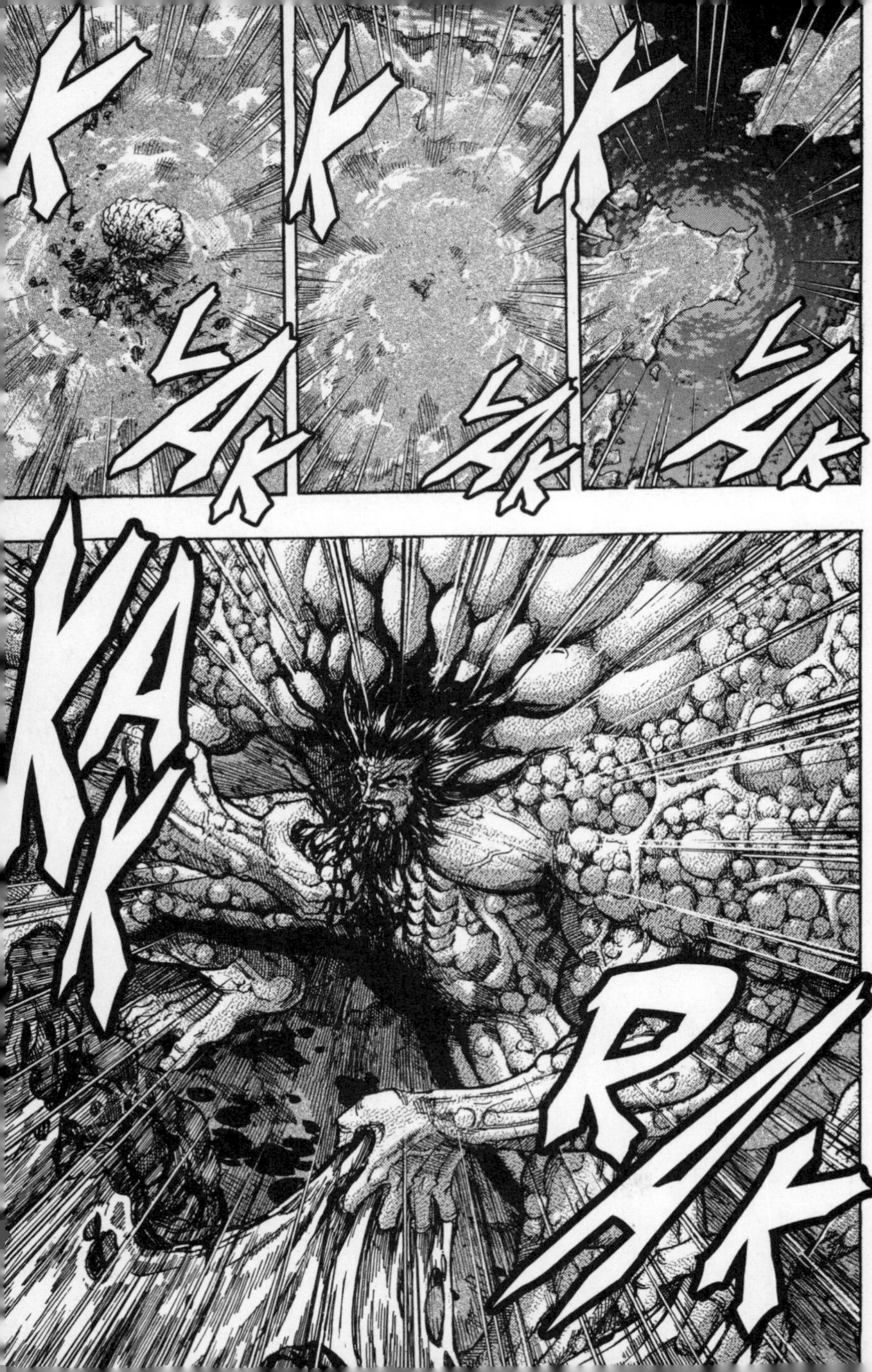
KRAK
KRAK
KRAK
KAKRAK

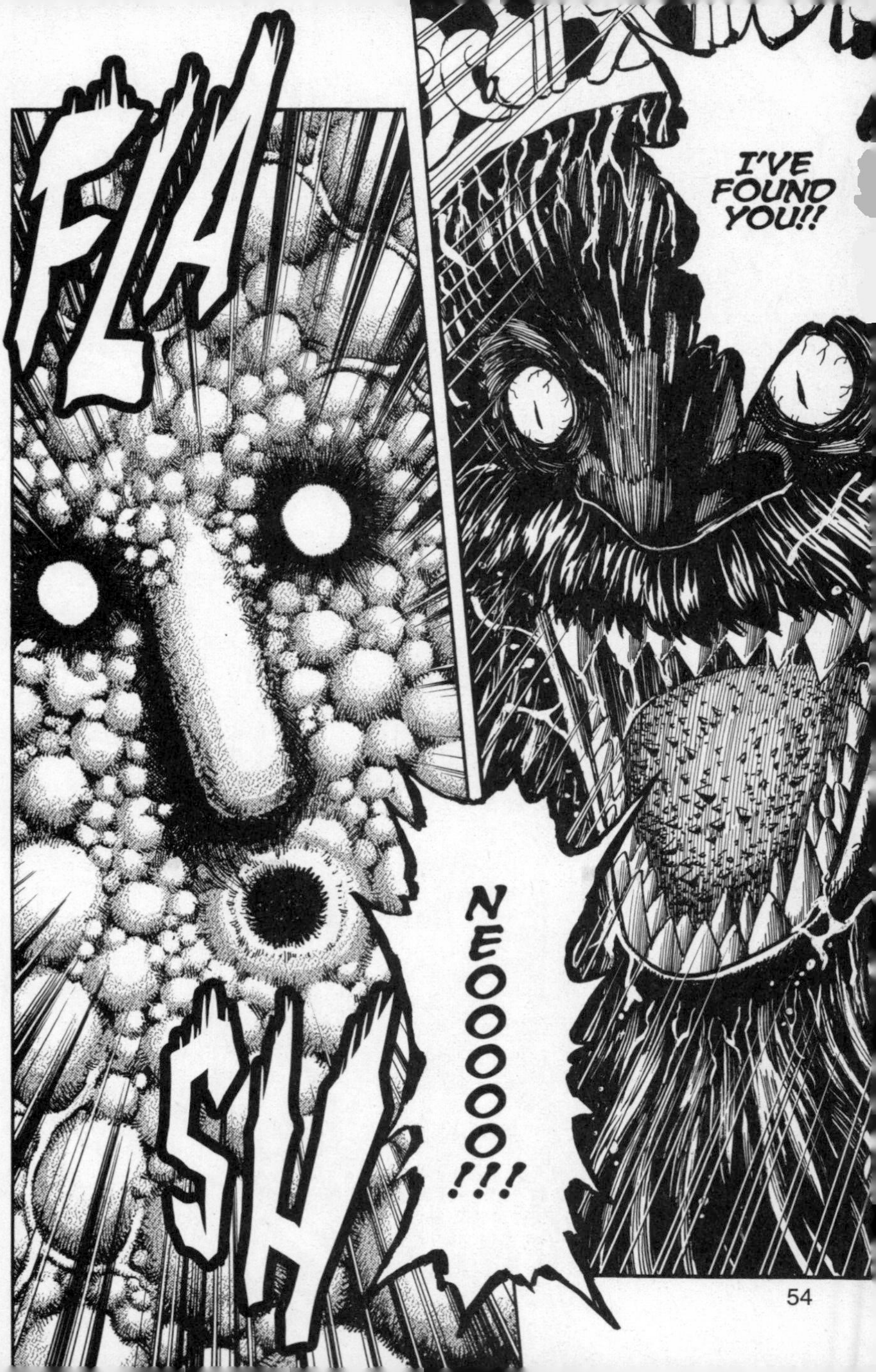
I'VE FOUND YOU!!
NEOOOOOO!!!
FLASH

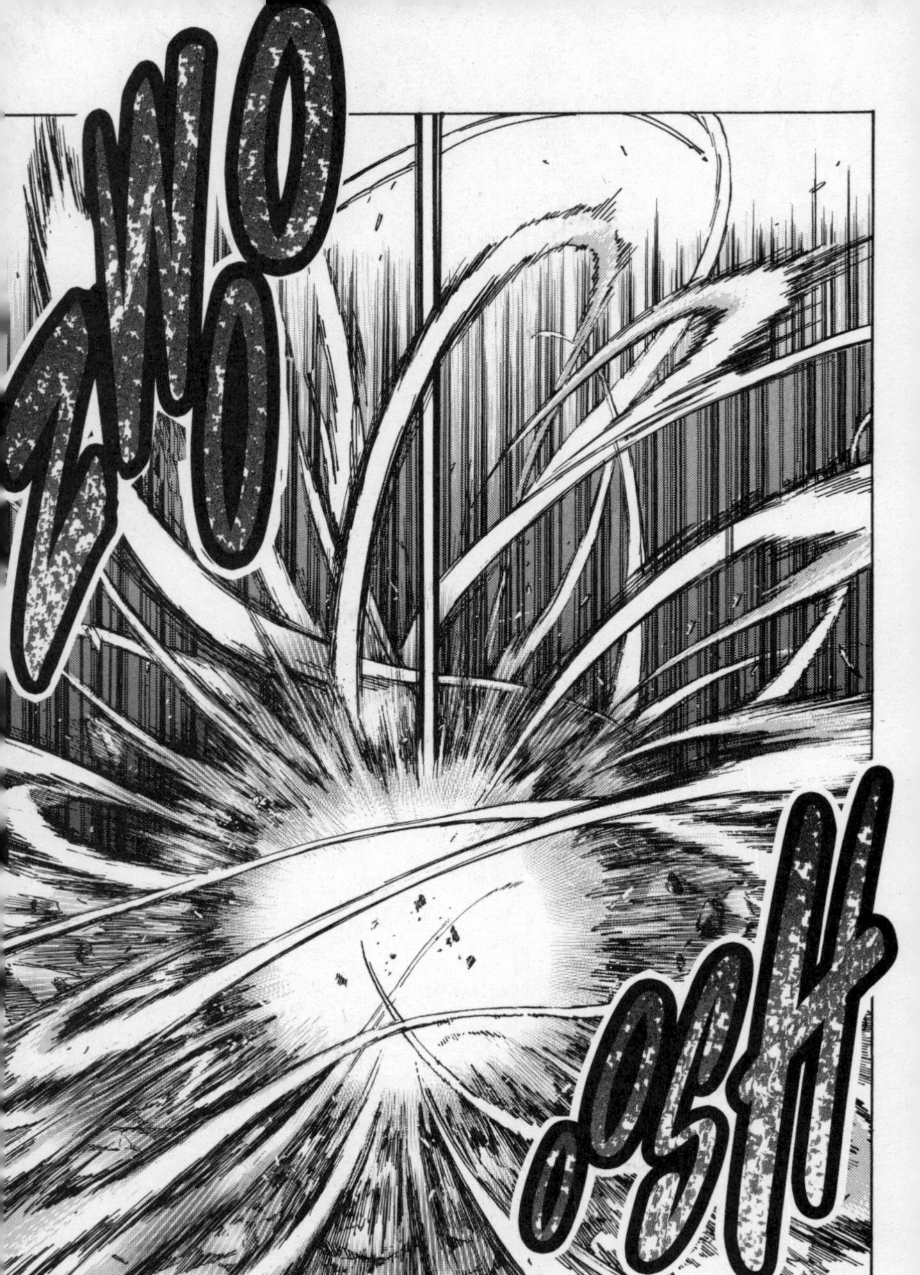

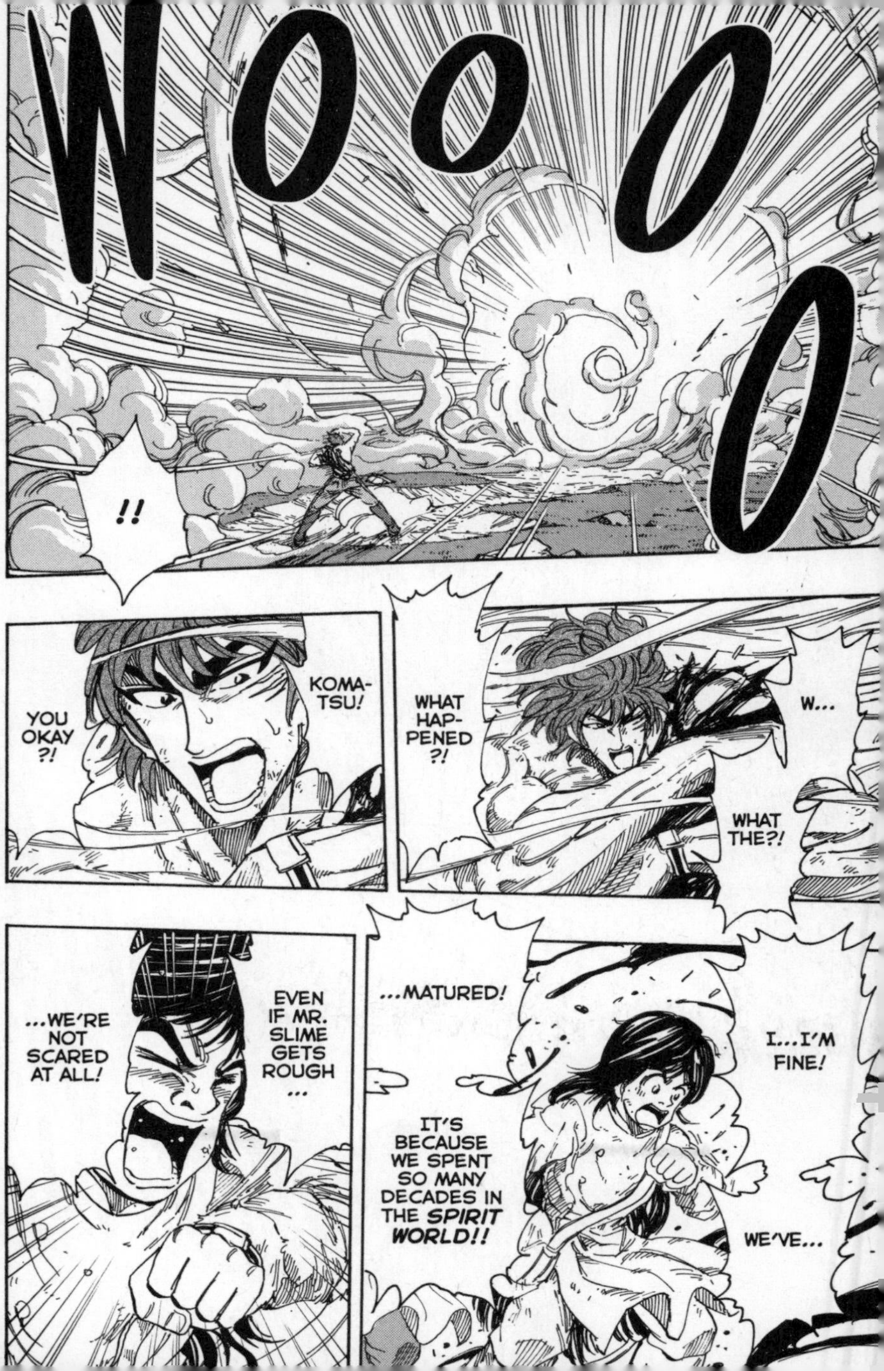
WOOOOO
!!
W...
WHAT THE?!
WHAT HAPPENED?!
KOMATSU!
YOU OKAY?!
I...I'M FINE!
WE'VE...
...MATURED!
IT'S BECAUSE WE SPENT SO MANY DECADES IN THE *SPIRIT WORLD!!*
EVEN IF MR. SLIME GETS ROUGH...
...WE'RE NOT SCARED AT ALL!

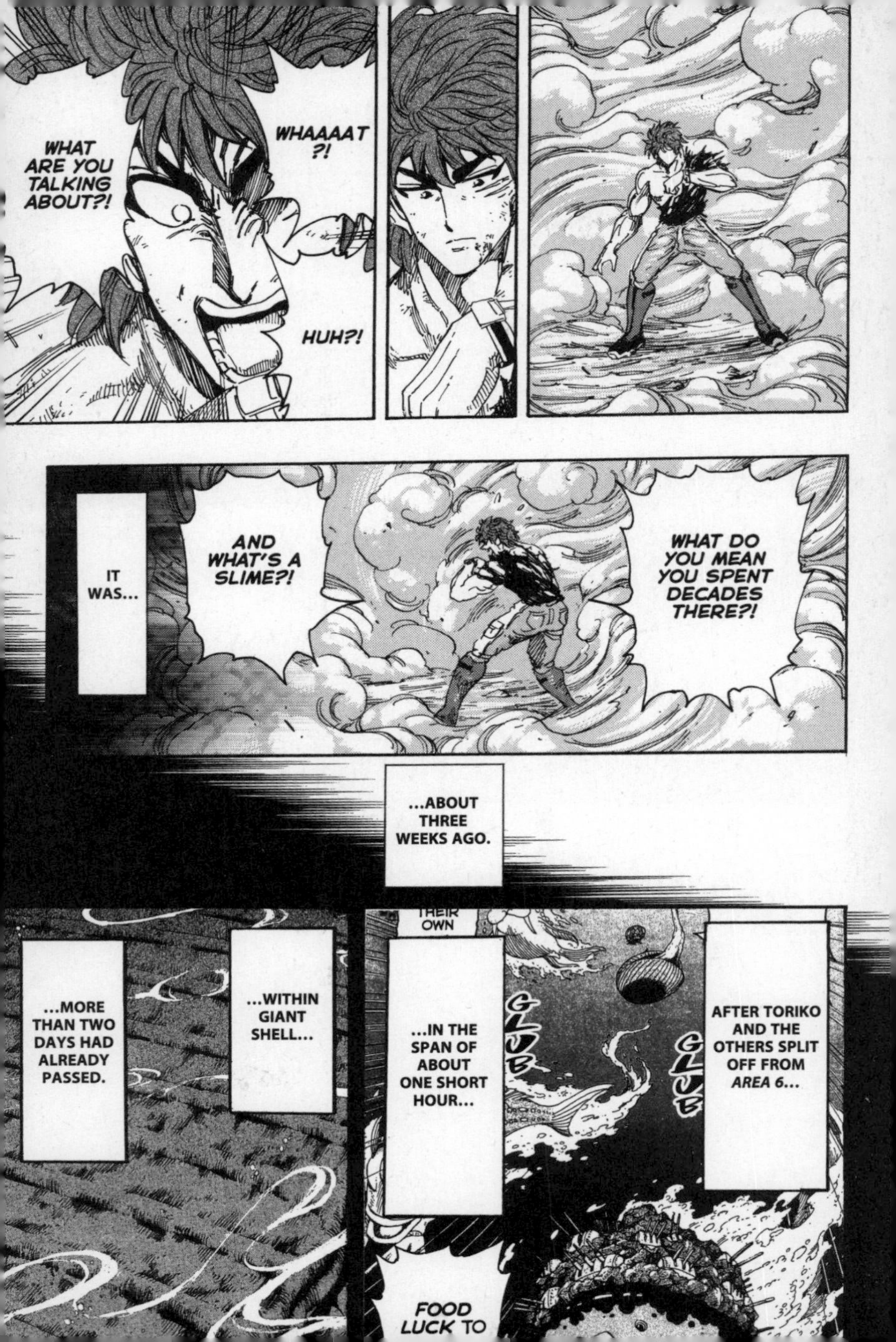
WHAAAAT ?!
HUH?!
WHAT ARE YOU TALKING ABOUT?!
WHAT DO YOU MEAN YOU SPENT DECADES THERE?!
AND WHAT'S A SLIME?!
IT WAS...
...ABOUT THREE WEEKS AGO.
AFTER TORIKO AND THE OTHERS SPLIT OFF FROM *AREA 6*...
GLUB
GLUB
THEIR OWN
...IN THE SPAN OF ABOUT ONE SHORT HOUR...
FOOD *LUCK* TO
...WITHIN GIANT SHELL...
...MORE THAN TWO DAYS HAD ALREADY PASSED.

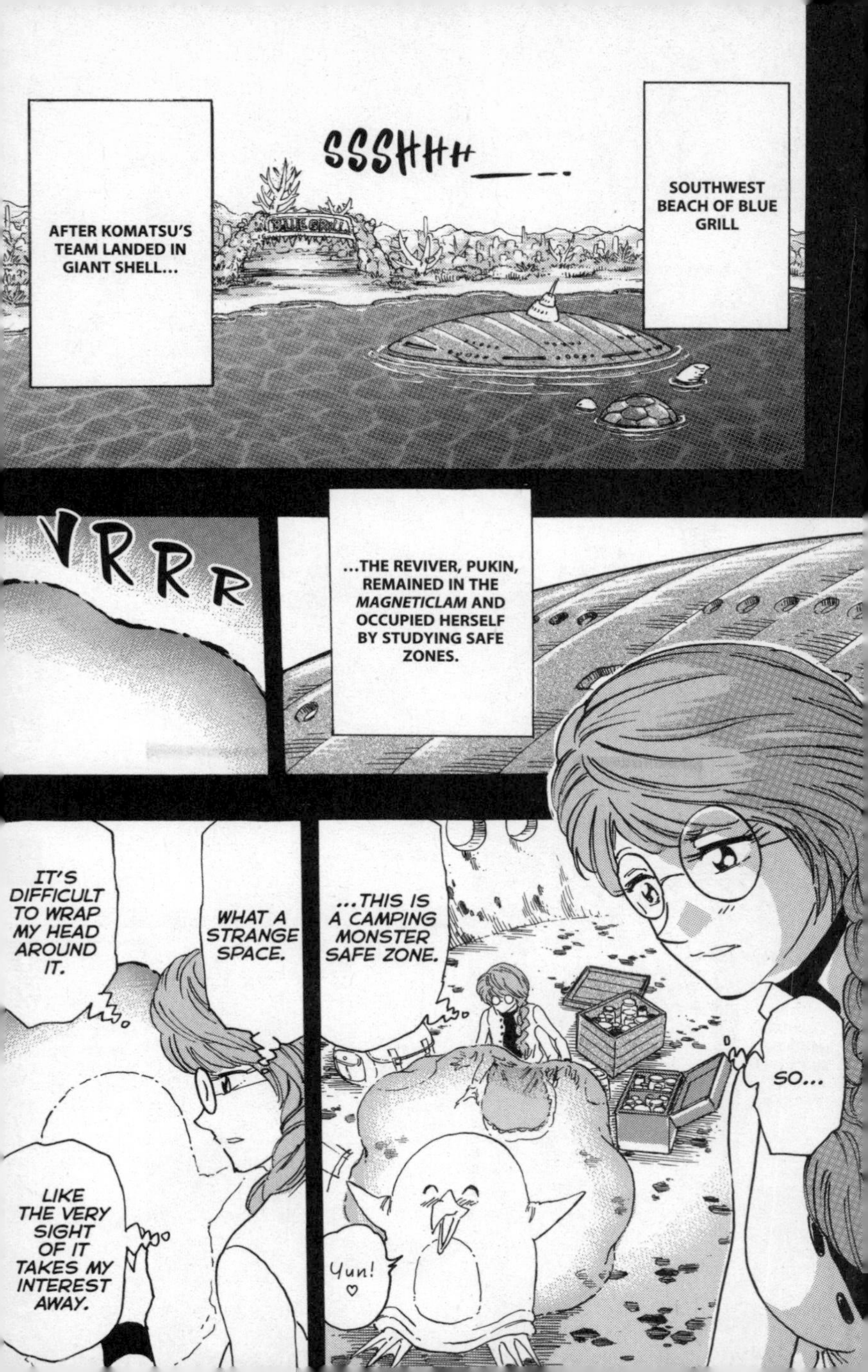
SOUTHWEST BEACH OF BLUE GRILL
SSSHHH
AFTER KOMATSU'S TEAM LANDED IN GIANT SHELL...
...THE REVIVER, PUKIN, REMAINED IN THE *MAGNETICLAM* AND OCCUPIED HERSELF BY STUDYING SAFE ZONES.
VRRRR
SO...
...THIS IS A CAMPING MONSTER SAFE ZONE.
Yun! ♡
WHAT A STRANGE SPACE.
IT'S DIFFICULT TO WRAP MY HEAD AROUND IT.
LIKE THE VERY SIGHT OF IT TAKES MY INTEREST AWAY.

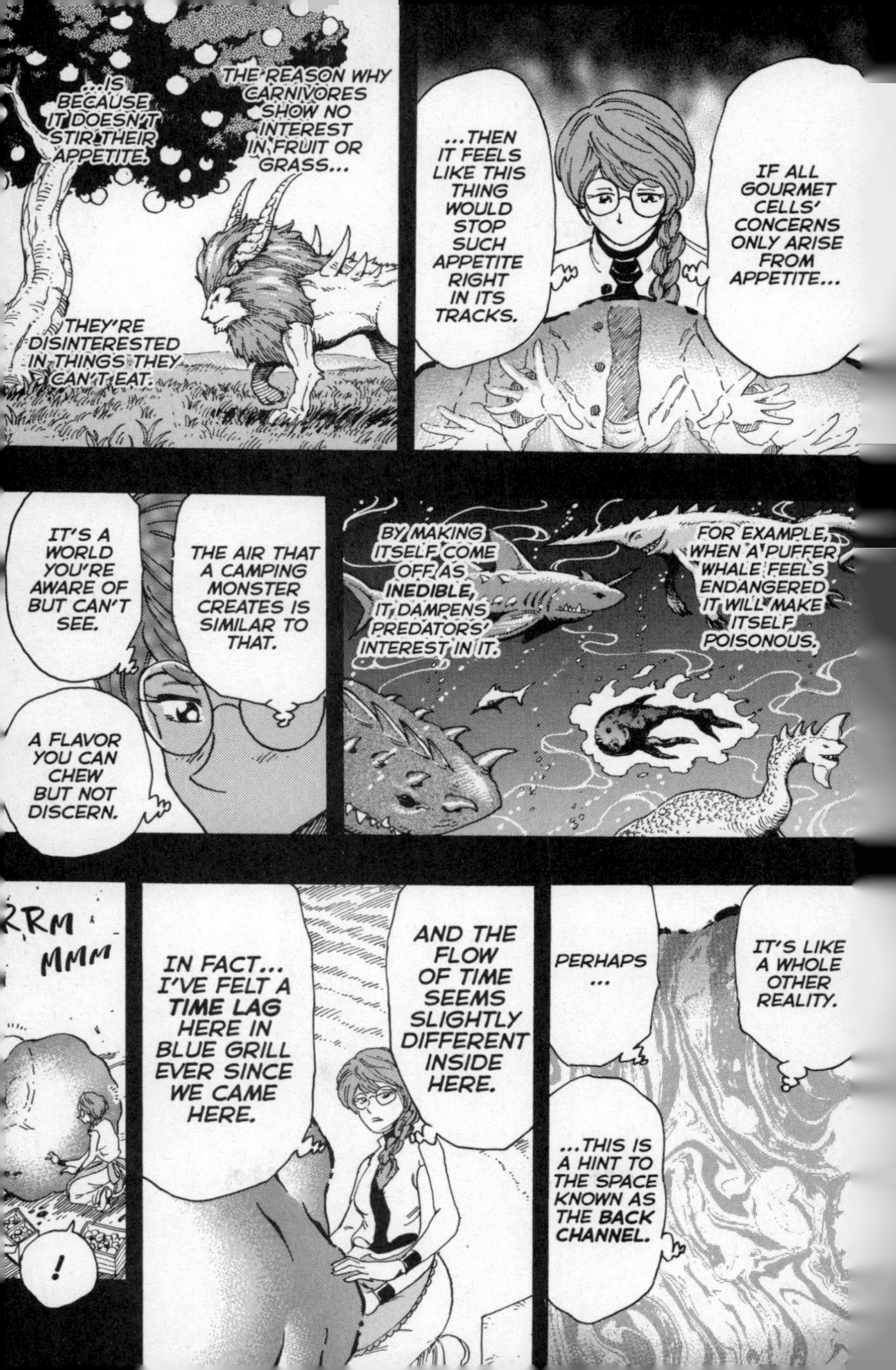
IF ALL GOURMET CELLS' CONCERNS ONLY ARISE FROM APPETITE...
...THEN IT FEELS LIKE THIS THING WOULD STOP SUCH APPETITE RIGHT IN ITS TRACKS.
THE REASON WHY CARNIVORES SHOW NO INTEREST IN FRUIT OR GRASS...
...IS BECAUSE IT DOESN'T STIR THEIR APPETITE.
THEY'RE DISINTERESTED IN THINGS THEY CAN'T EAT.
FOR EXAMPLE, WHEN A PUFFER WHALE FEELS ENDANGERED IT WILL MAKE ITSELF POISONOUS.
BY MAKING ITSELF COME OFF AS INEDIBLE, IT DAMPENS PREDATORS' INTEREST IN IT.
THE AIR THAT A CAMPING MONSTER CREATES IS SIMILAR TO THAT.
IT'S A WORLD YOU'RE AWARE OF BUT CAN'T SEE.
A FLAVOR YOU CAN CHEW BUT NOT DISCERN.
IT'S LIKE A WHOLE OTHER REALITY.
PERHAPS ...
...THIS IS A HINT TO THE SPACE KNOWN AS THE BACK CHANNEL.
AND THE FLOW OF TIME SEEMS SLIGHTLY DIFFERENT INSIDE HERE.
IN FACT... I'VE FELT A TIME LAG HERE IN BLUE GRILL EVER SINCE WE CAME HERE.
RRM
MMM
!

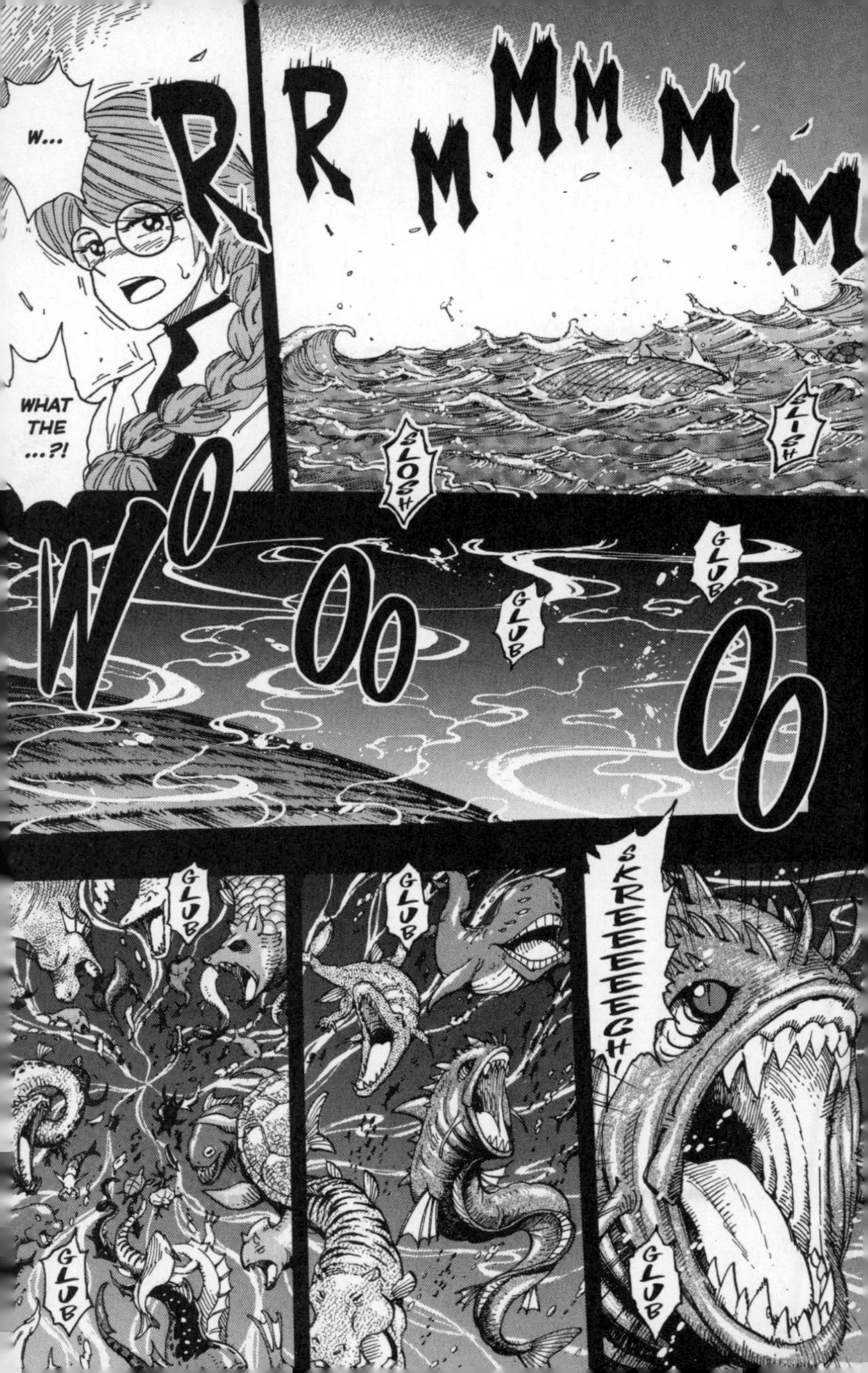
RRMMMMM
SLISH
SLOSH
W...
WHAT THE ...?!
WOOOOO
GLUB
GLUB
SKREEEEECH!
GLUB
GLUB
GLUB
GLUB
GLUB

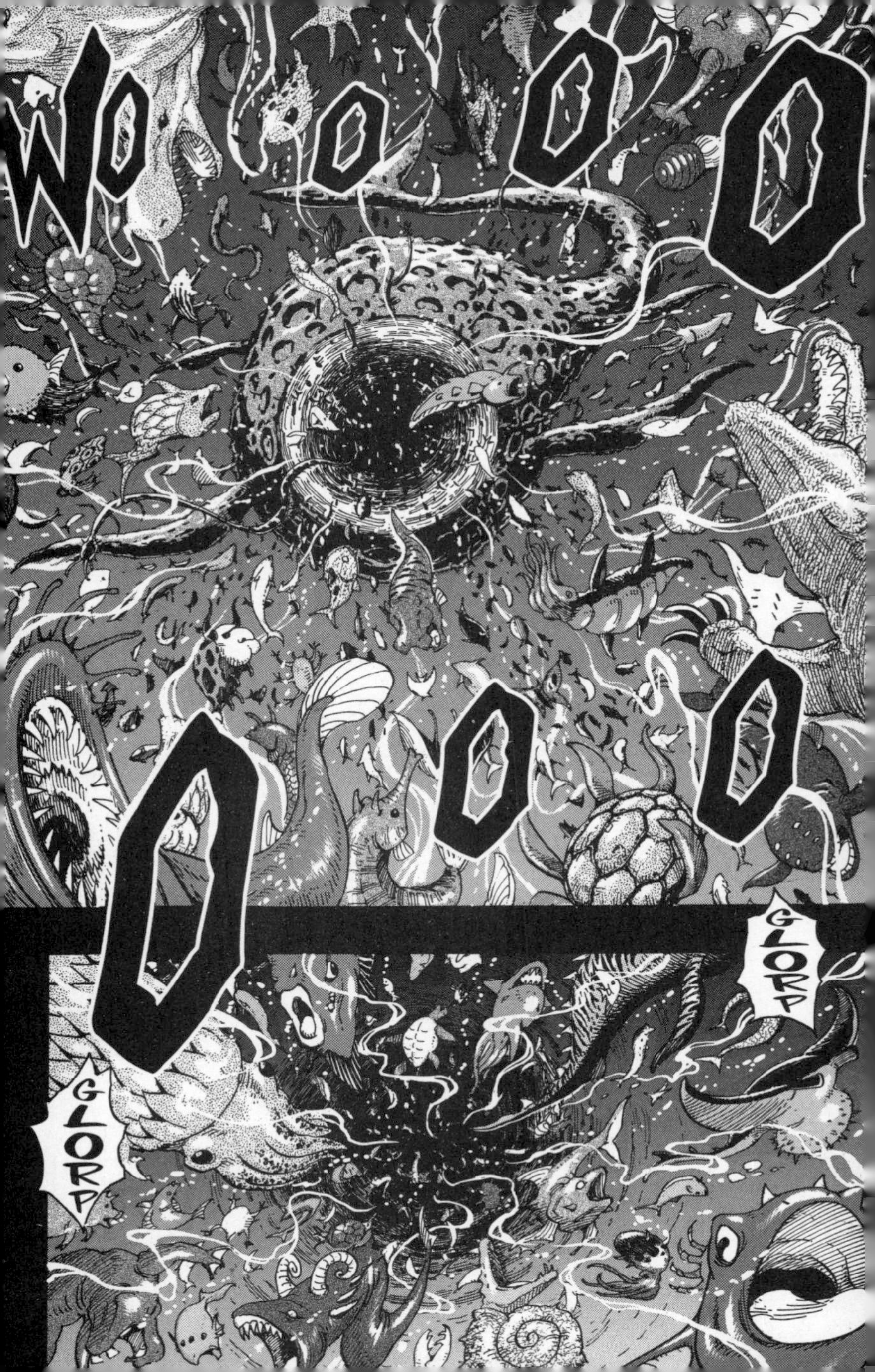
WOOOOOOOO
GLORP
GLORP

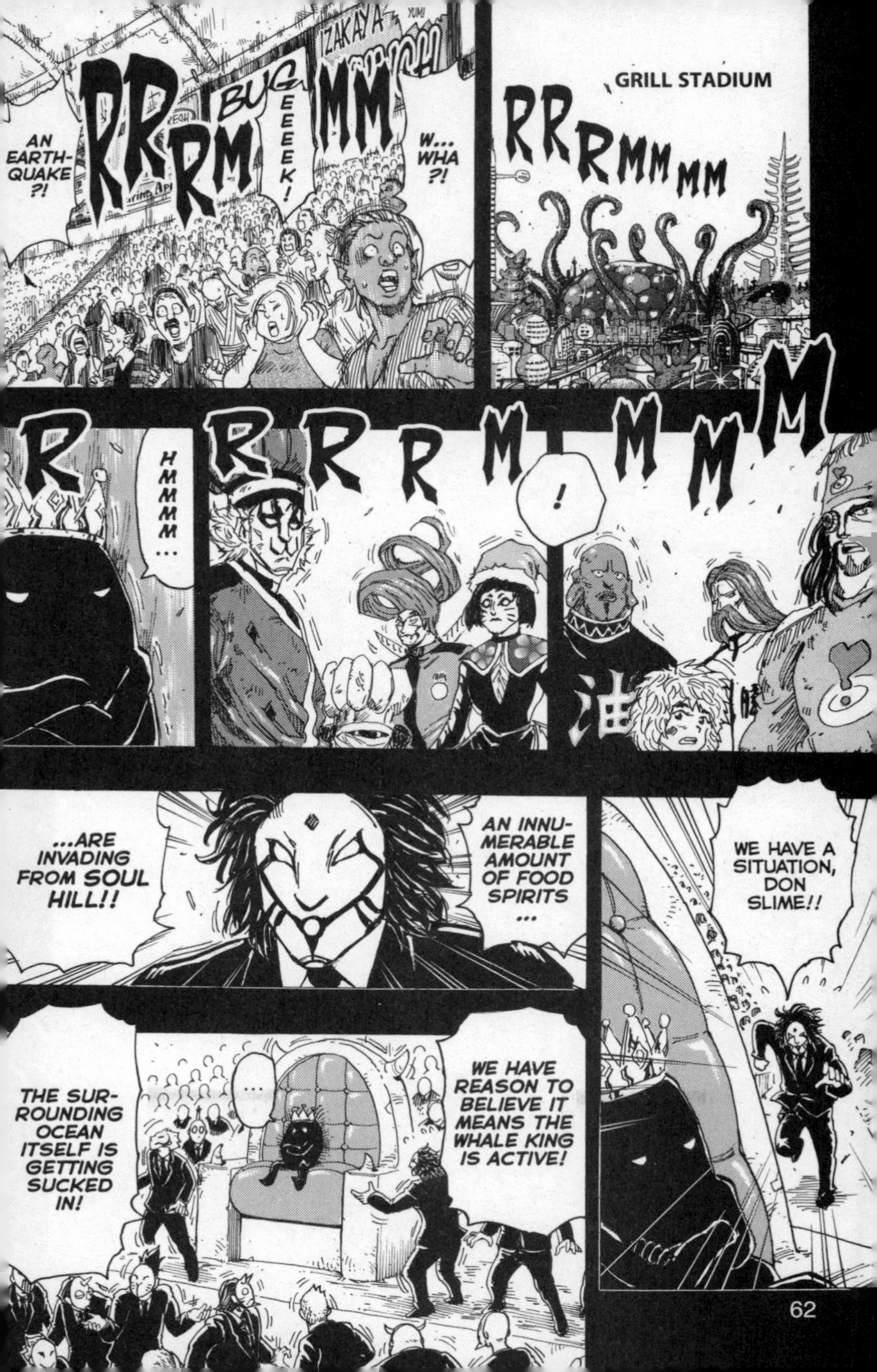
GRILL STADIUM
RRRMMMMM
IZAKAYA
YUM!
RRRM
MM
BUG
EEEEEK!
W... WHA?!
AN EARTHQUAKE?!
RRRRMMMMM
!
HMMMM...
WE HAVE A SITUATION, DON SLIME!!
AN INNUMERABLE AMOUNT OF FOOD SPIRITS...
...ARE INVADING FROM SOUL HILL!!
WE HAVE REASON TO BELIEVE IT MEANS THE WHALE KING IS ACTIVE!
...
THE SURROUNDING OCEAN ITSELF IS GETTING SUCKED IN!

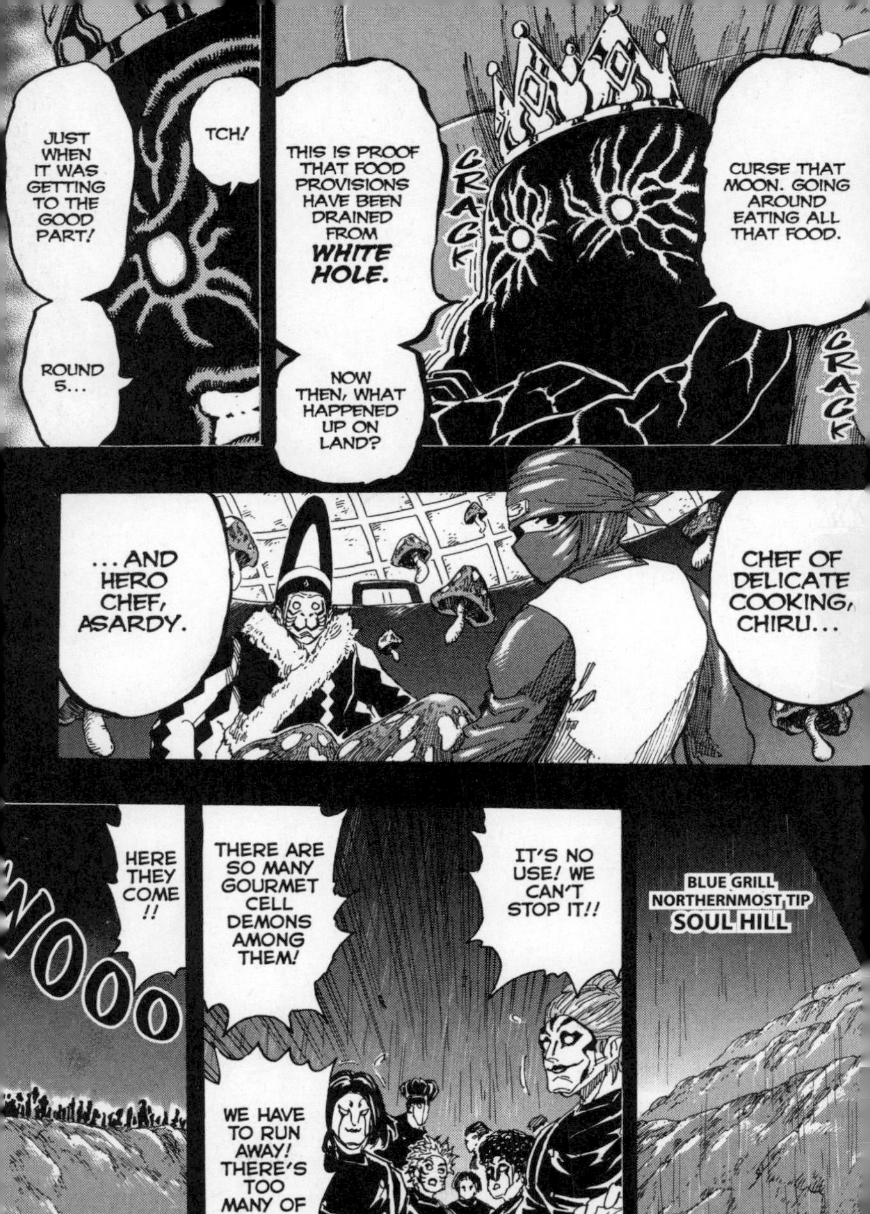
CRACK
CURSE THAT MOON. GOING AROUND EATING ALL THAT FOOD.
CRACK
THIS IS PROOF THAT FOOD PROVISIONS HAVE BEEN DRAINED FROM WHITE HOLE.
NOW THEN, WHAT HAPPENED UP ON LAND?
TCH!
JUST WHEN IT WAS GETTING TO THE GOOD PART!
ROUND 5...
CHEF OF DELICATE COOKING, CHIRU...
...AND HERO CHEF, ASARDY.
BLUE GRILL NORTHERNMOST TIP SOUL HILL
IT'S NO USE! WE CAN'T STOP IT!!
THERE ARE SO MANY GOURMET CELL DEMONS AMONG THEM!
WE HAVE TO RUN AWAY! THERE'S TOO MANY OF THEM!!
HERE THEY COME!!
WOOO

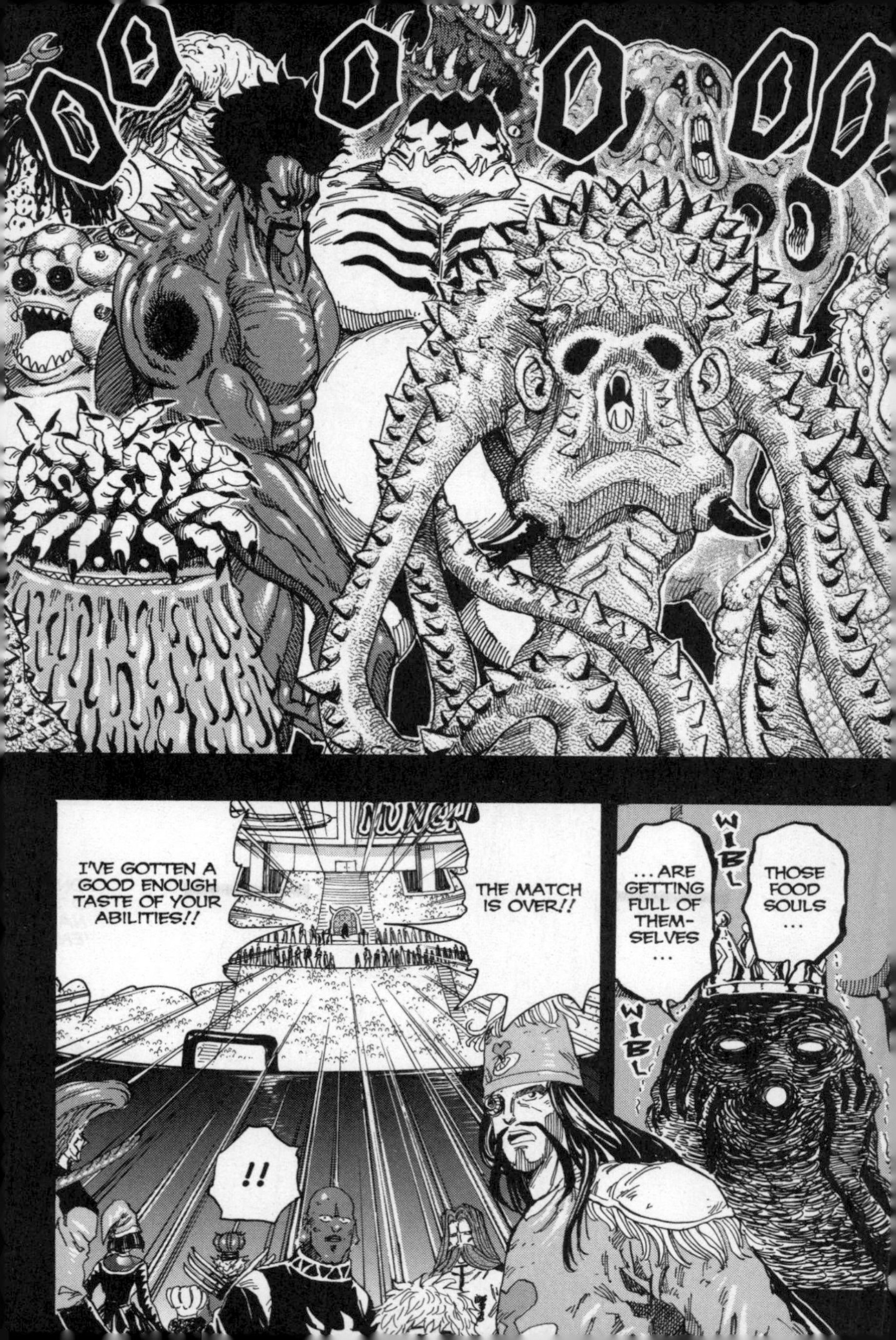
THOSE FOOD SOULS ...
WIBL
...ARE GETTING FULL OF THEM-SELVES ...
WIBL
THE MATCH IS OVER!!
I'VE GOTTEN A GOOD ENOUGH TASTE OF YOUR ABILITIES!!
!!

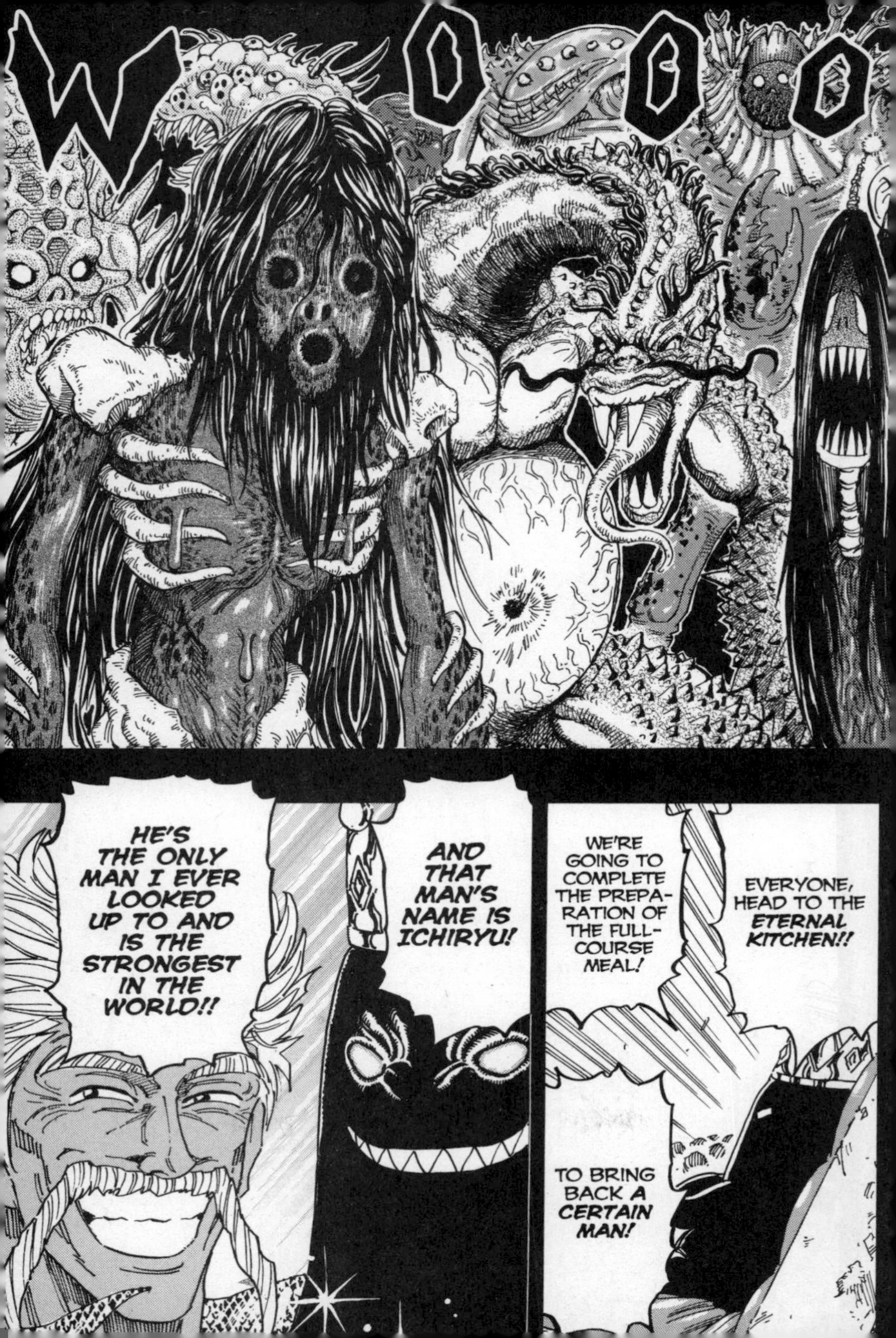
WOOOO
EVERYONE, HEAD TO THE ETERNAL KITCHEN!!
WE'RE GOING TO COMPLETE THE PREPARATION OF THE FULL-COURSE MEAL!
TO BRING BACK A CERTAIN MAN!
AND THAT MAN'S NAME IS ICHIRYU!
HE'S THE ONLY MAN I EVER LOOKED UP TO AND IS THE STRONGEST IN THE WORLD!!

TORIKO

GOURMET CHECKLIST

Vol. 373

 ### SUNDORIKO
(PLANT)

CAPTURE LEVEL: 1,000 THROUGH
IMPROVED BREEDING (2,500 IN THE
WILD)
HABITAT: AREA 7
SIZE: 60 CM (MORE THAN 30 M IN THE
WILD)
HEIGHT: ---
WEIGHT: 3 KG
PRICE: PRICELESS

SCALE

LONG AGO, THIS SUPER DANGEROUS PLANT DROVE THE GOURMET WORLD'S
AREA 7 INTO A MASS EXTINCTION, WIPING OUT THE MAJORITY OF LIVING THINGS
IN THE AREA. THE POLLEN OF THE SUNDORIKO CONTAINS AN ANTIGEN THAT CAUSES
A SEVERE ALLERGIC REACTION. ANY CREATURE THAT BREATHES IT IN EVEN ONCE
WILL EXPERIENCE EXTREME HAY FEVER. ONCE THE HAY FEVER HITS, EVEN THE
LARGEST ANIMALS EXPEL ALL THE FLUIDS FROM THEIR BODY IN A MATTER OF
SECONDS AND DIE. THE LETHALITY OF THE SUNDORIKO IN THE WILD IS SAID TO BE
100 PERCENT, AND MEMORIES OF FEAR AND TREPIDATION TOWARD THE SUNDORIKO
ARE APPARENTLY ETCHED INTO THE VERY GENES OF THE CREATURES LIVING ON THE
CONTINENT OF AREA 7. FOR THE RECORD, THE WILD SUNDORIKO IS A TASTY TREAT
AND COCO SECRETLY DECIDED TO MAKE IT THE APPETIZER IN HIS FULL-COURSE MEAL.

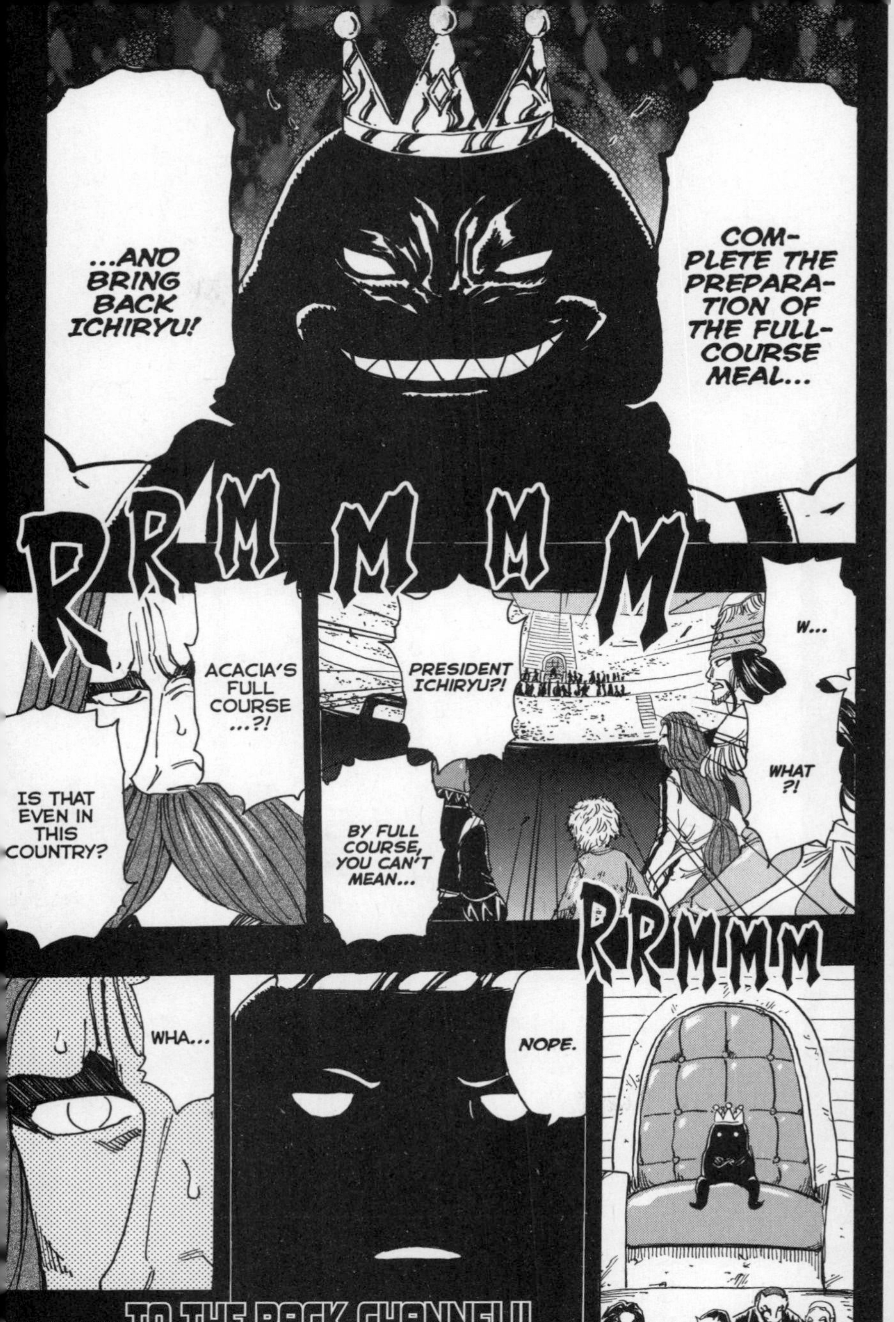
COM-PLETE THE PREPARA-TION OF THE FULL-COURSE MEAL...
...AND BRING BACK ICHIRYU!
RRMMMMM
W...
WHAT?!
PRESIDENT ICHIRYU?!
BY FULL COURSE, YOU CAN'T MEAN...
ACACIA'S FULL COURSE...?!
IS THAT EVEN IN THIS COUNTRY?
RRMMM
NOPE.
WHA...
GOURMET 344: TO THE BACK CHANNEL!!

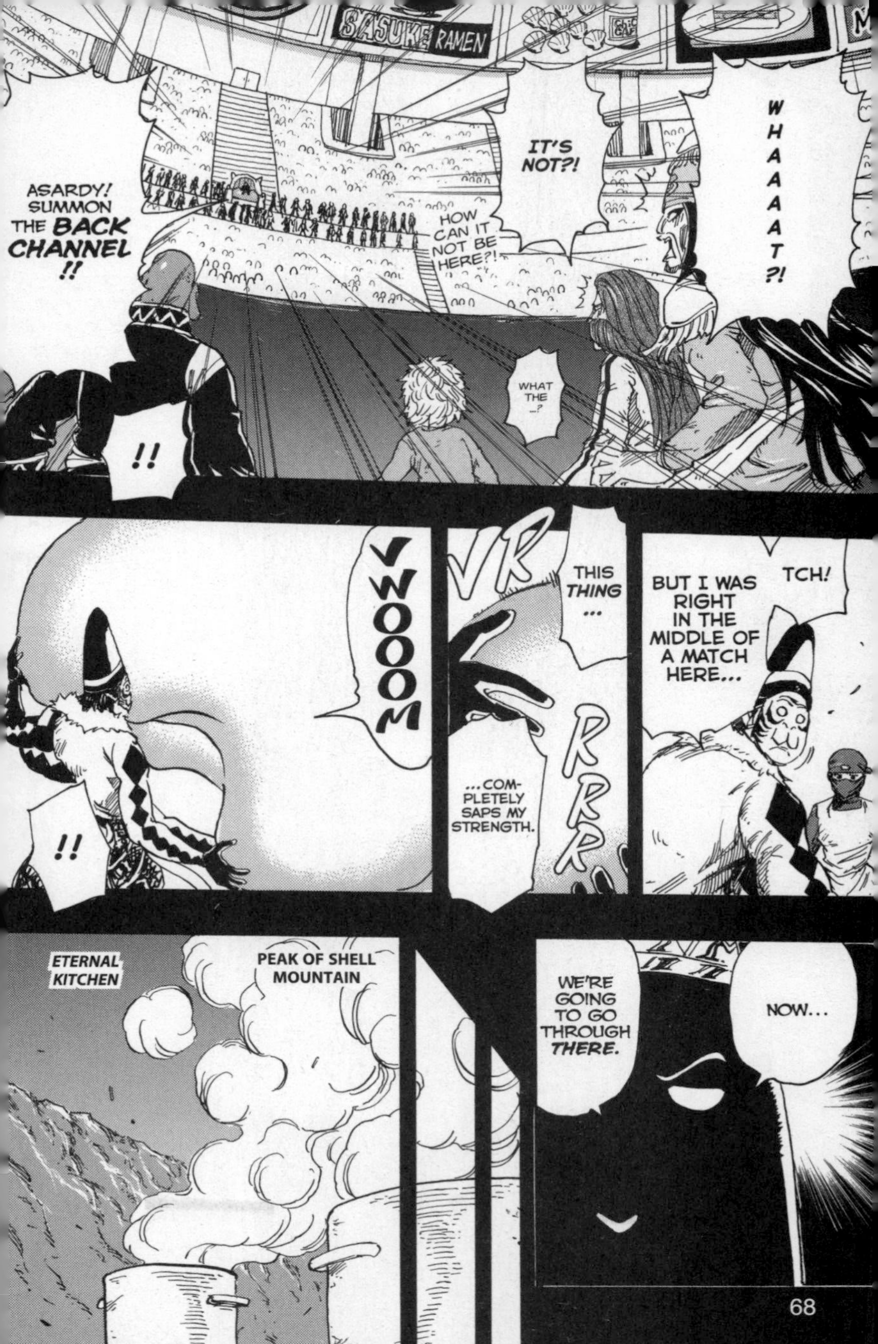
SASUKE RAMEN
WHAAAAAT?!
IT'S NOT?!
HOW CAN IT NOT BE HERE?!
WHAT THE ...?
ASARDY! SUMMON THE BACK CHANNEL!!
!!
TCH!
BUT I WAS RIGHT IN THE MIDDLE OF A MATCH HERE...
THIS THING...
VRRRRR
...COMPLETELY SAPS MY STRENGTH.
VWOOOOM
!!
NOW...
WE'RE GOING TO GO THROUGH THERE.
PEAK OF SHELL MOUNTAIN
ETERNAL KITCHEN

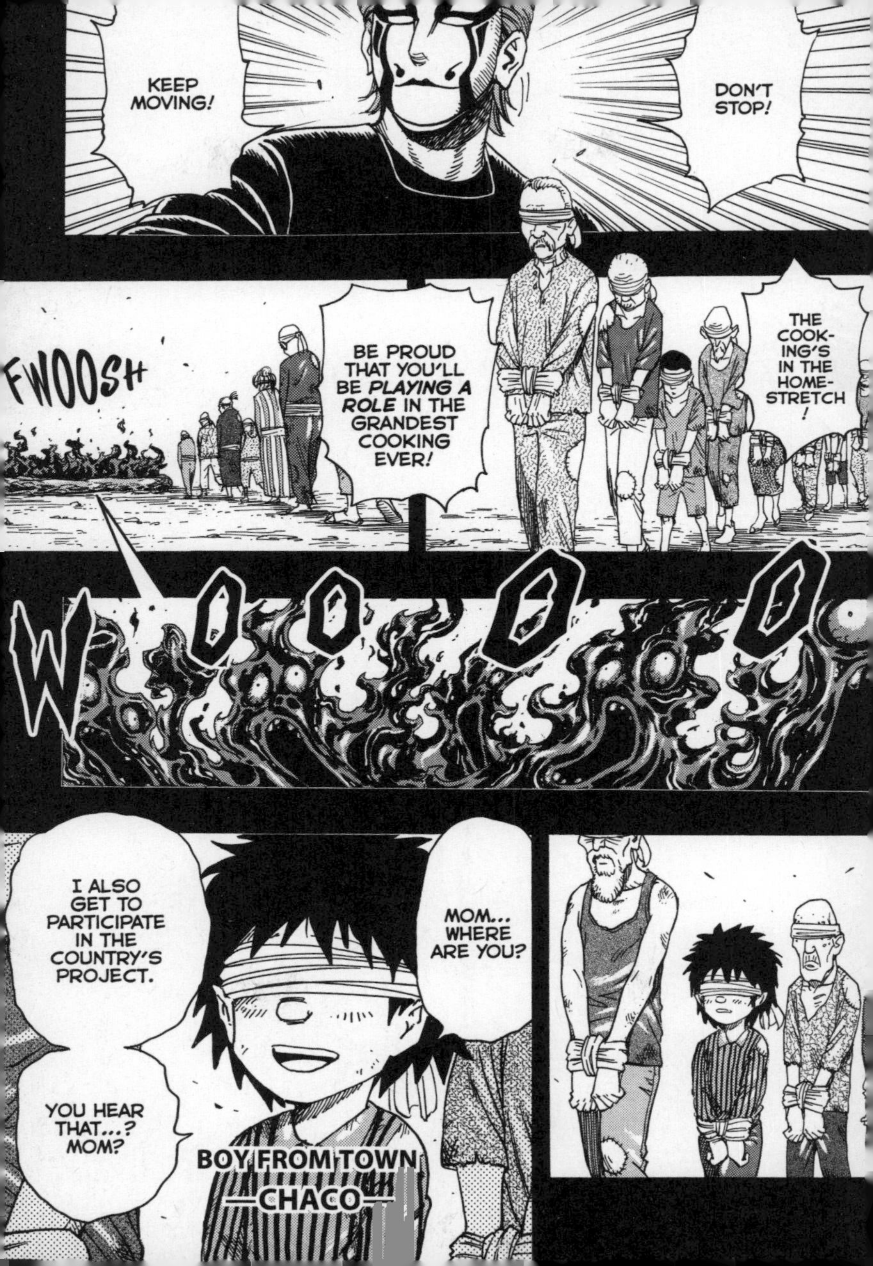
DON'T STOP!
KEEP MOVING!
THE COOKING'S IN THE HOMESTRETCH!
BE PROUD THAT YOU'LL BE PLAYING A ROLE IN THE GRANDEST COOKING EVER!
FWOOSH
WOOOOO
MOM... WHERE ARE YOU?
I ALSO GET TO PARTICIPATE IN THE COUNTRY'S PROJECT.
YOU HEAR THAT...? MOM?
BOY FROM TOWN
—CHACO—

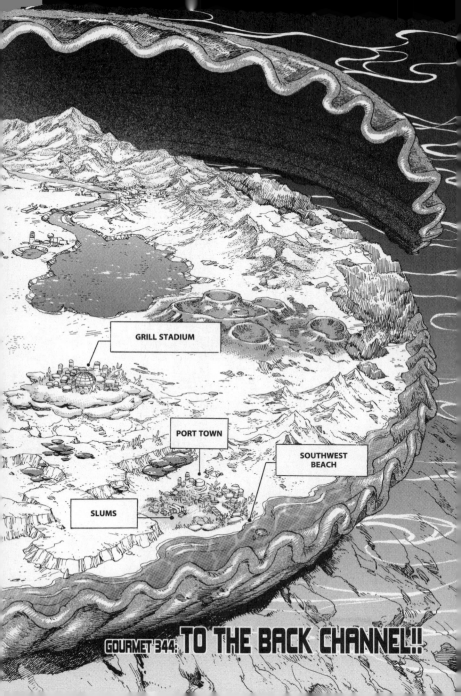

GRILL STADIUM

PORT TOWN

SOUTHWEST
BEACH

SLUMS

GOURMET 344: TO THE BACK CHANNEL!!

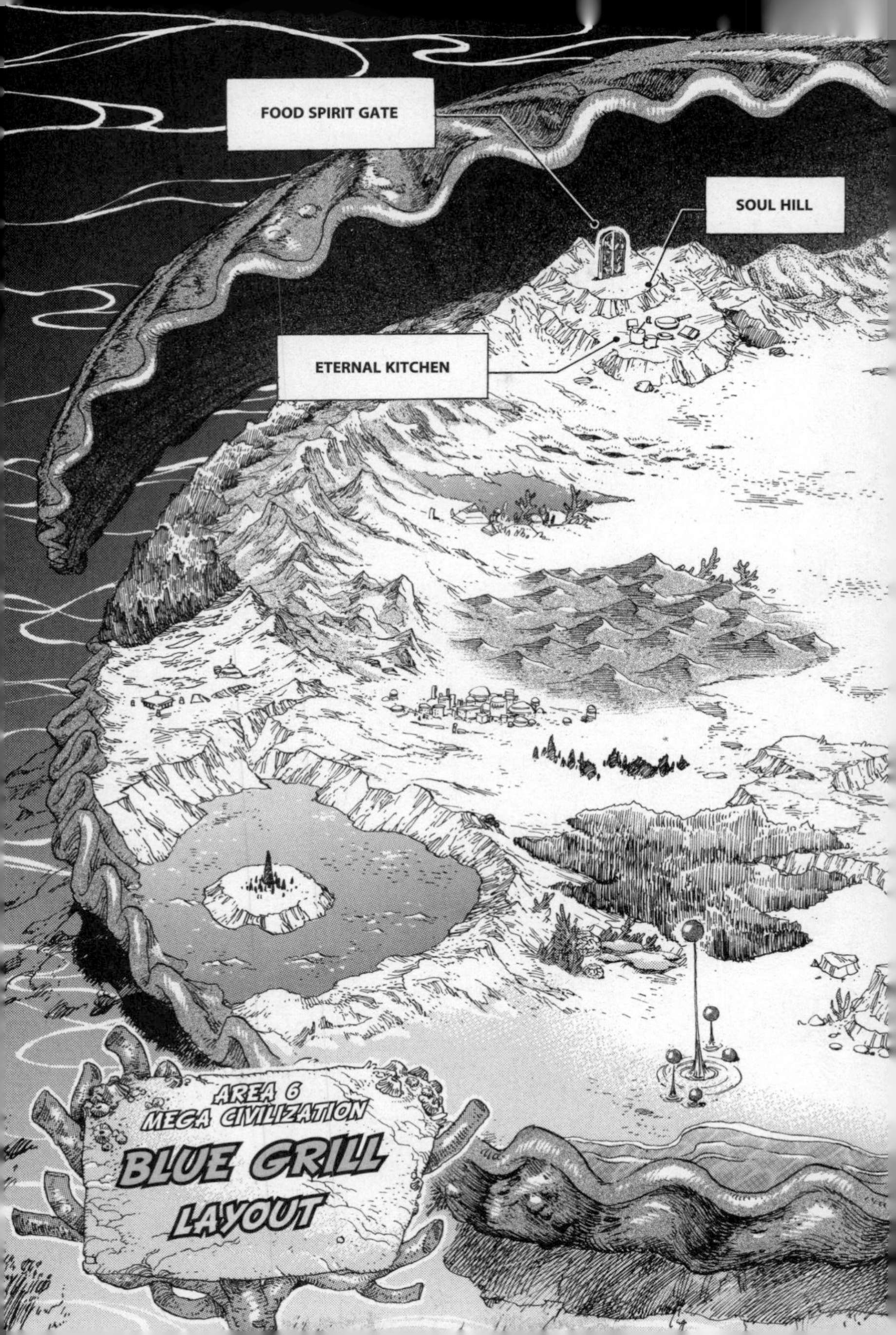
FOOD SPIRIT GATE
SOUL HILL
ETERNAL KITCHEN
AREA 6
MEGA CIVILIZATION
BLUE GRILL
LAYOUT

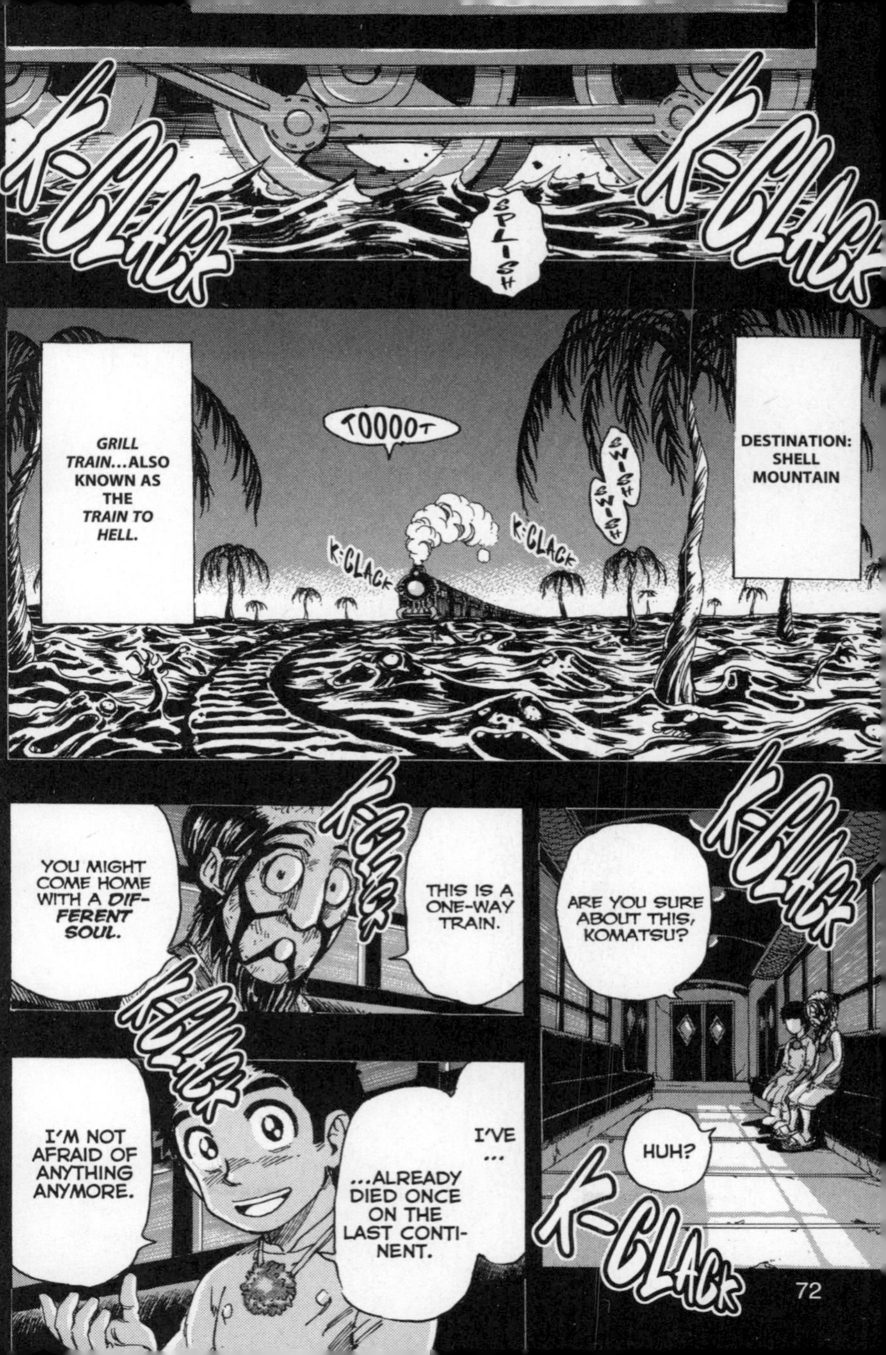
K-CLACK
SPLISH
K-CLACK
DESTINATION: SHELL MOUNTAIN
SWISH SWISH
K-CLACK
TOOOOT
K-CLACK
GRILL TRAIN...ALSO KNOWN AS THE *TRAIN TO HELL.*
K-CLACK
ARE YOU SURE ABOUT THIS, KOMATSU?
HUH?
K-CLACK
K-CLACK
THIS IS A ONE-WAY TRAIN.
YOU MIGHT COME HOME WITH A *DIFFERENT* SOUL.
K-CLACK
I'VE...
...ALREADY DIED ONCE ON THE LAST CONTINENT.
I'M NOT AFRAID OF ANYTHING ANYMORE.

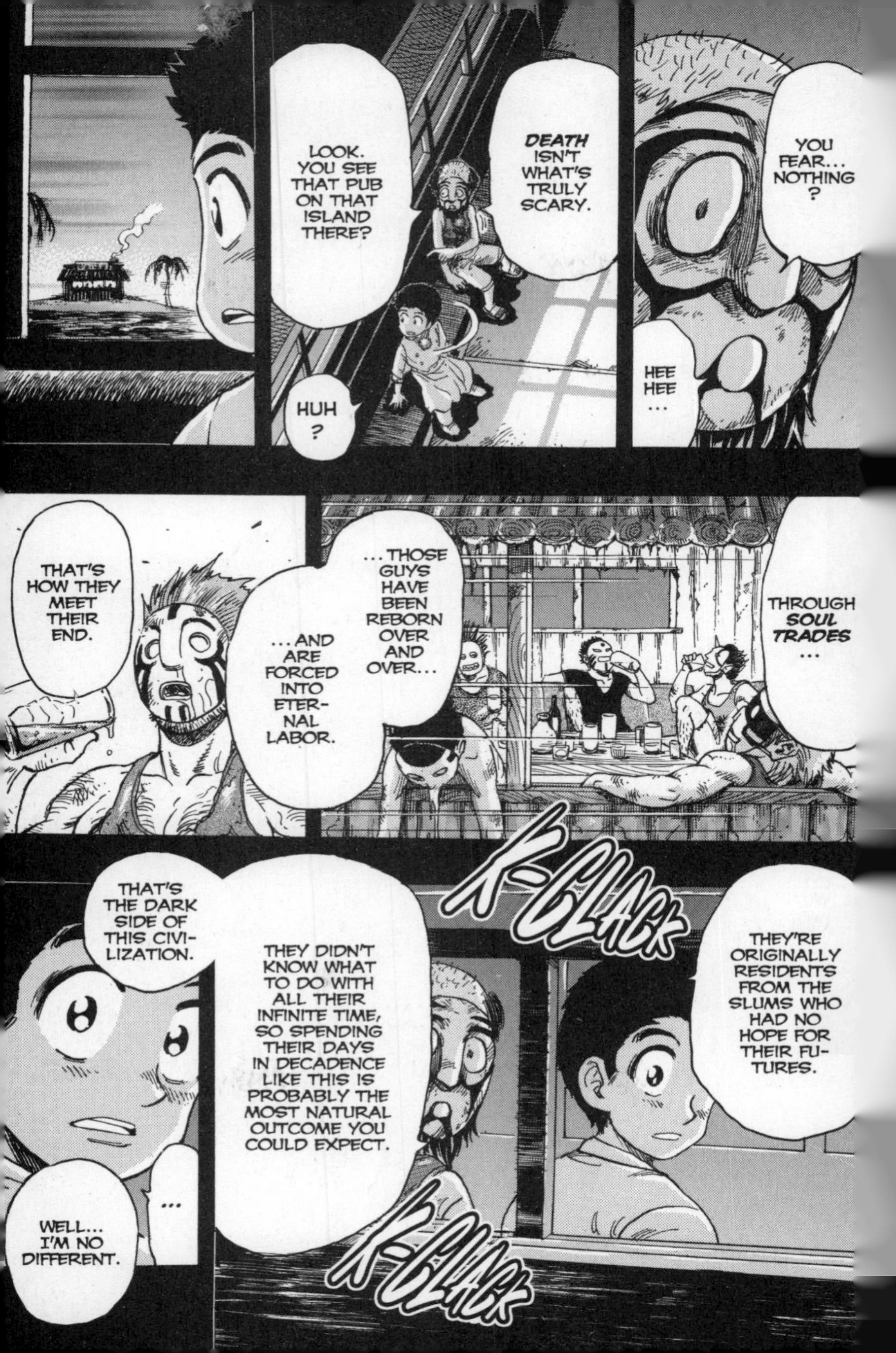
YOU FEAR... NOTHING?
HEE HEE...
DEATH ISN'T WHAT'S TRULY SCARY.
LOOK. YOU SEE THAT PUB ON THAT ISLAND THERE?
HUH?
THROUGH SOUL TRADES...
...THOSE GUYS HAVE BEEN REBORN OVER AND OVER...
...AND ARE FORCED INTO ETERNAL LABOR.
THAT'S HOW THEY MEET THEIR END.
THEY'RE ORIGINALLY RESIDENTS FROM THE SLUMS WHO HAD NO HOPE FOR THEIR FUTURES.
K-CLACK
THEY DIDN'T KNOW WHAT TO DO WITH ALL THEIR INFINITE TIME, SO SPENDING THEIR DAYS IN DECADENCE LIKE THIS IS PROBABLY THE MOST NATURAL OUTCOME YOU COULD EXPECT.
K-CLACK
THAT'S THE DARK SIDE OF THIS CIVILIZATION.
...
WELL... I'M NO DIFFERENT.

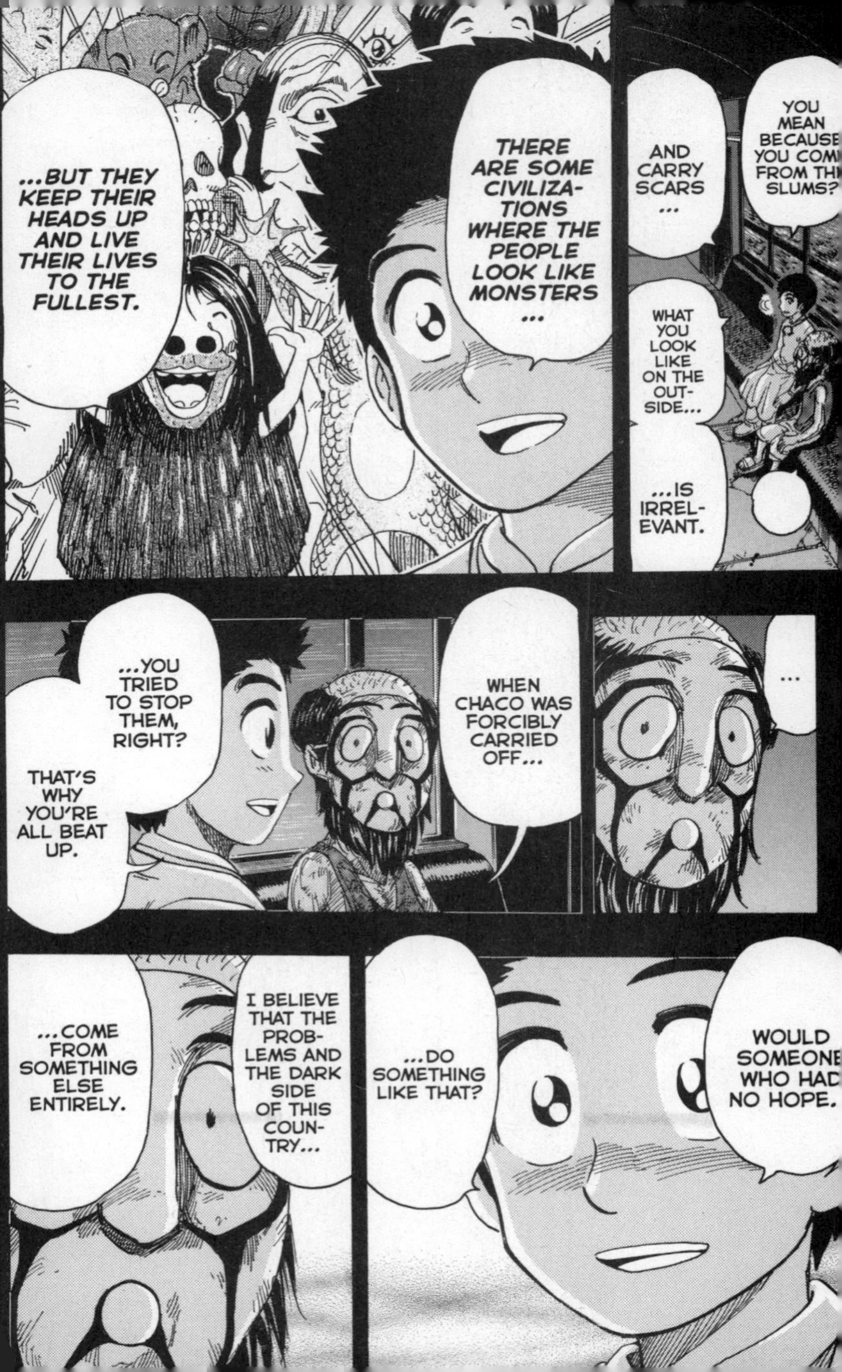
YOU MEAN BECAUSE YOU COM FROM TH SLUMS?
AND CARRY SCARS ...
WHAT YOU LOOK LIKE ON THE OUTSIDE...
...IS IRREL-EVANT.
THERE ARE SOME CIVILIZA-TIONS WHERE THE PEOPLE LOOK LIKE MONSTERS ...
...BUT THEY KEEP THEIR HEADS UP AND LIVE THEIR LIVES TO THE FULLEST.
...
WHEN CHACO WAS FORCIBLY CARRIED OFF...
...YOU TRIED TO STOP THEM, RIGHT?
THAT'S WHY YOU'RE ALL BEAT UP.
WOULD SOMEONE WHO HAD NO HOPE...
...DO SOMETHING LIKE THAT?
I BELIEVE THAT THE PROB-LEMS AND THE DARK SIDE OF THIS COUN-TRY...
...COME FROM SOMETHING ELSE ENTIRELY.

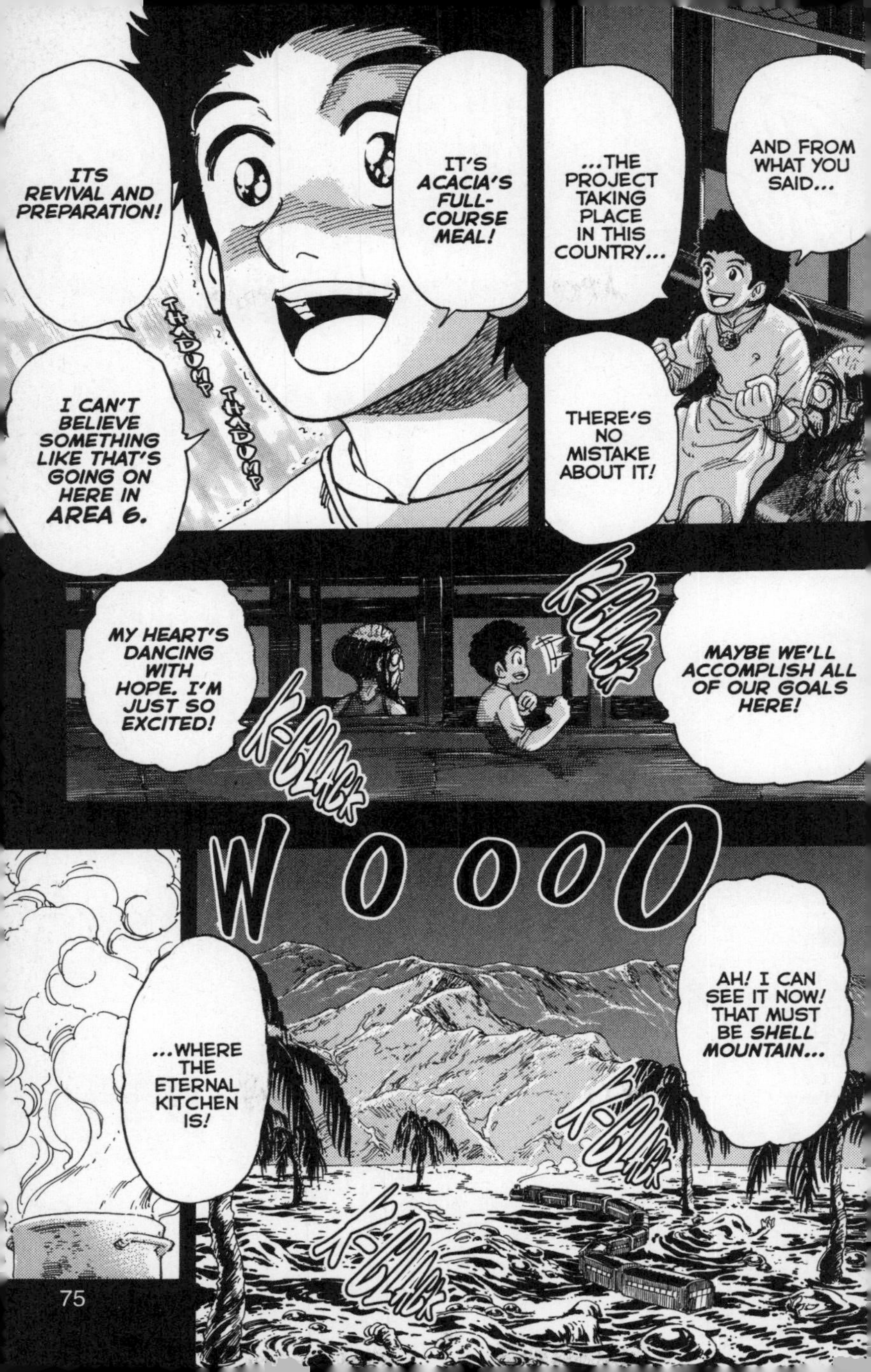

AND FROM WHAT YOU SAID...
...THE PROJECT TAKING PLACE IN THIS COUNTRY...
THERE'S NO MISTAKE ABOUT IT!
IT'S ACACIA'S FULL-COURSE MEAL!
ITS REVIVAL AND PREPARATION!
THADUMP THADUMP
I CAN'T BELIEVE SOMETHING LIKE THAT'S GOING ON HERE IN AREA 6.
K-CLACK
MAYBE WE'LL ACCOMPLISH ALL OF OUR GOALS HERE!
MY HEART'S DANCING WITH HOPE. I'M JUST SO EXCITED!
K-CLACK
WOOOO
AH! I CAN SEE IT NOW! THAT MUST BE SHELL MOUNTAIN...
K-CLACK
...WHERE THE ETERNAL KITCHEN IS!
K-CLACK

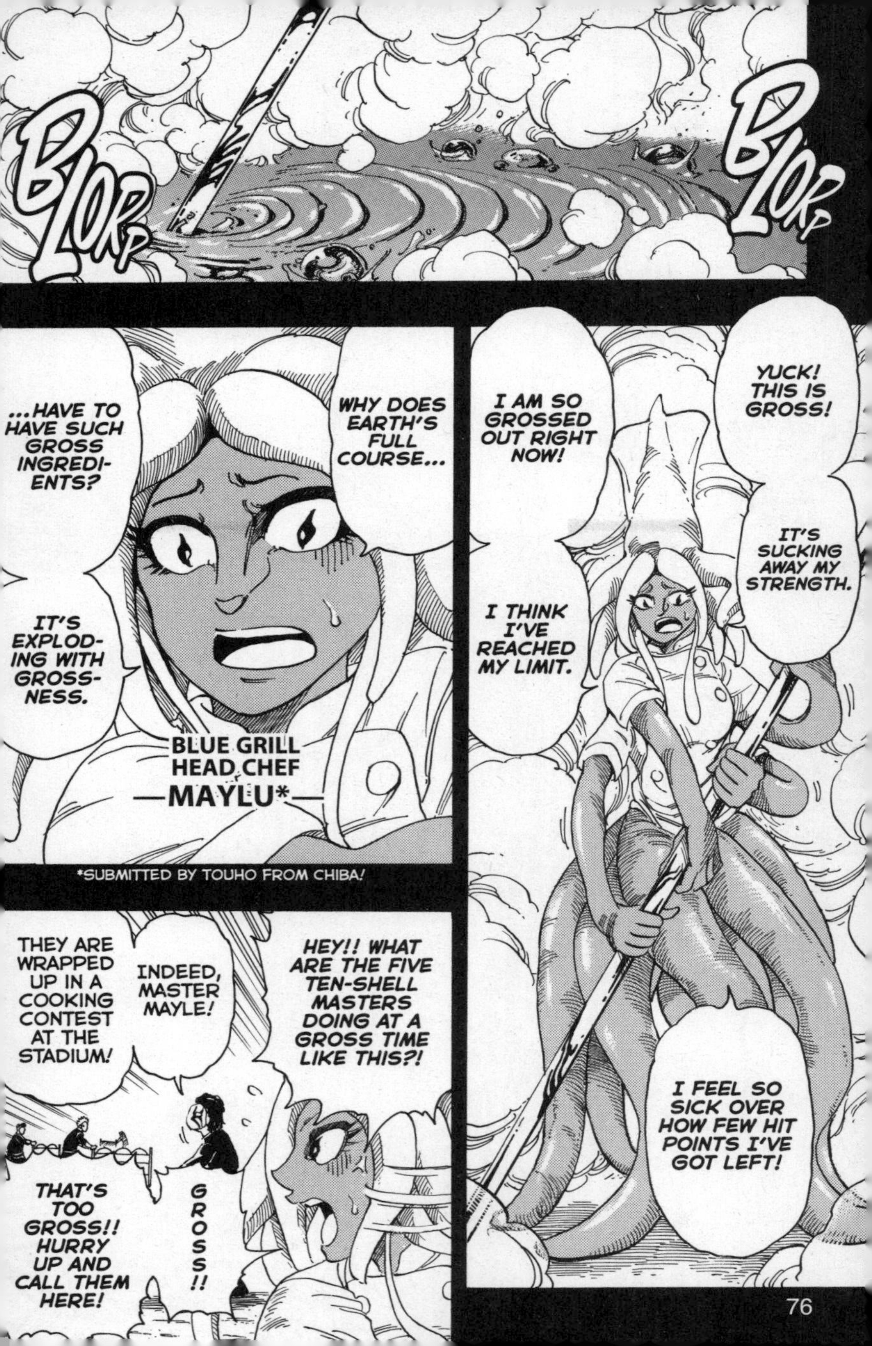
BLORP
BLORP
YUCK! THIS IS GROSS!
I AM SO GROSSED OUT RIGHT NOW!
IT'S SUCKING AWAY MY STRENGTH.
I THINK I'VE REACHED MY LIMIT.
I FEEL SO SICK OVER HOW FEW HIT POINTS I'VE GOT LEFT!
WHY DOES EARTH'S FULL COURSE...
...HAVE TO HAVE SUCH GROSS INGREDIENTS?
IT'S EXPLODING WITH GROSSNESS.
BLUE GRILL HEAD CHEF
—MAYLU*—
*SUBMITTED BY TOUHO FROM CHIBA!
HEY!! WHAT ARE THE FIVE TEN-SHELL MASTERS DOING AT A GROSS TIME LIKE THIS?!
INDEED, MASTER MAYLE!
THEY ARE WRAPPED UP IN A COOKING CONTEST AT THE STADIUM!
GROSS!!
THAT'S TOO GROSS!! HURRY UP AND CALL THEM HERE!

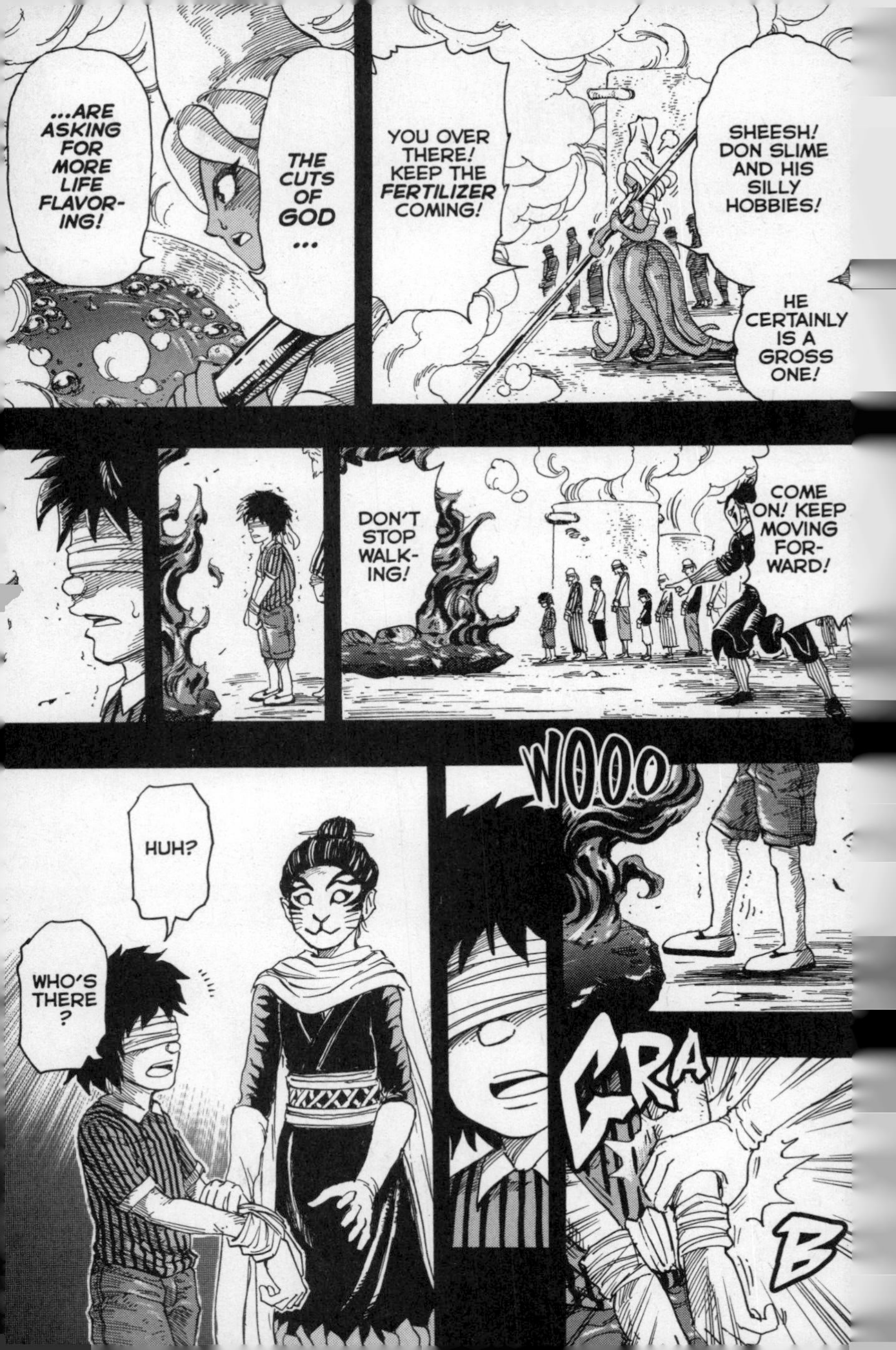
SHEESH! DON SLIME AND HIS SILLY HOBBIES!
HE CERTAINLY IS A GROSS ONE!
YOU OVER THERE! KEEP THE FERTILIZER COMING!
THE CUTS OF GOD...
...ARE ASKING FOR MORE LIFE FLAVORING!
COME ON! KEEP MOVING FORWARD!
DON'T STOP WALKING!
WOOO
GRA
B
HUH?
WHO'S THERE?

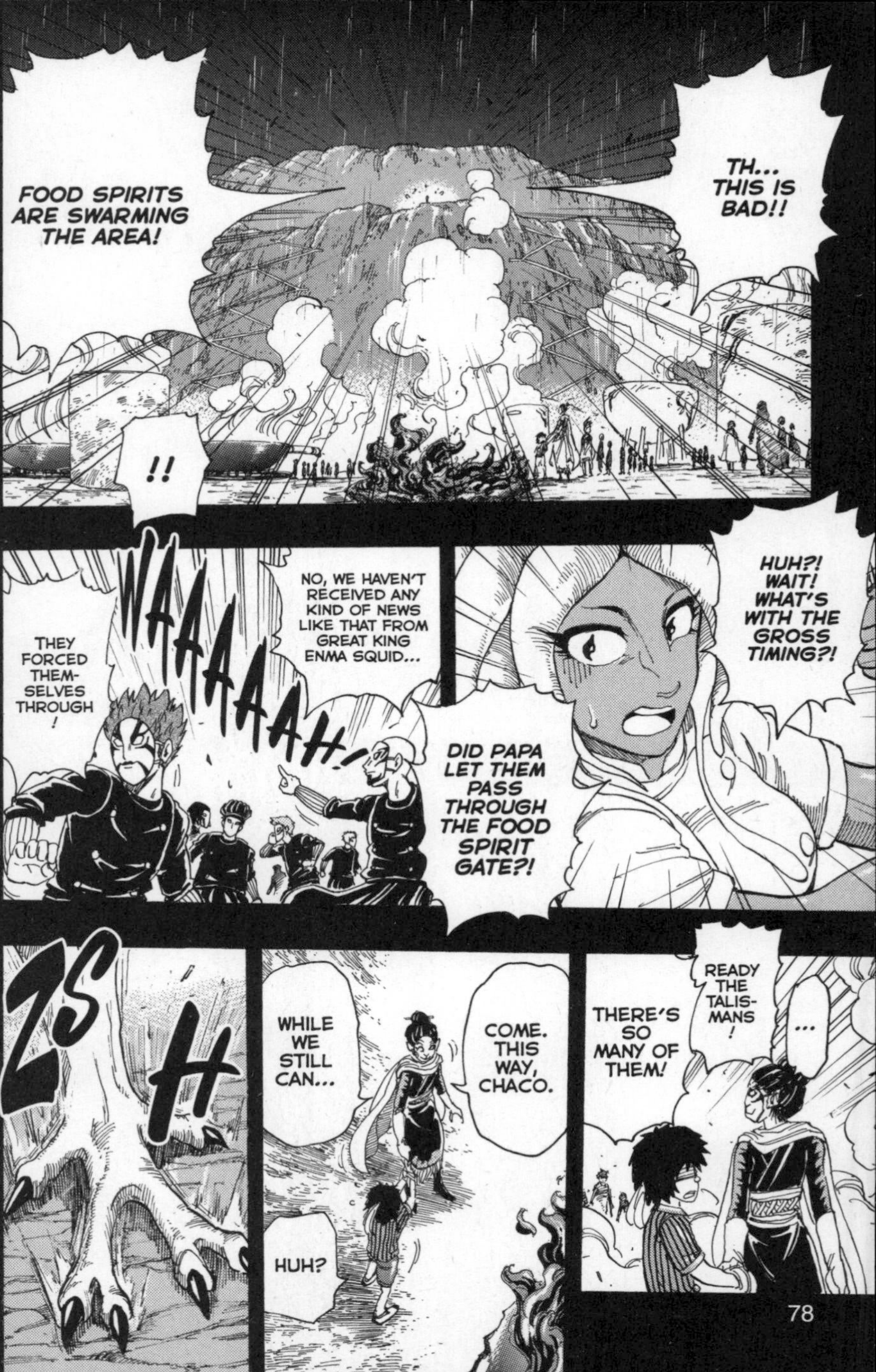

TH... THIS IS BAD!!
FOOD SPIRITS ARE SWARMING THE AREA!
!!
HUH?! WAIT! WHAT'S WITH THE GROSS TIMING?!
DID PAPA LET THEM PASS THROUGH THE FOOD SPIRIT GATE?!
NO, WE HAVEN'T RECEIVED ANY KIND OF NEWS LIKE THAT FROM GREAT KING ENMA SQUID...
WAAAAAAAH!
THEY FORCED THEM-SELVES THROUGH!
...
READY THE TALIS-MANS!
THERE'S SO MANY OF THEM!
COME. THIS WAY, CHACO.
WHILE WE STILL CAN...
HUH?
ZSH

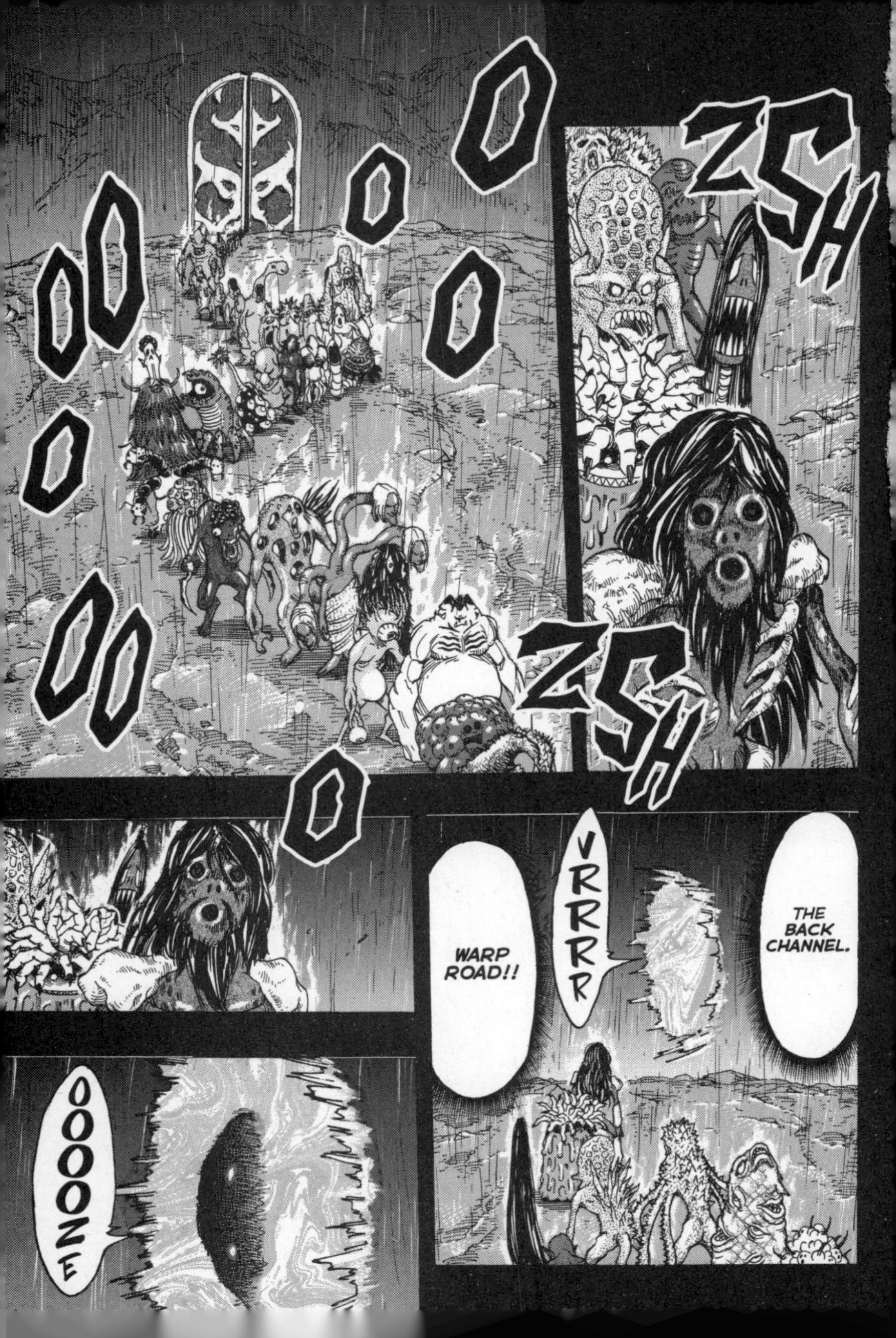
ZSH
ZSH
OOOOOOOOO
THE BACK CHANNEL.
VRRRR
WARP ROAD!!
OOOOOZE

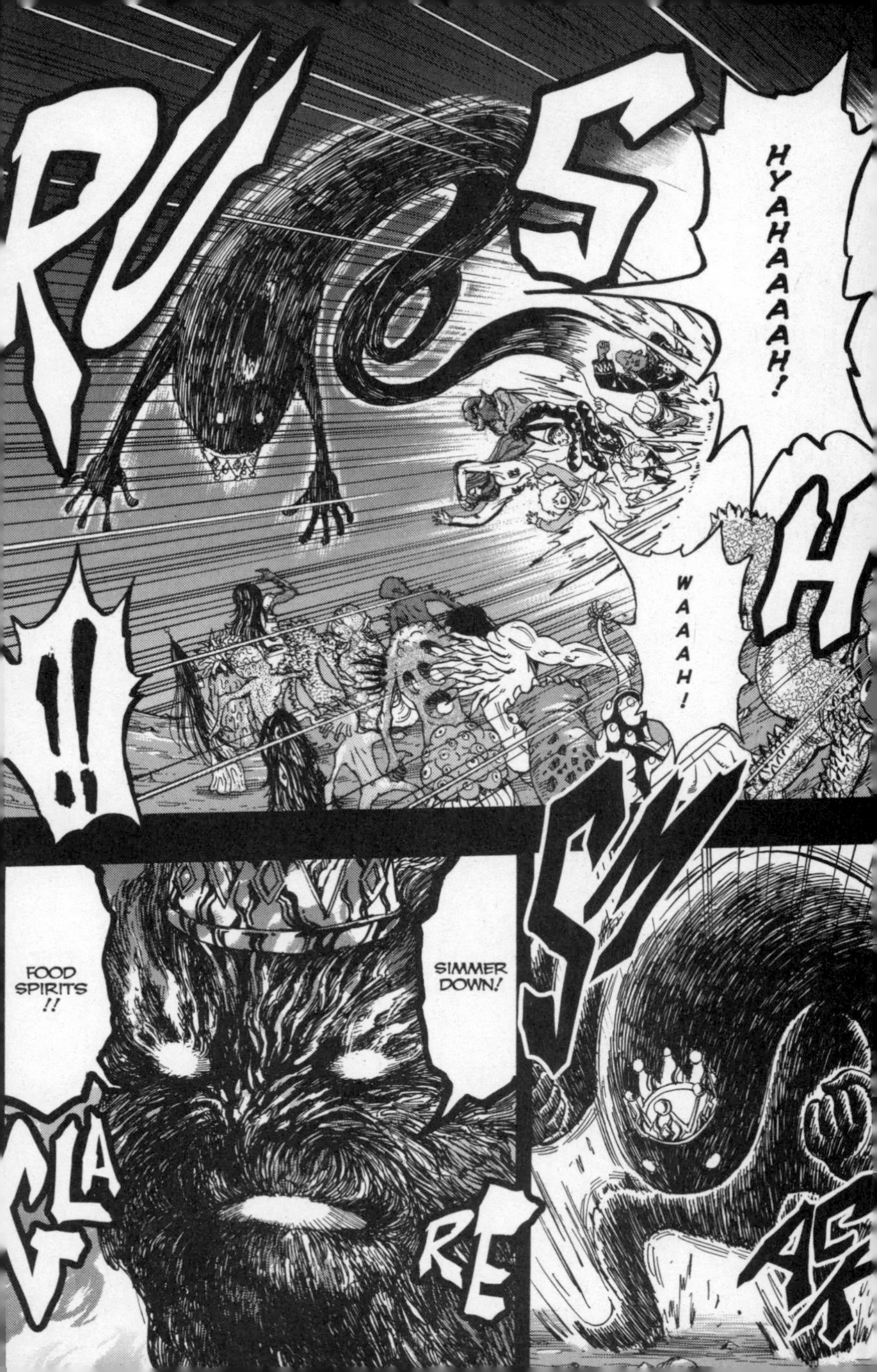
RU
S
H
HYAHAAAAAH!
WAAAAH!
!!
SW
AS
SIMMER DOWN!
FOOD SPIRITS !!
RE
LA

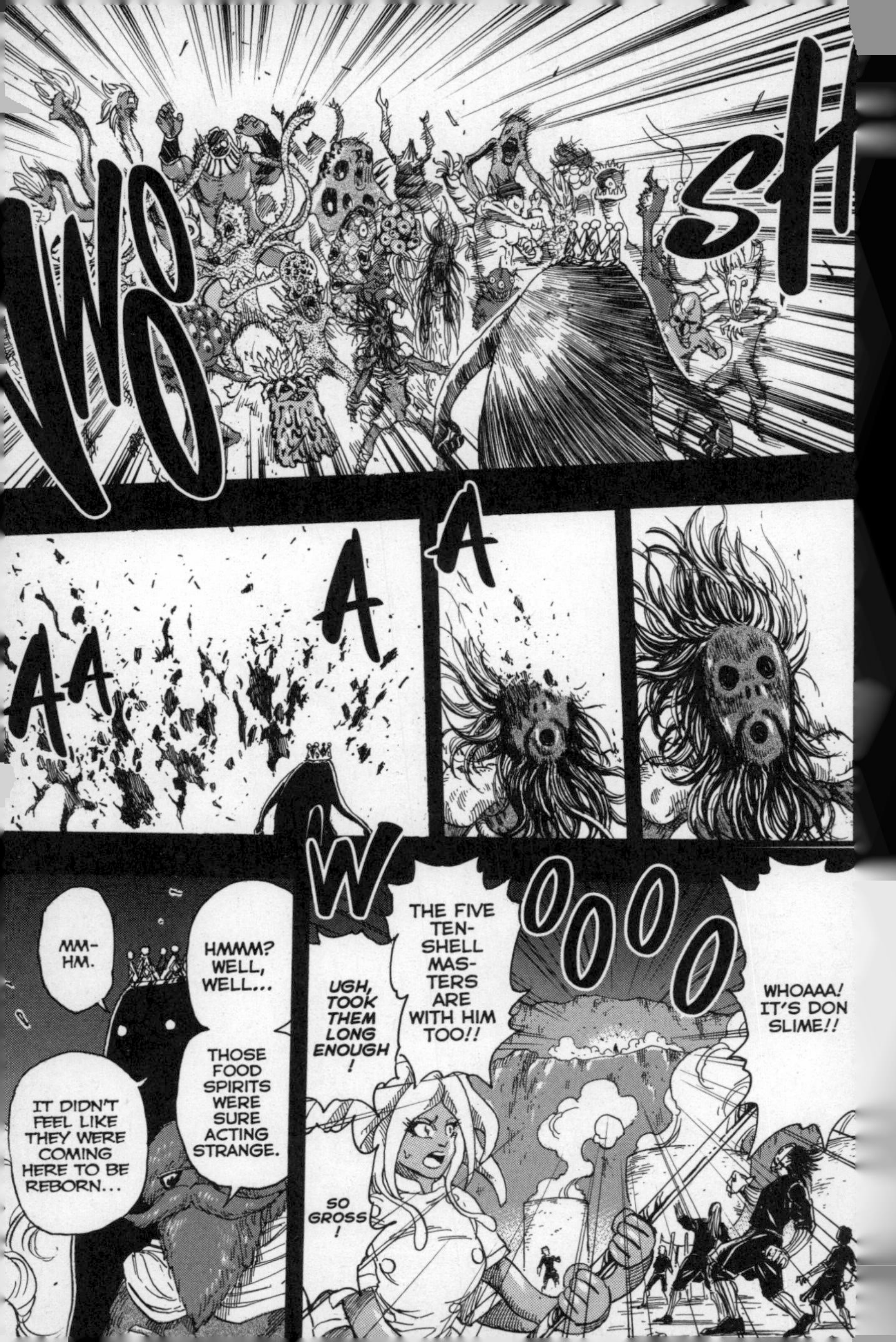
WOO
SH
A
AA
A
A
W
OOOOO
WHOAAA! IT'S DON SLIME!!
THE FIVE TEN-SHELL MASTERS ARE WITH HIM TOO!!
UGH, TOOK THEM LONG ENOUGH!
SO GROSS!
HMMM? WELL, WELL...
MM-HM.
THOSE FOOD SPIRITS WERE SURE ACTING STRANGE.
IT DIDN'T FEEL LIKE THEY WERE COMING HERE TO BE REBORN...

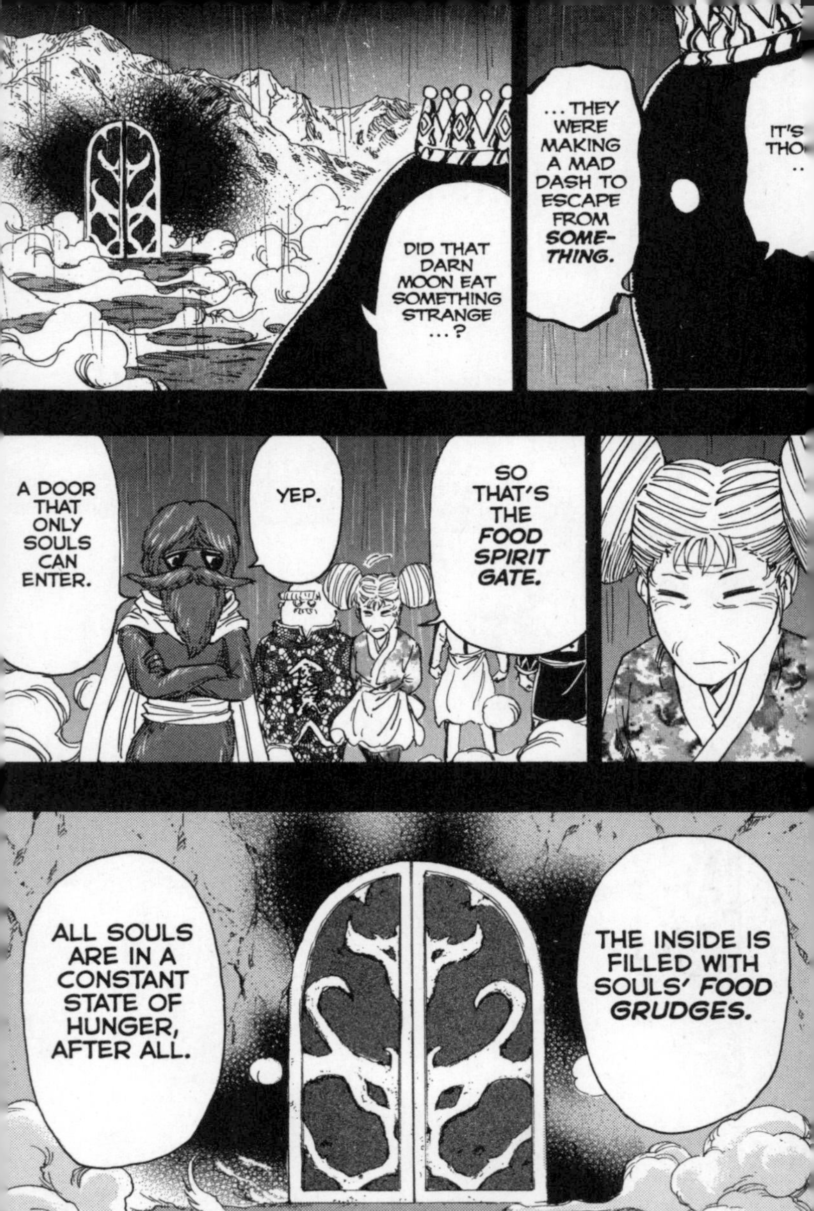
IT'S THO
...THEY WERE MAKING A MAD DASH TO ESCAPE FROM *SOMETHING*.
DID THAT DARN MOON EAT SOMETHING STRANGE ...?
SO THAT'S THE *FOOD SPIRIT GATE*.
YEP.
A DOOR THAT ONLY SOULS CAN ENTER.
THE INSIDE IS FILLED WITH SOULS' *FOOD GRUDGES*.
ALL SOULS ARE IN A CONSTANT STATE OF HUNGER, AFTER ALL.

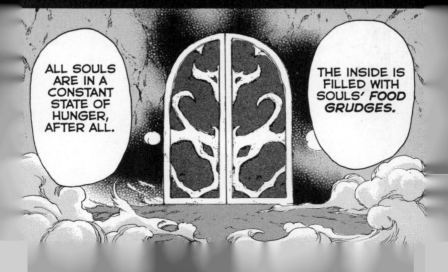

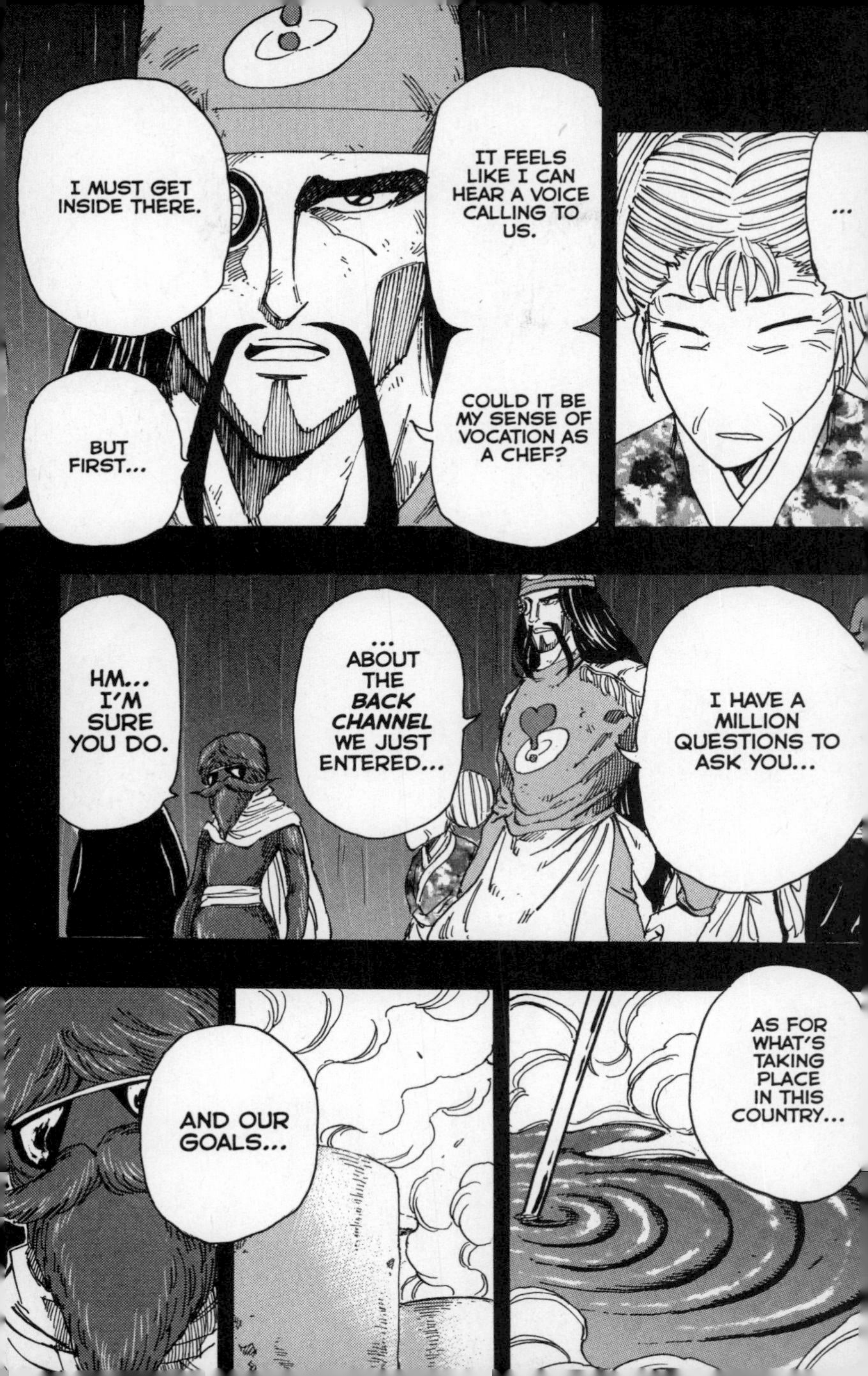
...
IT FEELS LIKE I CAN HEAR A VOICE CALLING TO US.
COULD IT BE MY SENSE OF VOCATION AS A CHEF?
I MUST GET INSIDE THERE.
BUT FIRST...
I HAVE A MILLION QUESTIONS TO ASK YOU...
... ABOUT THE *BACK CHANNEL* WE JUST ENTERED...
HM... I'M SURE YOU DO.
AS FOR WHAT'S TAKING PLACE IN THIS COUNTRY...
AND OUR GOALS...

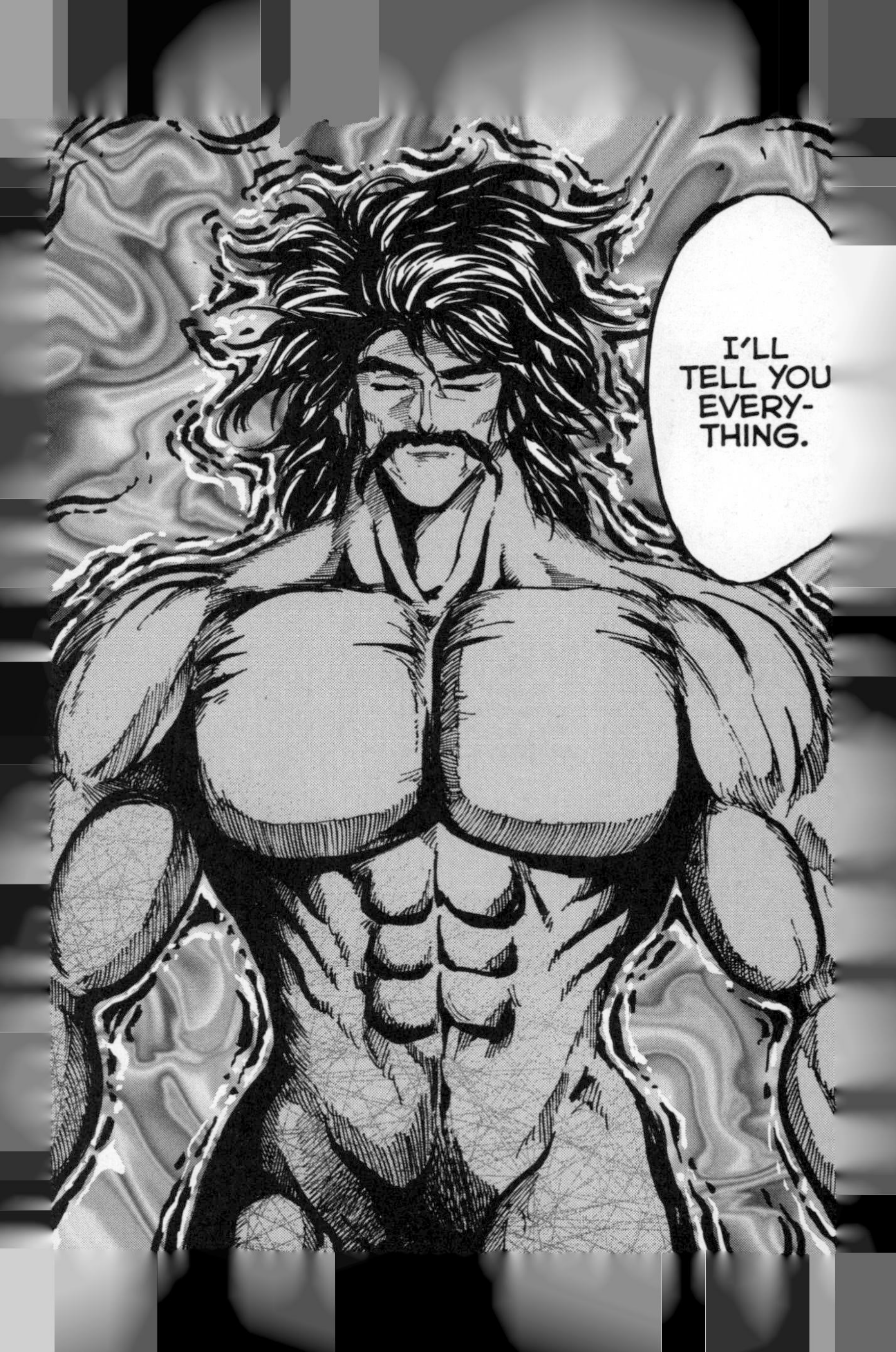
I'LL TELL YOU EVERY-THING.

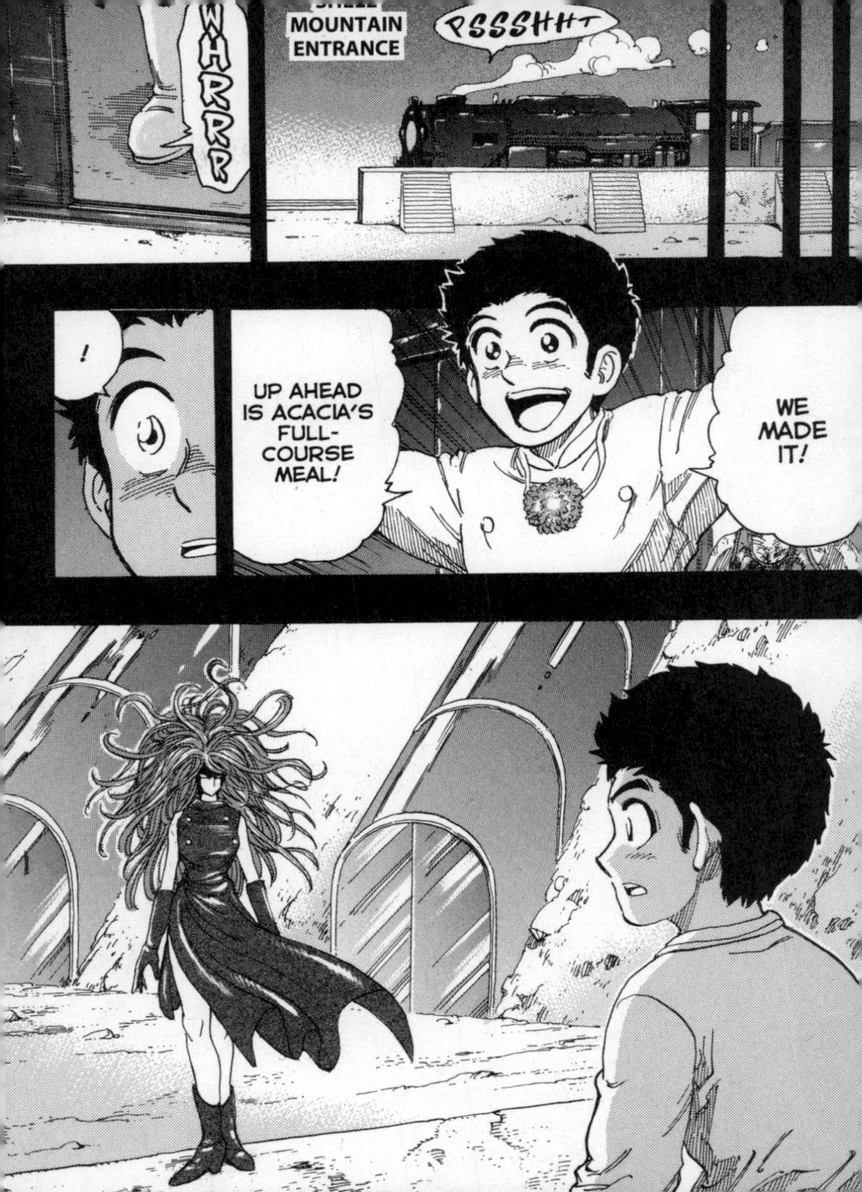
MOUNTAIN ENTRANCE
PSSSHHT
WHRRP
WE MADE IT!
UP AHEAD IS ACACIA'S FULL-COURSE MEAL!
!

TORIKO

GOURMET CHECKLIST

Vol. 374

MEGATON DANDELION
(GIANT PLANT)

CAPTURE LEVEL: 82
HABITAT: AREA 7
SIZE: ---
HEIGHT: 2,500 M
WEIGHT: 20 TONS
(ONE SEED IS 50 KG)
PRICE: NOT AN INGREDIENT

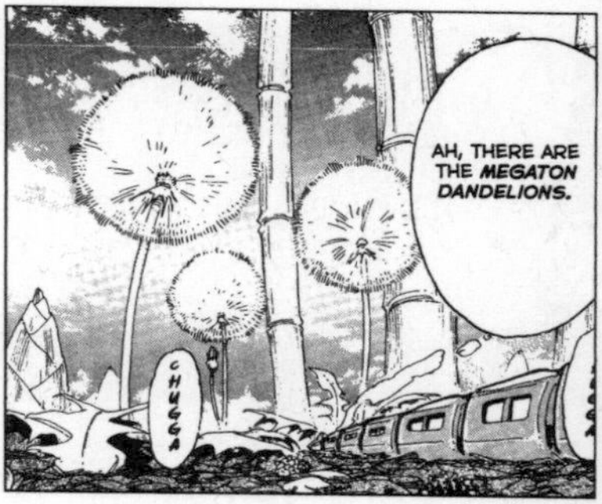
AH, THERE ARE THE *MEGATON* DANDELIONS.
CHUGGA

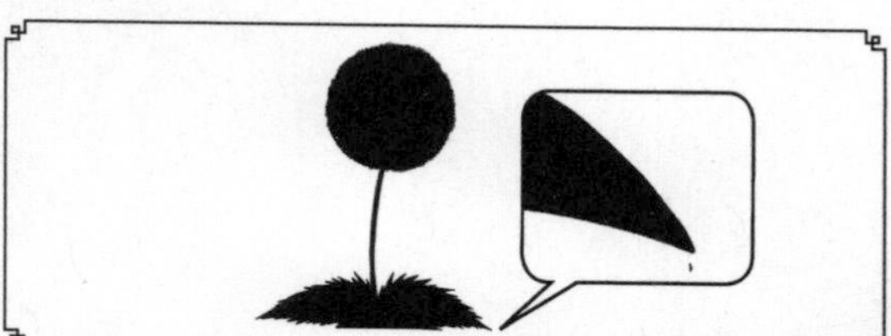

SCALE

A GIGANTIC DANDELION THAT GROWS IN THE GIANT LANDS OF THE GOURMET WORLD'S AREA 7, WHICH IS HOME TO THE FIVE LARGEST SPECIES ON THE PLANET. IF YOU GRAB ON TO THE GIANT FLUFF IN THE AIR, YOU CAN RIDE IT IN THE SKY LIKE A HOT AIR BALLOON. AREA 7 IS CRAWLING WITH DANGEROUS AND GIANT CREATURES, SO IF YOU CAN MANAGE TO MAKE USE OF THE THINGS AROUND YOU, YOU CAN TRAVERSE THE CONTINENT SAFELY, MAKING THIS ONE VERY HANDY PLANT.

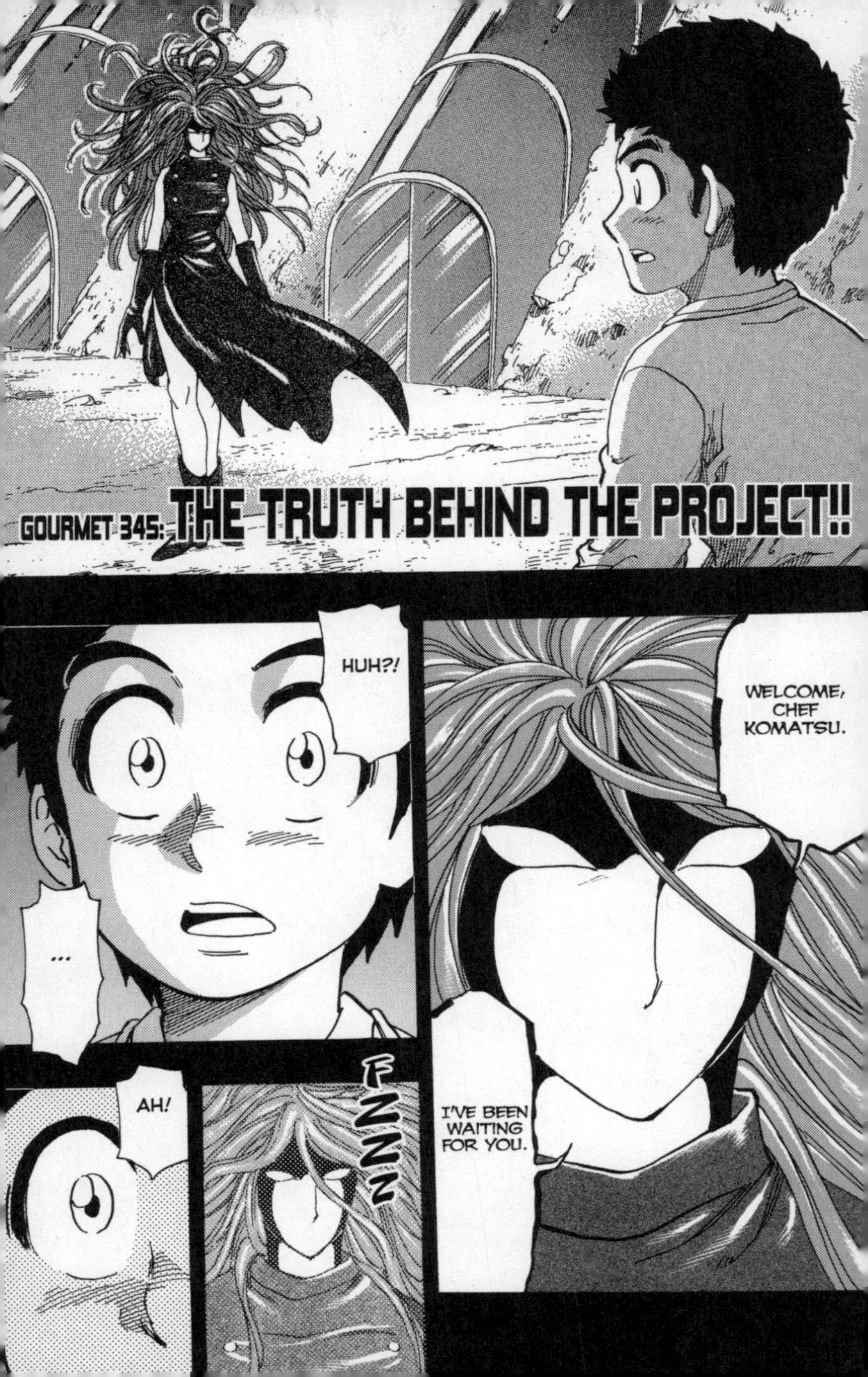
GOURMET 345: THE TRUTH BEHIND THE PROJECT!!
WELCOME, CHEF KOMATSU.
I'VE BEEN WAITING FOR YOU.
HUH?!
...
FZZZ
AH!

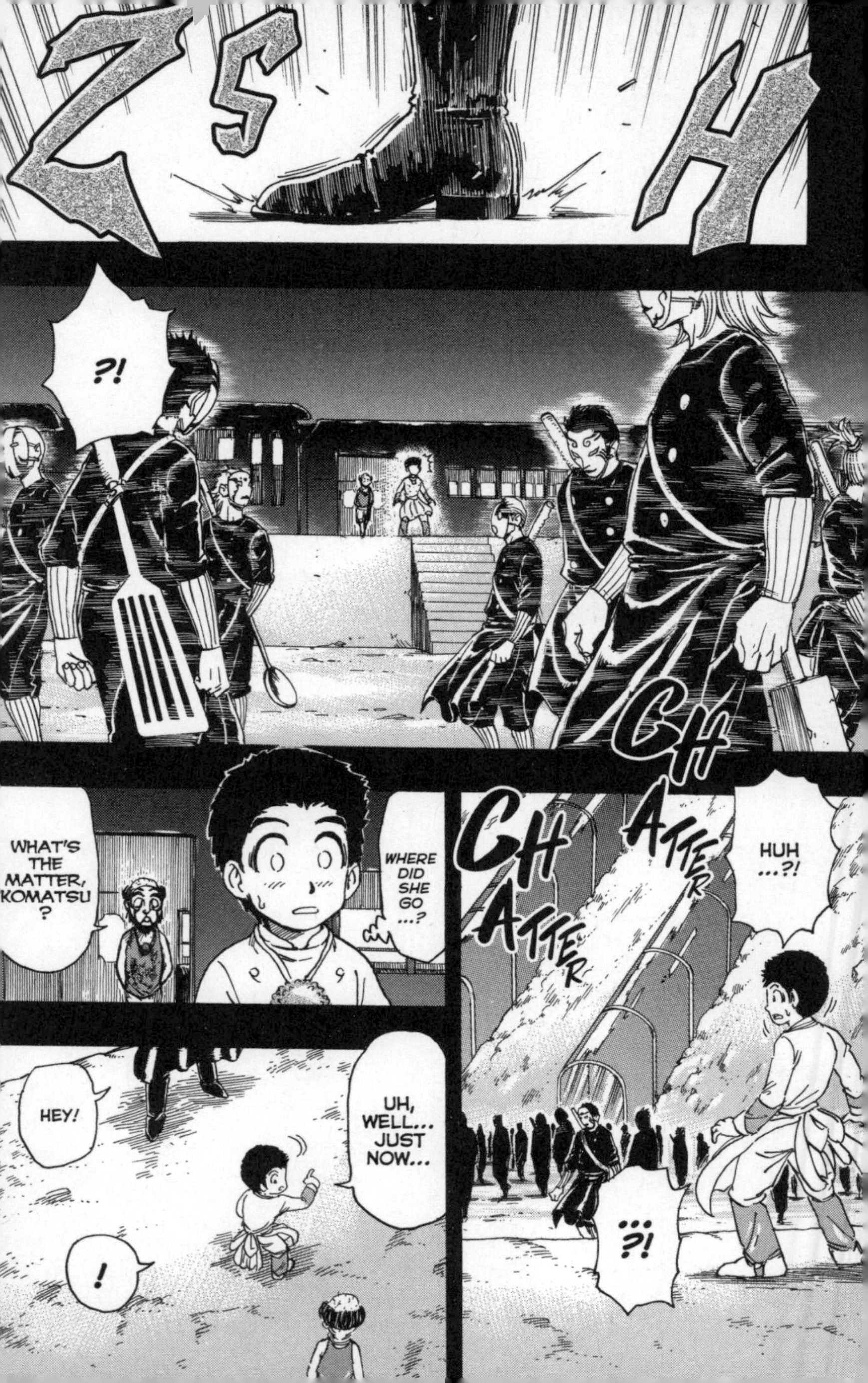

ZSH
?!
CHATTER
CHATTER
HUH ...?!
...?!
WHERE DID SHE GO ...?
WHAT'S THE MATTER, KOMATSU?
UH, WELL... JUST NOW...
HEY!
!

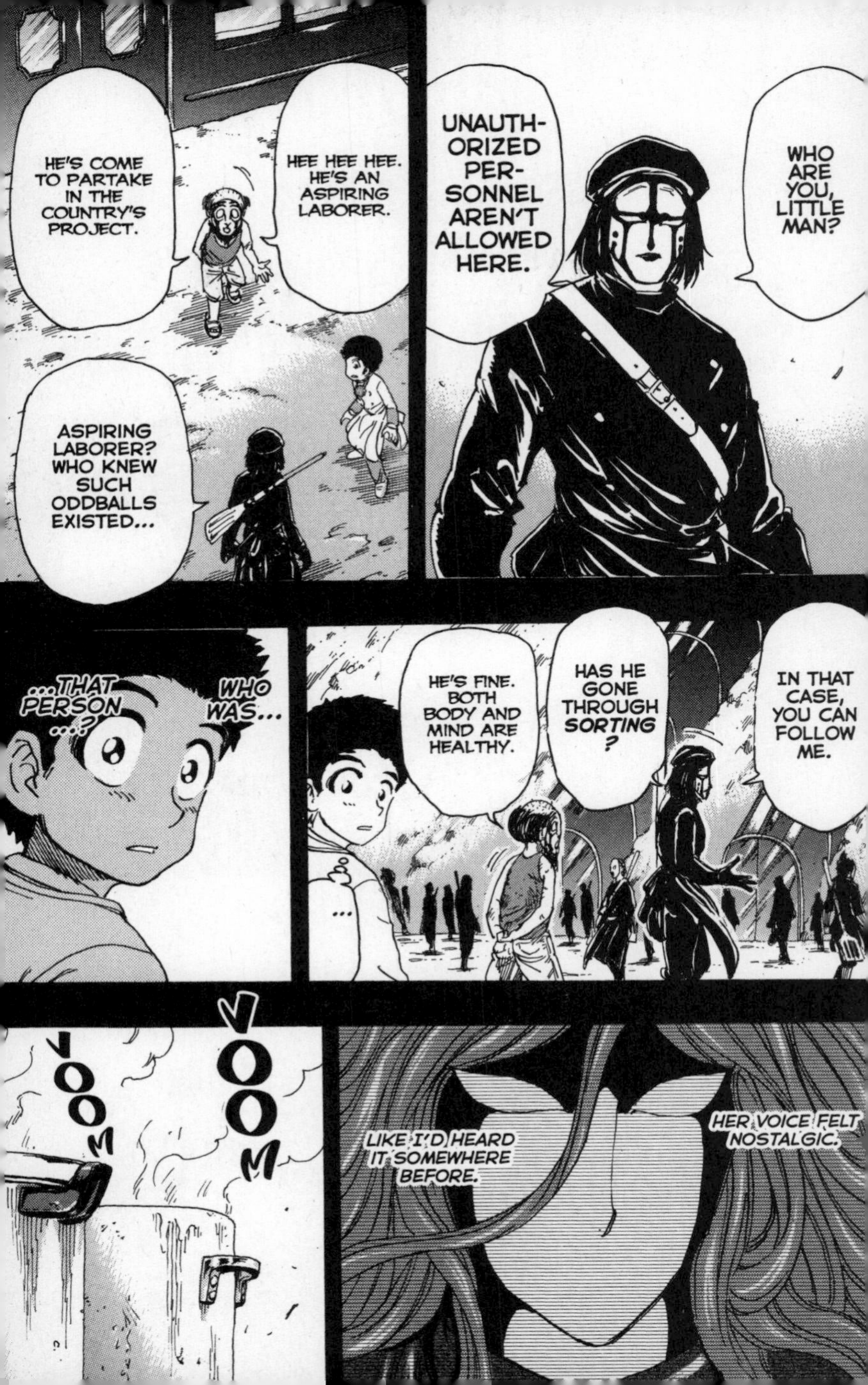
WHO ARE YOU, LITTLE MAN?
UNAUTH-ORIZED PER-SONNEL AREN'T ALLOWED HERE.
HEE HEE HEE. HE'S AN ASPIRING LABORER.
HE'S COME TO PARTAKE IN THE COUNTRY'S PROJECT.
ASPIRING LABORER? WHO KNEW SUCH ODDBALLS EXISTED...
IN THAT CASE, YOU CAN FOLLOW ME.
HAS HE GONE THROUGH *SORTING*?
HE'S FINE. BOTH BODY AND MIND ARE HEALTHY.
...
WHO WAS...
...THAT PERSON...?
HER VOICE FELT NOSTALGIC.
LIKE I'D HEARD IT SOMEWHERE BEFORE.
VOOM
VOOM

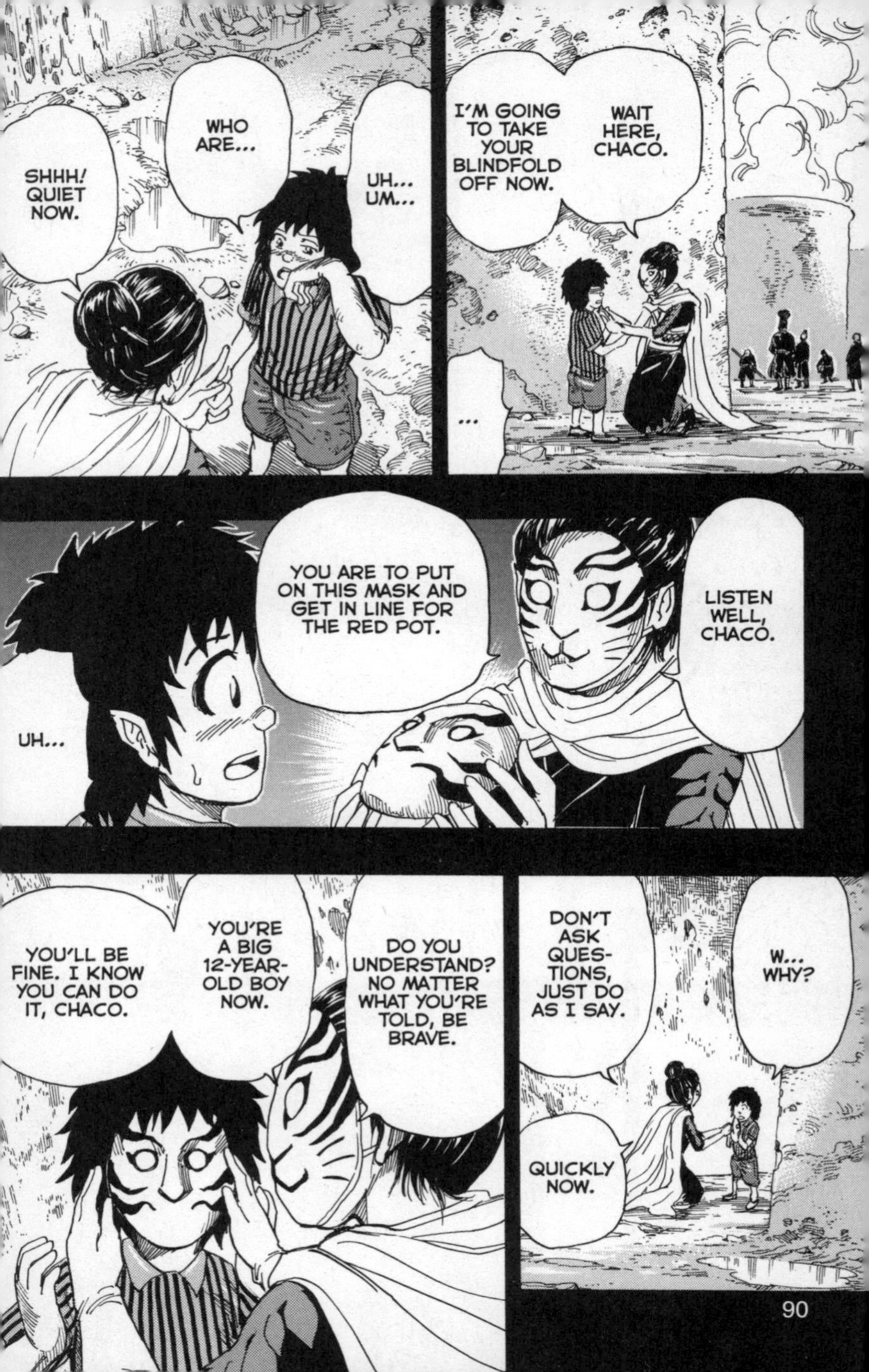
WAIT HERE, CHACO.
I'M GOING TO TAKE YOUR BLINDFOLD OFF NOW.
...
UH... UM...
WHO ARE...
SHHH! QUIET NOW.
LISTEN WELL, CHACO.
YOU ARE TO PUT ON THIS MASK AND GET IN LINE FOR THE RED POT.
UH...
W... WHY?
DON'T ASK QUES-TIONS, JUST DO AS I SAY.
QUICKLY NOW.
DO YOU UNDERSTAND? NO MATTER WHAT YOU'RE TOLD, BE BRAVE.
YOU'RE A BIG 12-YEAR-OLD BOY NOW.
YOU'LL BE FINE. I KNOW YOU CAN DO IT, CHACO.

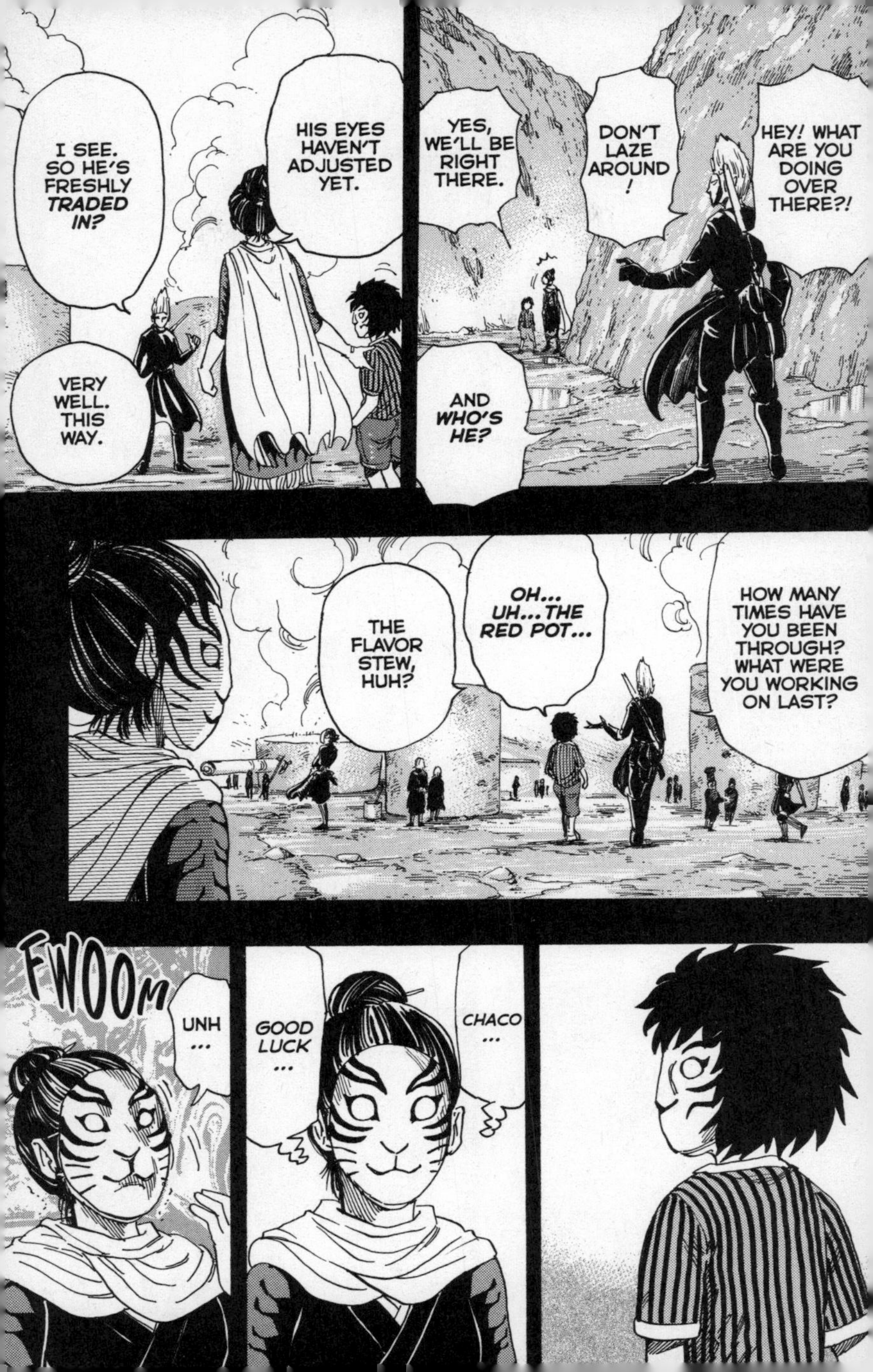
HEY! WHAT ARE YOU DOING OVER THERE?!
DON'T LAZE AROUND!
YES, WE'LL BE RIGHT THERE.
AND *WHO'S* HE?
HIS EYES HAVEN'T ADJUSTED YET.
I SEE. SO HE'S FRESHLY *TRADED IN?*
VERY WELL. THIS WAY.
HOW MANY TIMES HAVE YOU BEEN THROUGH? WHAT WERE YOU WORKING ON LAST?
OH... UH...THE RED POT...
THE FLAVOR STEW, HUH?
CHACO ...
GOOD LUCK ...
FWOOM
UNH ...

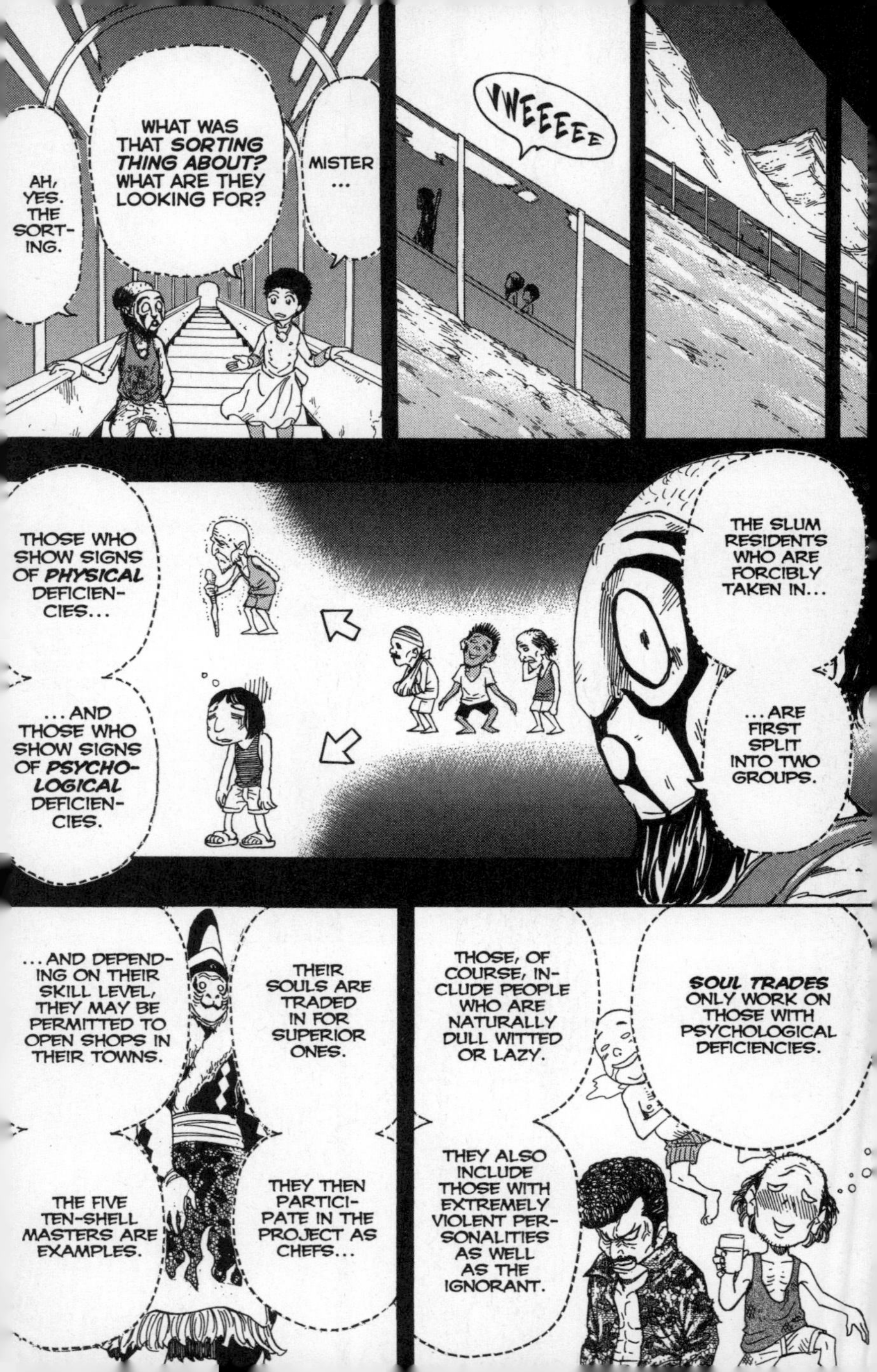
VWEEEEEE
MISTER ...
WHAT WAS THAT SORTING THING ABOUT? WHAT ARE THEY LOOKING FOR?
AH, YES. THE SORTING.
THE SLUM RESIDENTS WHO ARE FORCIBLY TAKEN IN...
...ARE FIRST SPLIT INTO TWO GROUPS.
THOSE WHO SHOW SIGNS OF PHYSICAL DEFICIENCIES...
...AND THOSE WHO SHOW SIGNS OF PSYCHOLOGICAL DEFICIENCIES.
SOUL TRADES ONLY WORK ON THOSE WITH PSYCHOLOGICAL DEFICIENCIES.
THOSE, OF COURSE, INCLUDE PEOPLE WHO ARE NATURALLY DULL WITTED OR LAZY.
THEY ALSO INCLUDE THOSE WITH EXTREMELY VIOLENT PERSONALITIES AS WELL AS THE IGNORANT.
THEIR SOULS ARE TRADED IN FOR SUPERIOR ONES.
...AND DEPENDING ON THEIR SKILL LEVEL, THEY MAY BE PERMITTED TO OPEN SHOPS IN THEIR TOWNS.
THEY THEN PARTICIPATE IN THE PROJECT AS CHEFS...
THE FIVE TEN-SHELL MASTERS ARE EXAMPLES.

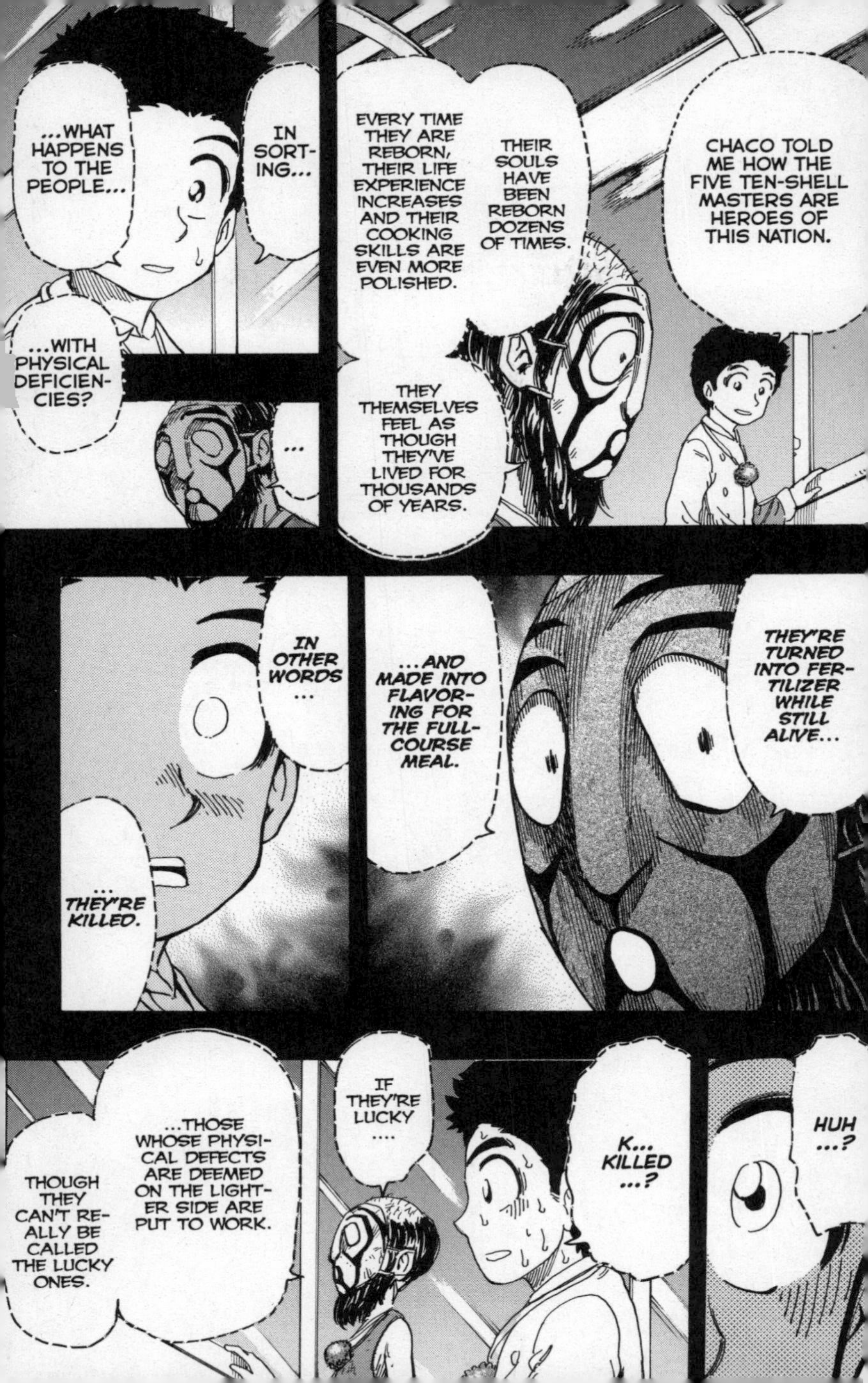
CHACO TOLD ME HOW THE FIVE TEN-SHELL MASTERS ARE HEROES OF THIS NATION.
THEIR SOULS HAVE BEEN REBORN DOZENS OF TIMES.
EVERY TIME THEY ARE REBORN, THEIR LIFE EXPERIENCE INCREASES AND THEIR COOKING SKILLS ARE EVEN MORE POLISHED.
THEY THEMSELVES FEEL AS THOUGH THEY'VE LIVED FOR THOUSANDS OF YEARS.
IN SORTING...
...WHAT HAPPENS TO THE PEOPLE...
...WITH PHYSICAL DEFICIENCIES?
...
THEY'RE TURNED INTO FERTILIZER WHILE STILL ALIVE...
...AND MADE INTO FLAVORING FOR THE FULL-COURSE MEAL.
IN OTHER WORDS...
...THEY'RE KILLED.
HUH...?
K... KILLED...?
IF THEY'RE LUCKY....
...THOSE WHOSE PHYSICAL DEFECTS ARE DEEMED ON THE LIGHTER SIDE ARE PUT TO WORK.
THOUGH THEY CAN'T REALLY BE CALLED THE LUCKY ONES.

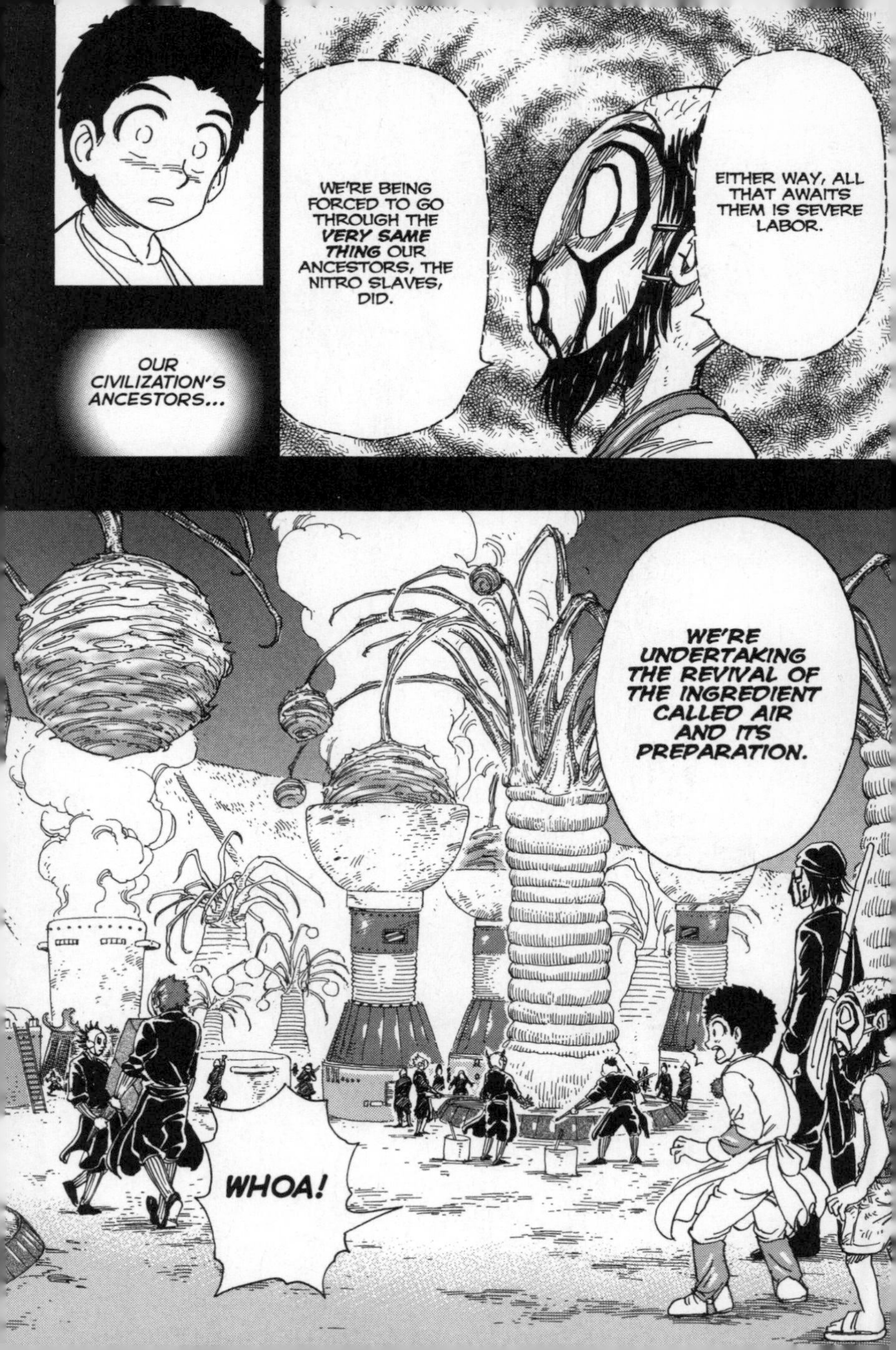
EITHER WAY, ALL THAT AWAITS THEM IS SEVERE LABOR.
WE'RE BEING FORCED TO GO THROUGH THE ***VERY SAME THING*** OUR ANCESTORS, THE NITRO SLAVES, DID.
OUR CIVILIZATION'S ANCESTORS...
WE'RE UNDERTAKING THE REVIVAL OF THE INGREDIENT CALLED AIR AND ITS PREPARATION.
WHOA!

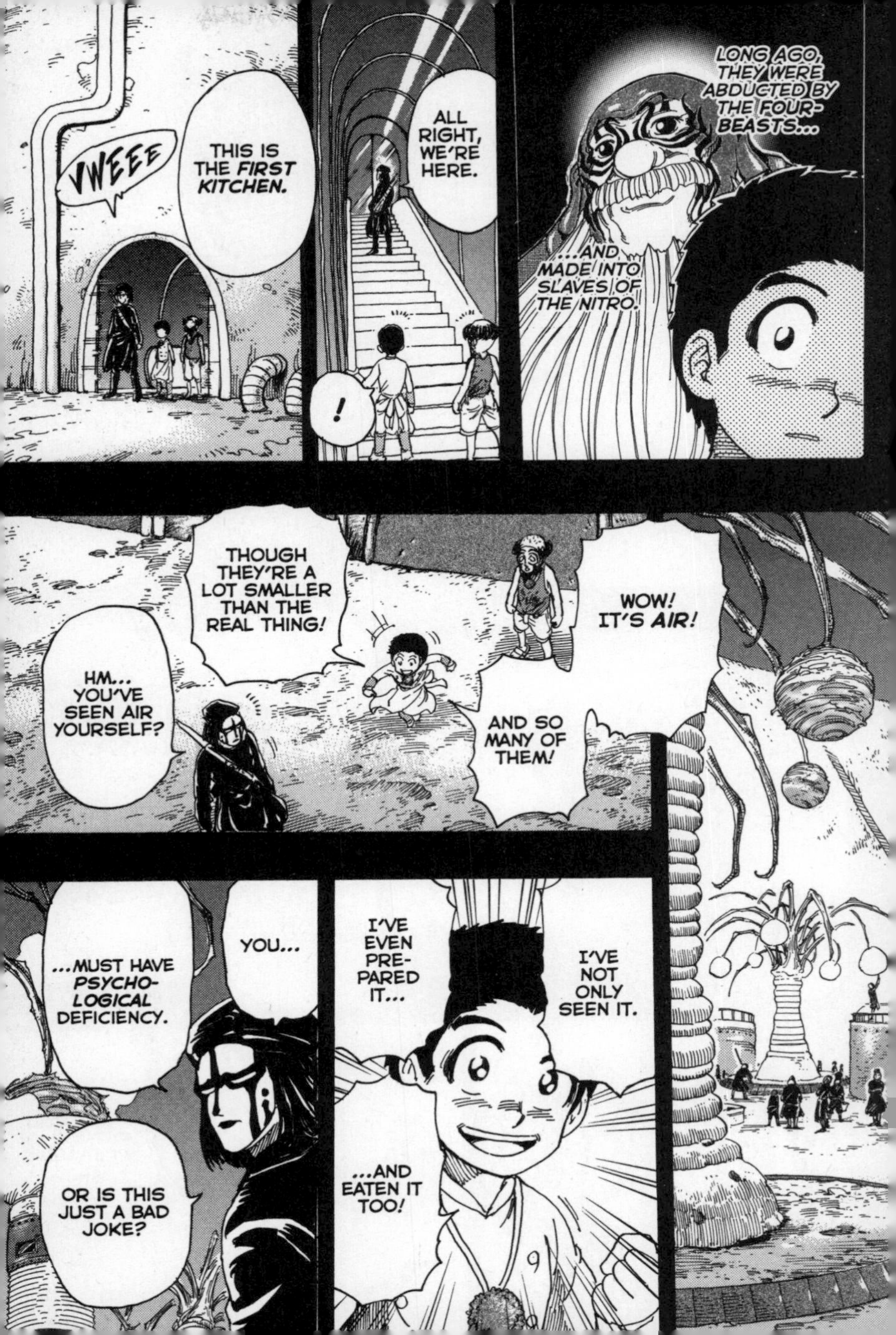
LONG AGO, THEY WERE ABDUCTED BY THE FOUR-BEASTS...
...AND MADE INTO SLAVES OF THE NITRO.
ALL RIGHT, WE'RE HERE.
!
THIS IS THE *FIRST KITCHEN.*
VWEEE
WOW! IT'S *AIR!*
AND SO MANY OF THEM!
THOUGH THEY'RE A LOT SMALLER THAN THE REAL THING!
HM... YOU'VE SEEN AIR YOURSELF?
I'VE NOT ONLY SEEN IT.
I'VE EVEN PRE-PARED IT...
...AND EATEN IT TOO!
YOU...
...MUST HAVE *PSYCHO-LOGICAL* DEFICIENCY.
OR IS THIS JUST A BAD JOKE?

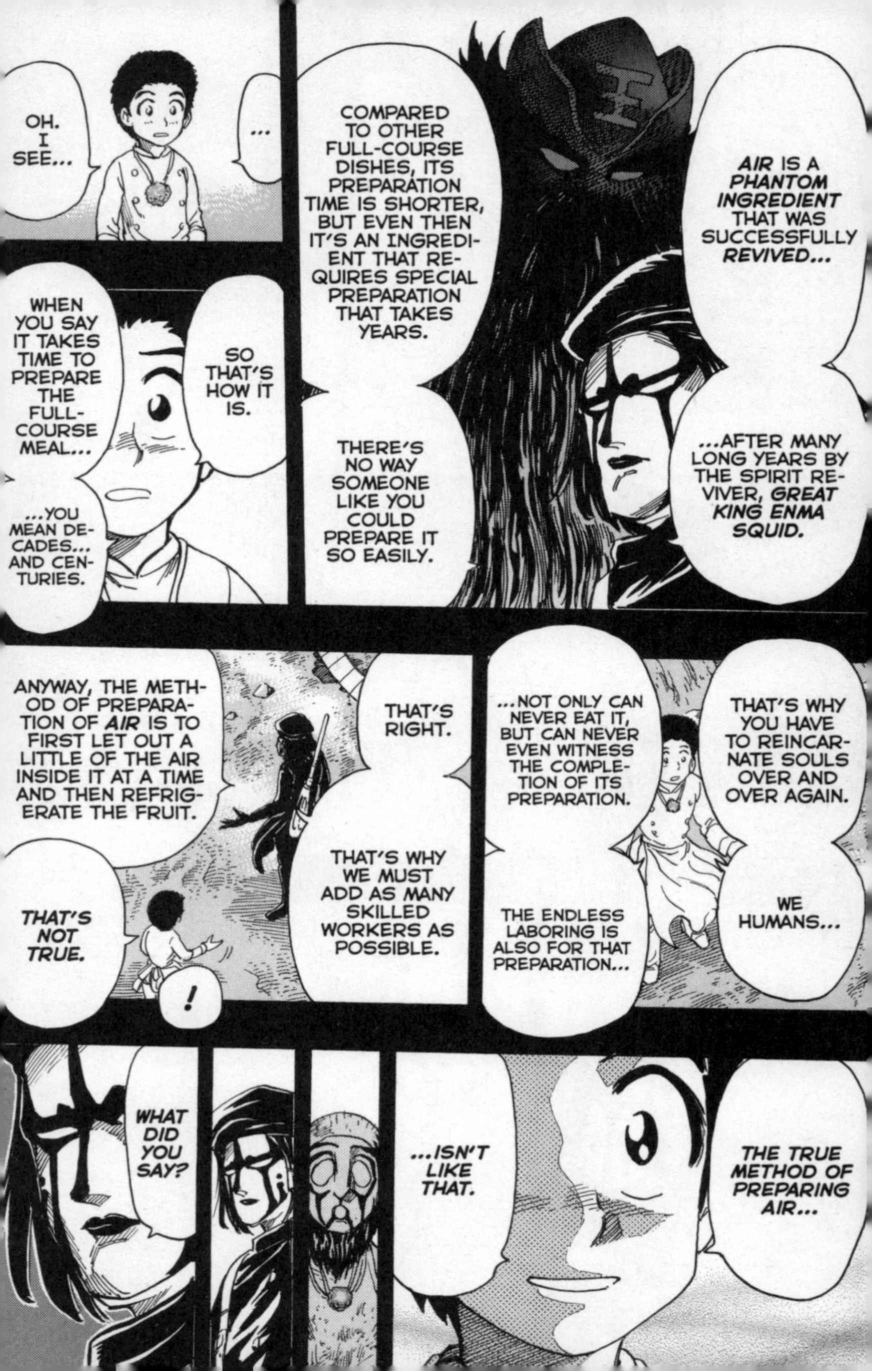
AIR IS A PHANTOM INGREDIENT THAT WAS SUCCESSFULLY REVIVED...
...AFTER MANY LONG YEARS BY THE SPIRIT REVIVER, GREAT KING ENMA SQUID.
COMPARED TO OTHER FULL-COURSE DISHES, ITS PREPARATION TIME IS SHORTER, BUT EVEN THEN IT'S AN INGREDIENT THAT REQUIRES SPECIAL PREPARATION THAT TAKES YEARS.
THERE'S NO WAY SOMEONE LIKE YOU COULD PREPARE IT SO EASILY.
...
OH. I SEE...
SO THAT'S HOW IT IS.
WHEN YOU SAY IT TAKES TIME TO PREPARE THE FULL-COURSE MEAL...
...YOU MEAN DECADES... AND CENTURIES.
THAT'S WHY YOU HAVE TO REINCARNATE SOULS OVER AND OVER AGAIN.
WE HUMANS...
...NOT ONLY CAN NEVER EAT IT, BUT CAN NEVER EVEN WITNESS THE COMPLETION OF ITS PREPARATION.
THE ENDLESS LABORING IS ALSO FOR THAT PREPARATION...
THAT'S RIGHT.
THAT'S WHY WE MUST ADD AS MANY SKILLED WORKERS AS POSSIBLE.
ANYWAY, THE METHOD OF PREPARATION OF AIR IS TO FIRST LET OUT A LITTLE OF THE AIR INSIDE IT AT A TIME AND THEN REFRIGERATE THE FRUIT.
THAT'S NOT TRUE.
!
THE TRUE METHOD OF PREPARING AIR...
...ISN'T LIKE THAT.
WHAT DID YOU SAY?

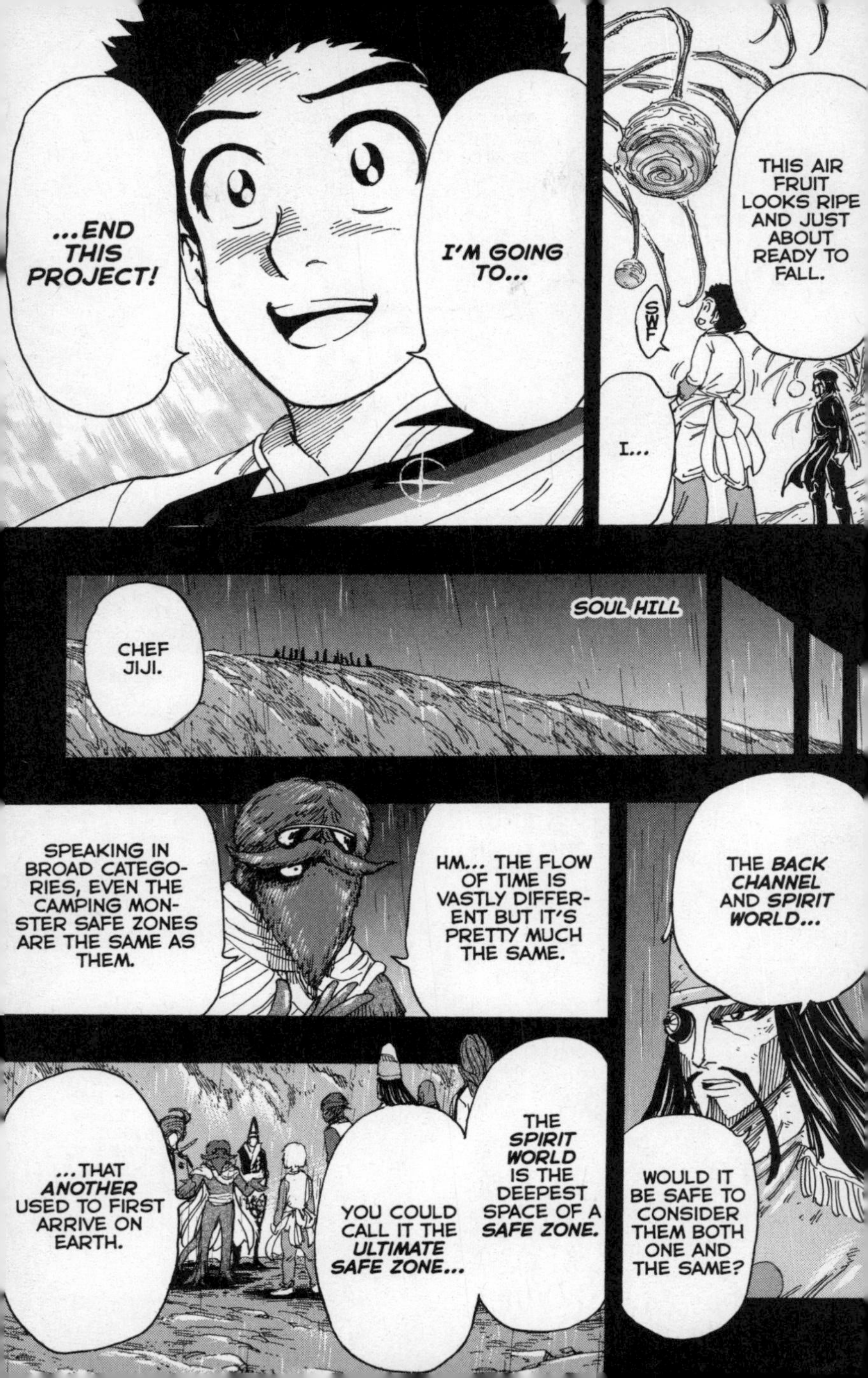

THIS AIR FRUIT LOOKS RIPE AND JUST ABOUT READY TO FALL.
SWF
I...
I'M GOING TO...
...END THIS PROJECT!
SOUL HILL
CHEF JIJI.
THE BACK CHANNEL AND SPIRIT WORLD...
WOULD IT BE SAFE TO CONSIDER THEM BOTH ONE AND THE SAME?
HM... THE FLOW OF TIME IS VASTLY DIFFERENT BUT IT'S PRETTY MUCH THE SAME.
SPEAKING IN BROAD CATEGORIES, EVEN THE CAMPING MONSTER SAFE ZONES ARE THE SAME AS THEM.
THE SPIRIT WORLD IS THE DEEPEST SPACE OF A SAFE ZONE.
YOU COULD CALL IT THE ULTIMATE SAFE ZONE...
...THAT ANOTHER USED TO FIRST ARRIVE ON EARTH.

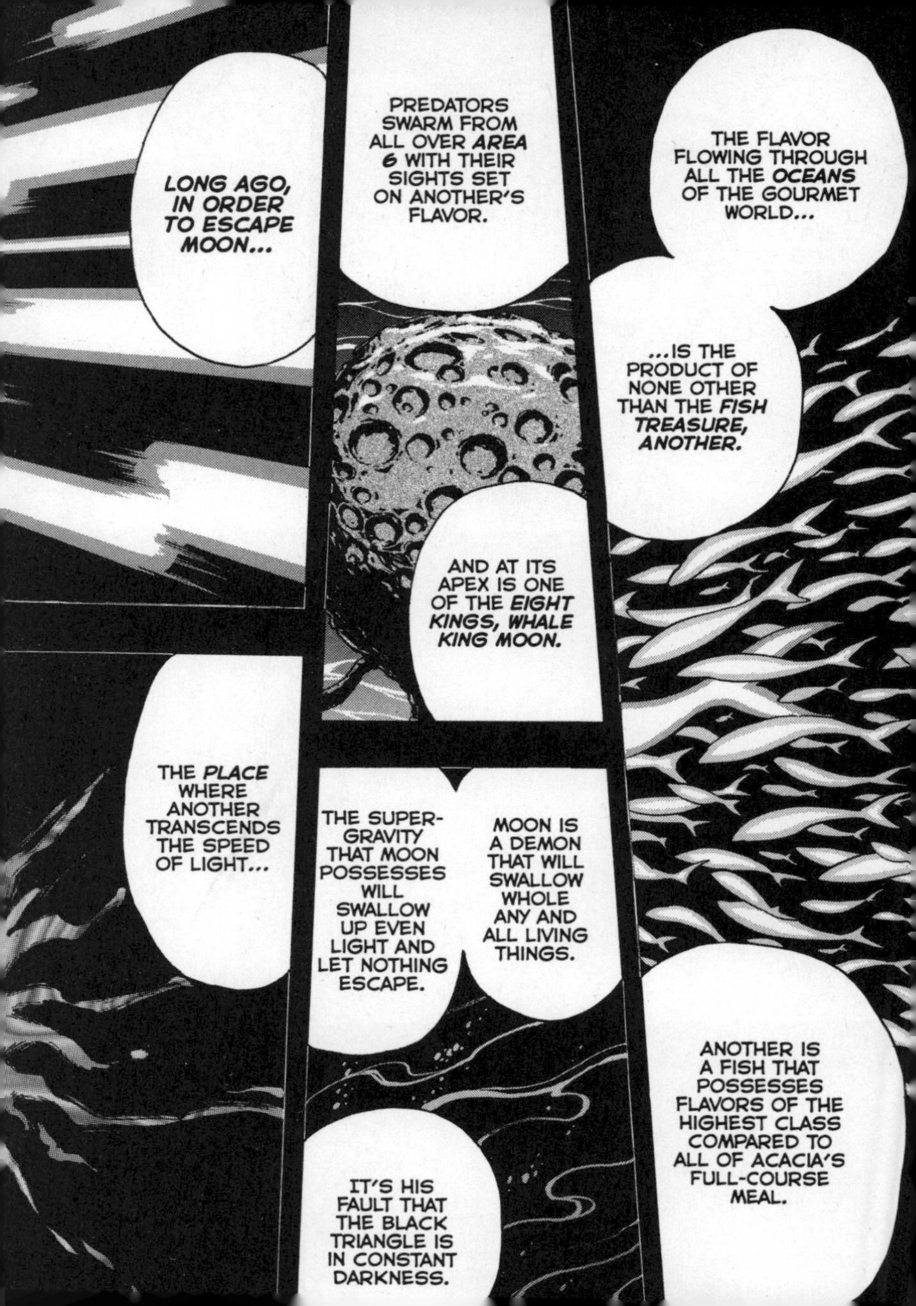
THE FLAVOR FLOWING THROUGH ALL THE *OCEANS* OF THE GOURMET WORLD...
...IS THE PRODUCT OF NONE OTHER THAN THE *FISH TREASURE, ANOTHER.*
ANOTHER IS A FISH THAT POSSESSES FLAVORS OF THE HIGHEST CLASS COMPARED TO ALL OF ACACIA'S FULL-COURSE MEAL.
PREDATORS SWARM FROM ALL OVER *AREA 6* WITH THEIR SIGHTS SET ON ANOTHER'S FLAVOR.
AND AT ITS APEX IS ONE OF THE *EIGHT KINGS, WHALE KING MOON.*
LONG AGO, IN ORDER TO ESCAPE MOON...
MOON IS A DEMON THAT WILL SWALLOW WHOLE ANY AND ALL LIVING THINGS.
THE SUPER-GRAVITY THAT MOON POSSESSES WILL SWALLOW UP EVEN LIGHT AND LET NOTHING ESCAPE.
IT'S HIS FAULT THAT THE BLACK TRIANGLE IS IN CONSTANT DARKNESS.
THE *PLACE* WHERE ANOTHER TRANSCENDS THE SPEED OF LIGHT...

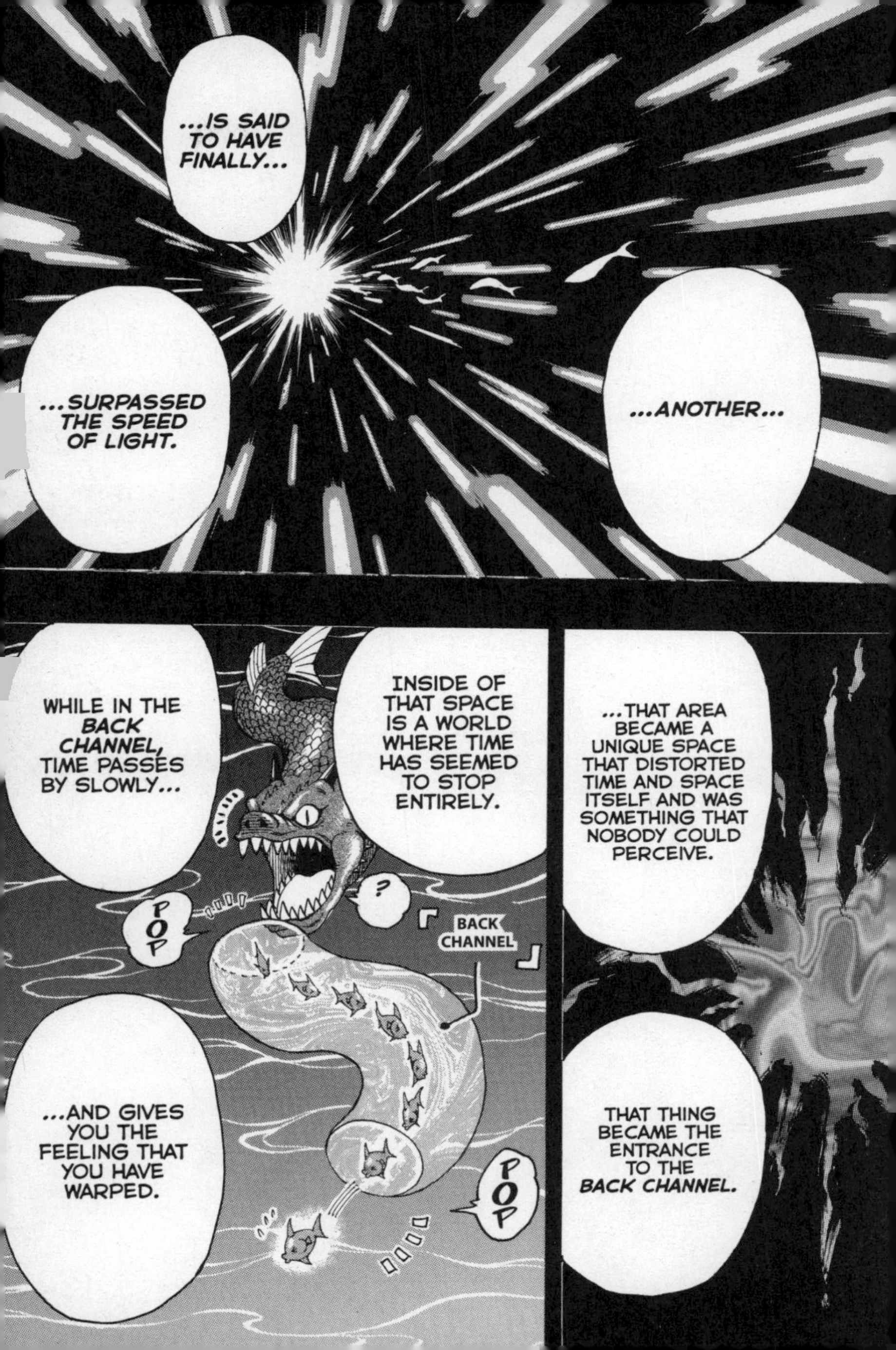
...IS SAID TO HAVE FINALLY...
...SURPASSED THE SPEED OF LIGHT.
...ANOTHER...
...THAT AREA BECAME A UNIQUE SPACE THAT DISTORTED TIME AND SPACE ITSELF AND WAS SOMETHING THAT NOBODY COULD PERCEIVE.
THAT THING BECAME THE ENTRANCE TO THE BACK CHANNEL.
INSIDE OF THAT SPACE IS A WORLD WHERE TIME HAS SEEMED TO STOP ENTIRELY.
WHILE IN THE BACK CHANNEL, TIME PASSES BY SLOWLY...
?
POP
BACK CHANNEL
...AND GIVES YOU THE FEELING THAT YOU HAVE WARPED.
POP

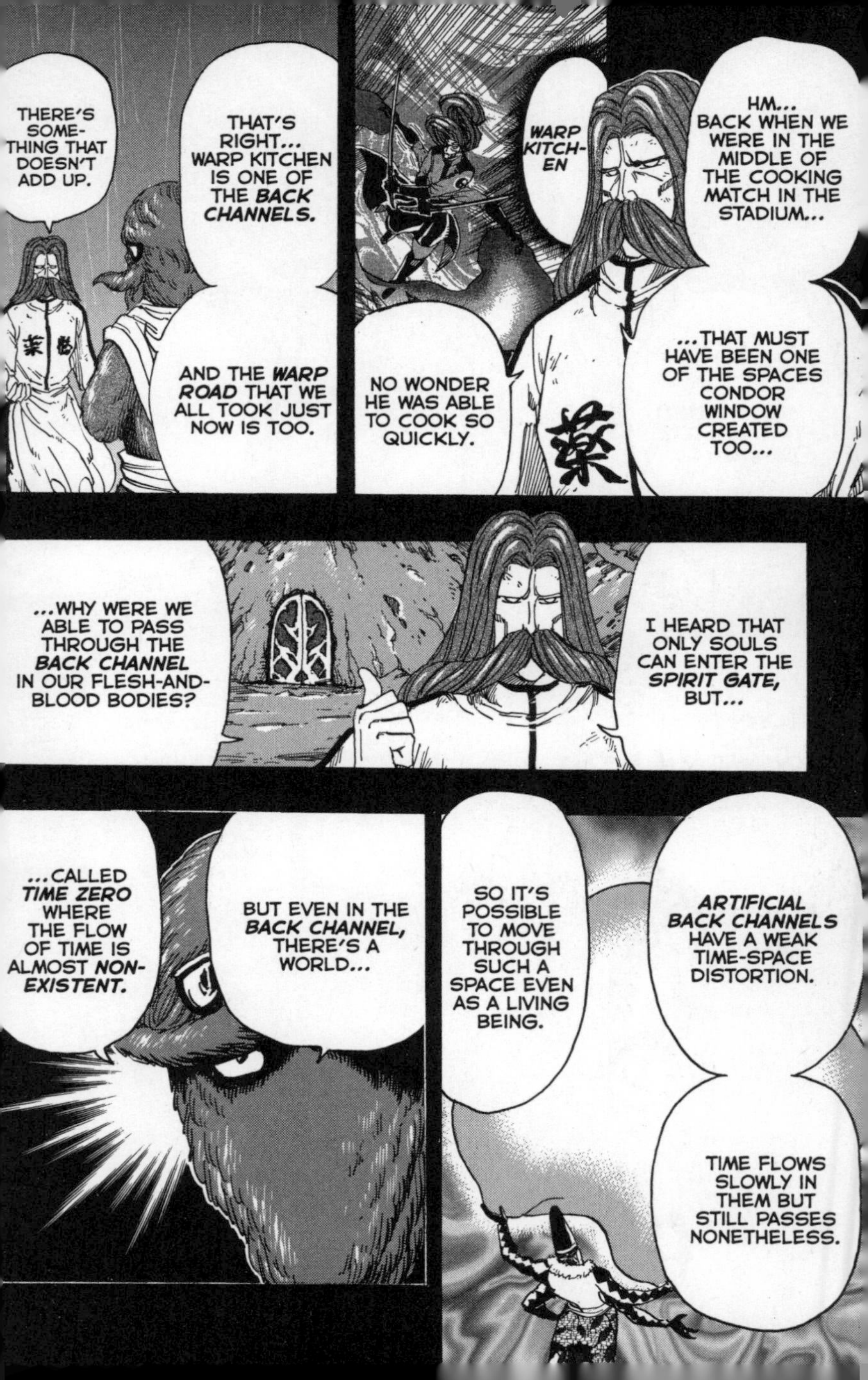
HM... BACK WHEN WE WERE IN THE MIDDLE OF THE COOKING MATCH IN THE STADIUM...
WARP KITCHEN
...THAT MUST HAVE BEEN ONE OF THE SPACES CONDOR WINDOW CREATED TOO...
NO WONDER HE WAS ABLE TO COOK SO QUICKLY.
THAT'S RIGHT... WARP KITCHEN IS ONE OF THE BACK CHANNELS.
AND THE WARP ROAD THAT WE ALL TOOK JUST NOW IS TOO.
THERE'S SOMETHING THAT DOESN'T ADD UP.
I HEARD THAT ONLY SOULS CAN ENTER THE SPIRIT GATE, BUT...
...WHY WERE WE ABLE TO PASS THROUGH THE BACK CHANNEL IN OUR FLESH-AND-BLOOD BODIES?
ARTIFICIAL BACK CHANNELS HAVE A WEAK TIME-SPACE DISTORTION.
TIME FLOWS SLOWLY IN THEM BUT STILL PASSES NONETHELESS.
SO IT'S POSSIBLE TO MOVE THROUGH SUCH A SPACE EVEN AS A LIVING BEING.
BUT EVEN IN THE BACK CHANNEL, THERE'S A WORLD...
...CALLED TIME ZERO WHERE THE FLOW OF TIME IS ALMOST NON-EXISTENT.

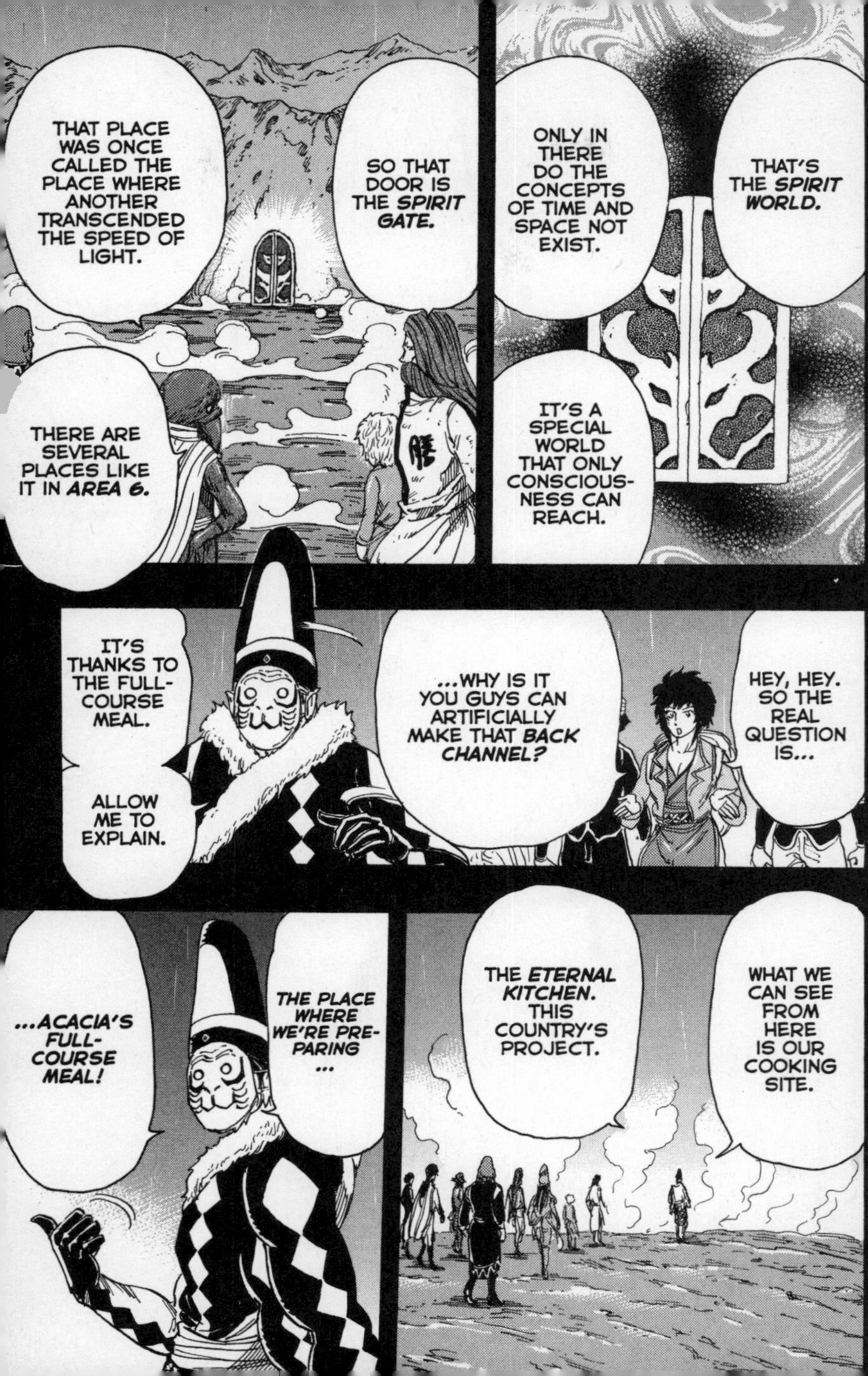
THAT'S THE SPIRIT WORLD.
ONLY IN THERE DO THE CONCEPTS OF TIME AND SPACE NOT EXIST.
IT'S A SPECIAL WORLD THAT ONLY CONSCIOUSNESS CAN REACH.
SO THAT DOOR IS THE SPIRIT GATE.
THAT PLACE WAS ONCE CALLED THE PLACE WHERE ANOTHER TRANSCENDED THE SPEED OF LIGHT.
THERE ARE SEVERAL PLACES LIKE IT IN AREA 6.
HEY, HEY. SO THE REAL QUESTION IS...
...WHY IS IT YOU GUYS CAN ARTIFICIALLY MAKE THAT BACK CHANNEL?
IT'S THANKS TO THE FULL-COURSE MEAL.
ALLOW ME TO EXPLAIN.
WHAT WE CAN SEE FROM HERE IS OUR COOKING SITE.
THE ETERNAL KITCHEN. THIS COUNTRY'S PROJECT.
THE PLACE WHERE WE'RE PREPARING...
...ACACIA'S FULL-COURSE MEAL!

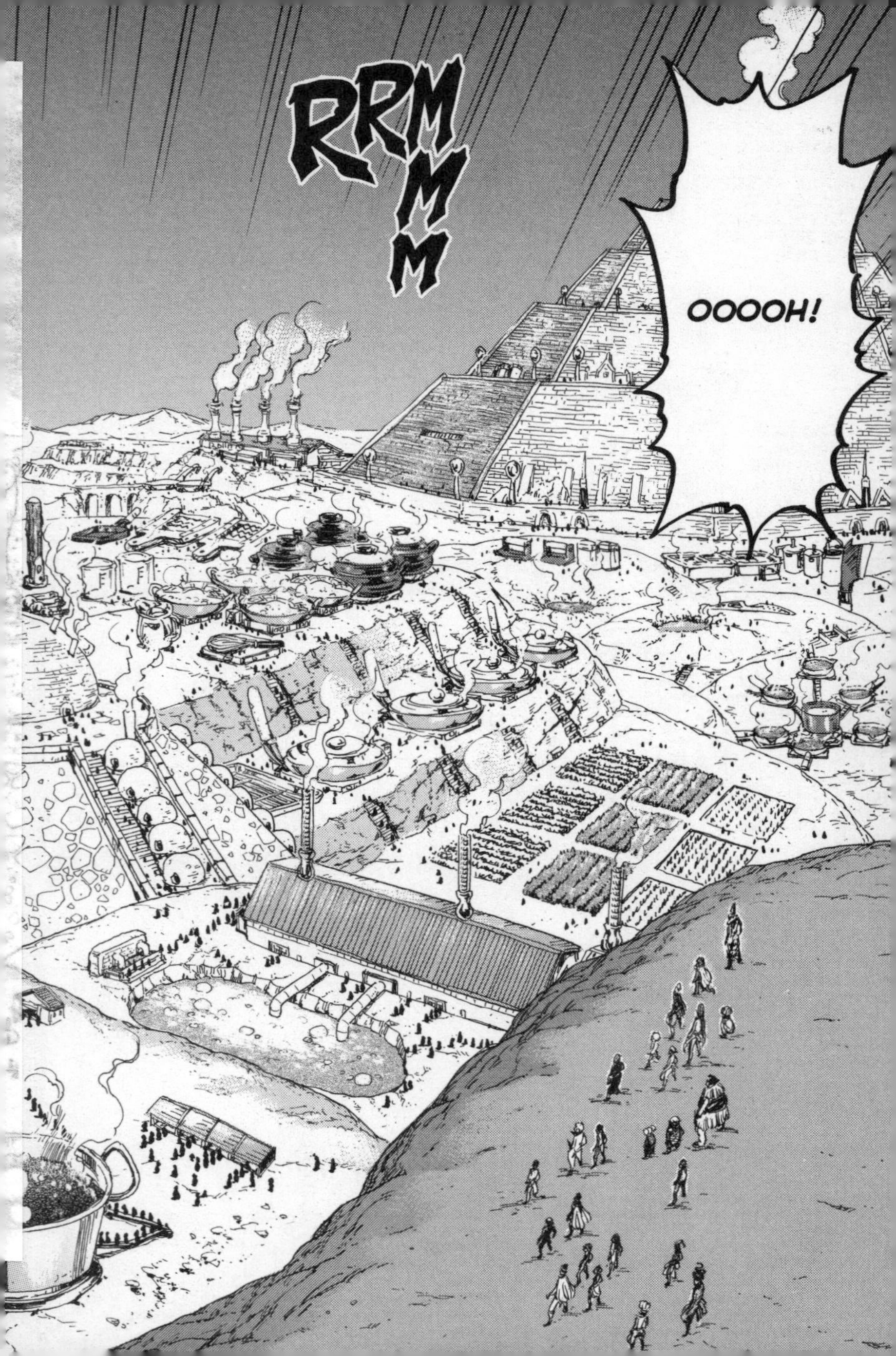
OOOOH!
RRMMMM

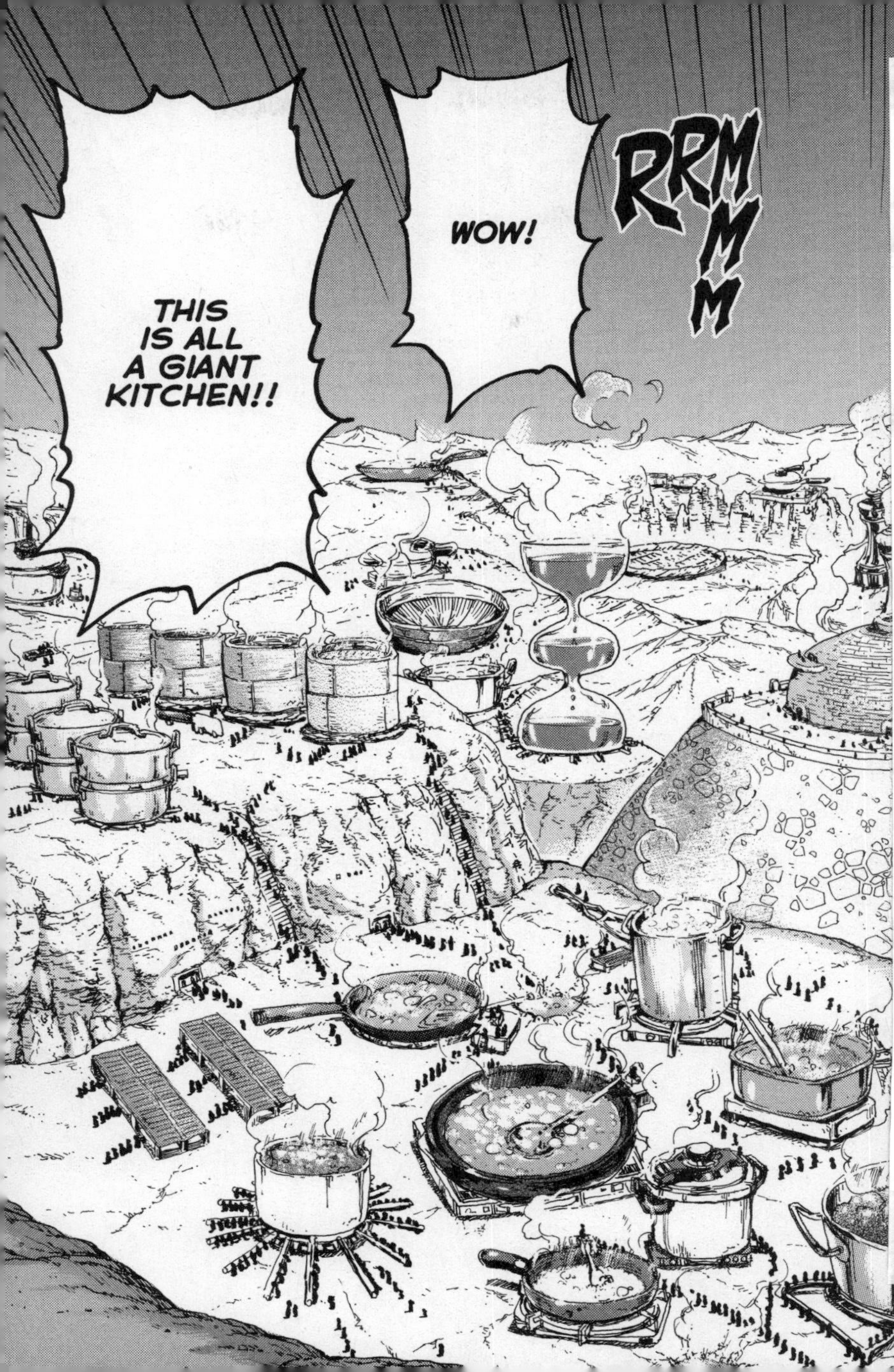
RRMMMM
WOW!
THIS IS ALL A GIANT KITCHEN!!

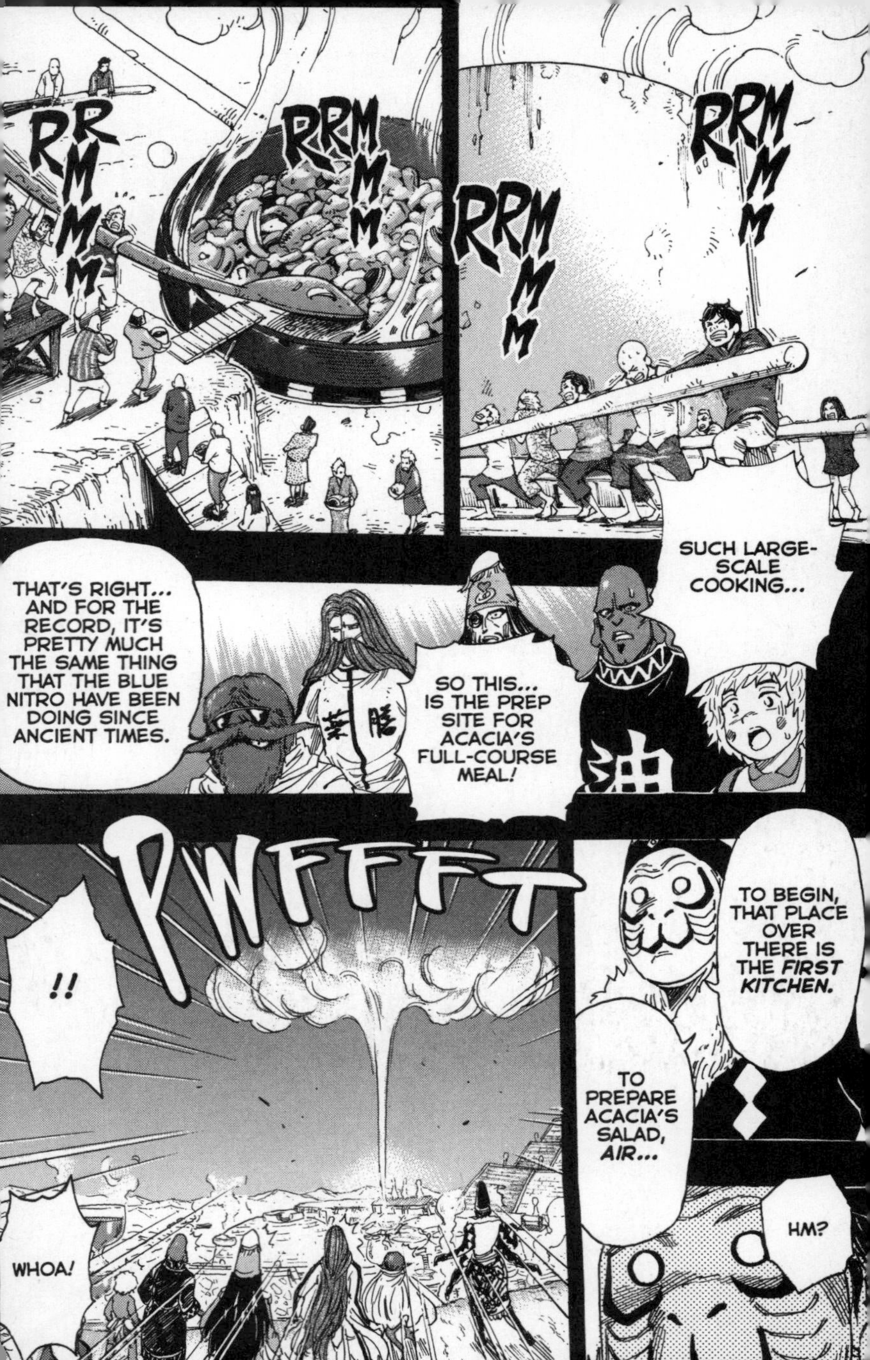
RRMMM
RRMMMM
RRMMMM
RRMMMM
SUCH LARGE-SCALE COOKING...
SO THIS... IS THE PREP SITE FOR ACACIA'S FULL-COURSE MEAL!
THAT'S RIGHT... AND FOR THE RECORD, IT'S PRETTY MUCH THE SAME THING THAT THE BLUE NITRO HAVE BEEN DOING SINCE ANCIENT TIMES.
TO BEGIN, THAT PLACE OVER THERE IS THE *FIRST KITCHEN.*
TO PREPARE ACACIA'S SALAD, *AIR...*
HM?
PWFFFT
!!
WHOA!

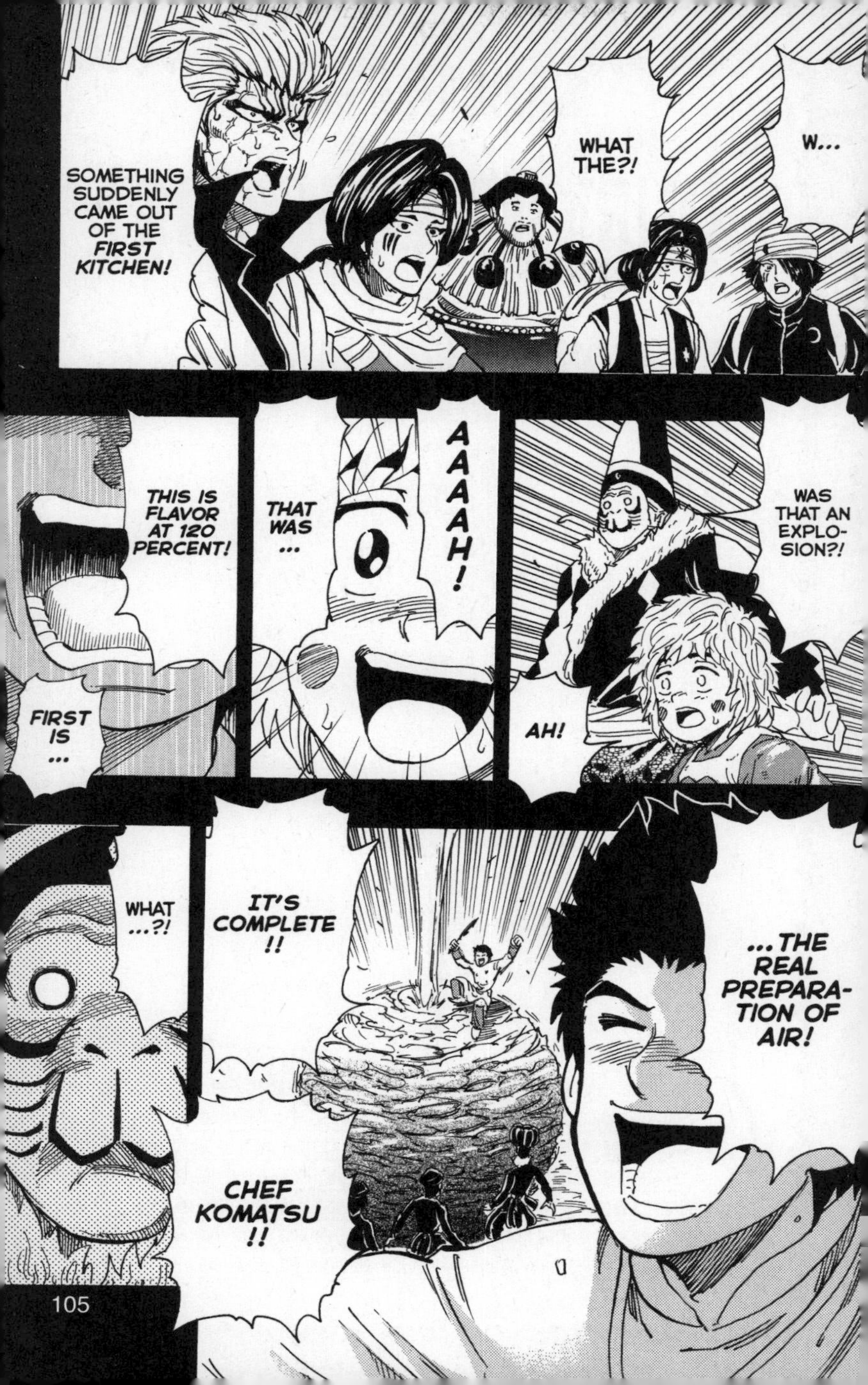
W...
WHAT THE?!
SOMETHING SUDDENLY CAME OUT OF THE *FIRST* KITCHEN!
WAS THAT AN EXPLOSION?!
AH!
AAAAAH!
THAT WAS ...
THIS IS FLAVOR AT 120 PERCENT!
FIRST IS ...
...THE REAL PREPARATION OF AIR!
IT'S COMPLETE !!
CHEF KOMATSU !!
WHAT ...?!

TORIKO

GOURMET CHECKLIST

Vol. 375

CONSOMME MAGMA
(BEVERAGE MAGMA)

CAPTURE LEVEL: 2,800
HABITAT: AREA 7
SIZE: ---
HEIGHT: ---
WEIGHT: ---
PRICE: 20 MILLION YEN PER GLASS

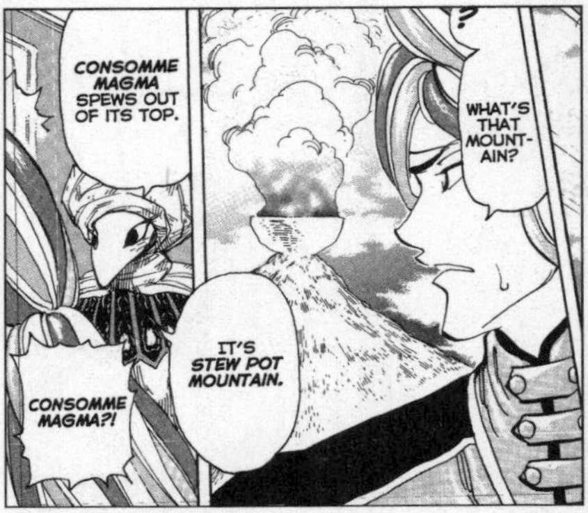
?
WHAT'S THAT MOUNTAIN?
IT'S STEW POT MOUNTAIN.
CONSOMME MAGMA SPEWS OUT OF ITS TOP.
CONSOMME MAGMA?!

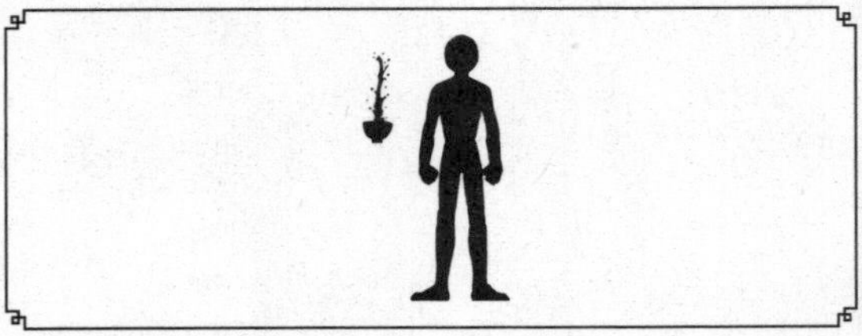

SCALE

ONE OF THE ITEMS IN KNOCKING MASTER JIRO'S FULL-MEAL COURSE, THIS PHANTOM HIGH-GRADE SOUP ERUPTS FROM THE MOUTH OF STEW POT MOUNTAIN FOUND IN THE NORTHERN MOUNTAIN AREA IN AREA 7. METICULOUS TEMPERATURE CONTROL IS NEEDED TO CONSUME IT, BUT ONCE PROPERLY PREPARED, IT HAS A HIGH-CLASS FLAVOR INCONGRUENT WITH ITS NAME AND IS A TRULY FITTING MEAL FOR KNOCKING MASTER JIRO'S SOUP DISH. IT'S ALSO SAID THAT THE MONKEY KING BAMBINA LIKES TO GO TO STEW POT MOUNTAIN AND ENJOY THE MAGMA AS A HOT SPRING.

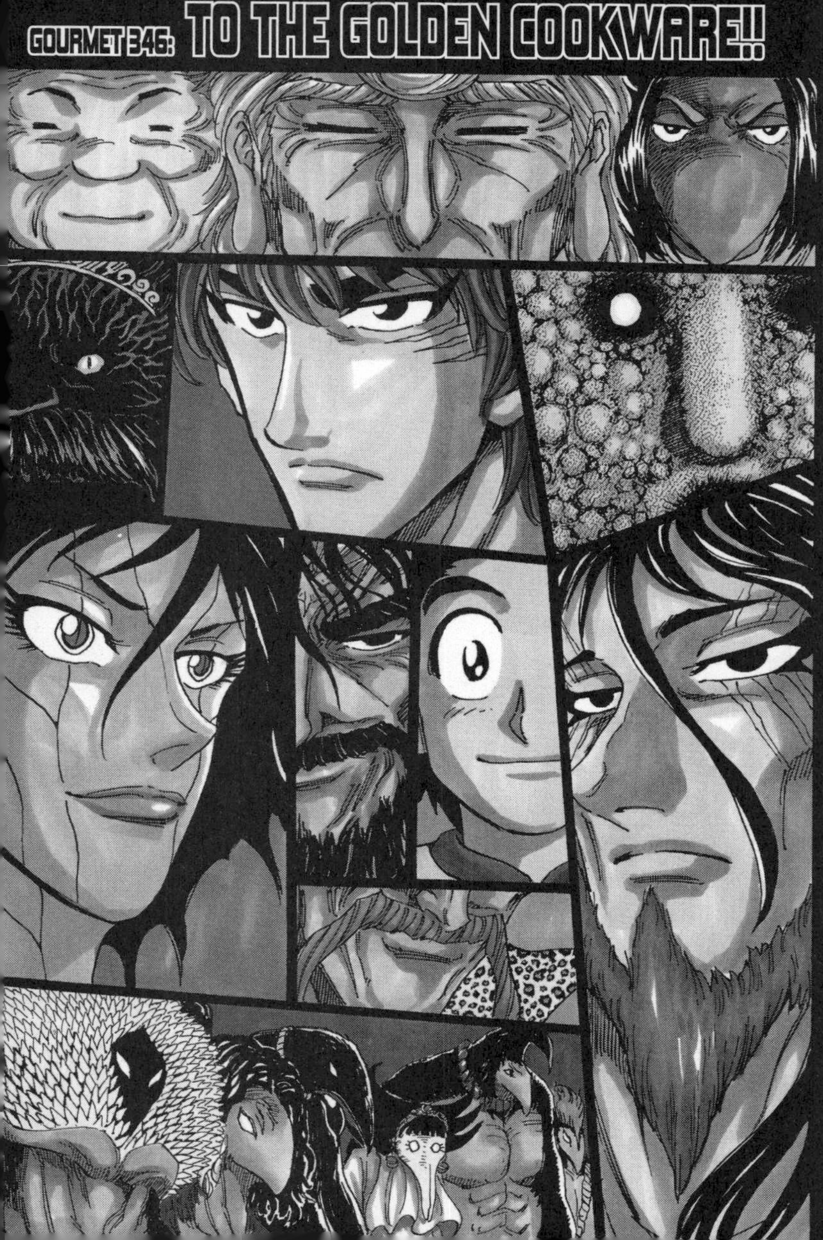
GOURMET 346: TO THE GOLDEN COOKWARE!!

GOURMET CHECKLIST

Vol. 376

GORILLA TAURUS
(MAMMAL)

WE'RE IN THE NORTH MOUNTAIN AREA.
THE RULER HERE IS MASTER GORILLA TAURUS.
IN FACT, THE ONES WHO CAME UP WITH THE RULES FOR THIS CONTINENT ARE THE FOUR MASTERS.
100 G MOUNTAIN

CAPTURE LEVEL: 1,405
HABITAT: NORTHERN MOUNTAIN AREA IN AREA 7
SIZE: 3,800 M
HEIGHT: 4,000 M
WEIGHT: 10 BILLION TONS
PRICE: PRICELESS

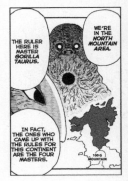

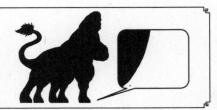

SCALE

OF ALL THE PRIMATES THAT LIVE IN MONKEY RESTAURANT, THIS IS ONE OF THE FOUR MASTERS WHO IS ALLOWED TO PREY ON WHATEVER IT WANTS. IN ADDITION TO HAVING MASTERED A HIGH LEVEL OF MONKEY MARTIAL ARTS, IT CAN ALSO REGENERATE AND REFINE ANTIBODIES AGAINST POISONS. WHEN THE GORILLA TAURUS WAS BEATEN BY TORIKO AND THE GANG, THE RULES OF THE NORTH MOUNTAIN AREA FELL APART AND THE POWER BALANCE IN AREA 7 CRUMBLED.

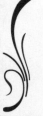

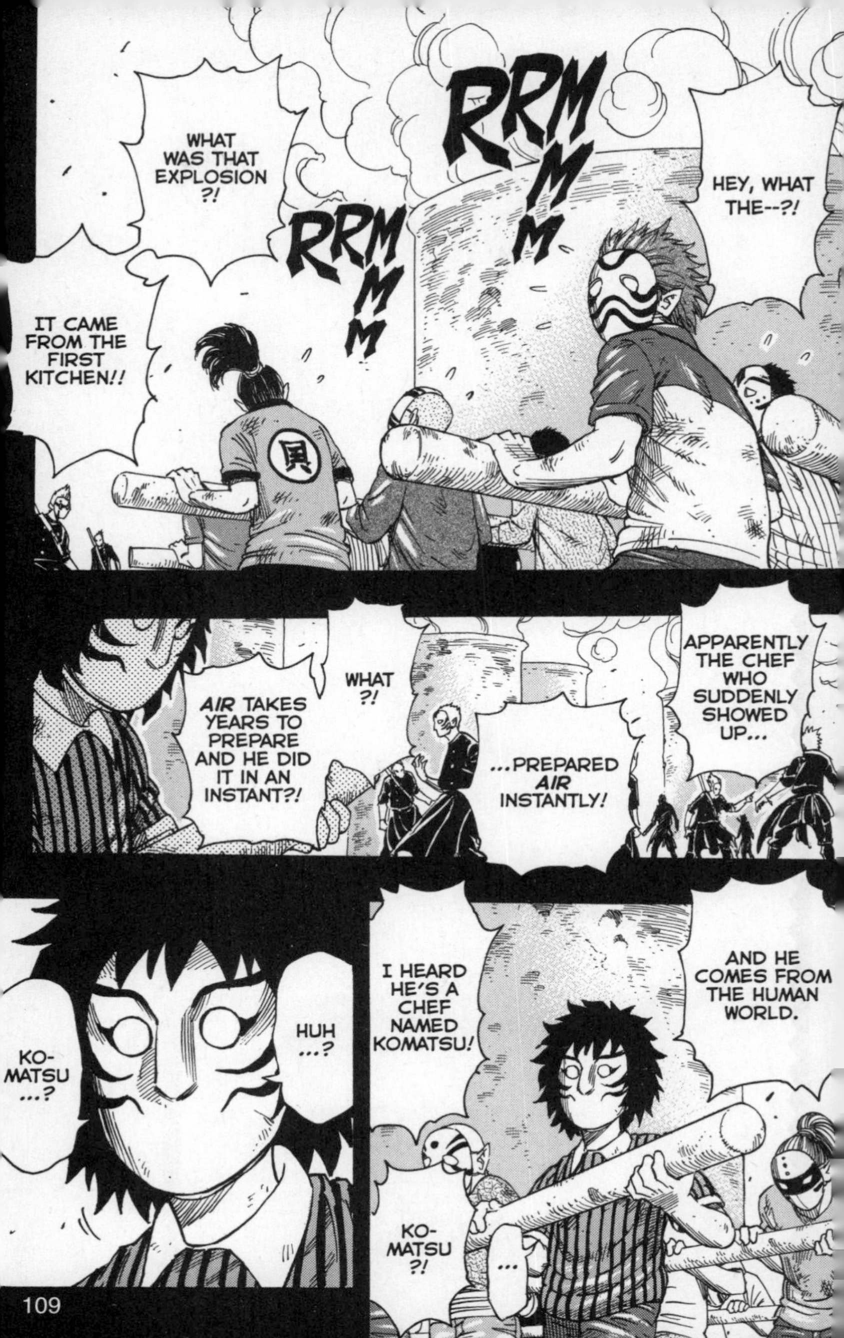
HEY, WHAT THE--?!
RRMMMM
RRMMMM
WHAT WAS THAT EXPLOSION?!
IT CAME FROM THE FIRST KITCHEN!!
APPARENTLY THE CHEF WHO SUDDENLY SHOWED UP...
...PREPARED *AIR* INSTANTLY!
WHAT?!
AIR TAKES YEARS TO PREPARE AND HE DID IT IN AN INSTANT?!
AND HE COMES FROM THE HUMAN WORLD.
I HEARD HE'S A CHEF NAMED KOMATSU!
KO-MATSU?!
...
HUH...?
KO-MATSU...?

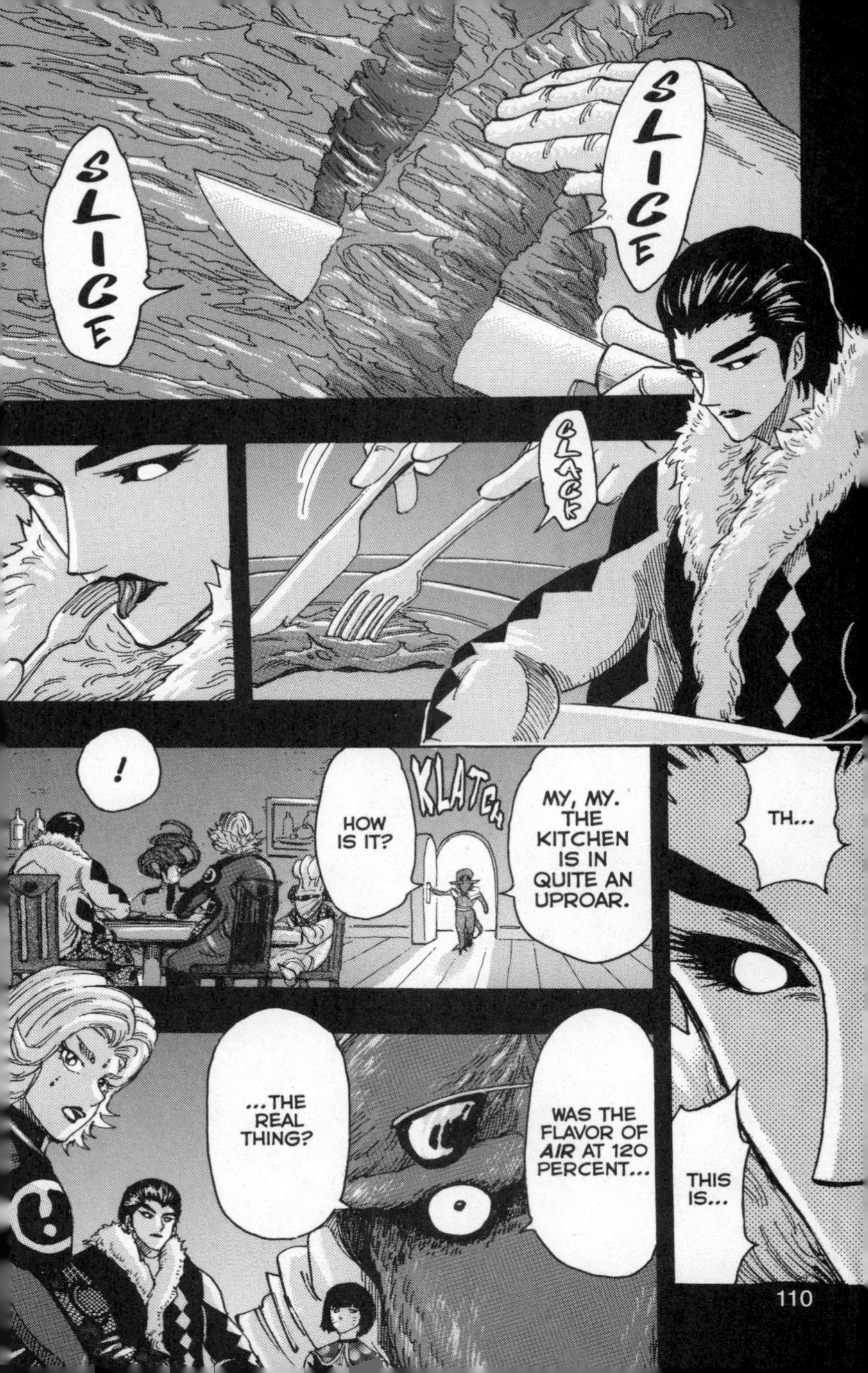

SLICE
SLICE
BLACK
TH...
THIS IS...
MY, MY. THE KITCHEN IS IN QUITE AN UPROAR.
KLATCH
HOW IS IT?
!
WAS THE FLAVOR OF *AIR* AT 120 PERCENT...
...THE REAL THING?

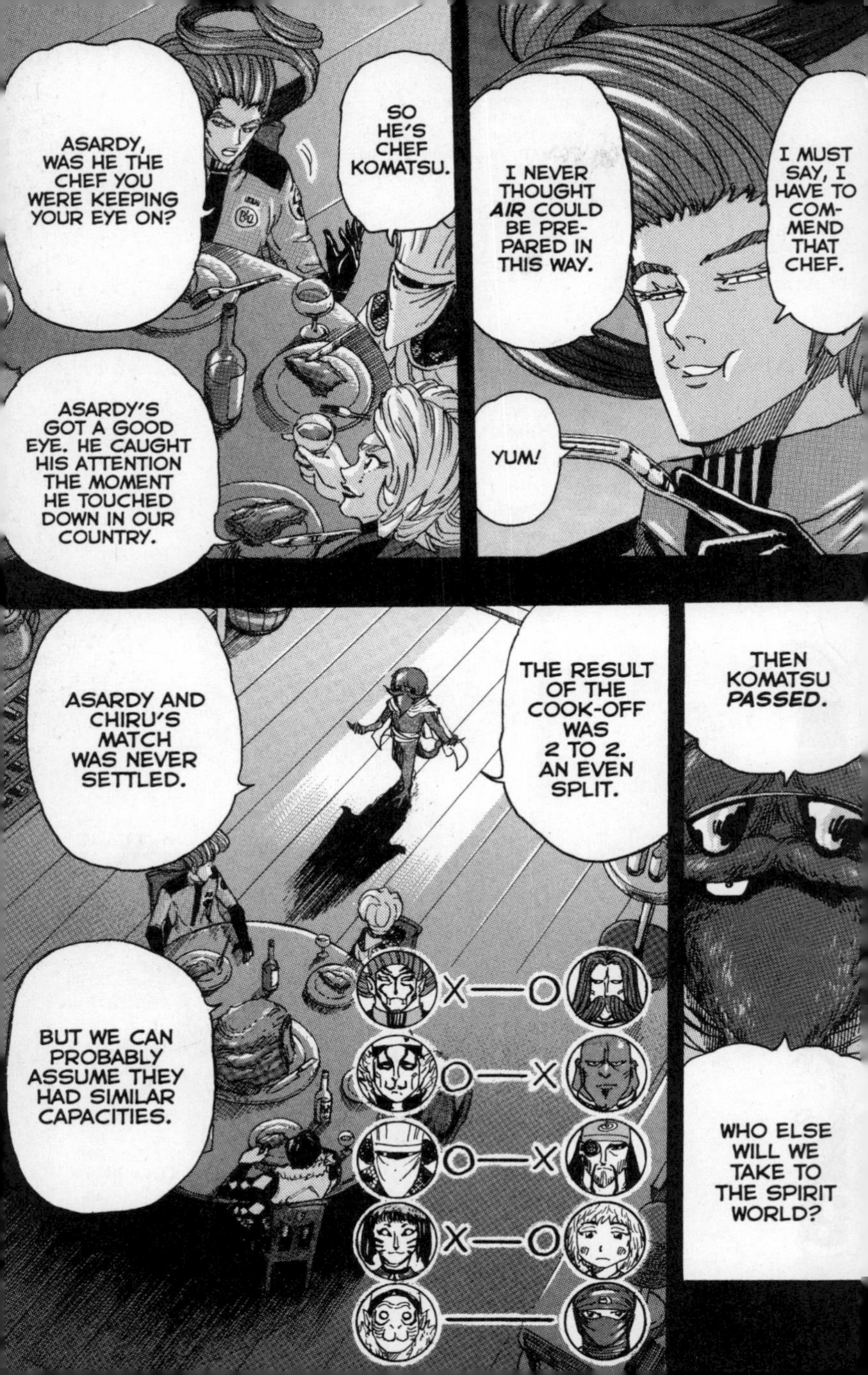
I MUST SAY, I HAVE TO COMMEND THAT CHEF.
I NEVER THOUGHT *AIR* COULD BE PREPARED IN THIS WAY.
YUM!
SO HE'S CHEF KOMATSU.
ASARDY, WAS HE THE CHEF YOU WERE KEEPING YOUR EYE ON?
ASARDY'S GOT A GOOD EYE. HE CAUGHT HIS ATTENTION THE MOMENT HE TOUCHED DOWN IN OUR COUNTRY.
THEN KOMATSU *PASSED*.
WHO ELSE WILL WE TAKE TO THE SPIRIT WORLD?
THE RESULT OF THE COOK-OFF WAS 2 TO 2. AN EVEN SPLIT.
ASARDY AND CHIRU'S MATCH WAS NEVER SETTLED.
BUT WE CAN PROBABLY ASSUME THEY HAD SIMILAR CAPACITIES.

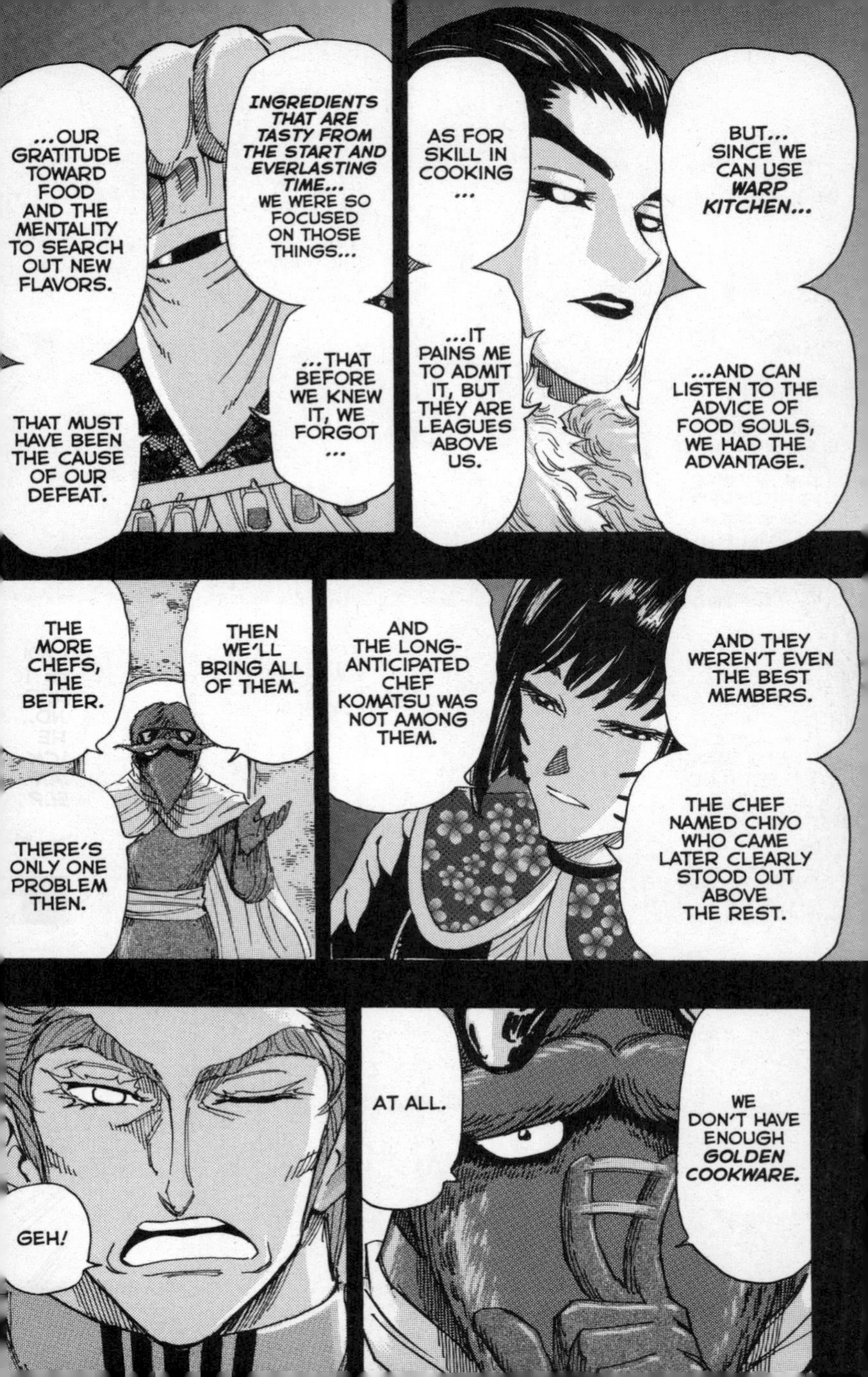
BUT... SINCE WE CAN USE *WARP KITCHEN...*
...AND CAN LISTEN TO THE ADVICE OF FOOD SOULS, WE HAD THE ADVANTAGE.
AS FOR SKILL IN COOKING...
...IT PAINS ME TO ADMIT IT, BUT THEY ARE LEAGUES ABOVE US.
INGREDIENTS THAT ARE TASTY FROM THE START AND EVERLASTING TIME... WE WERE SO FOCUSED ON THOSE THINGS...
...THAT BEFORE WE KNEW IT, WE FORGOT...
...OUR GRATITUDE TOWARD FOOD AND THE MENTALITY TO SEARCH OUT NEW FLAVORS.
THAT MUST HAVE BEEN THE CAUSE OF OUR DEFEAT.
AND THEY WEREN'T EVEN THE BEST MEMBERS.
THE CHEF NAMED CHIYO WHO CAME LATER CLEARLY STOOD OUT ABOVE THE REST.
AND THE LONG-ANTICIPATED CHEF KOMATSU WAS NOT AMONG THEM.
THEN WE'LL BRING ALL OF THEM.
THE MORE CHEFS, THE BETTER.
THERE'S ONLY ONE PROBLEM THEN.
WE DON'T HAVE ENOUGH *GOLDEN COOKWARE.*
AT ALL.
GEH!

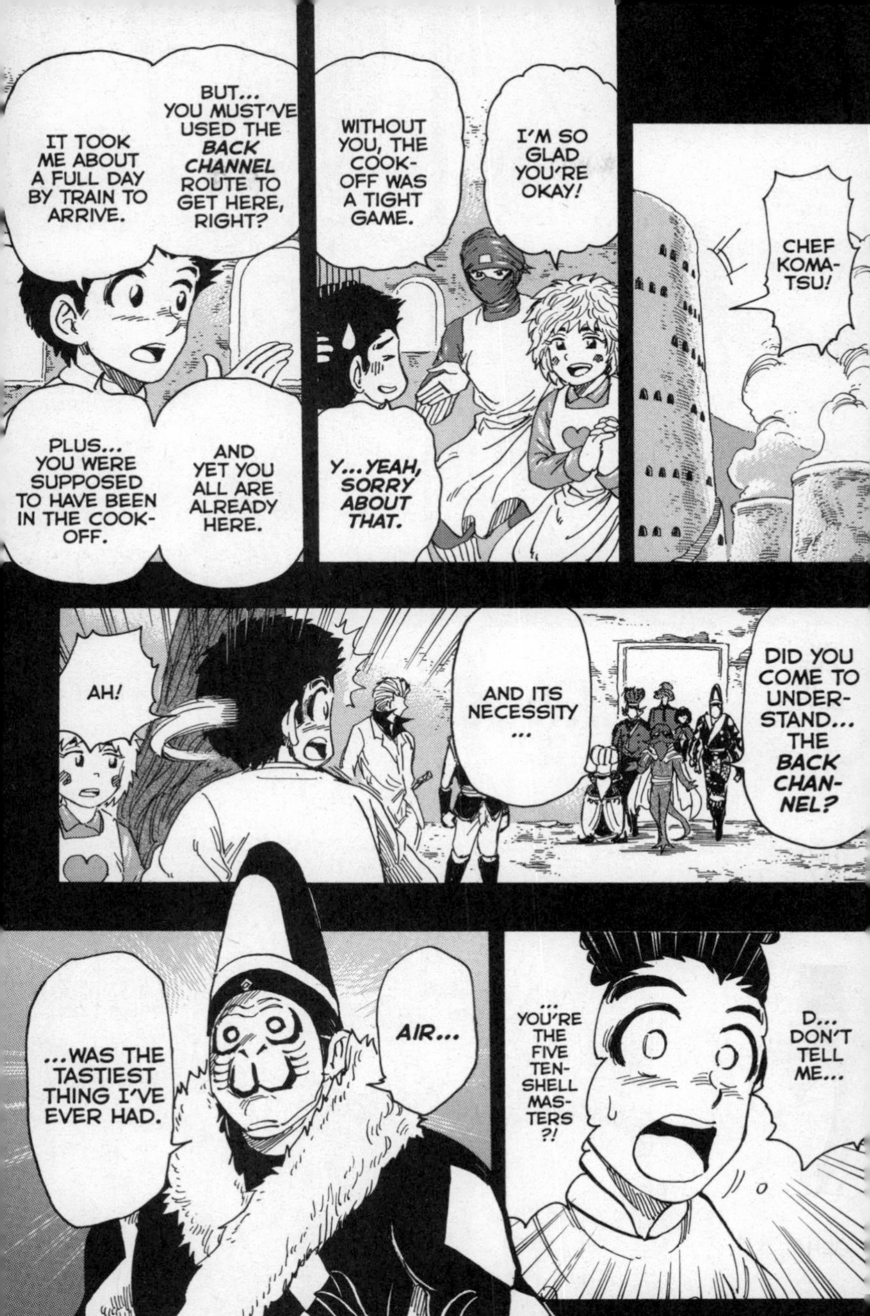
CHEF KOMATSU!
I'M SO GLAD YOU'RE OKAY!
WITHOUT YOU, THE COOK-OFF WAS A TIGHT GAME.
Y...YEAH, SORRY ABOUT THAT.
BUT... YOU MUST'VE USED THE BACK CHANNEL ROUTE TO GET HERE, RIGHT?
IT TOOK ME ABOUT A FULL DAY BY TRAIN TO ARRIVE.
AND YET YOU ALL ARE ALREADY HERE.
PLUS... YOU WERE SUPPOSED TO HAVE BEEN IN THE COOK-OFF.
DID YOU COME TO UNDERSTAND... THE BACK CHANNEL?
AND ITS NECESSITY ...
AH!
D... DON'T TELL ME...
... YOU'RE THE FIVE TEN-SHELL MASTERS?!
AIR...
...WAS THE TASTIEST THING I'VE EVER HAD.

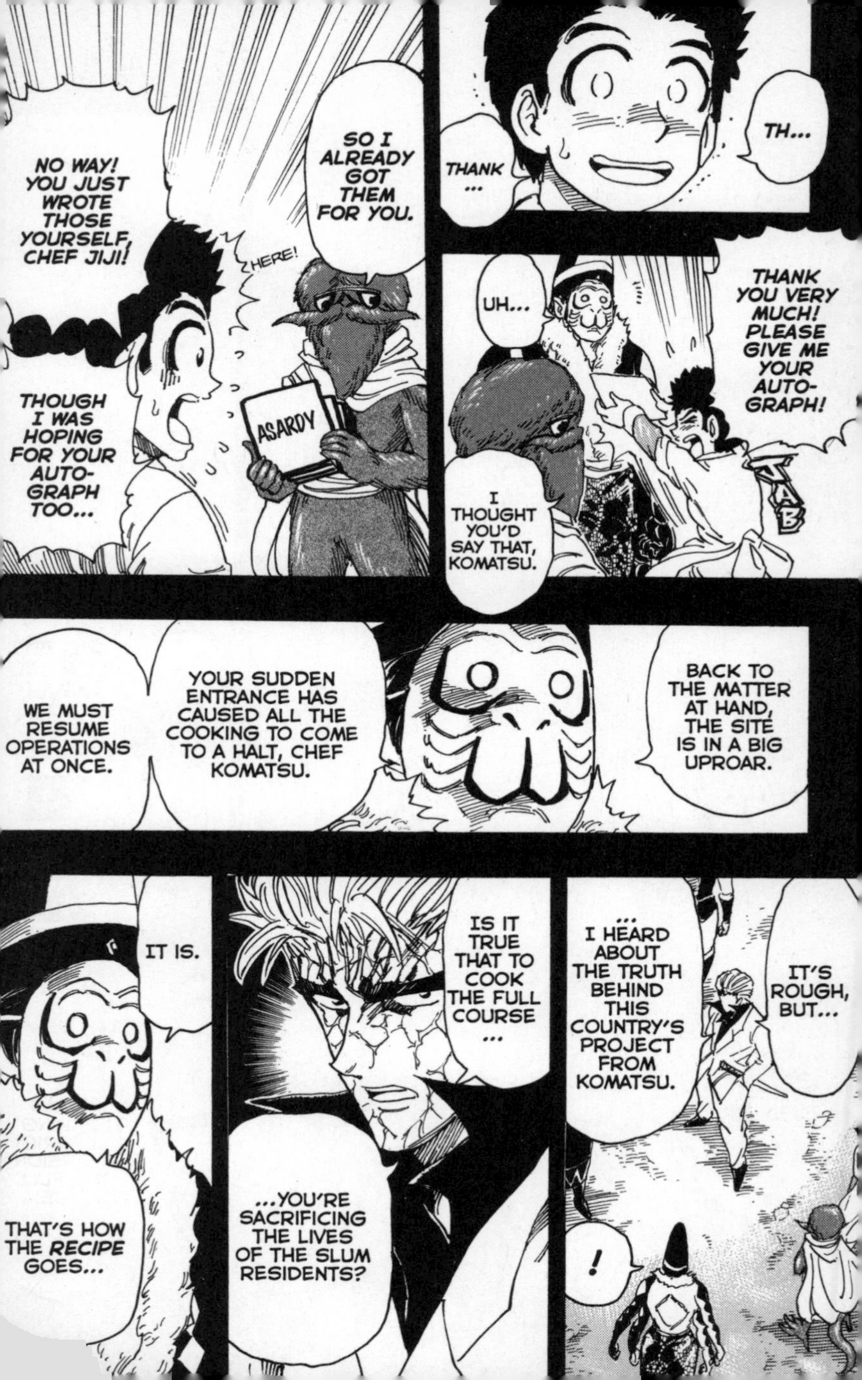
TH...
THANK ...
THANK YOU VERY MUCH! PLEASE GIVE ME YOUR AUTOGRAPH!
TAB
UH...
I THOUGHT YOU'D SAY THAT, KOMATSU.
SO I ALREADY GOT THEM FOR YOU.
HERE!
ASARDY
NO WAY! YOU JUST WROTE THOSE YOURSELF, CHEF JIJI!
THOUGH I WAS HOPING FOR YOUR AUTOGRAPH TOO...
BACK TO THE MATTER AT HAND, THE SITE IS IN A BIG UPROAR.
YOUR SUDDEN ENTRANCE HAS CAUSED ALL THE COOKING TO COME TO A HALT, CHEF KOMATSU.
WE MUST RESUME OPERATIONS AT ONCE.
IT'S ROUGH, BUT...
... I HEARD ABOUT THE TRUTH BEHIND THIS COUNTRY'S PROJECT FROM KOMATSU.
!
IS IT TRUE THAT TO COOK THE FULL COURSE ...
...YOU'RE SACRIFICING THE LIVES OF THE SLUM RESIDENTS?
IT IS.
THAT'S HOW THE *RECIPE* GOES...

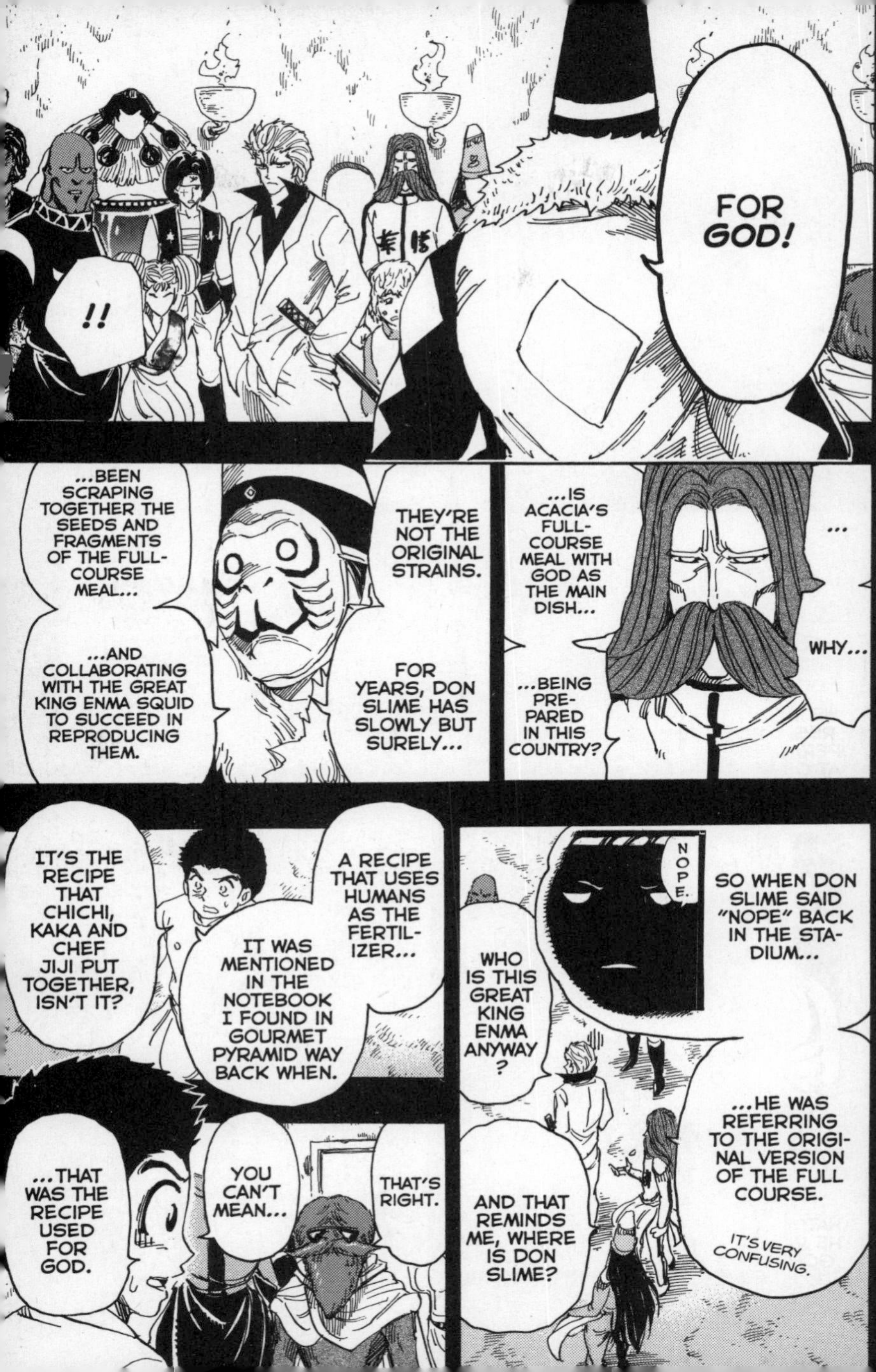
FOR GOD!
!!
...
WHY...
...IS ACACIA'S FULL-COURSE MEAL WITH GOD AS THE MAIN DISH...
...BEING PRE-PARED IN THIS COUNTRY?
THEY'RE NOT THE ORIGINAL STRAINS.
FOR YEARS, DON SLIME HAS SLOWLY BUT SURELY...
...BEEN SCRAPING TOGETHER THE SEEDS AND FRAGMENTS OF THE FULL-COURSE MEAL...
...AND COLLABORATING WITH THE GREAT KING ENMA SQUID TO SUCCEED IN REPRODUCING THEM.
SO WHEN DON SLIME SAID "NOPE" BACK IN THE STA-DIUM...
NOPE.
...HE WAS REFERRING TO THE ORIGI-NAL VERSION OF THE FULL COURSE.
IT'S VERY CONFUSING.
WHO IS THIS GREAT KING ENMA ANYWAY?
AND THAT REMINDS ME, WHERE IS DON SLIME?
A RECIPE THAT USES HUMANS AS THE FERTIL-IZER...
IT'S THE RECIPE THAT CHICHI, KAKA AND CHEF JIJI PUT TOGETHER, ISN'T IT?
IT WAS MENTIONED IN THE NOTEBOOK I FOUND IN GOURMET PYRAMID WAY BACK WHEN.
THAT'S RIGHT.
YOU CAN'T MEAN...
...THAT WAS THE RECIPE USED FOR GOD.

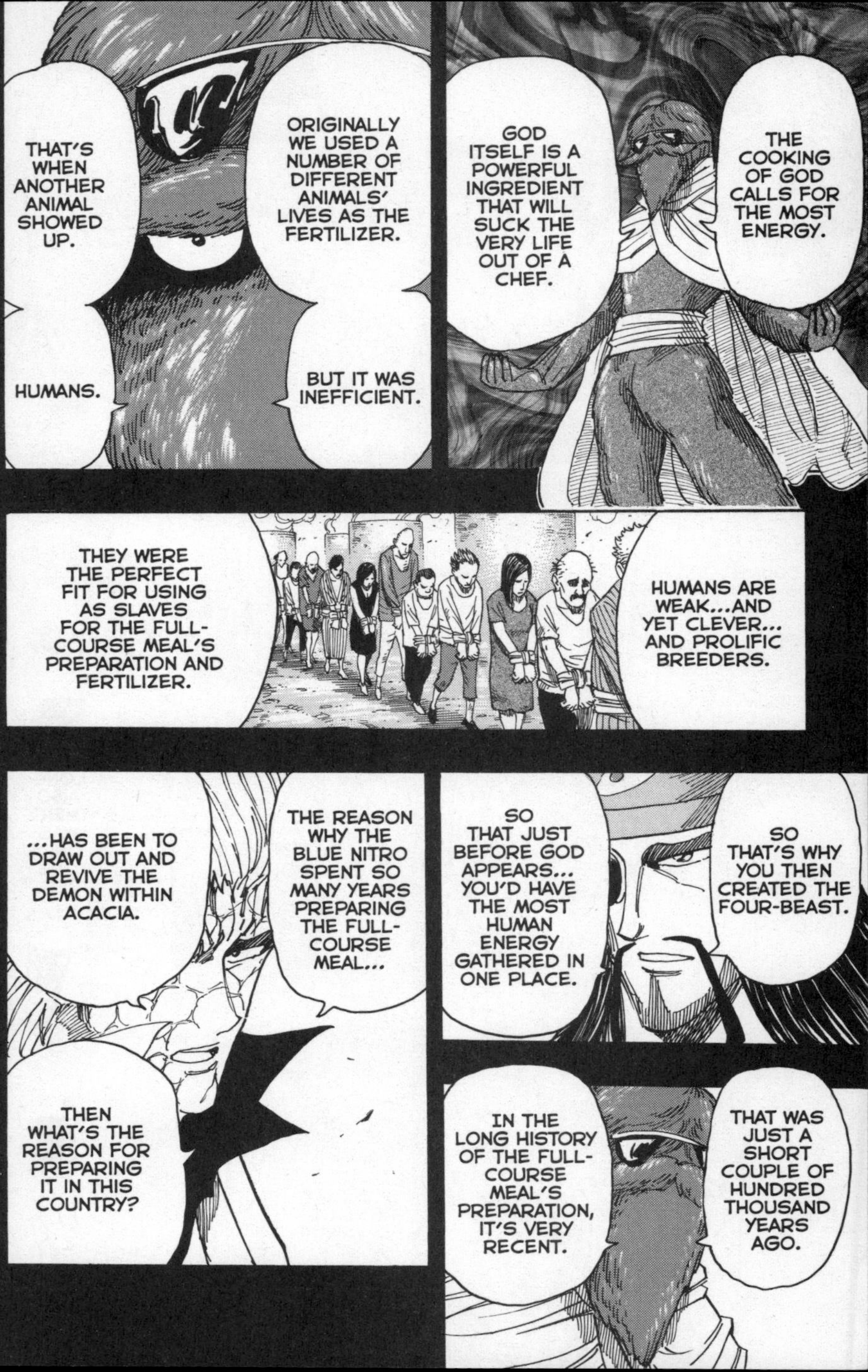
THE COOKING OF GOD CALLS FOR THE MOST ENERGY.
GOD ITSELF IS A POWERFUL INGREDIENT THAT WILL SUCK THE VERY LIFE OUT OF A CHEF.
ORIGINALLY WE USED A NUMBER OF DIFFERENT ANIMALS' LIVES AS THE FERTILIZER.
BUT IT WAS INEFFICIENT.
THAT'S WHEN ANOTHER ANIMAL SHOWED UP.
HUMANS.
HUMANS ARE WEAK...AND YET CLEVER... AND PROLIFIC BREEDERS.
THEY WERE THE PERFECT FIT FOR USING AS SLAVES FOR THE FULL-COURSE MEAL'S PREPARATION AND FERTILIZER.
SO THAT'S WHY YOU THEN CREATED THE FOUR-BEAST.
SO THAT JUST BEFORE GOD APPEARS... YOU'D HAVE THE MOST HUMAN ENERGY GATHERED IN ONE PLACE.
THAT WAS JUST A SHORT COUPLE OF HUNDRED THOUSAND YEARS AGO.
IN THE LONG HISTORY OF THE FULL-COURSE MEAL'S PREPARATION, IT'S VERY RECENT.
THE REASON WHY THE BLUE NITRO SPENT SO MANY YEARS PREPARING THE FULL-COURSE MEAL...
...HAS BEEN TO DRAW OUT AND REVIVE THE DEMON WITHIN ACACIA.
THEN WHAT'S THE REASON FOR PREPARING IT IN THIS COUNTRY?

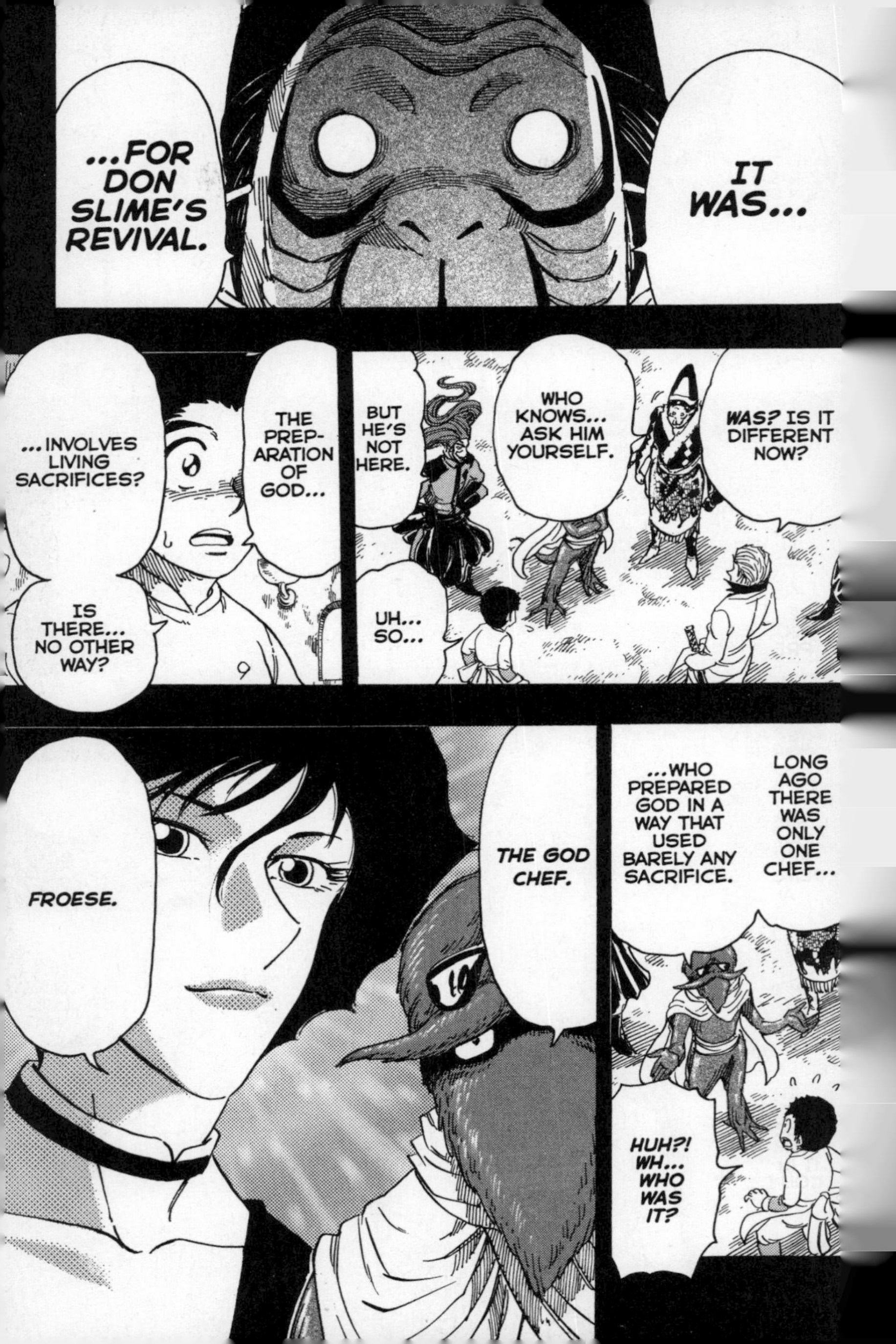
IT WAS...
...FOR DON SLIME'S REVIVAL.
WAS? IS IT DIFFERENT NOW?
WHO KNOWS... ASK HIM YOURSELF.
BUT HE'S NOT HERE.
UH... SO...
THE PREPARATION OF GOD...
...INVOLVES LIVING SACRIFICES?
IS THERE... NO OTHER WAY?
LONG AGO THERE WAS ONLY ONE CHEF...
...WHO PREPARED GOD IN A WAY THAT USED BARELY ANY SACRIFICE.
HUH?! WH... WHO WAS IT?
THE GOD CHEF.
FROESE.

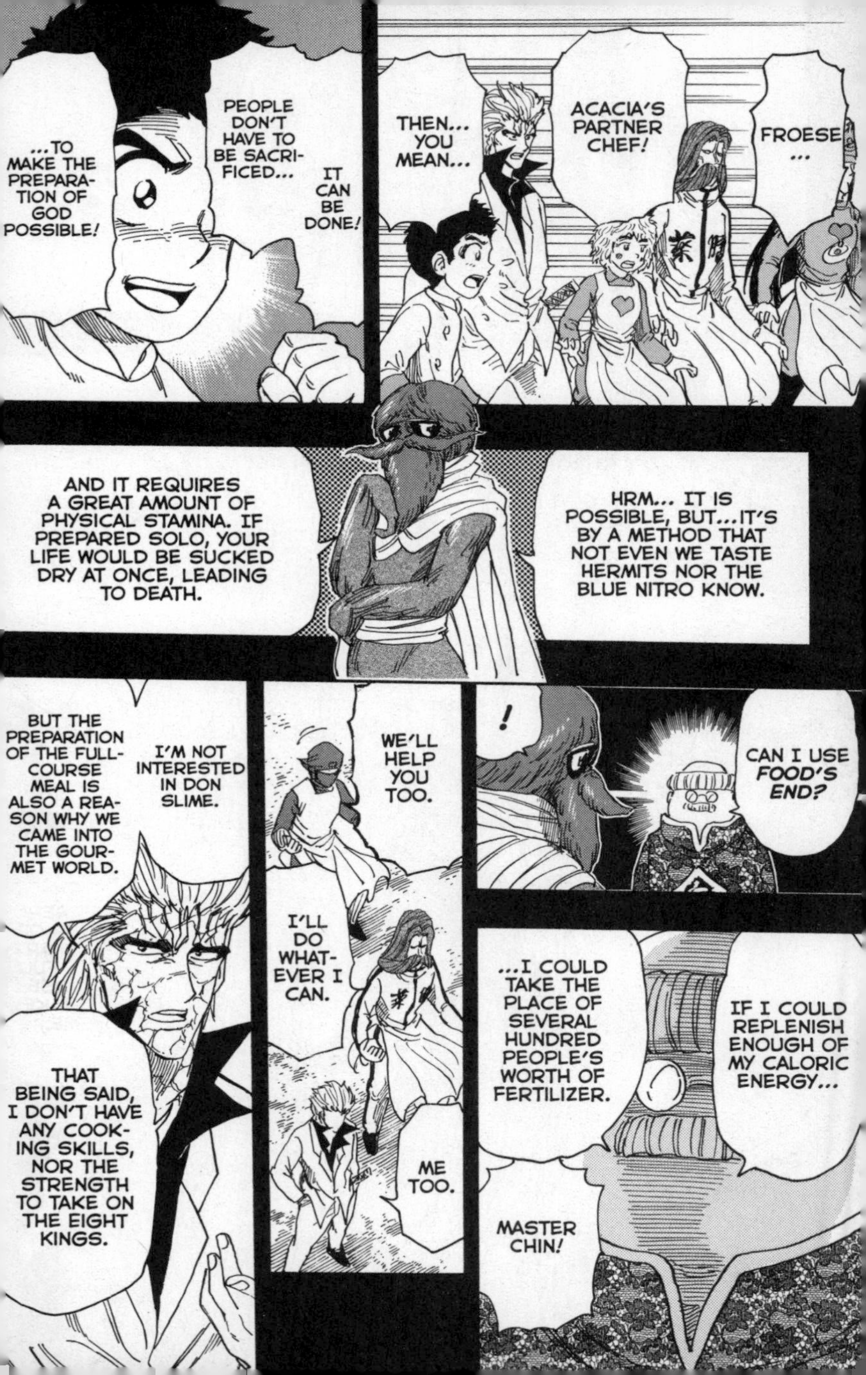
FROESE...
ACACIA'S PARTNER CHEF!
THEN... YOU MEAN...
IT CAN BE DONE!
PEOPLE DON'T HAVE TO BE SACRIFICED...
...TO MAKE THE PREPARATION OF GOD POSSIBLE!
HRM... IT IS POSSIBLE, BUT...IT'S BY A METHOD THAT NOT EVEN WE TASTE HERMITS NOR THE BLUE NITRO KNOW.
AND IT REQUIRES A GREAT AMOUNT OF PHYSICAL STAMINA. IF PREPARED SOLO, YOUR LIFE WOULD BE SUCKED DRY AT ONCE, LEADING TO DEATH.
CAN I USE *FOOD'S END?*
!
IF I COULD REPLENISH ENOUGH OF MY CALORIC ENERGY...
...I COULD TAKE THE PLACE OF SEVERAL HUNDRED PEOPLE'S WORTH OF FERTILIZER.
MASTER CHIN!
WE'LL HELP YOU TOO.
I'LL DO WHATEVER I CAN.
ME TOO.
I'M NOT INTERESTED IN DON SLIME.
BUT THE PREPARATION OF THE FULL-COURSE MEAL IS ALSO A REASON WHY WE CAME INTO THE GOURMET WORLD.
THAT BEING SAID, I DON'T HAVE ANY COOKING SKILLS, NOR THE STRENGTH TO TAKE ON THE EIGHT KINGS.

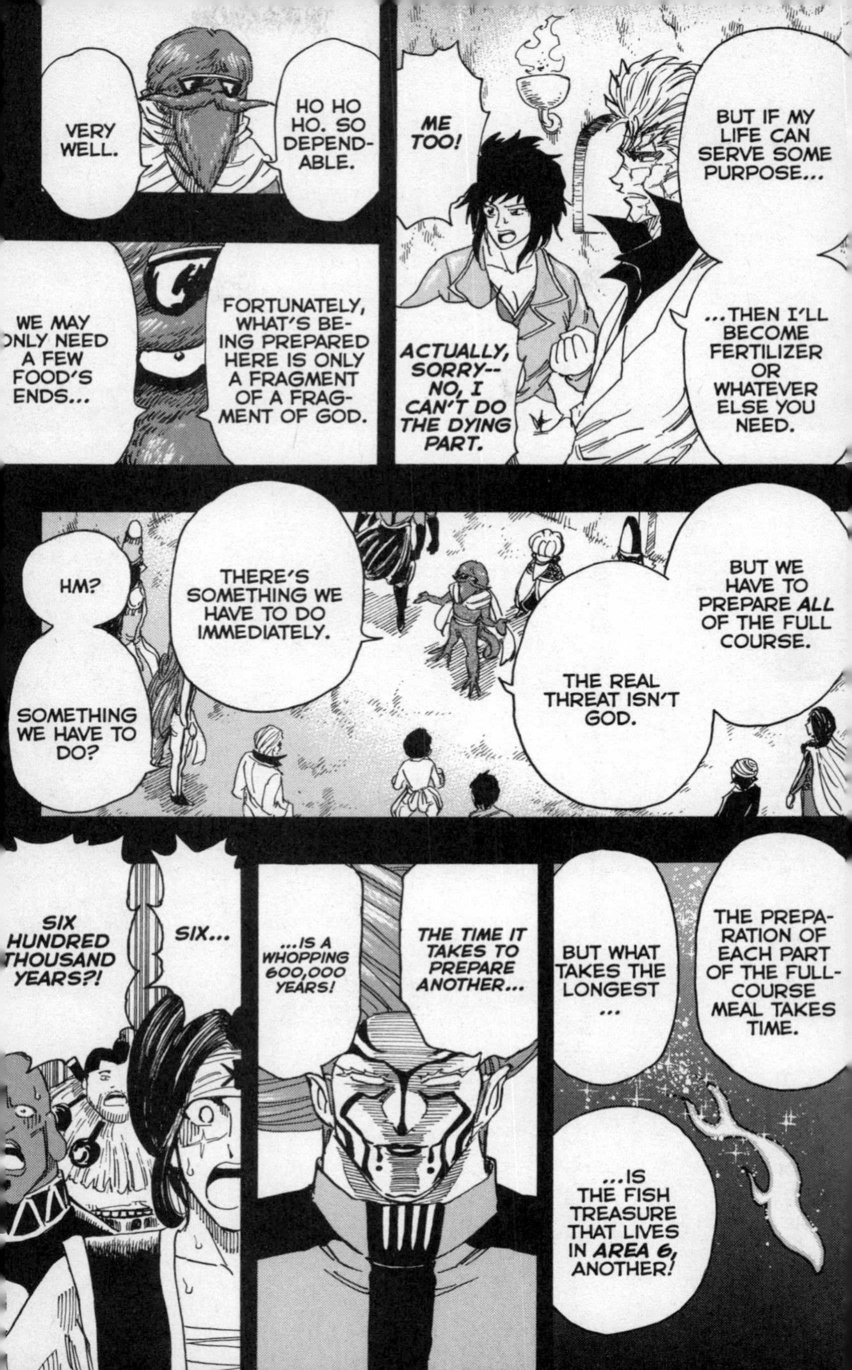
BUT IF MY LIFE CAN SERVE SOME PURPOSE...
...THEN I'LL BECOME FERTILIZER OR WHATEVER ELSE YOU NEED.
ME TOO!
ACTUALLY, SORRY-- NO, I CAN'T DO THE DYING PART.
HO HO HO. SO DEPENDABLE.
VERY WELL.
FORTUNATELY, WHAT'S BEING PREPARED HERE IS ONLY A FRAGMENT OF A FRAGMENT OF GOD.
WE MAY ONLY NEED A FEW FOOD'S ENDS...
BUT WE HAVE TO PREPARE ALL OF THE FULL COURSE.
THE REAL THREAT ISN'T GOD.
THERE'S SOMETHING WE HAVE TO DO IMMEDIATELY.
HM?
SOMETHING WE HAVE TO DO?
THE PREPARATION OF EACH PART OF THE FULL-COURSE MEAL TAKES TIME.
BUT WHAT TAKES THE LONGEST ...
...IS THE FISH TREASURE THAT LIVES IN AREA 6, ANOTHER!
THE TIME IT TAKES TO PREPARE ANOTHER...
...IS A WHOPPING 600,000 YEARS!
SIX...
SIX HUNDRED THOUSAND YEARS?!

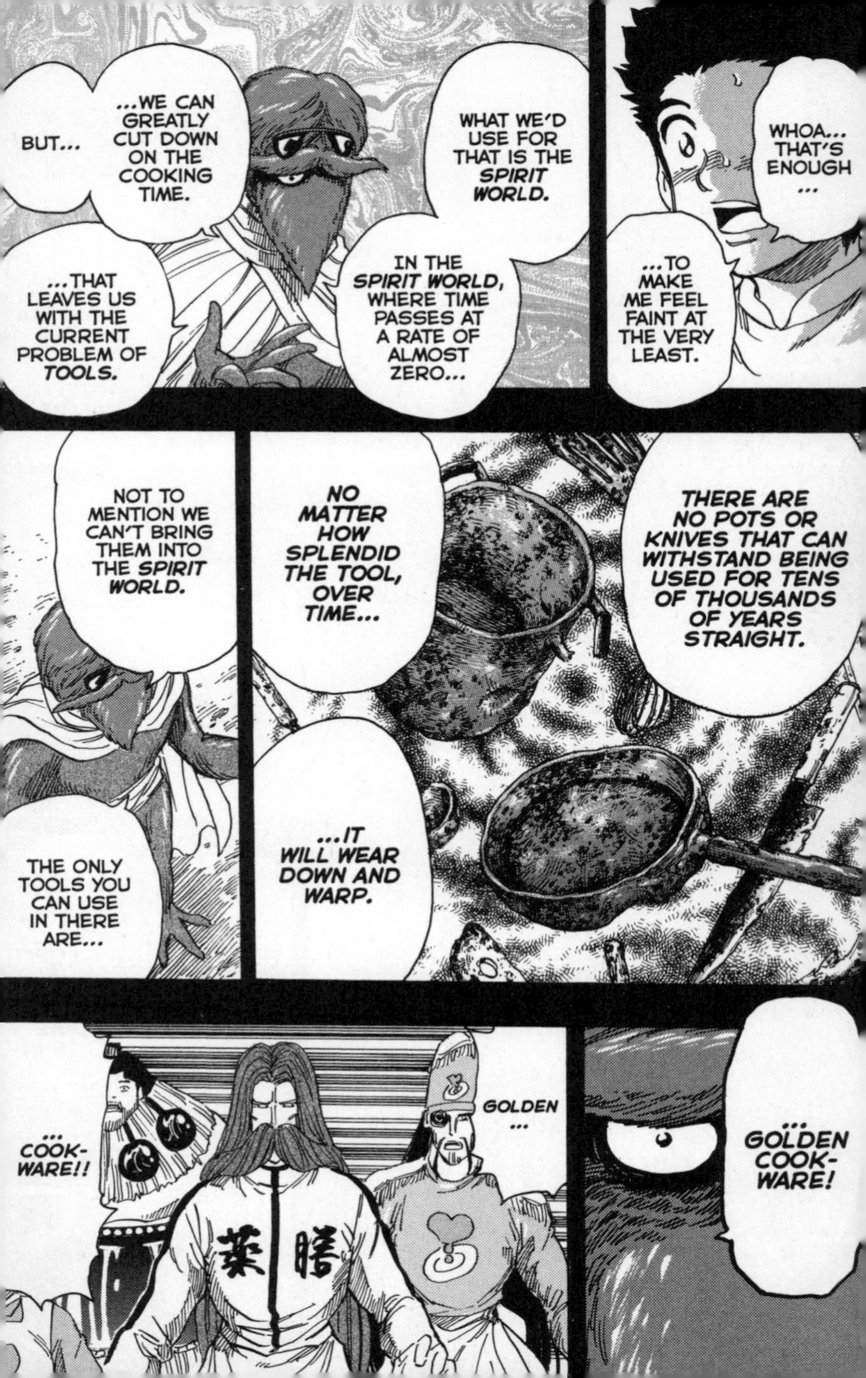
WHOA... THAT'S ENOUGH ...
...TO MAKE ME FEEL FAINT AT THE VERY LEAST.
WHAT WE'D USE FOR THAT IS THE *SPIRIT WORLD.*
IN THE *SPIRIT WORLD,* WHERE TIME PASSES AT A RATE OF ALMOST ZERO...
...WE CAN GREATLY CUT DOWN ON THE COOKING TIME.
BUT...
...THAT LEAVES US WITH THE CURRENT PROBLEM OF *TOOLS.*
THERE ARE NO POTS OR KNIVES THAT CAN WITHSTAND BEING USED FOR TENS OF THOUSANDS OF YEARS STRAIGHT.
NO MATTER HOW SPLENDID THE TOOL, OVER TIME...
...IT WILL WEAR DOWN AND WARP.
NOT TO MENTION WE CAN'T BRING THEM INTO THE *SPIRIT WORLD.*
THE ONLY TOOLS YOU CAN USE IN THERE ARE...
...GOLDEN COOK-WARE!
GOLDEN ...
...COOK-WARE!!
薬膳

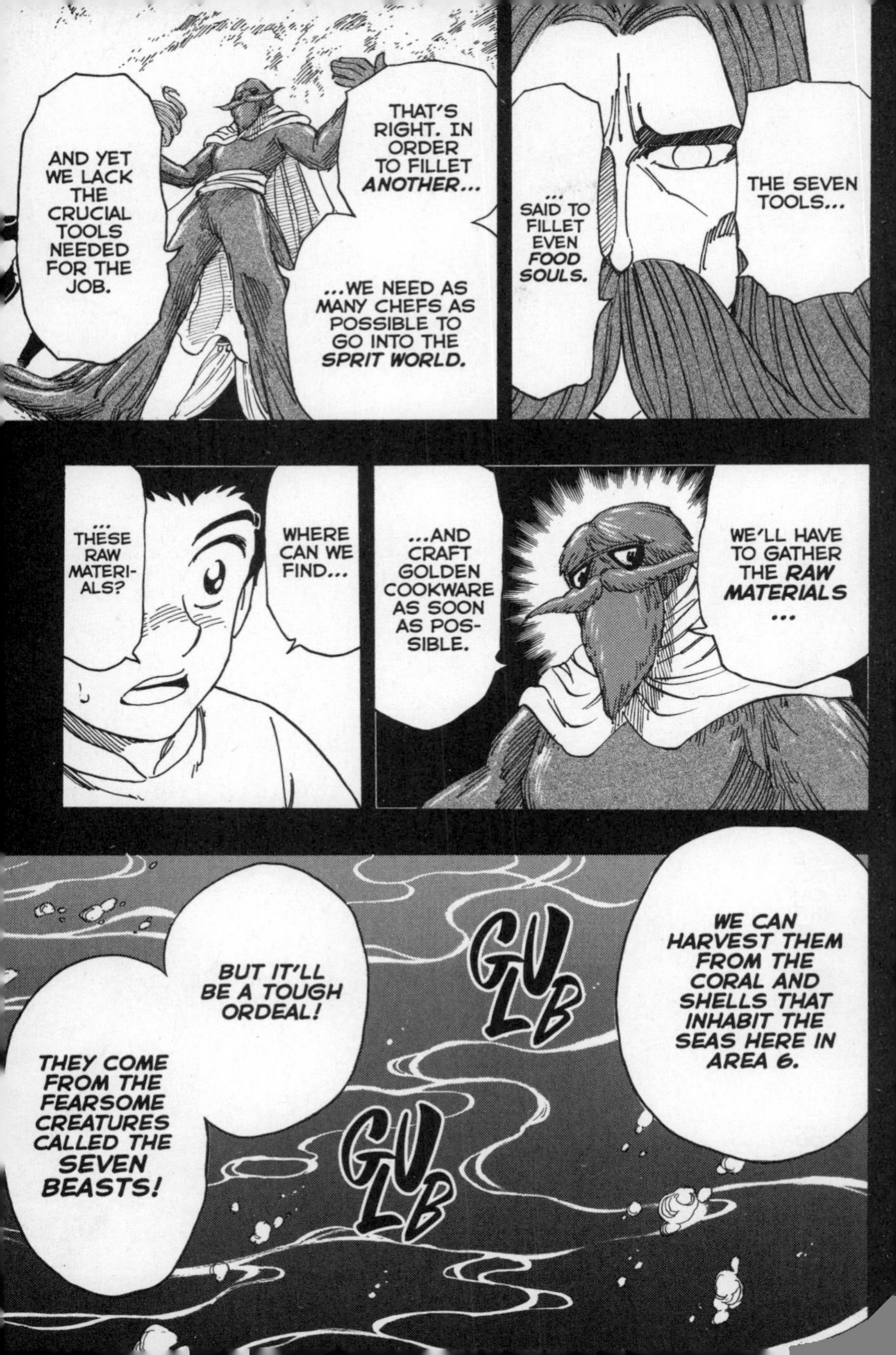
THE SEVEN TOOLS...
...SAID TO FILLET EVEN FOOD SOULS.
THAT'S RIGHT. IN ORDER TO FILLET ANOTHER...
...WE NEED AS MANY CHEFS AS POSSIBLE TO GO INTO THE SPRIT WORLD.
AND YET WE LACK THE CRUCIAL TOOLS NEEDED FOR THE JOB.
WE'LL HAVE TO GATHER THE RAW MATERIALS...
...AND CRAFT GOLDEN COOKWARE AS SOON AS POSSIBLE.
WHERE CAN WE FIND...
...THESE RAW MATERIALS?
WE CAN HARVEST THEM FROM THE CORAL AND SHELLS THAT INHABIT THE SEAS HERE IN AREA 6.
GLUB
GLUB
BUT IT'LL BE A TOUGH ORDEAL!
THEY COME FROM THE FEARSOME CREATURES CALLED THE SEVEN BEASTS!

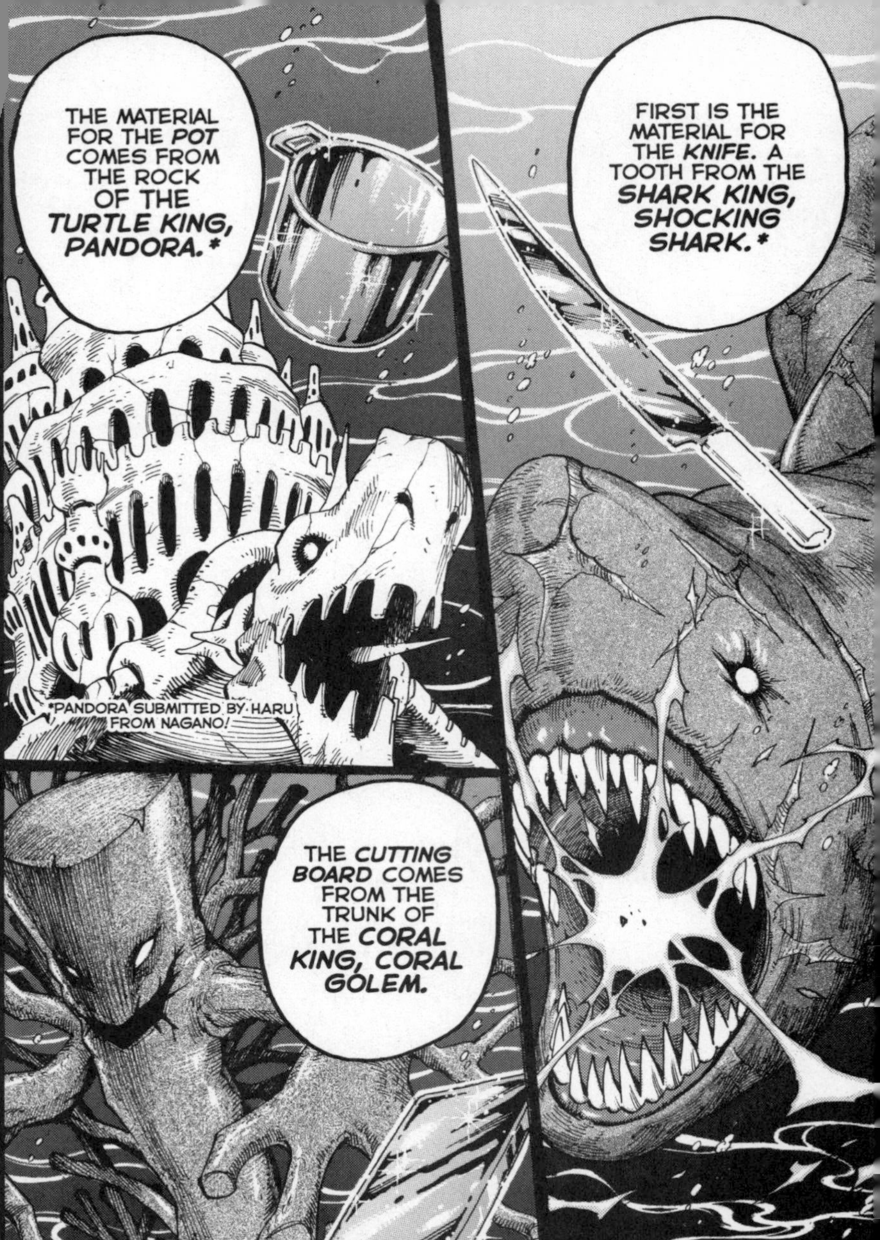
FIRST IS THE MATERIAL FOR THE KNIFE. A TOOTH FROM THE SHARK KING, SHOCKING SHARK.*
*SHOCKING SHARK SUBMITTED BY HIROYUKI MORITA FROM ISHIKAWA!
THE MATERIAL FOR THE POT COMES FROM THE ROCK OF THE TURTLE KING, PANDORA.*
*PANDORA SUBMITTED BY HARU FROM NAGANO!
THE CUTTING BOARD COMES FROM THE TRUNK OF THE CORAL KING, CORAL GOLEM.

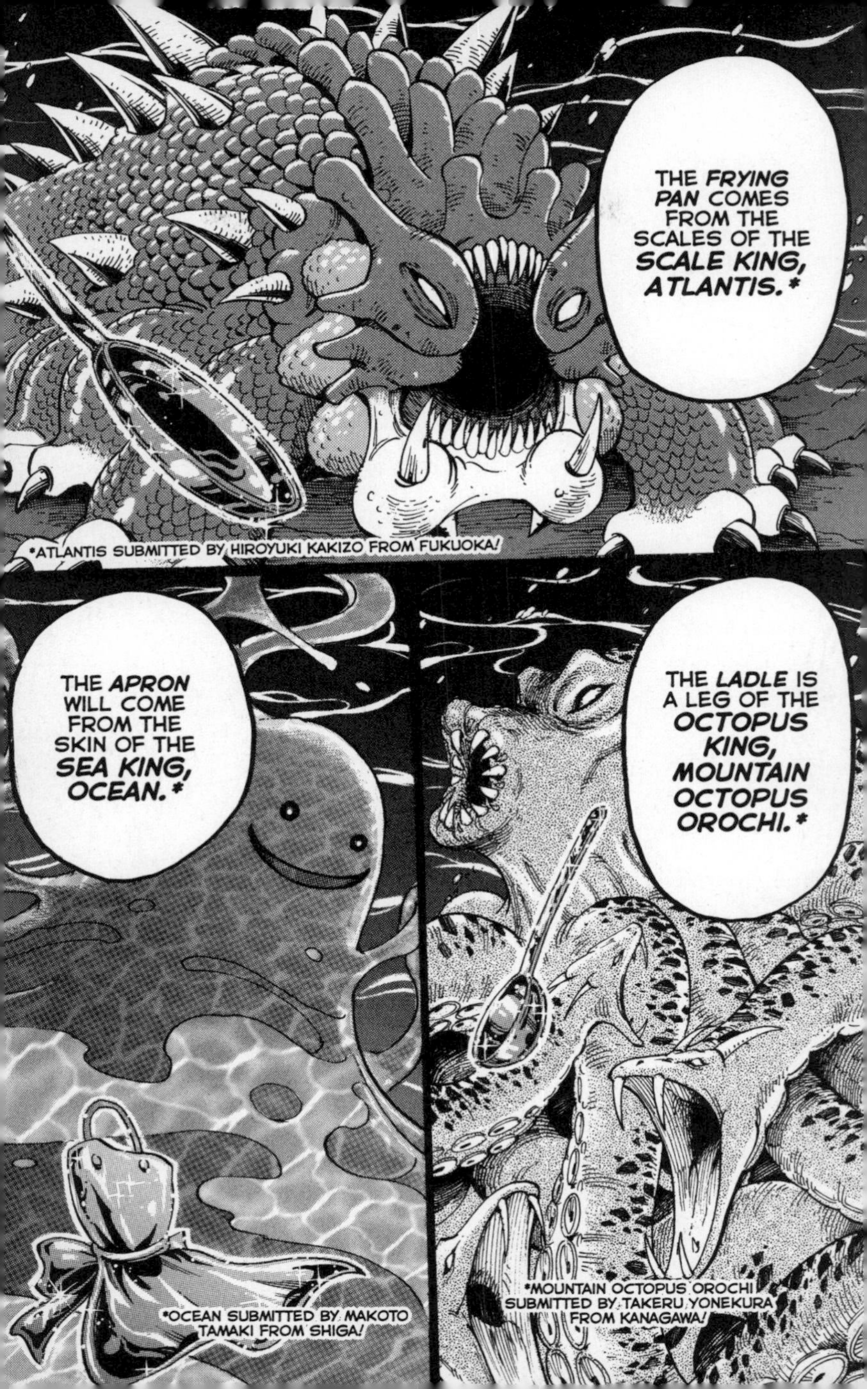
THE FRYING PAN COMES FROM THE SCALES OF THE SCALE KING, ATLANTIS.*
*ATLANTIS SUBMITTED BY HIROYUKI KAKIZO FROM FUKUOKA!
THE LADLE IS A LEG OF THE OCTOPUS KING, MOUNTAIN OCTOPUS OROCHI.*
*MOUNTAIN OCTOPUS OROCHI SUBMITTED BY TAKERU YONEKURA FROM KANAGAWA!
THE APRON WILL COME FROM THE SKIN OF THE SEA KING, OCEAN.*
*OCEAN SUBMITTED BY MAKOTO TAMAKI FROM SHIGA!

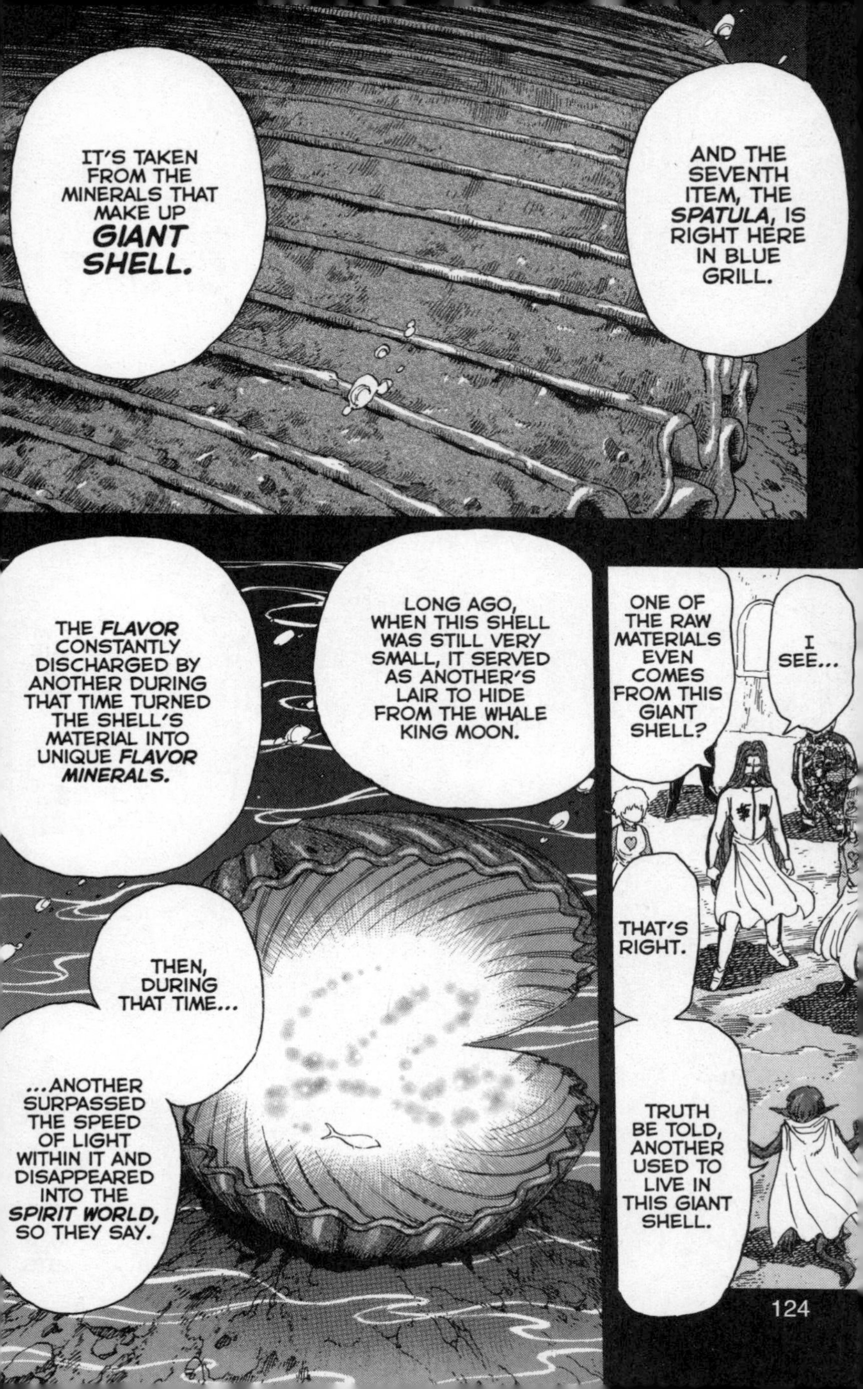
AND THE SEVENTH ITEM, THE *SPATULA*, IS RIGHT HERE IN BLUE GRILL.
IT'S TAKEN FROM THE MINERALS THAT MAKE UP **GIANT SHELL.**
I SEE...
ONE OF THE RAW MATERIALS EVEN COMES FROM THIS GIANT SHELL?
THAT'S RIGHT.
TRUTH BE TOLD, ANOTHER USED TO LIVE IN THIS GIANT SHELL.
LONG AGO, WHEN THIS SHELL WAS STILL VERY SMALL, IT SERVED AS ANOTHER'S LAIR TO HIDE FROM THE WHALE KING MOON.
THE *FLAVOR* CONSTANTLY DISCHARGED BY ANOTHER DURING THAT TIME TURNED THE SHELL'S MATERIAL INTO UNIQUE *FLAVOR MINERALS.*
THEN, DURING THAT TIME...
...ANOTHER SURPASSED THE SPEED OF LIGHT WITHIN IT AND DISAPPEARED INTO THE *SPIRIT WORLD,* SO THEY SAY.

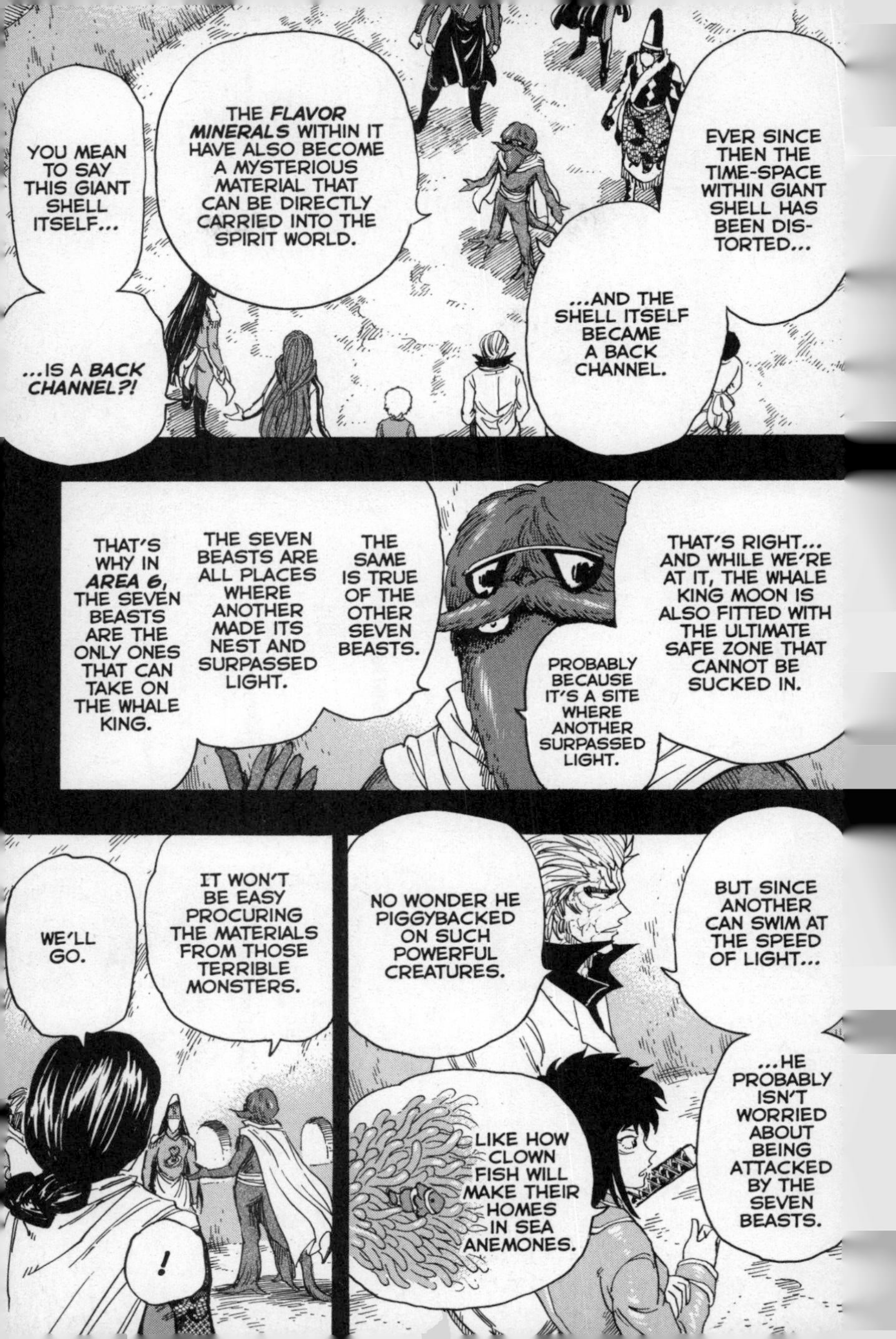
EVER SINCE THEN THE TIME-SPACE WITHIN GIANT SHELL HAS BEEN DIS-TORTED...
...AND THE SHELL ITSELF BECAME A BACK CHANNEL.
THE *FLAVOR MINERALS* WITHIN IT HAVE ALSO BECOME A MYSTERIOUS MATERIAL THAT CAN BE DIRECTLY CARRIED INTO THE SPIRIT WORLD.
YOU MEAN TO SAY THIS GIANT SHELL ITSELF...
...IS A *BACK CHANNEL?!*
THAT'S RIGHT... AND WHILE WE'RE AT IT, THE WHALE KING MOON IS ALSO FITTED WITH THE ULTIMATE SAFE ZONE THAT CANNOT BE SUCKED IN.
PROBABLY BECAUSE IT'S A SITE WHERE ANOTHER SURPASSED LIGHT.
THE SAME IS TRUE OF THE OTHER SEVEN BEASTS.
THE SEVEN BEASTS ARE ALL PLACES WHERE ANOTHER MADE ITS NEST AND SURPASSED LIGHT.
THAT'S WHY IN *AREA 6*, THE SEVEN BEASTS ARE THE ONLY ONES THAT CAN TAKE ON THE WHALE KING.
BUT SINCE ANOTHER CAN SWIM AT THE SPEED OF LIGHT...
...HE PROBABLY ISN'T WORRIED ABOUT BEING ATTACKED BY THE SEVEN BEASTS.
NO WONDER HE PIGGYBACKED ON SUCH POWERFUL CREATURES.
LIKE HOW CLOWN FISH WILL MAKE THEIR HOMES IN SEA ANEMONES.
IT WON'T BE EASY PROCURING THE MATERIALS FROM THOSE TERRIBLE MONSTERS.
WE'LL GO.
!

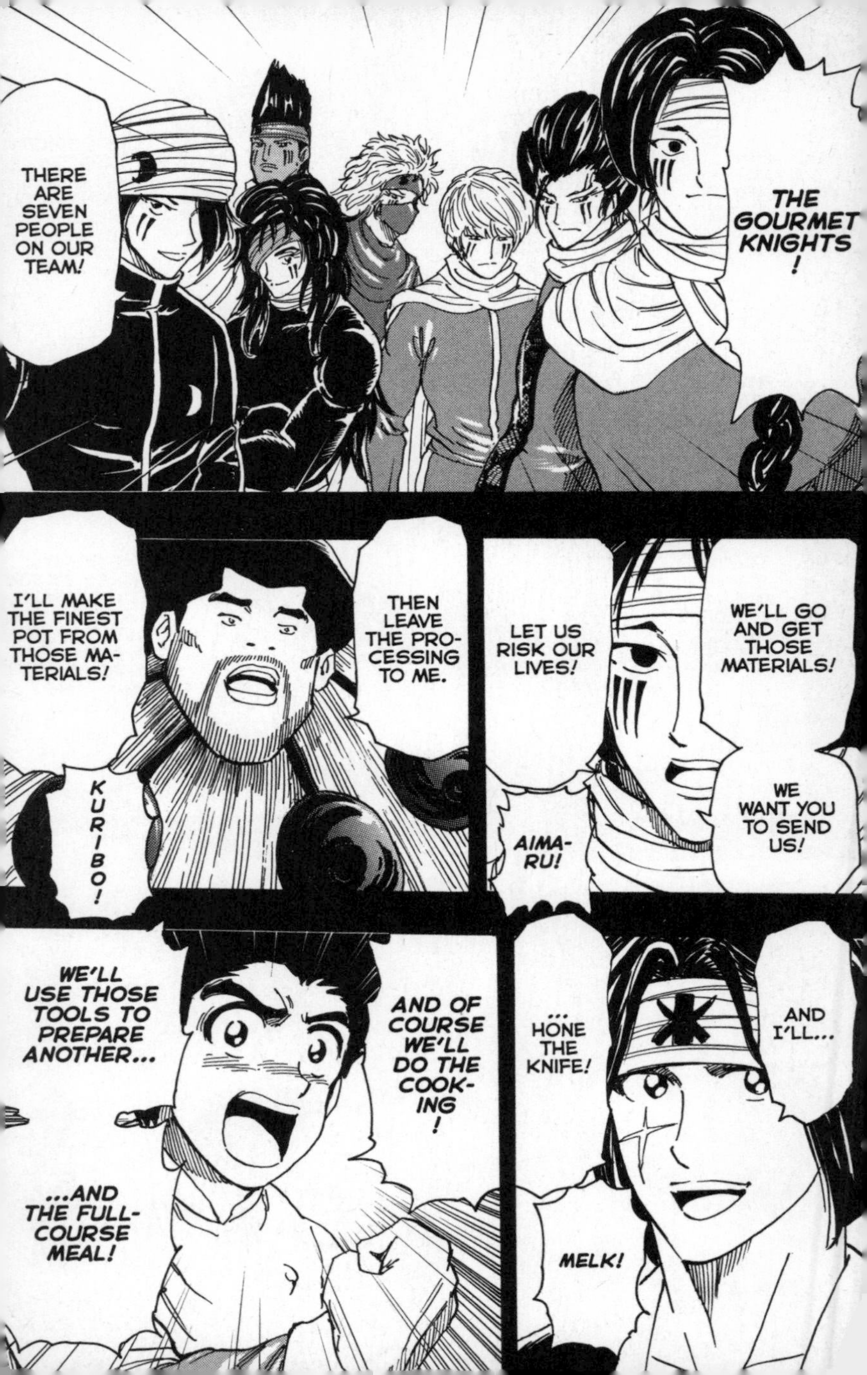

THE GOURMET KNIGHTS!
THERE ARE SEVEN PEOPLE ON OUR TEAM!
WE'LL GO AND GET THOSE MATERIALS!
WE WANT YOU TO SEND US!
LET US RISK OUR LIVES!
AIMARU!
THEN LEAVE THE PROCESSING TO ME.
I'LL MAKE THE FINEST POT FROM THOSE MATERIALS!
KURIBO!
AND I'LL...
...HONE THE KNIFE!
MELK!
AND OF COURSE WE'LL DO THE COOKING!
WE'LL USE THOSE TOOLS TO PREPARE ANOTHER...
...AND THE FULL-COURSE MEAL!

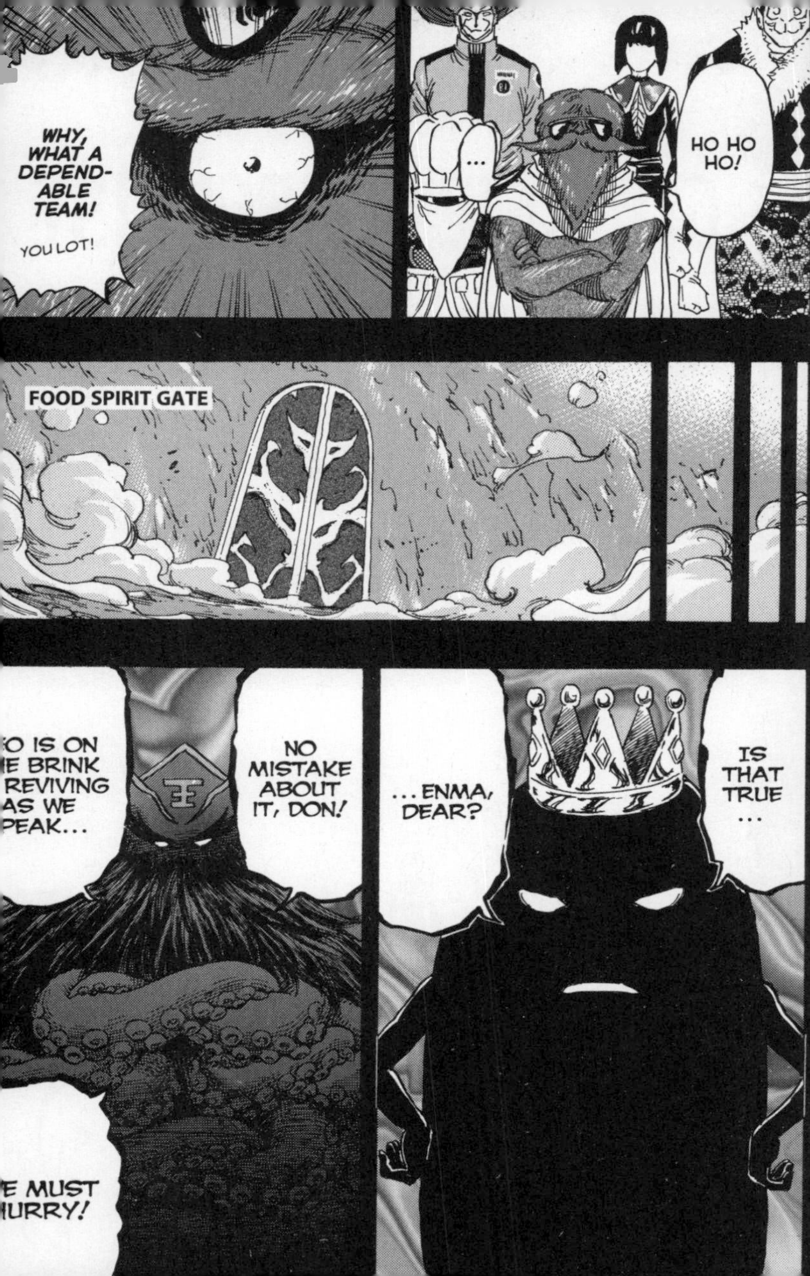
...
HO HO HO!
WHY, WHAT A DEPEND-ABLE TEAM!
YOU LOT!
FOOD SPIRIT GATE
IS THAT TRUE...
...ENMA, DEAR?
NO MISTAKE ABOUT IT, DON!
O IS ON E BRINK REVIVING AS WE PEAK...
E MUST HURRY!

TORIKO

GOURMET CHECKLIST

Vol. 377

B.B. PILL BUG
(SPECIAL INSECT BEAST)

CAPTURE LEVEL: 1,750
HABITAT: 100 G MOUNTAIN IN AREA 7
SIZE: 10 CM
HEIGHT: ---
WEIGHT: 1.5 KG BY DEFAULT
PRICE: NOT PRICED

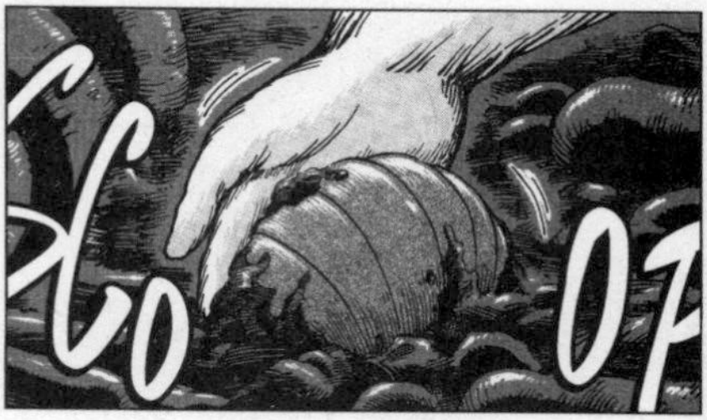

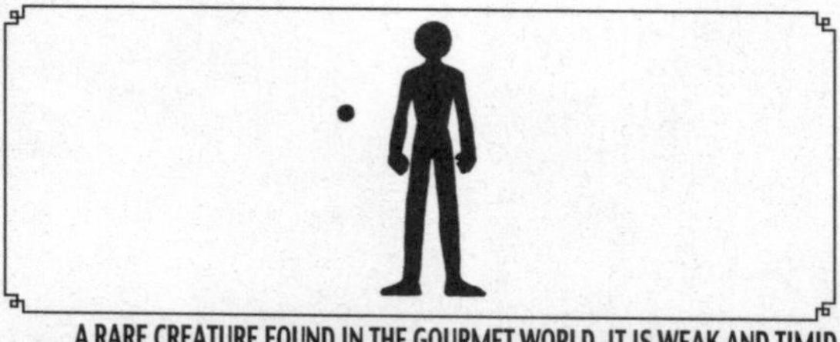

SCALE

A RARE CREATURE FOUND IN THE GOURMET WORLD, IT IS WEAK AND TIMID, AND ONCE FRIGHTENED IT WILL CURL UP INTO A BALL AND DEMONSTRATE ITS IMPRESSIVE POWERS OF SELF-DEFENSE. IT CAN ROLL AT TREMENDOUS SPEEDS, BECOME SO HEAVY THAT IT CANNOT BE LIFTED, BECOME LIGHT ENOUGH TO BE CARRIED AWAY BY THE WIND, STOP IN MID-MOTION, LET OFF A TERRIBLE SMELL AND RELEASE POISONS. AT THE SAME TIME, THE MORE YOU SPIN IT AROUND LIKE A BALL, THE TASTIER IT BECOMES. THOSE VERY SAME PECULIAR LIFE FUNCTIONS ARE WHAT ENABLED TORIKO AND THE GANG TO TRAIN IN MONKEY MARTIAL ARTS, MAKING IT AN INGREDIENT THEY SHOULD BE THANKFUL FOR.

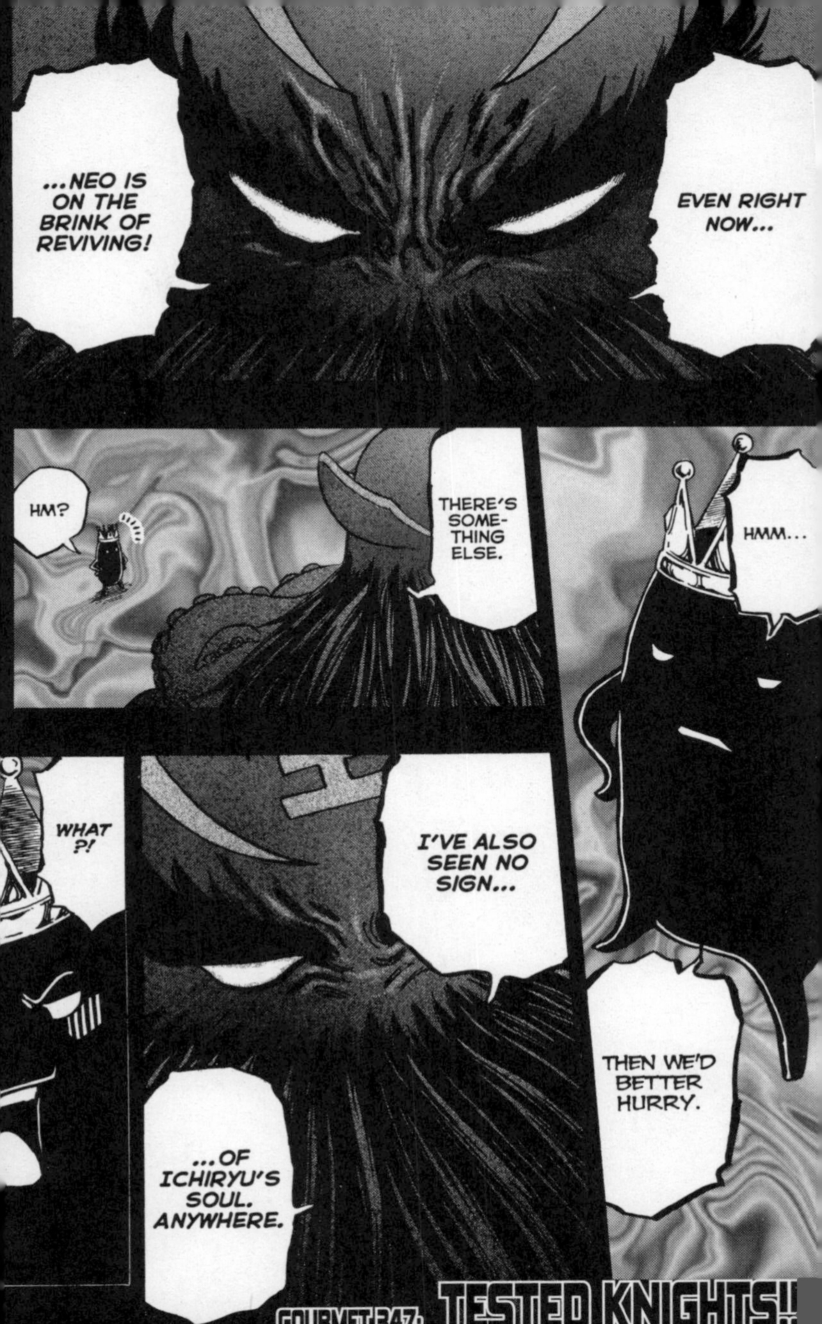
EVEN RIGHT NOW...
...NEO IS ON THE BRINK OF REVIVING!
THERE'S SOMETHING ELSE.
HM?
I'VE ALSO SEEN NO SIGN...
...OF ICHIRYU'S SOUL. ANYWHERE.
WHAT?!
HMM...
THEN WE'D BETTER HURRY.

GOURMET 347: TESTED KNIGHTS!!

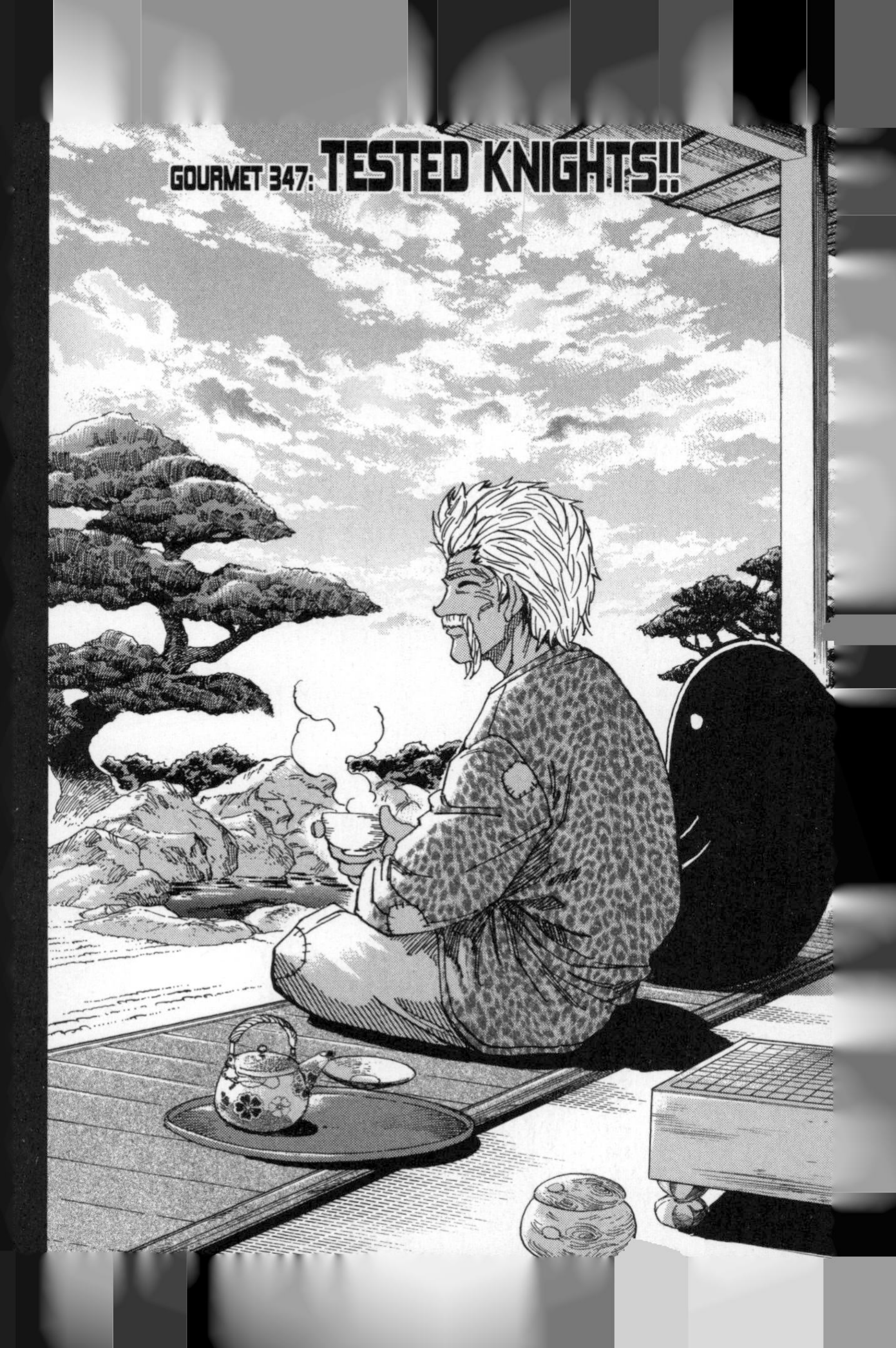
GOURMET 347: TESTED KNIGHTS!!

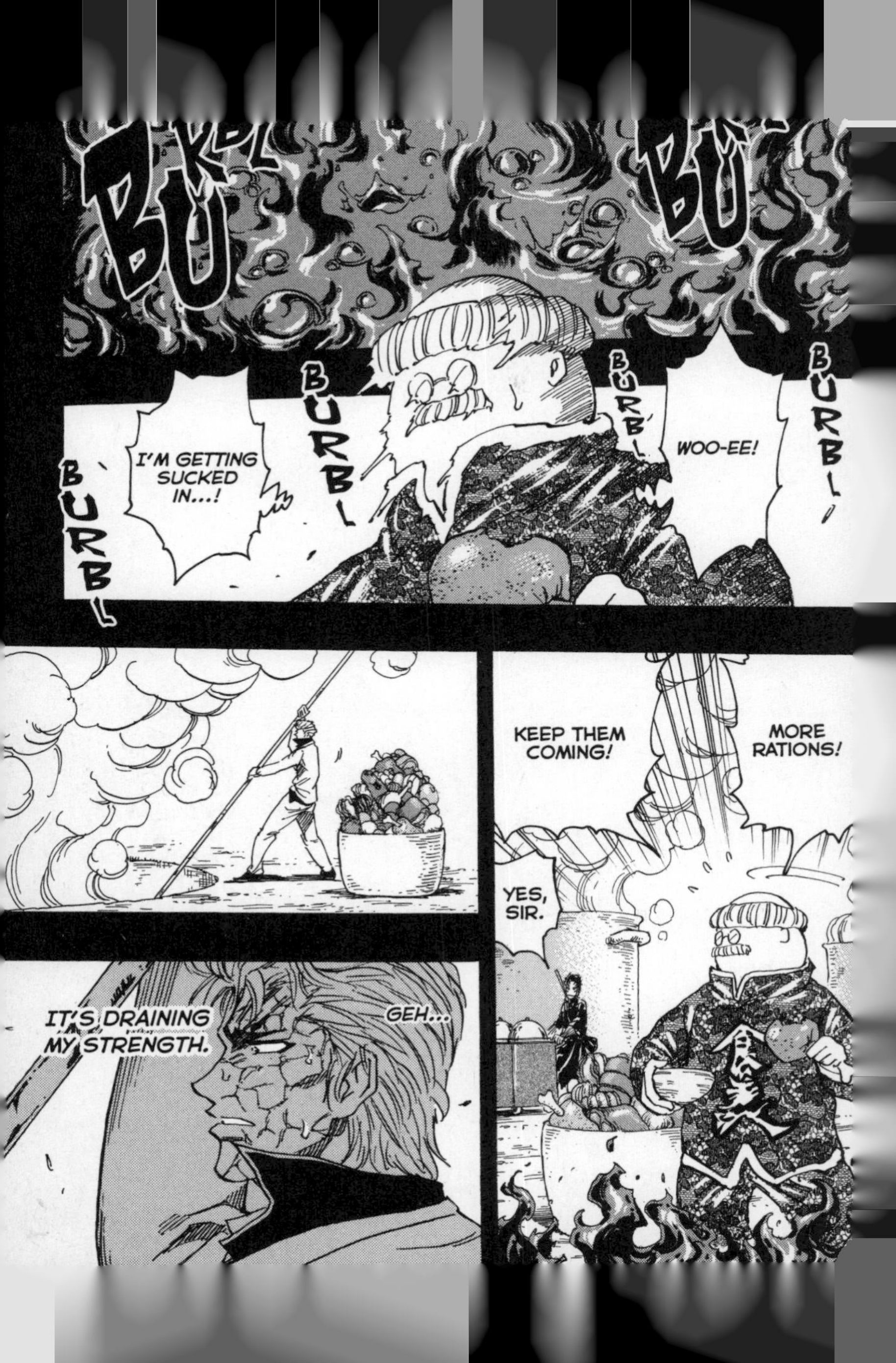
BURBL
BURBL
WOO-EE!
BURBL
BURBL
I'M GETTING SUCKED IN...!
BURBL
MORE RATIONS!
KEEP THEM COMING!
YES, SIR.
GEH...
IT'S DRAINING MY STRENGTH.

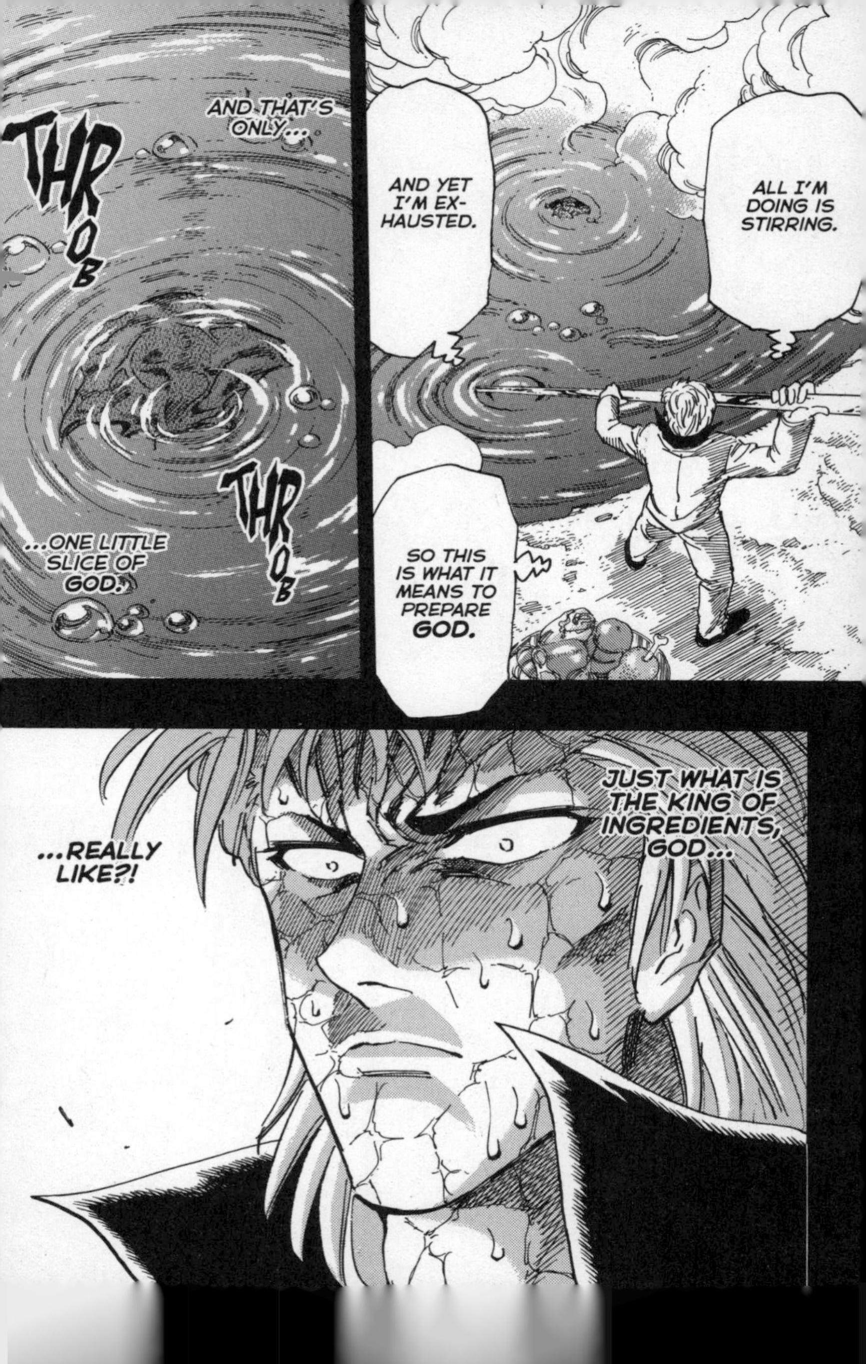
ALL I'M DOING IS STIRRING.
AND YET I'M EXHAUSTED.
SO THIS IS WHAT IT MEANS TO PREPARE GOD.
AND THAT'S ONLY...
THROB
THROB
...ONE LITTLE SLICE OF GOD.
JUST WHAT IS THE KING OF INGREDIENTS, GOD...
...REALLY LIKE?!

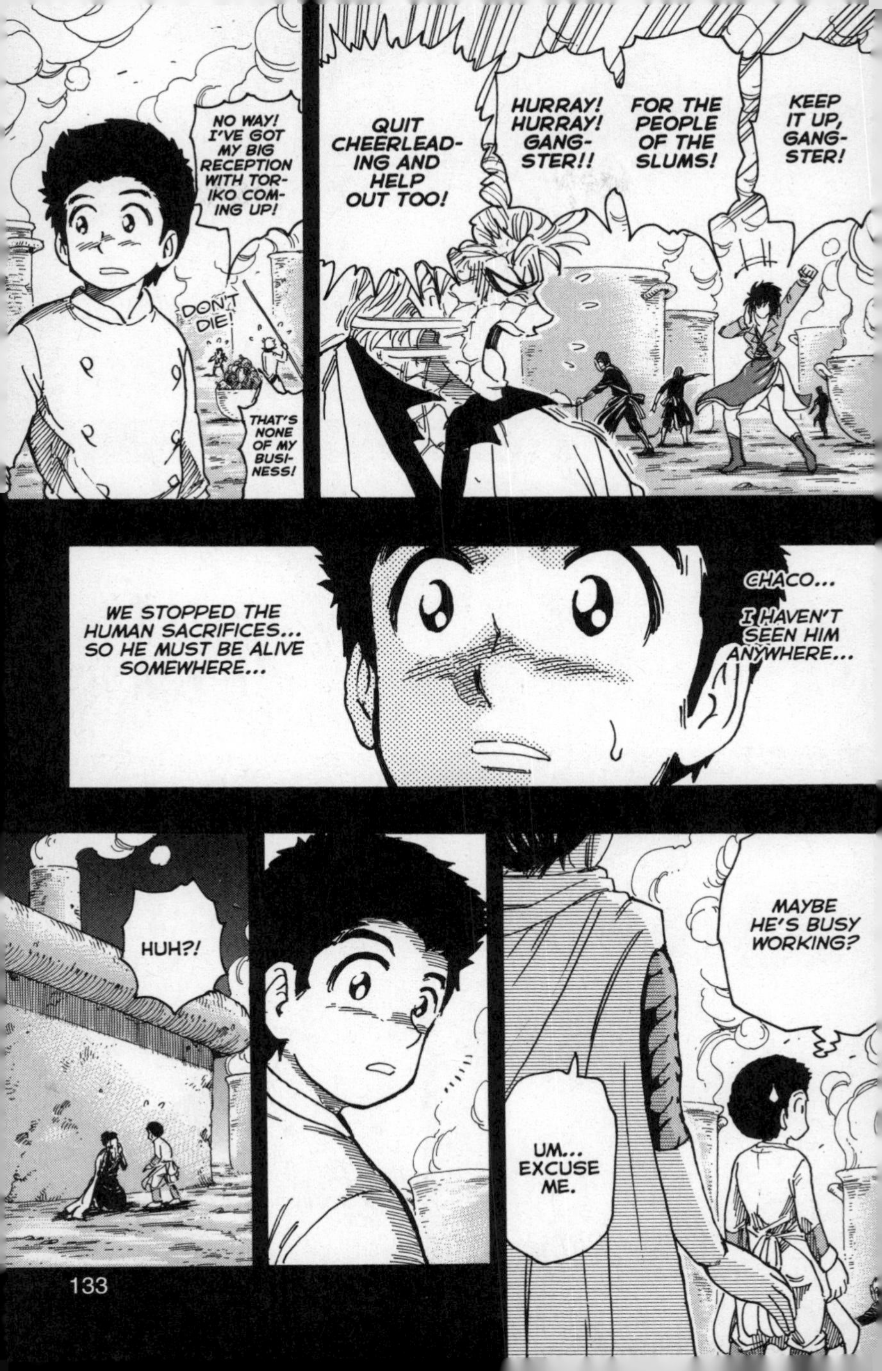
KEEP IT UP, GANGSTER!
FOR THE PEOPLE OF THE SLUMS!
HURRAY! HURRAY! GANGSTER!!
QUIT CHEERLEADING AND HELP OUT TOO!
NO WAY! I'VE GOT MY BIG RECEPTION WITH TORIKO COMING UP!
DON'T DIE!
THAT'S NONE OF MY BUSINESS!
CHACO...
I HAVEN'T SEEN HIM ANYWHERE...
WE STOPPED THE HUMAN SACRIFICES... SO HE MUST BE ALIVE SOMEWHERE...
MAYBE HE'S BUSY WORKING?
UM... EXCUSE ME.
HUH?!

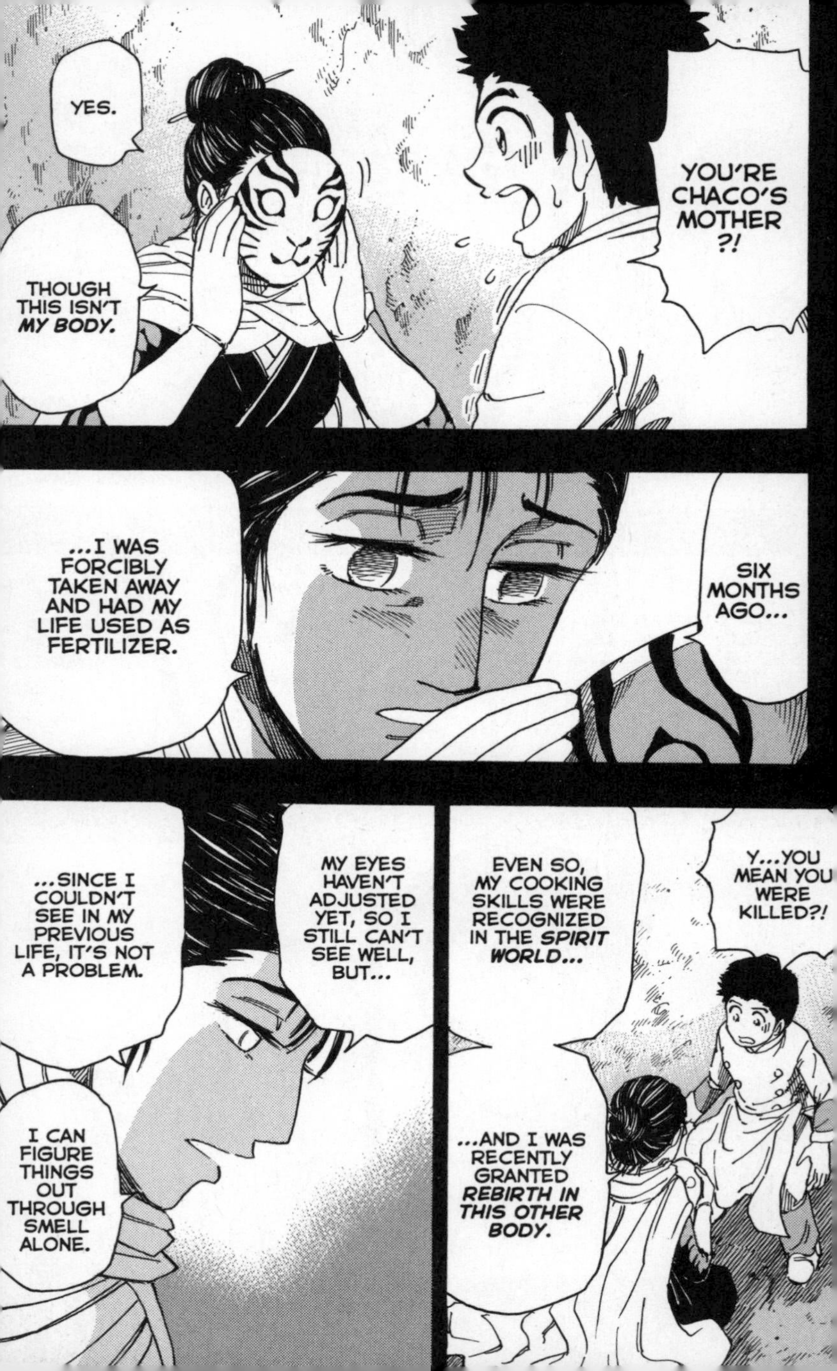
YOU'RE CHACO'S MOTHER ?!
YES.
THOUGH THIS ISN'T *MY BODY.*
SIX MONTHS AGO...
...I WAS FORCIBLY TAKEN AWAY AND HAD MY LIFE USED AS FERTILIZER.
Y...YOU MEAN YOU WERE KILLED?!
EVEN SO, MY COOKING SKILLS WERE RECOGNIZED IN THE *SPIRIT WORLD...*
...AND I WAS RECENTLY GRANTED *REBIRTH IN THIS OTHER BODY.*
MY EYES HAVEN'T ADJUSTED YET, SO I STILL CAN'T SEE WELL, BUT...
...SINCE I COULDN'T SEE IN MY PREVIOUS LIFE, IT'S NOT A PROBLEM.
I CAN FIGURE THINGS OUT THROUGH SMELL ALONE.

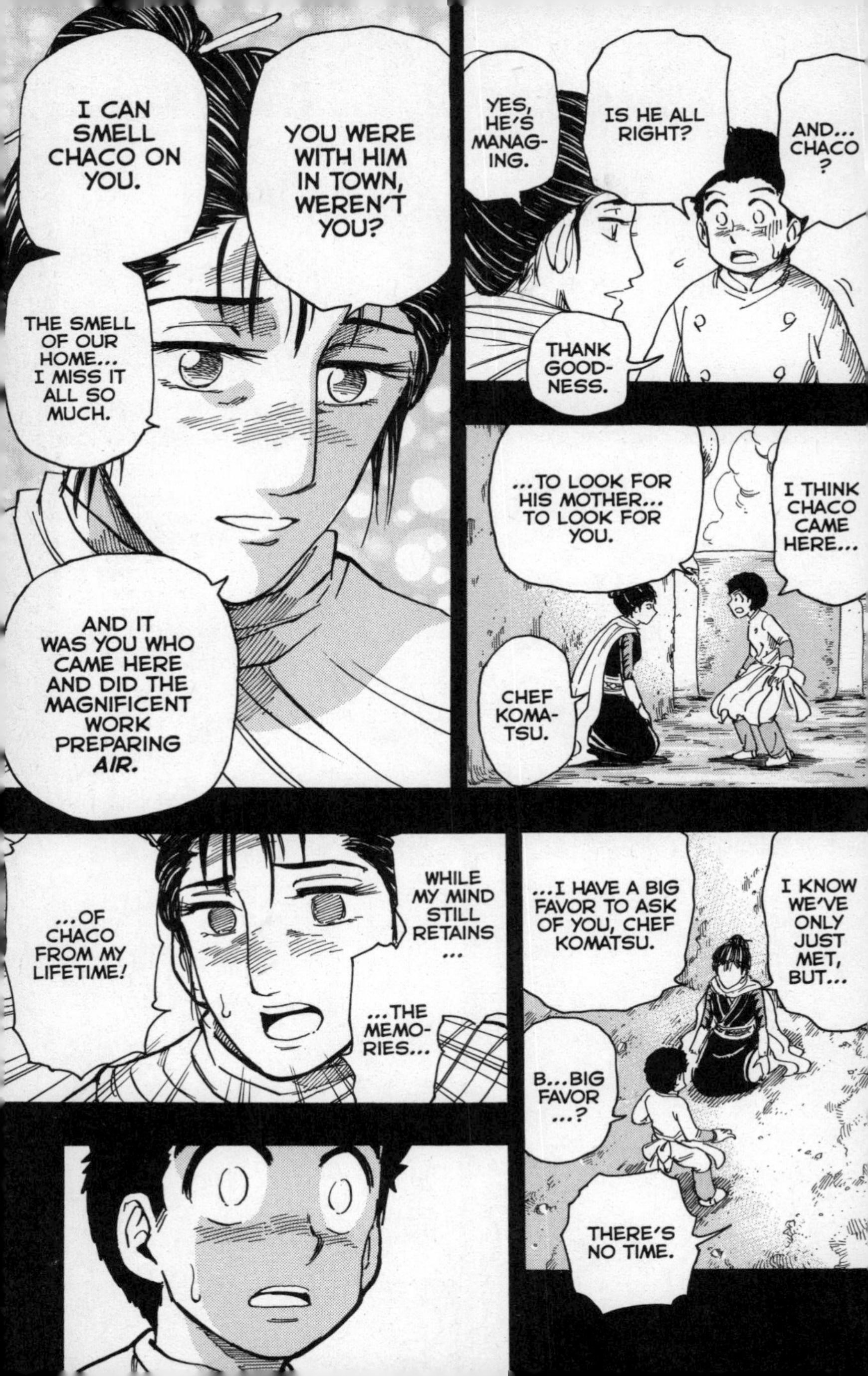
AND... CHACO?
IS HE ALL RIGHT?
YES, HE'S MANAGING.
THANK GOODNESS.
I THINK CHACO CAME HERE...
...TO LOOK FOR HIS MOTHER... TO LOOK FOR YOU.
CHEF KOMATSU.
YOU WERE WITH HIM IN TOWN, WEREN'T YOU?
I CAN SMELL CHACO ON YOU.
THE SMELL OF OUR HOME... I MISS IT ALL SO MUCH.
AND IT WAS YOU WHO CAME HERE AND DID THE MAGNIFICENT WORK PREPARING *AIR.*
I KNOW WE'VE ONLY JUST MET, BUT...
...I HAVE A BIG FAVOR TO ASK OF YOU, CHEF KOMATSU.
B...BIG FAVOR...?
THERE'S NO TIME.
WHILE MY MIND STILL RETAINS...
...THE MEMORIES...
...OF CHACO FROM MY LIFETIME!

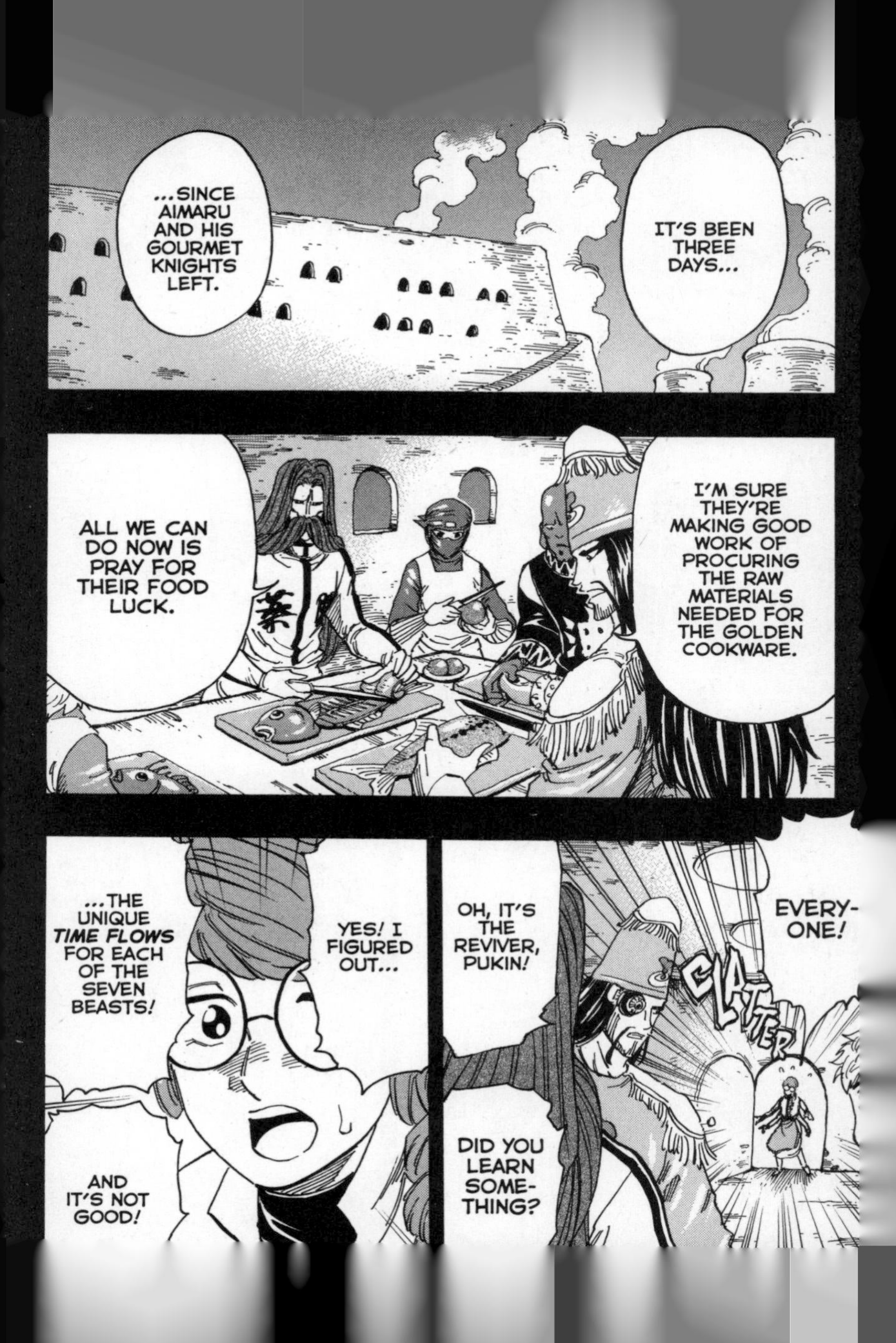

IT'S BEEN THREE DAYS...
...SINCE AIMARU AND HIS GOURMET KNIGHTS LEFT.
I'M SURE THEY'RE MAKING GOOD WORK OF PROCURING THE RAW MATERIALS NEEDED FOR THE GOLDEN COOKWARE.
ALL WE CAN DO NOW IS PRAY FOR THEIR FOOD LUCK.
EVERY-ONE!
CLATTER
OH, IT'S THE REVIVER, PUKIN!
DID YOU LEARN SOME-THING?
YES! I FIGURED OUT...
...THE UNIQUE *TIME FLOWS* FOR EACH OF THE SEVEN BEASTS!
AND IT'S NOT GOOD!

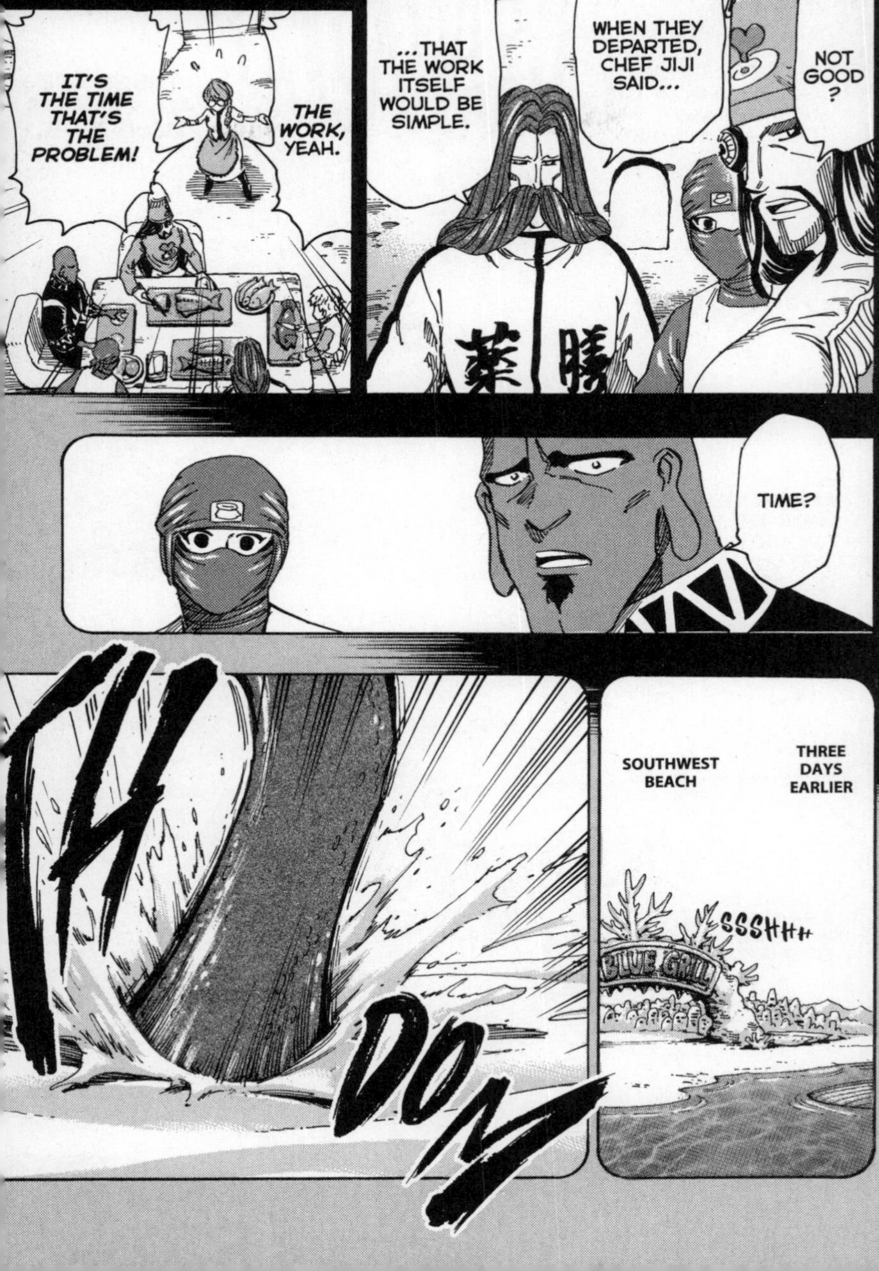
NOT GOOD?
WHEN THEY DEPARTED, CHEF JIJI SAID...
...THAT THE WORK ITSELF WOULD BE SIMPLE.
THE WORK, YEAH.
IT'S THE TIME THAT'S THE PROBLEM!
TIME?
THREE DAYS EARLIER
SOUTHWEST BEACH
BLUE GRILL
SSSHHH
DOM

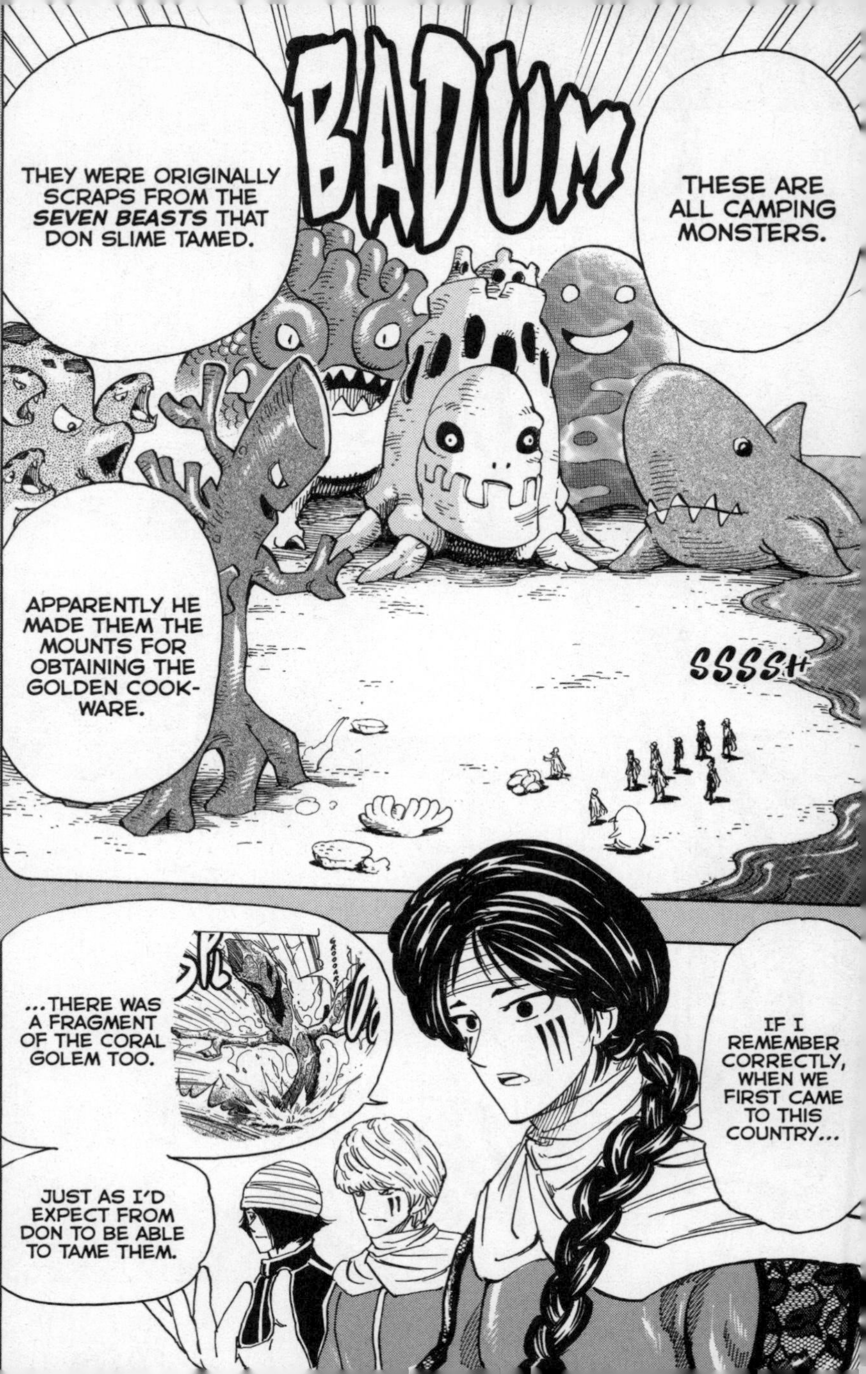
THESE ARE ALL CAMPING MONSTERS.
BADUM
THEY WERE ORIGINALLY SCRAPS FROM THE *SEVEN BEASTS* THAT DON SLIME TAMED.
APPARENTLY HE MADE THEM THE MOUNTS FOR OBTAINING THE GOLDEN COOK-WARE.
SSSSH
IF I REMEMBER CORRECTLY, WHEN WE FIRST CAME TO THIS COUNTRY...
...THERE WAS A FRAGMENT OF THE CORAL GOLEM TOO.
JUST AS I'D EXPECT FROM DON TO BE ABLE TO TAME THEM.

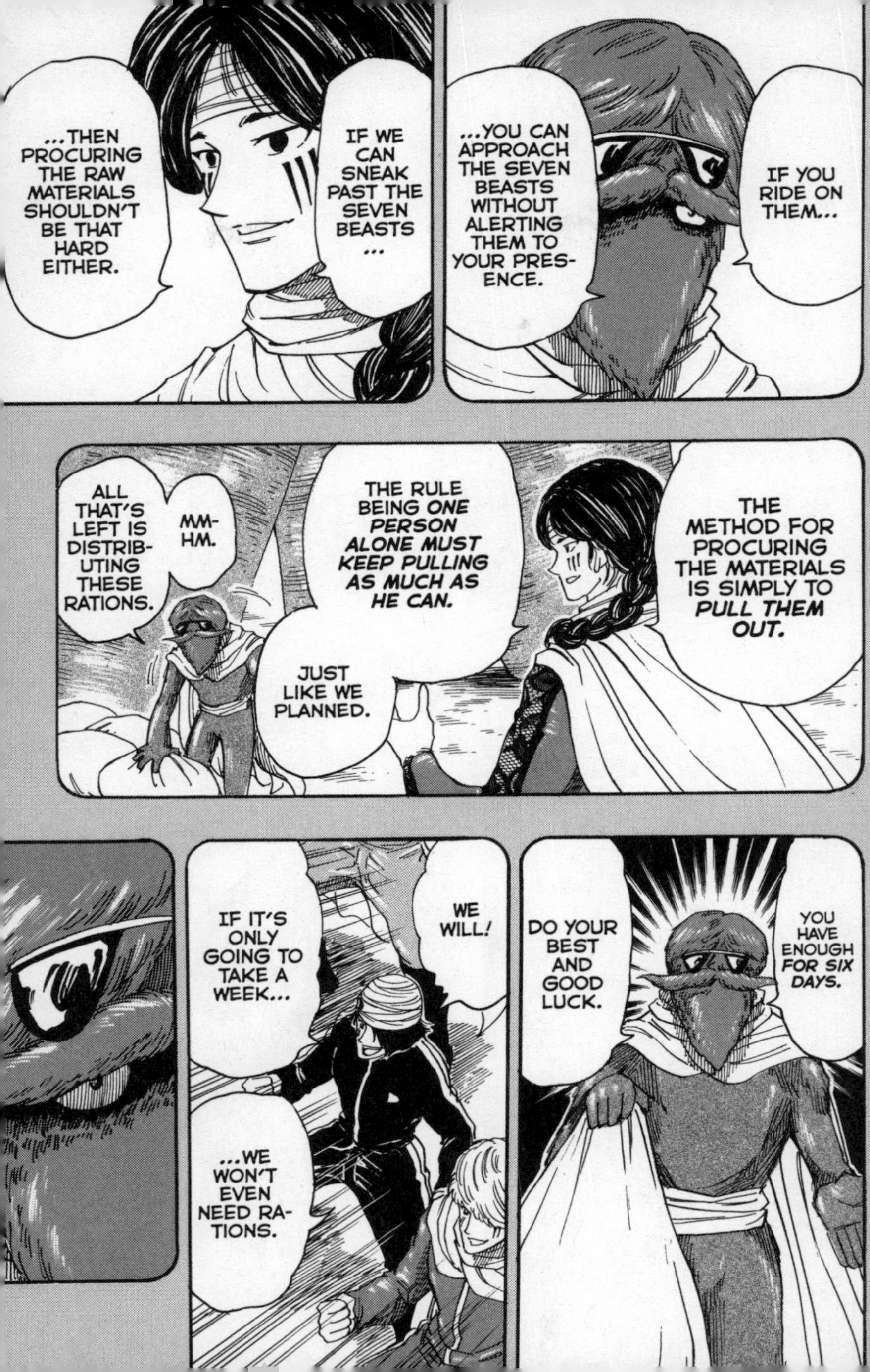
IF YOU RIDE ON THEM...
...YOU CAN APPROACH THE SEVEN BEASTS WITHOUT ALERTING THEM TO YOUR PRESENCE.
IF WE CAN SNEAK PAST THE SEVEN BEASTS...
...THEN PROCURING THE RAW MATERIALS SHOULDN'T BE THAT HARD EITHER.
THE METHOD FOR PROCURING THE MATERIALS IS SIMPLY TO *PULL THEM OUT.*
THE RULE BEING *ONE PERSON ALONE MUST KEEP PULLING AS MUCH AS HE CAN.*
JUST LIKE WE PLANNED.
MM-HM.
ALL THAT'S LEFT IS DISTRIBUTING THESE RATIONS.
YOU HAVE ENOUGH *FOR SIX DAYS.*
DO YOUR BEST AND GOOD LUCK.
WE WILL!
IF IT'S ONLY GOING TO TAKE A WEEK...
...WE WON'T EVEN NEED RATIONS.

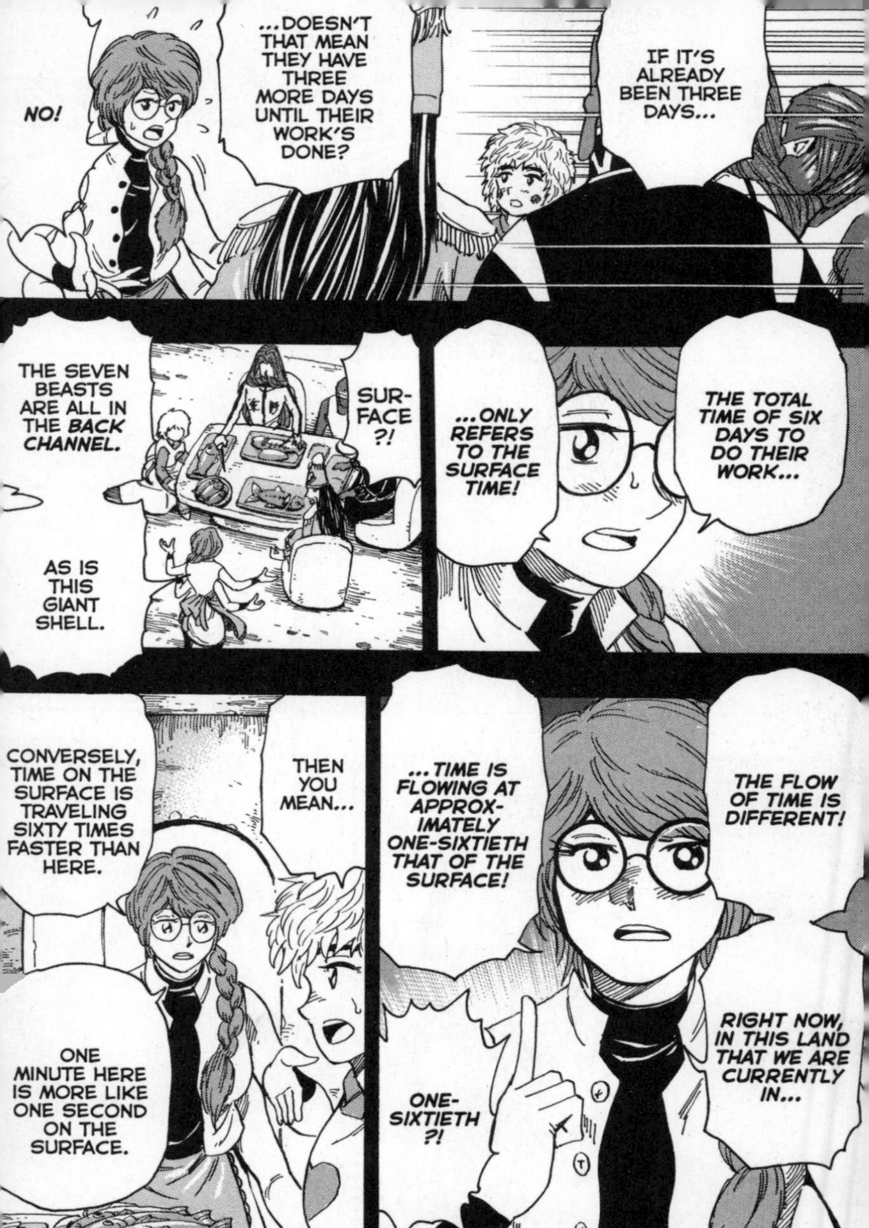
IF IT'S ALREADY BEEN THREE DAYS...
...DOESN'T THAT MEAN THEY HAVE THREE MORE DAYS UNTIL THEIR WORK'S DONE?
NO!
THE TOTAL TIME OF SIX DAYS TO DO THEIR WORK...
...ONLY REFERS TO THE SURFACE TIME!
SUR-FACE ?!
THE SEVEN BEASTS ARE ALL IN THE BACK CHANNEL.
AS IS THIS GIANT SHELL.
THE FLOW OF TIME IS DIFFERENT!
RIGHT NOW, IN THIS LAND THAT WE ARE CURRENTLY IN...
...TIME IS FLOWING AT APPROX-IMATELY ONE-SIXTIETH THAT OF THE SURFACE!
ONE-SIXTIETH ?!
THEN YOU MEAN...
CONVERSELY, TIME ON THE SURFACE IS TRAVELING SIXTY TIMES FASTER THAN HERE.
ONE MINUTE HERE IS MORE LIKE ONE SECOND ON THE SURFACE.

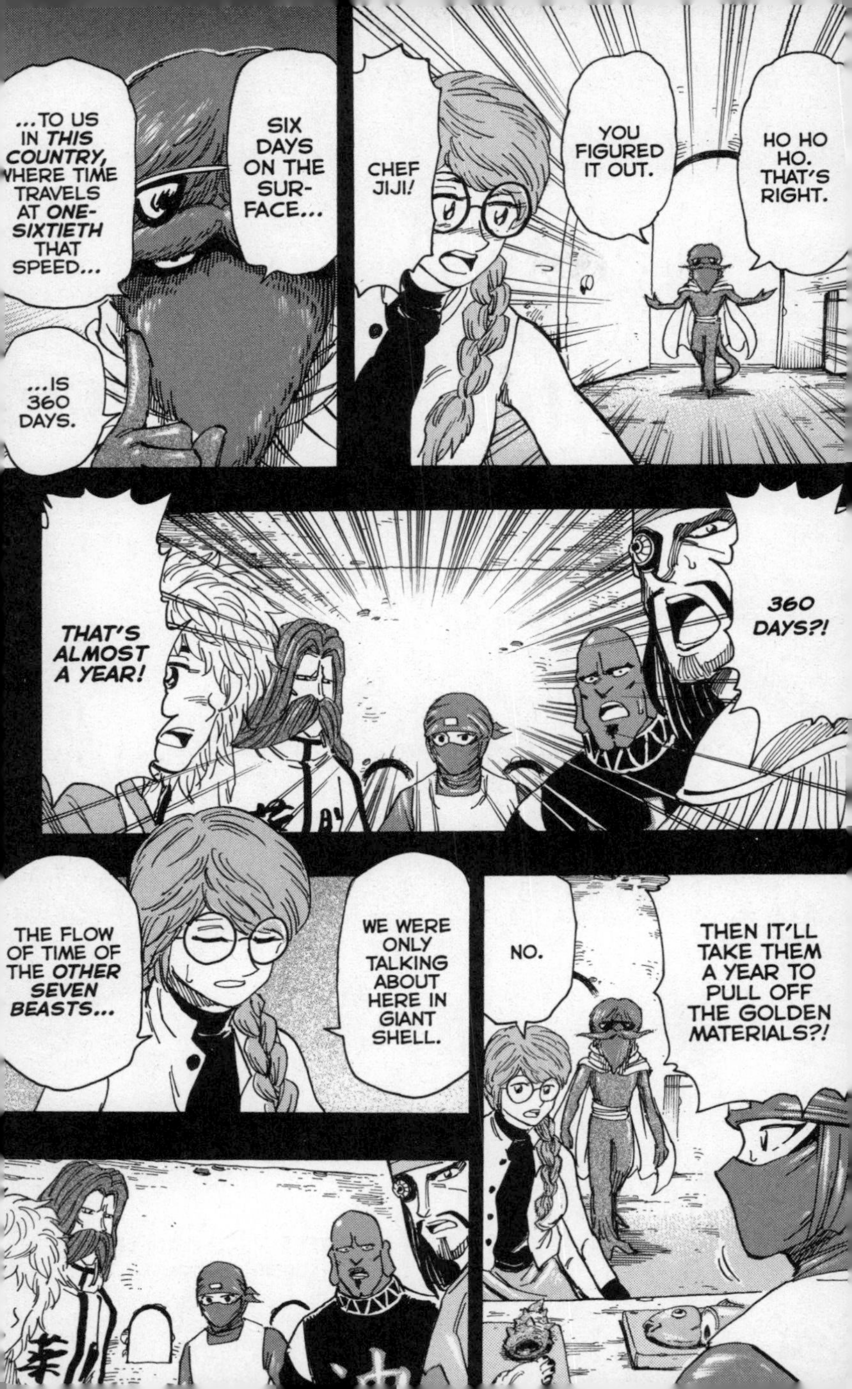
HO HO HO. THAT'S RIGHT.
YOU FIGURED IT OUT.
CHEF JIJI!
SIX DAYS ON THE SURFACE...
...TO US IN *THIS COUNTRY,* WHERE TIME TRAVELS AT *ONE-SIXTIETH* THAT SPEED...
...IS 360 DAYS.
360 DAYS?!
THAT'S ALMOST A YEAR!
THEN IT'LL TAKE THEM A YEAR TO PULL OFF THE GOLDEN MATERIALS?!
NO.
WE WERE ONLY TALKING ABOUT HERE IN GIANT SHELL.
THE FLOW OF TIME OF THE *OTHER SEVEN BEASTS...*

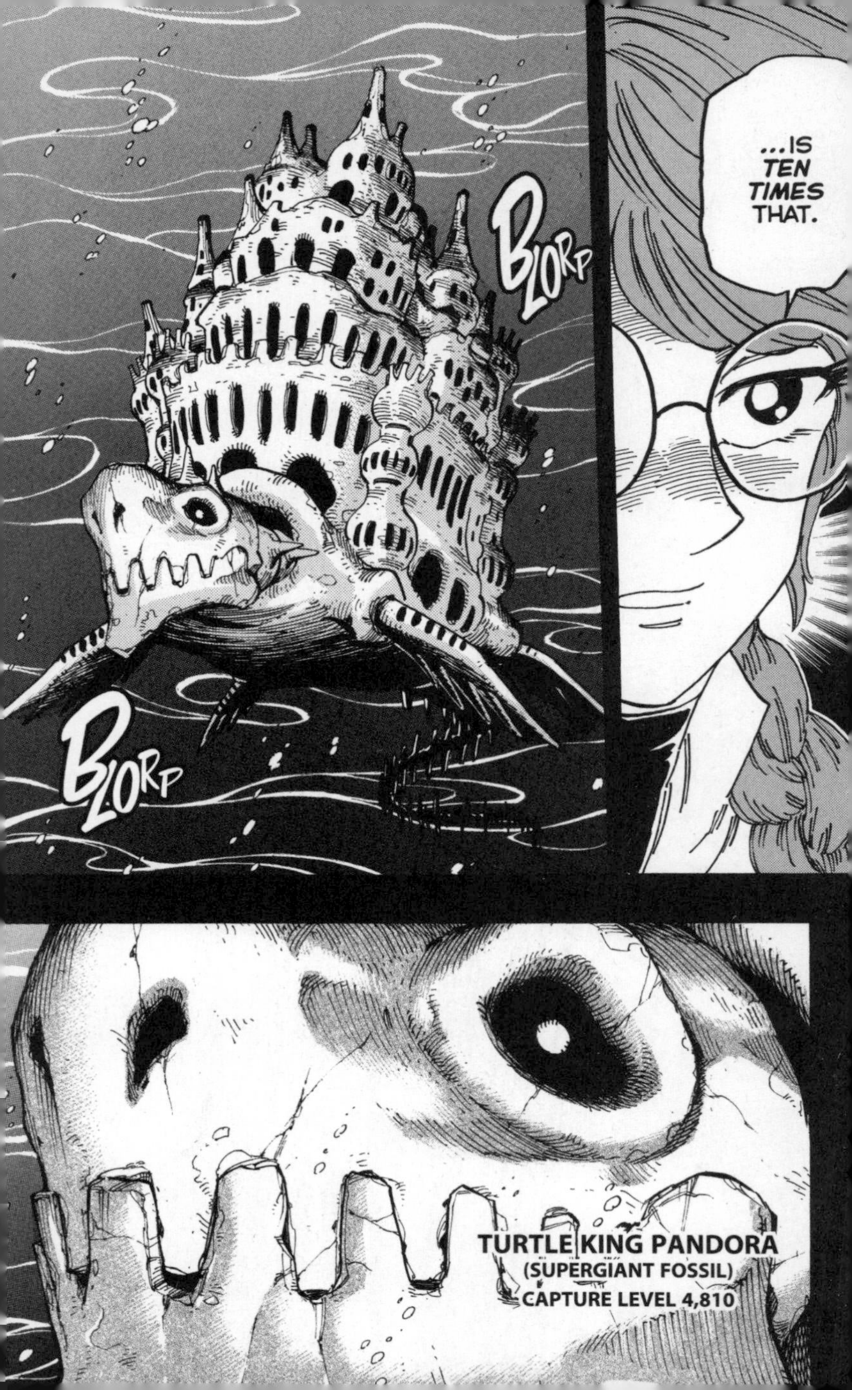
...IS TEN TIMES THAT.
BLORP
BLORP
TURTLE KING PANDORA
(SUPERGIANT FOSSIL)
CAPTURE LEVEL 4,810

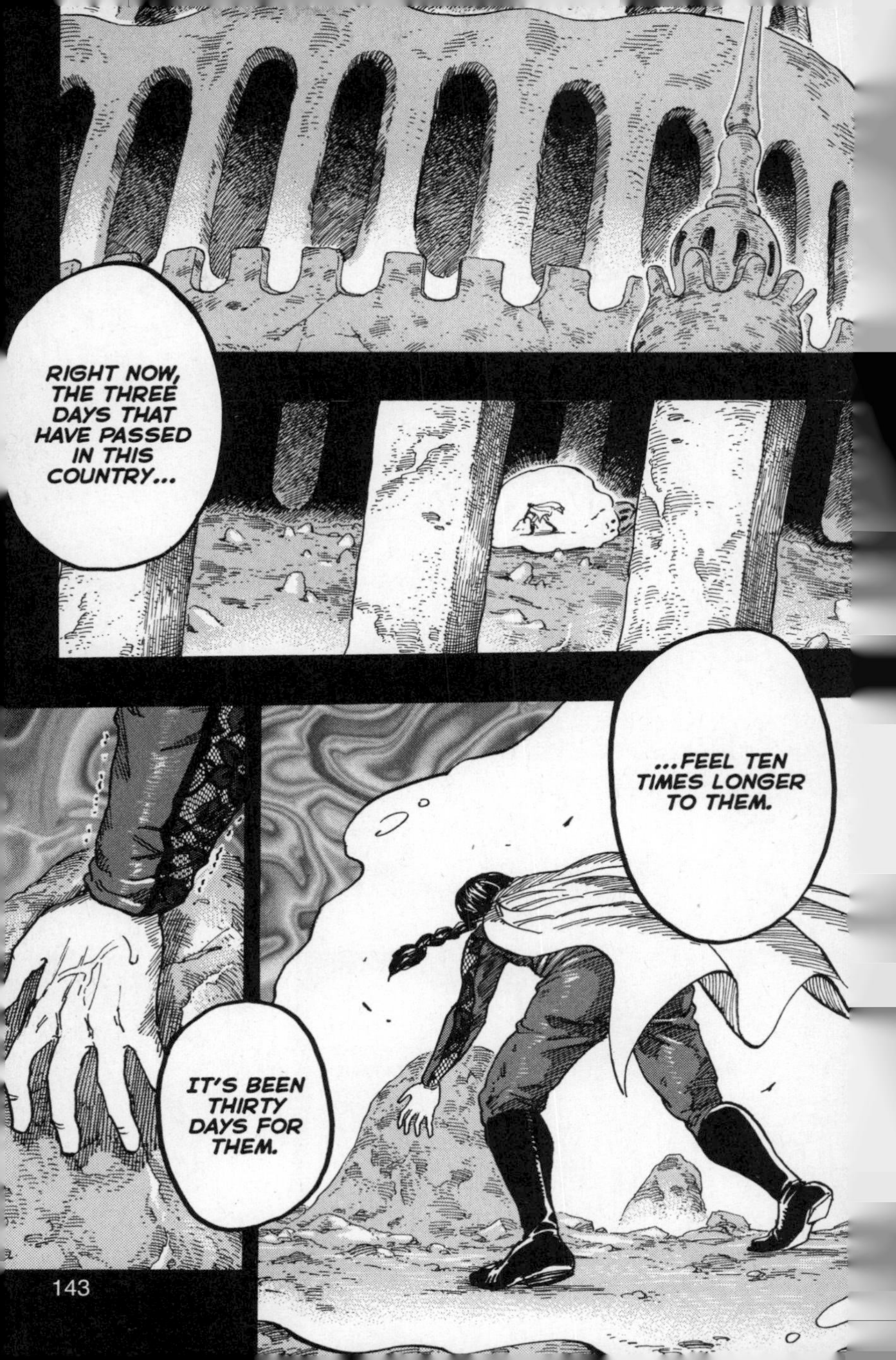
RIGHT NOW, THE THREE DAYS THAT HAVE PASSED IN THIS COUNTRY...
...FEEL TEN TIMES LONGER TO THEM.
IT'S BEEN THIRTY DAYS FOR THEM.

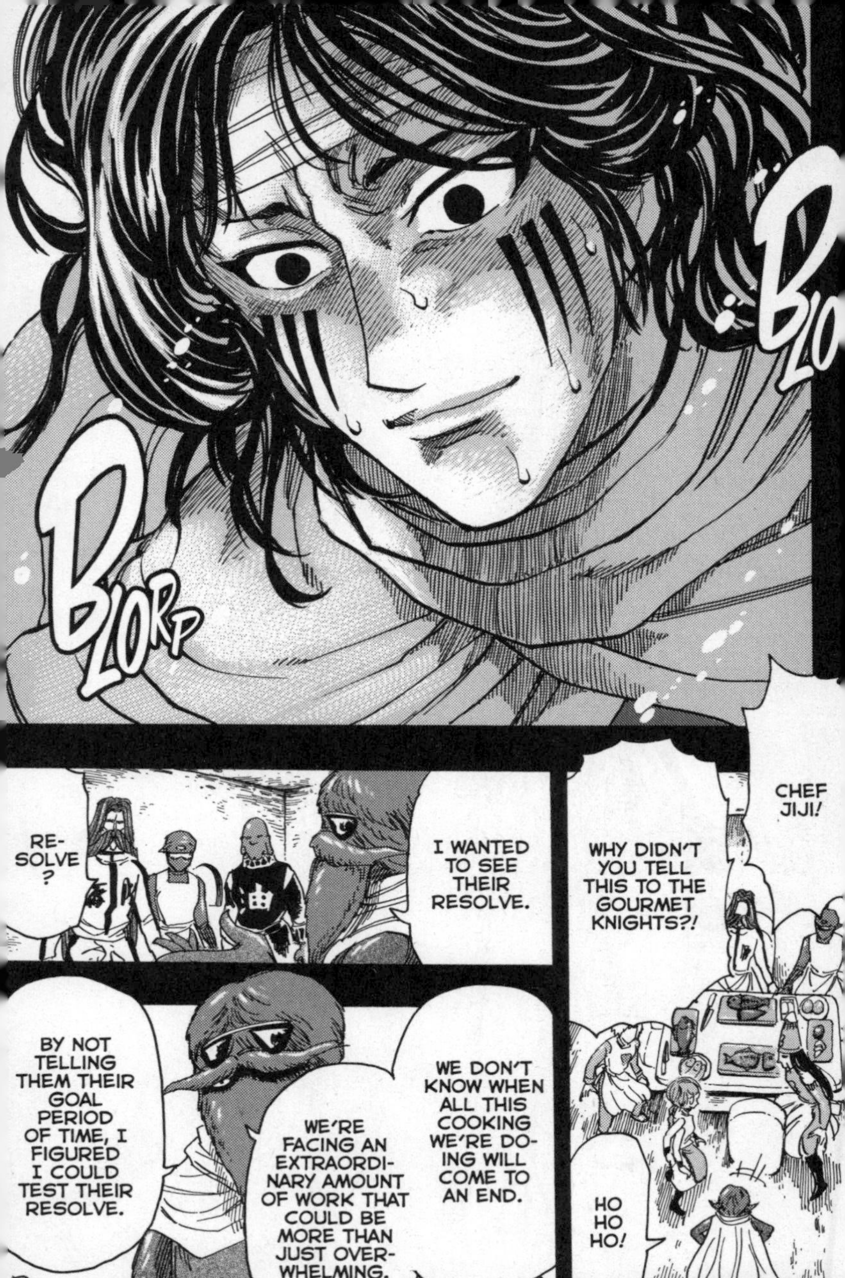
BLO
BLORP
CHEF JIJI!
WHY DIDN'T YOU TELL THIS TO THE GOURMET KNIGHTS?!
HO HO HO!
I WANTED TO SEE THEIR RESOLVE.
RE-SOLVE?
WE DON'T KNOW WHEN ALL THIS COOKING WE'RE DO-ING WILL COME TO AN END.
WE'RE FACING AN EXTRAORDI-NARY AMOUNT OF WORK THAT COULD BE MORE THAN JUST OVER-WHELMING.
BY NOT TELLING THEM THEIR GOAL PERIOD OF TIME, I FIGURED I COULD TEST THEIR RESOLVE.

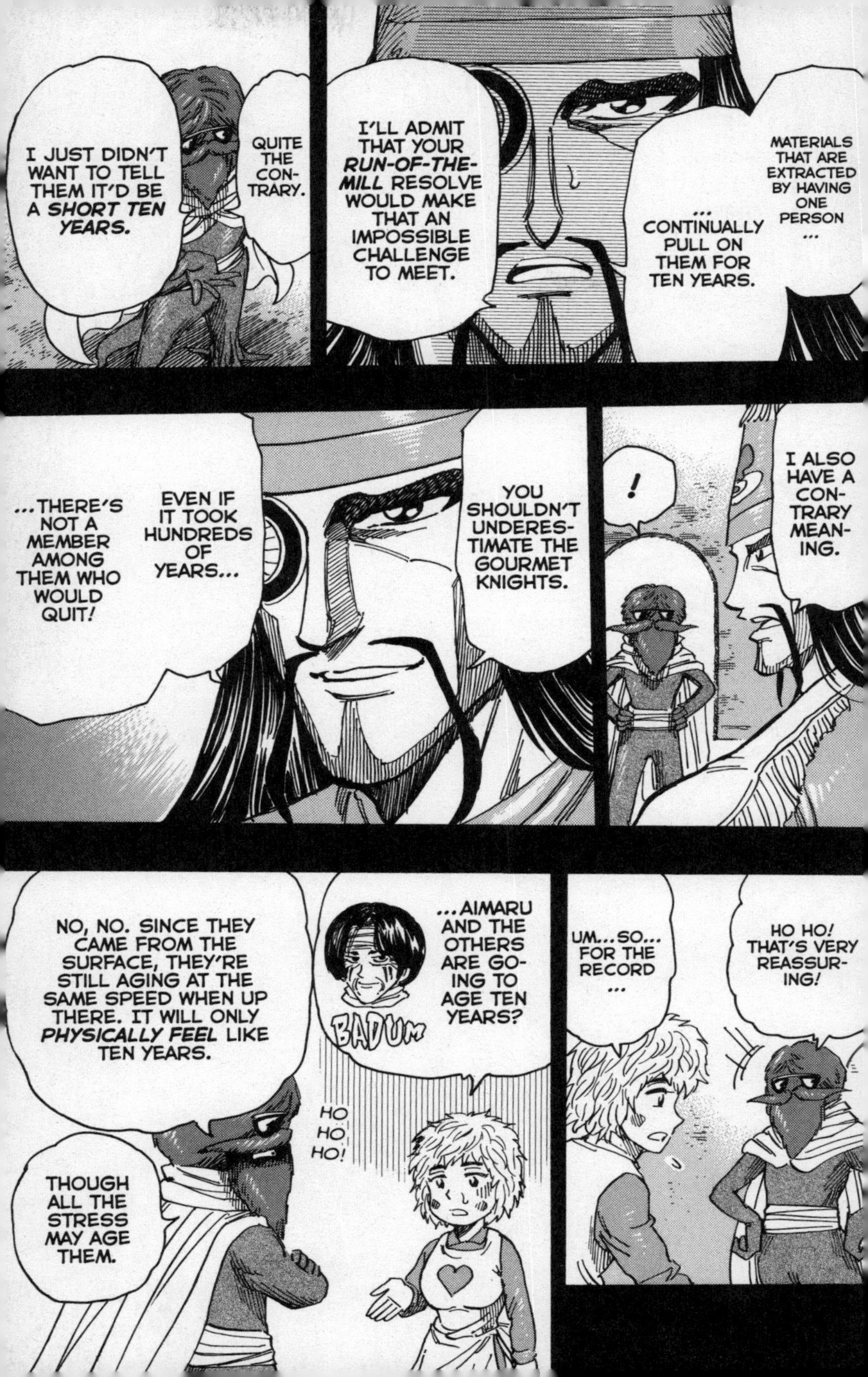
MATERIALS THAT ARE EXTRACTED BY HAVING ONE PERSON ...
... CONTINUALLY PULL ON THEM FOR TEN YEARS.
I'LL ADMIT THAT YOUR *RUN-OF-THE-MILL* RESOLVE WOULD MAKE THAT AN IMPOSSIBLE CHALLENGE TO MEET.
QUITE THE CON-TRARY.
I JUST DIDN'T WANT TO TELL THEM IT'D BE A *SHORT TEN YEARS.*
I ALSO HAVE A CON-TRARY MEAN-ING.
!
YOU SHOULDN'T UNDERES-TIMATE THE GOURMET KNIGHTS.
EVEN IF IT TOOK HUNDREDS OF YEARS...
...THERE'S NOT A MEMBER AMONG THEM WHO WOULD QUIT!
HO HO! THAT'S VERY REASSUR-ING!
UM...SO... FOR THE RECORD ...
...AIMARU AND THE OTHERS ARE GO-ING TO AGE TEN YEARS?
BADUM
NO, NO. SINCE THEY CAME FROM THE SURFACE, THEY'RE STILL AGING AT THE SAME SPEED WHEN UP THERE. IT WILL ONLY *PHYSICALLY FEEL* LIKE TEN YEARS.
HO HO HO!
THOUGH ALL THE STRESS MAY AGE THEM.

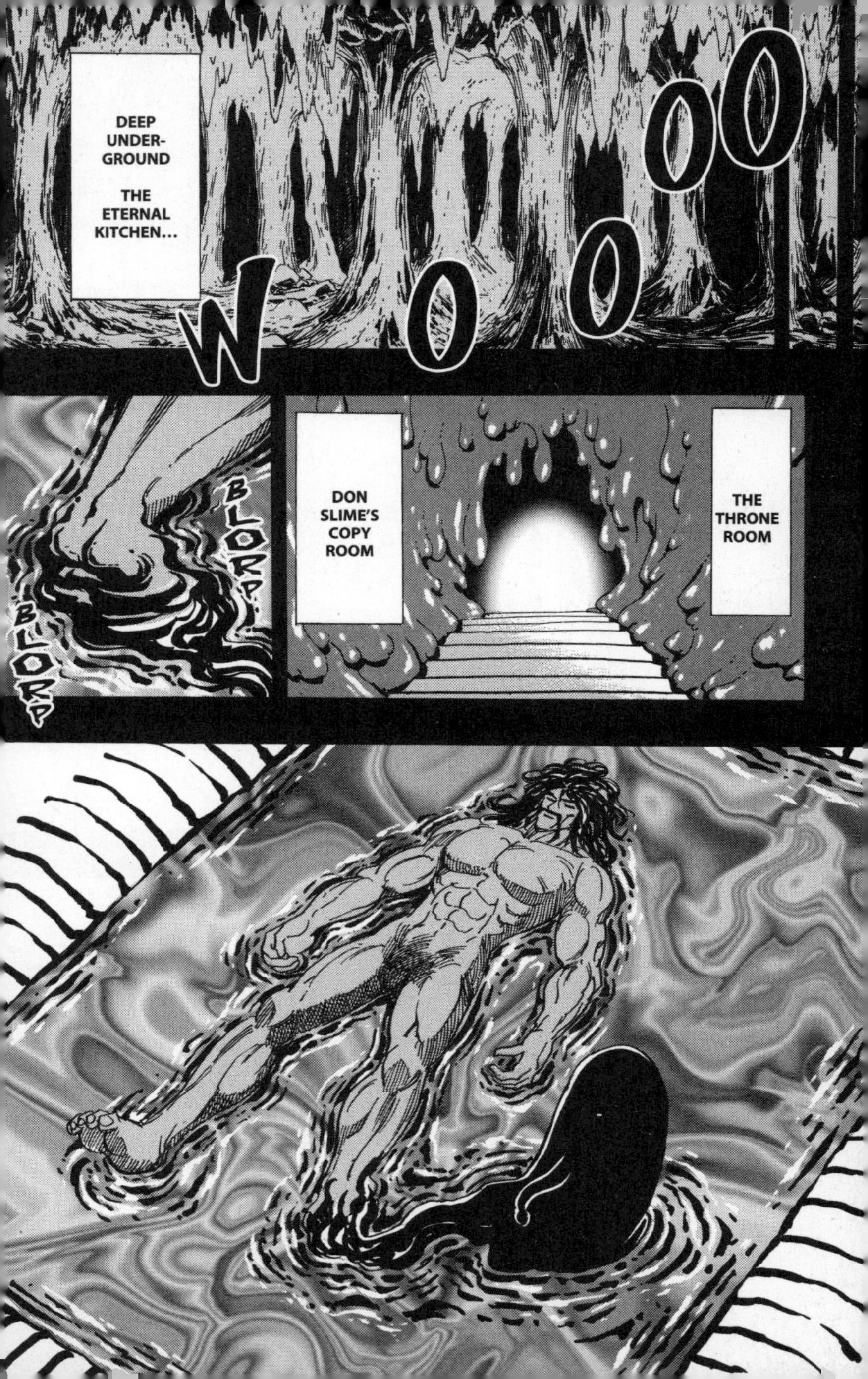
DEEP UNDER-GROUND
THE ETERNAL KITCHEN…
WOOOO
THE THRONE ROOM
DON SLIME'S COPY ROOM
BLORP
BLORP

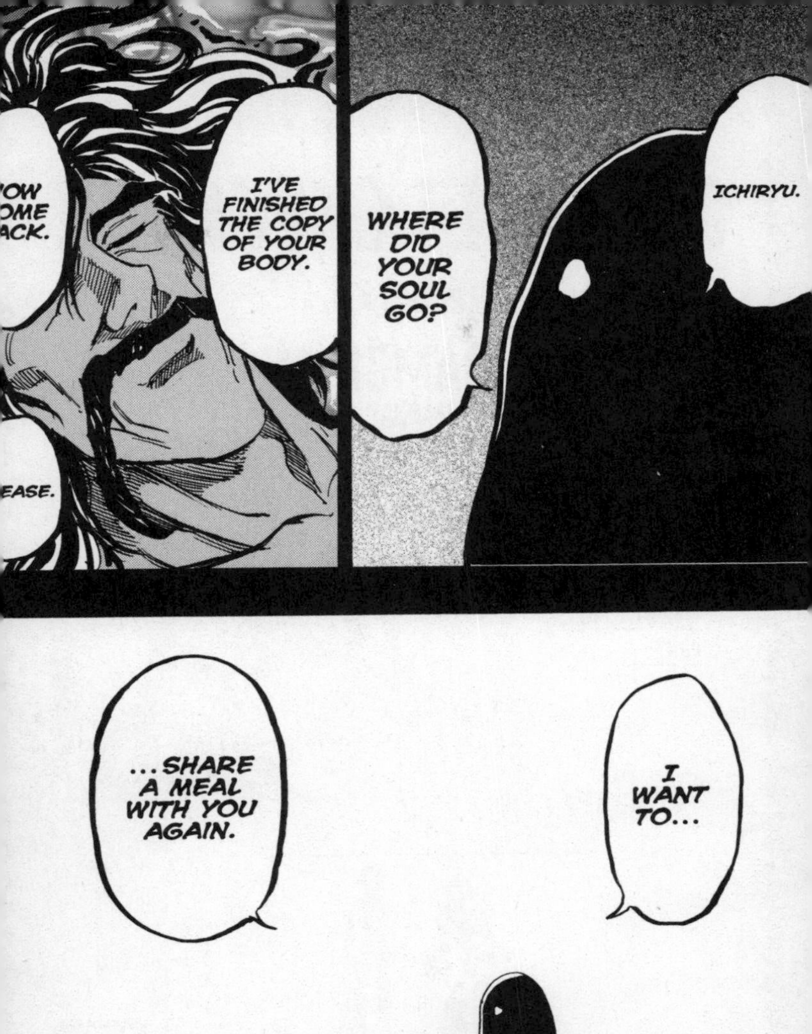
ICHIRYU.
WHERE DID YOUR SOUL GO?
I'VE FINISHED THE COPY OF YOUR BODY.
I WANT TO...
...SHARE A MEAL WITH YOU AGAIN.

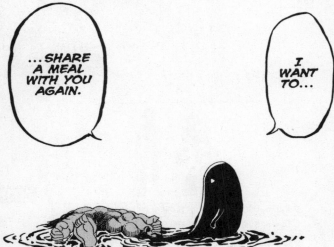

TORIKO

GOURMET CHECKLIST

Vol. 378

BAMBINA
(MAMMAL KING)

CAPTURE LEVEL: 6,000

HABITAT: AREA 7

SIZE: ---

HEIGHT: 150 CM

WEIGHT: 25 TONS

PRICE: ---

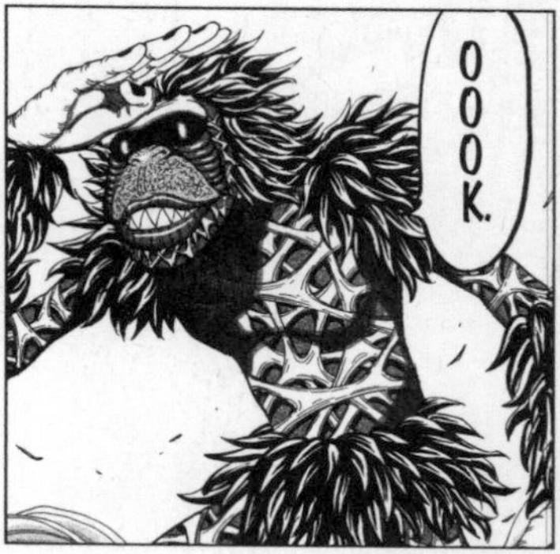
OOOOK.

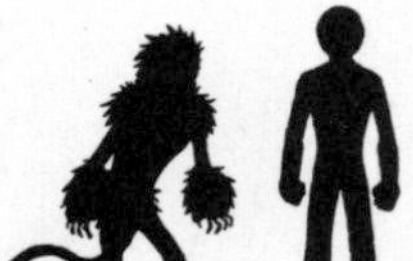

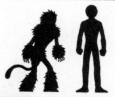

SCALE

ONE OF THE EIGHT KINGS THAT RULES ONE OF THE EIGHT CONTINENTS IN THE GOURMENT WORLD AND IS AT THE APEX OF THE MONKEY MARTIAL ARTS HIERARCHY—THE MONKEY KING! HE'S KNOWN TO BE THE PROBLEM CHILD OF THE EIGHT KINGS, BUT HIS ABILITIES ARE BY FAR THE BEST AND BECAUSE HE'S THAT POWERFUL, FIGHTS ARE JUST GAMES TO HIM. THAT SAME GAME DEVELOPED INTO MONKEY MARTIAL ARTS. EVEN THE MONKEY DANCE, WHICH IS SAID TO BE THE ORIGINS OF MONKEY MARTIAL ARTS, WAS JUST A DANCE HE DID WITH HIS BELOVED LONG AGO. BY DOING THE MONKEY DANCE, THE PROBLEM CHILD BECOMES A ROMANTIC AND REMEMBERS THE GOOD TIMES WITH HIS LATE LOVER.

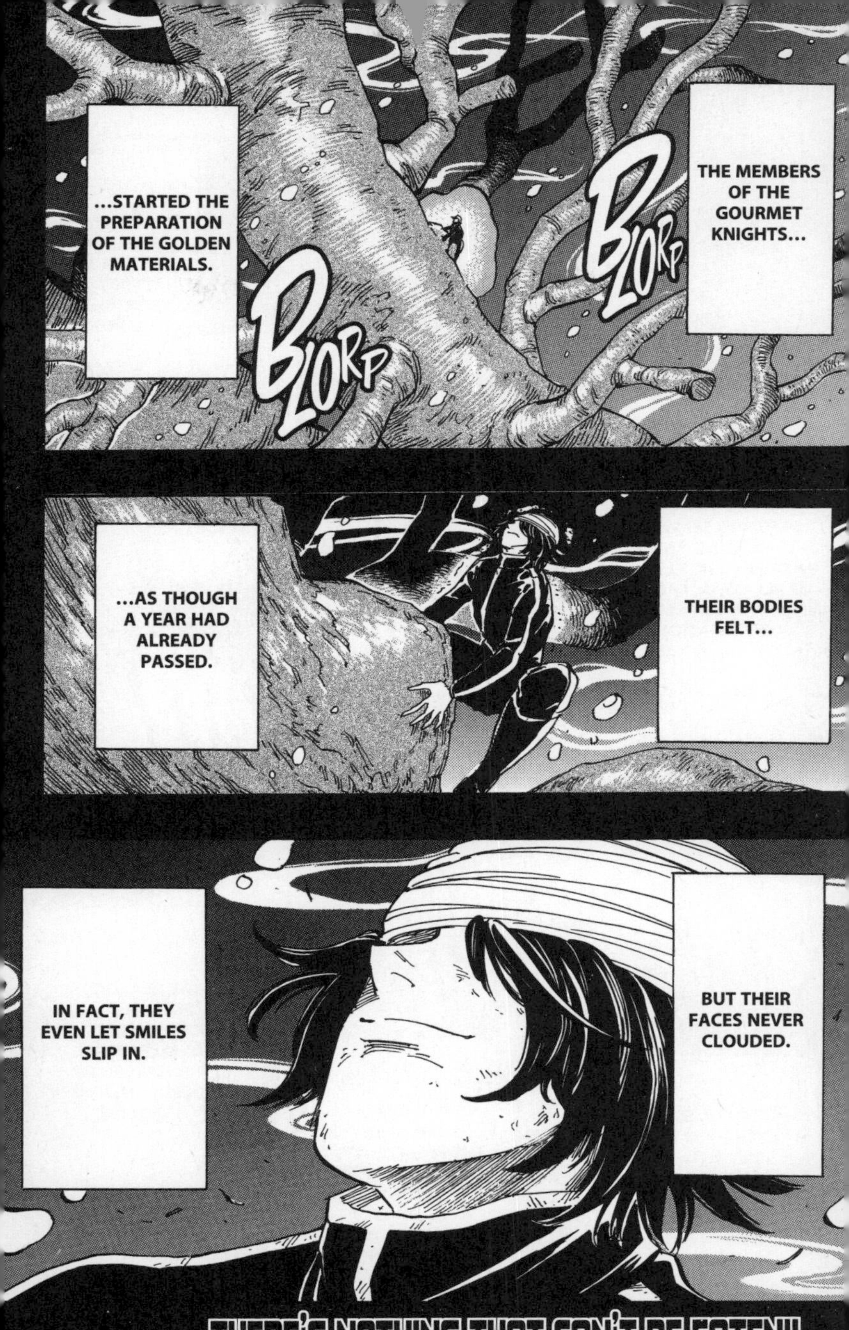
THE MEMBERS OF THE GOURMET KNIGHTS...
BLORP
...STARTED THE PREPARATION OF THE GOLDEN MATERIALS.
BLORP
THEIR BODIES FELT...
...AS THOUGH A YEAR HAD ALREADY PASSED.
BUT THEIR FACES NEVER CLOUDED.
IN FACT, THEY EVEN LET SMILES SLIP IN.

GOURMET 348: THERE'S NOTHING THAT CAN'T BE EATEN!!

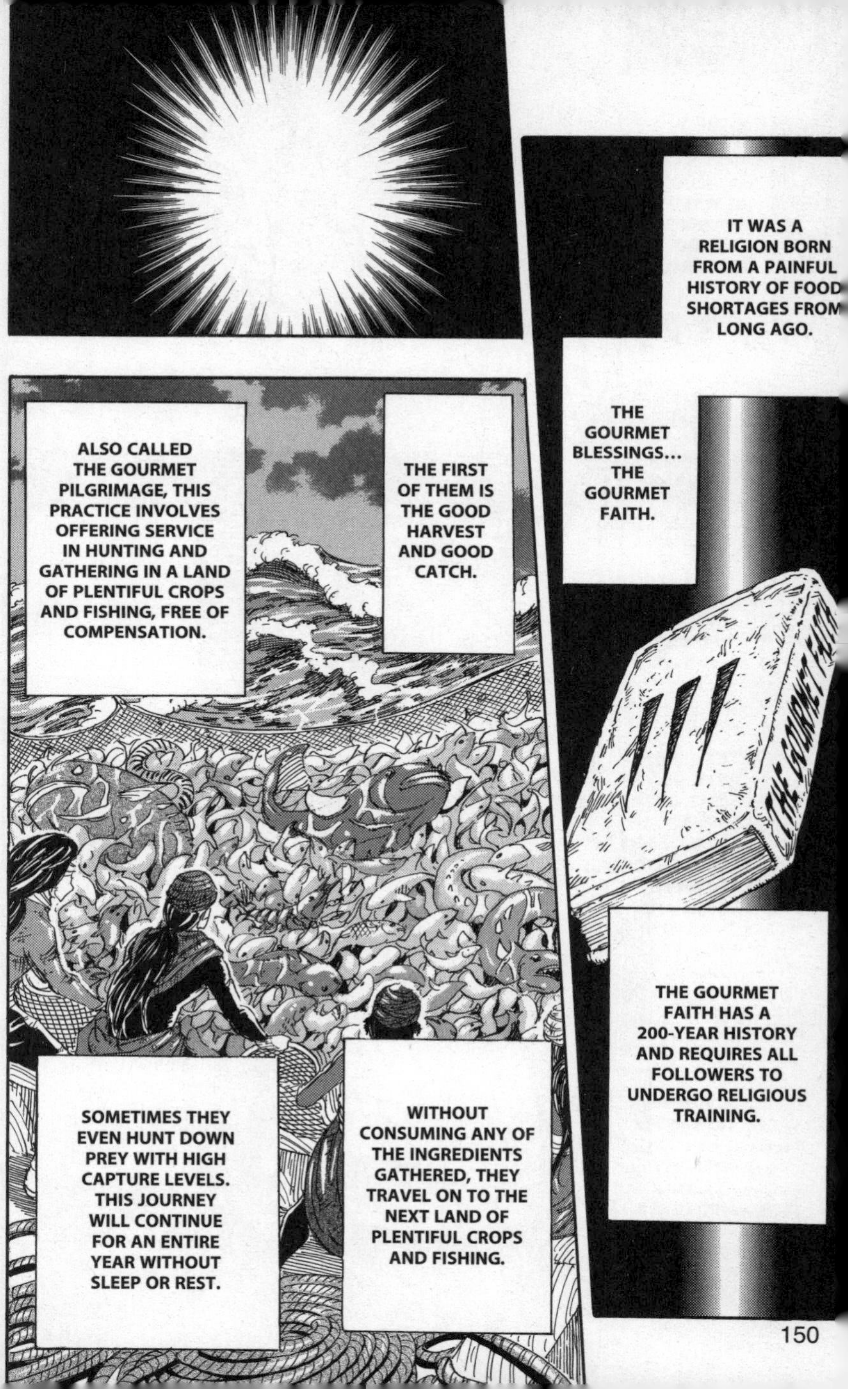
IT WAS A RELIGION BORN FROM A PAINFUL HISTORY OF FOOD SHORTAGES FROM LONG AGO.
THE GOURMET BLESSINGS... THE GOURMET FAITH.
THE GOURMET FAITH
THE GOURMET FAITH HAS A 200-YEAR HISTORY AND REQUIRES ALL FOLLOWERS TO UNDERGO RELIGIOUS TRAINING.
THE FIRST OF THEM IS THE GOOD HARVEST AND GOOD CATCH.
ALSO CALLED THE GOURMET PILGRIMAGE, THIS PRACTICE INVOLVES OFFERING SERVICE IN HUNTING AND GATHERING IN A LAND OF PLENTIFUL CROPS AND FISHING, FREE OF COMPENSATION.
WITHOUT CONSUMING ANY OF THE INGREDIENTS GATHERED, THEY TRAVEL ON TO THE NEXT LAND OF PLENTIFUL CROPS AND FISHING.
SOMETIMES THEY EVEN HUNT DOWN PREY WITH HIGH CAPTURE LEVELS. THIS JOURNEY WILL CONTINUE FOR AN ENTIRE YEAR WITHOUT SLEEP OR REST.

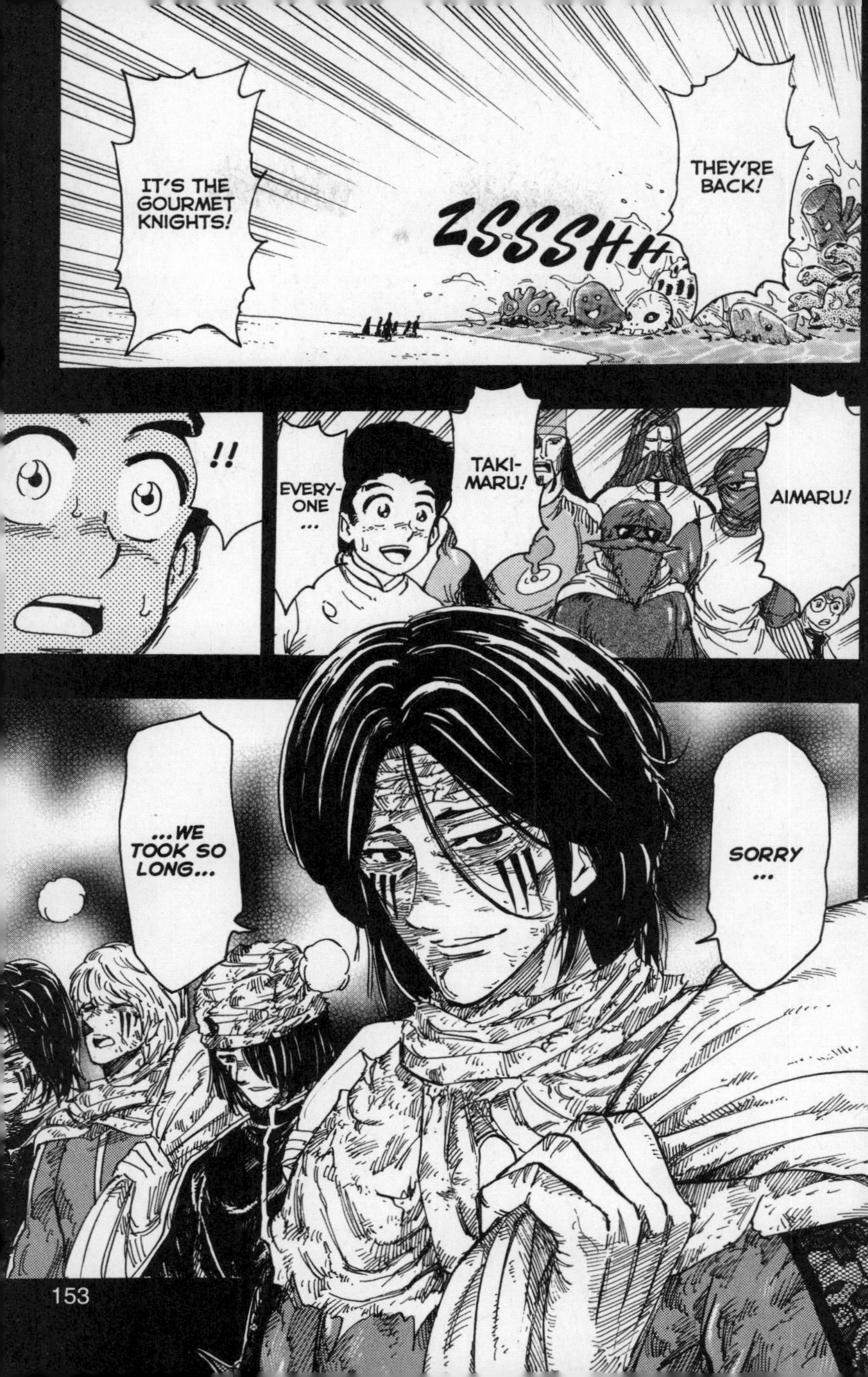
THEY'RE BACK!
ZSSSHH
IT'S THE GOURMET KNIGHTS!
AIMARU!
TAKI-MARU!
EVERY-ONE ...
!!
SORRY ...
...WE TOOK SO LONG...

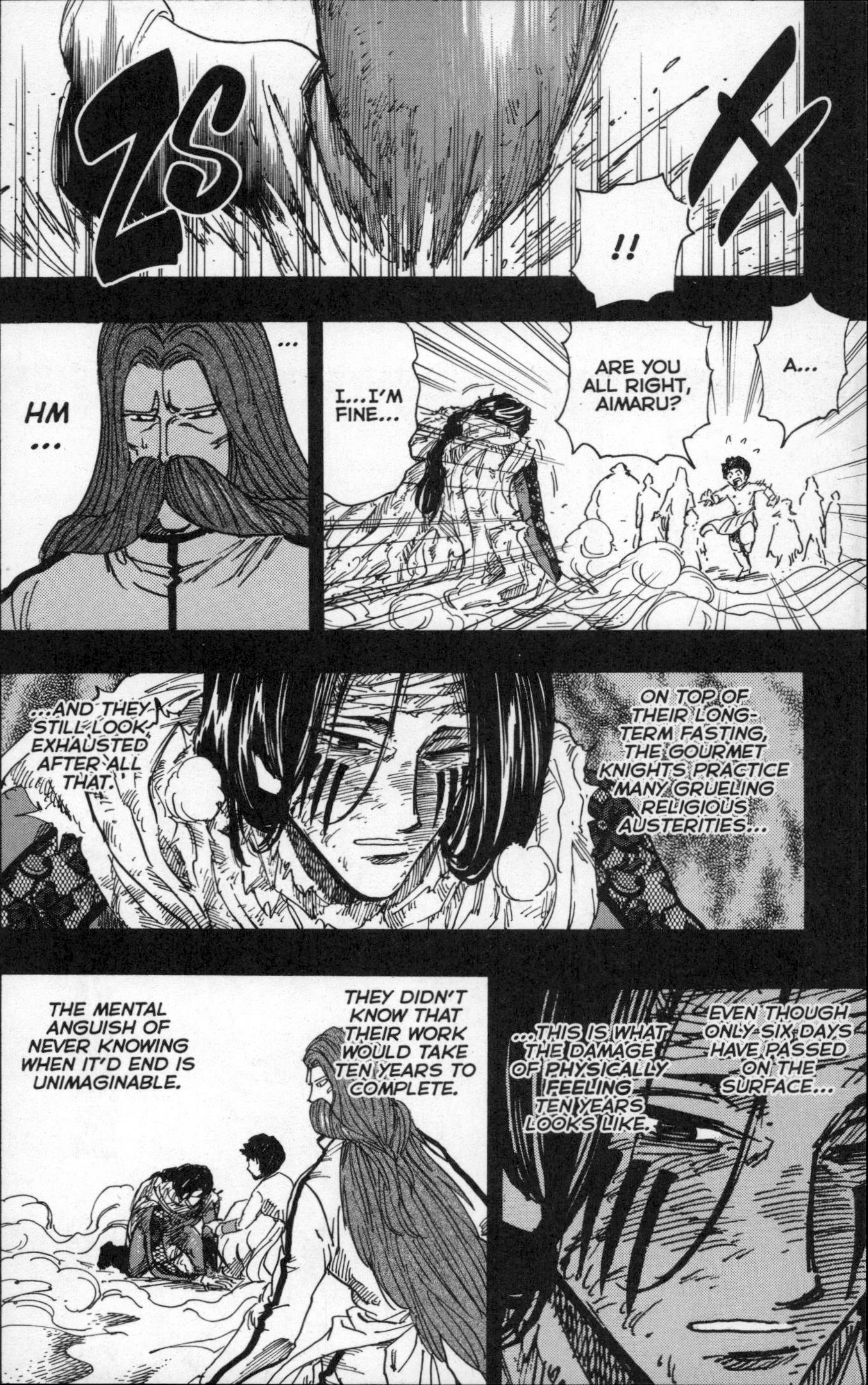
!!
ZS
A...
ARE YOU ALL RIGHT, AIMARU?
I...I'M FINE...
...
HM ...
ON TOP OF THEIR LONG-TERM FASTING, THE GOURMET KNIGHTS PRACTICE MANY GRUELING RELIGIOUS AUSTERITIES...
...AND THEY STILL LOOK EXHAUSTED AFTER ALL THAT.
EVEN THOUGH ONLY SIX DAYS HAVE PASSED ON THE SURFACE...
...THIS IS WHAT THE DAMAGE OF PHYSICALLY FEELING TEN YEARS LOOKS LIKE.
THEY DIDN'T KNOW THAT THEIR WORK WOULD TAKE TEN YEARS TO COMPLETE.
THE MENTAL ANGUISH OF NEVER KNOWING WHEN IT'D END IS UNIMAGINABLE.

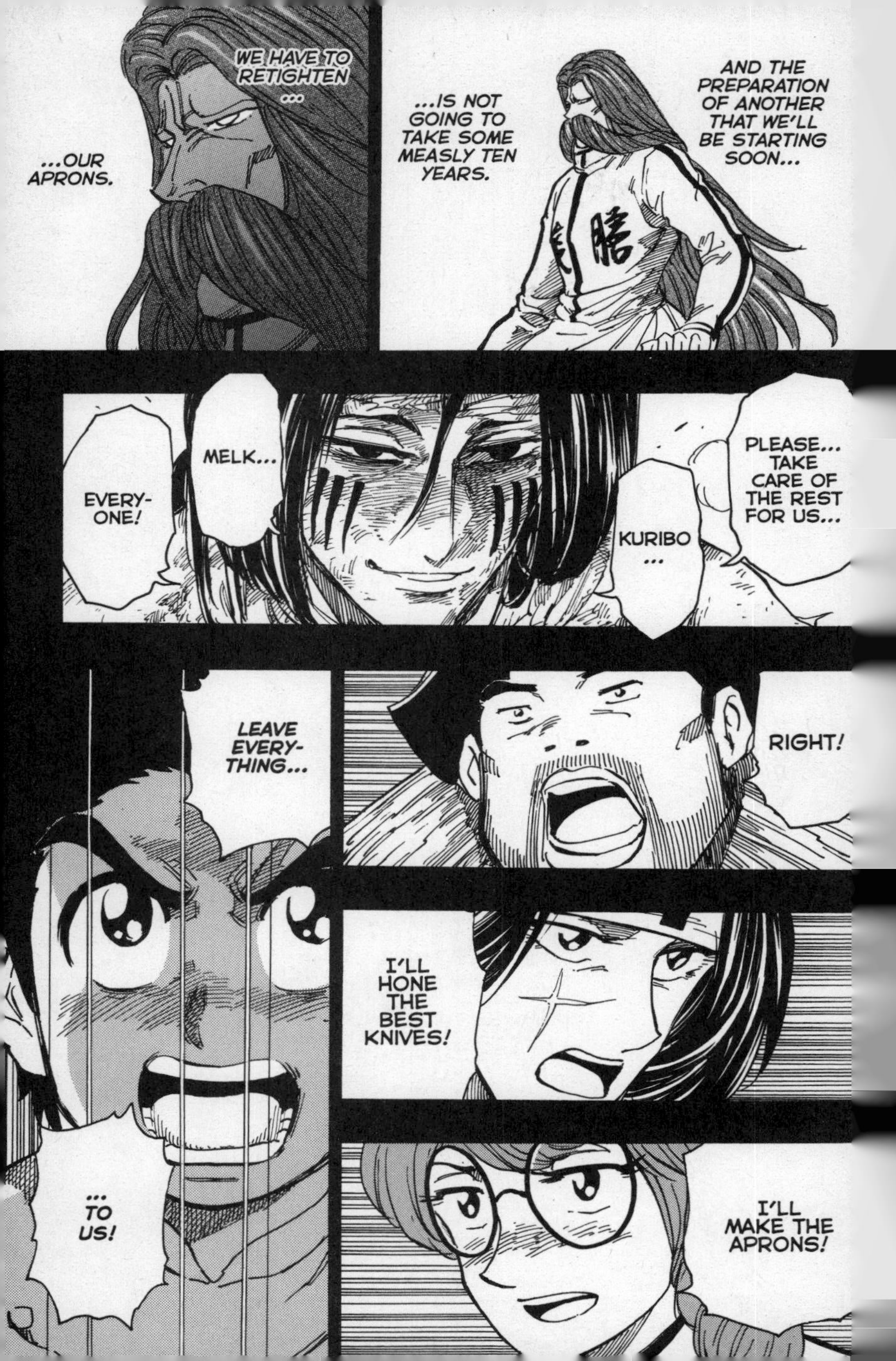
AND THE PREPARATION OF ANOTHER THAT WE'LL BE STARTING SOON...
...IS NOT GOING TO TAKE SOME MEASLY TEN YEARS.
WE HAVE TO RETIGHTEN ...
...OUR APRONS.
PLEASE... TAKE CARE OF THE REST FOR US...
KURIBO ...
MELK...
EVERY-ONE!
RIGHT!
I'LL HONE THE BEST KNIVES!
I'LL MAKE THE APRONS!
LEAVE EVERY-THING...
... TO US!

GOURMET 348: THERE'S NOTHING THAT CAN'T BE EATEN!!

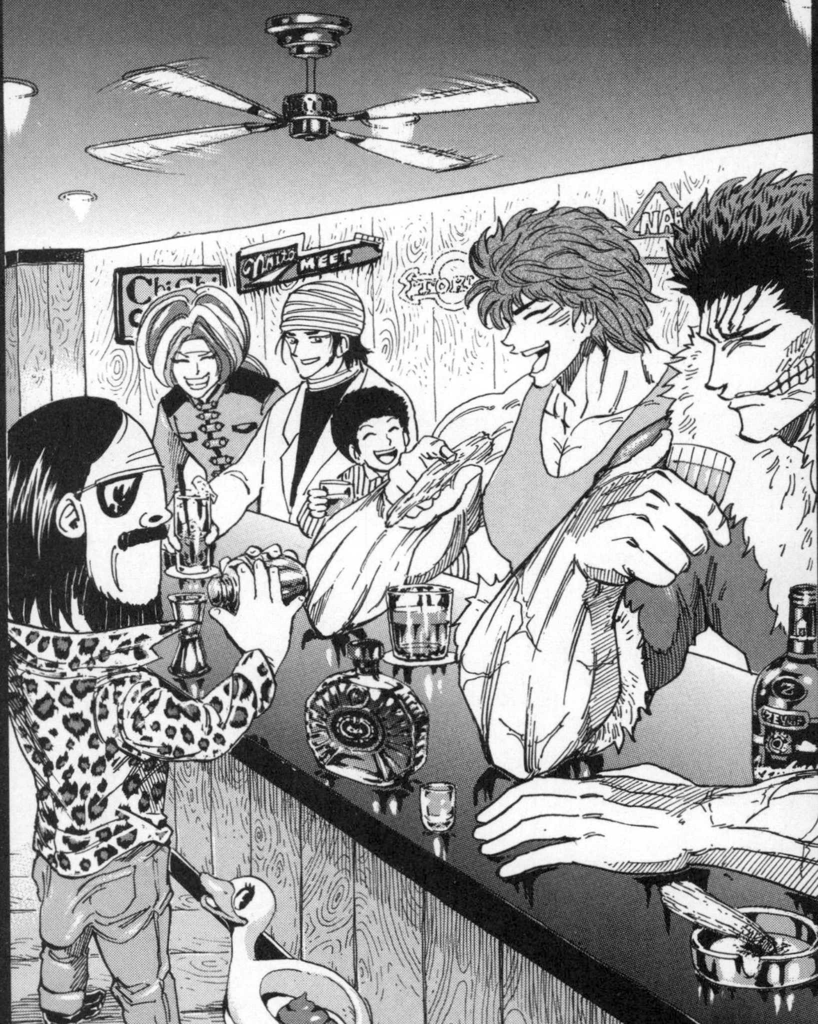
MEET

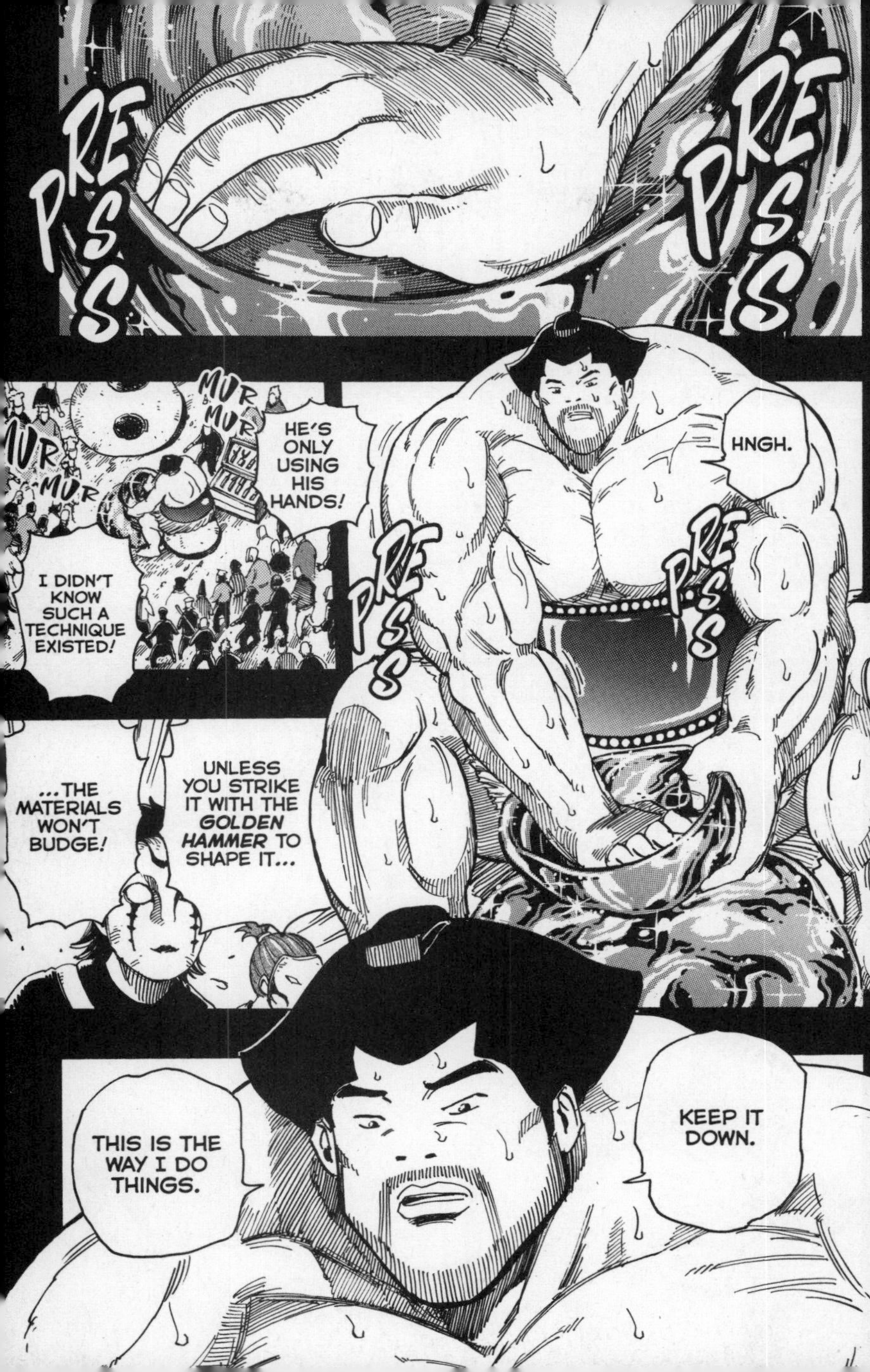
PRESS
PRESS
HNGH.
PRESS
PRESS
MUR MUR
MUR MUR
HE'S ONLY USING HIS HANDS!
I DIDN'T KNOW SUCH A TECHNIQUE EXISTED!
UNLESS YOU STRIKE IT WITH THE *GOLDEN HAMMER* TO SHAPE IT...
...THE MATERIALS WON'T BUDGE!
KEEP IT DOWN.
THIS IS THE WAY I DO THINGS.

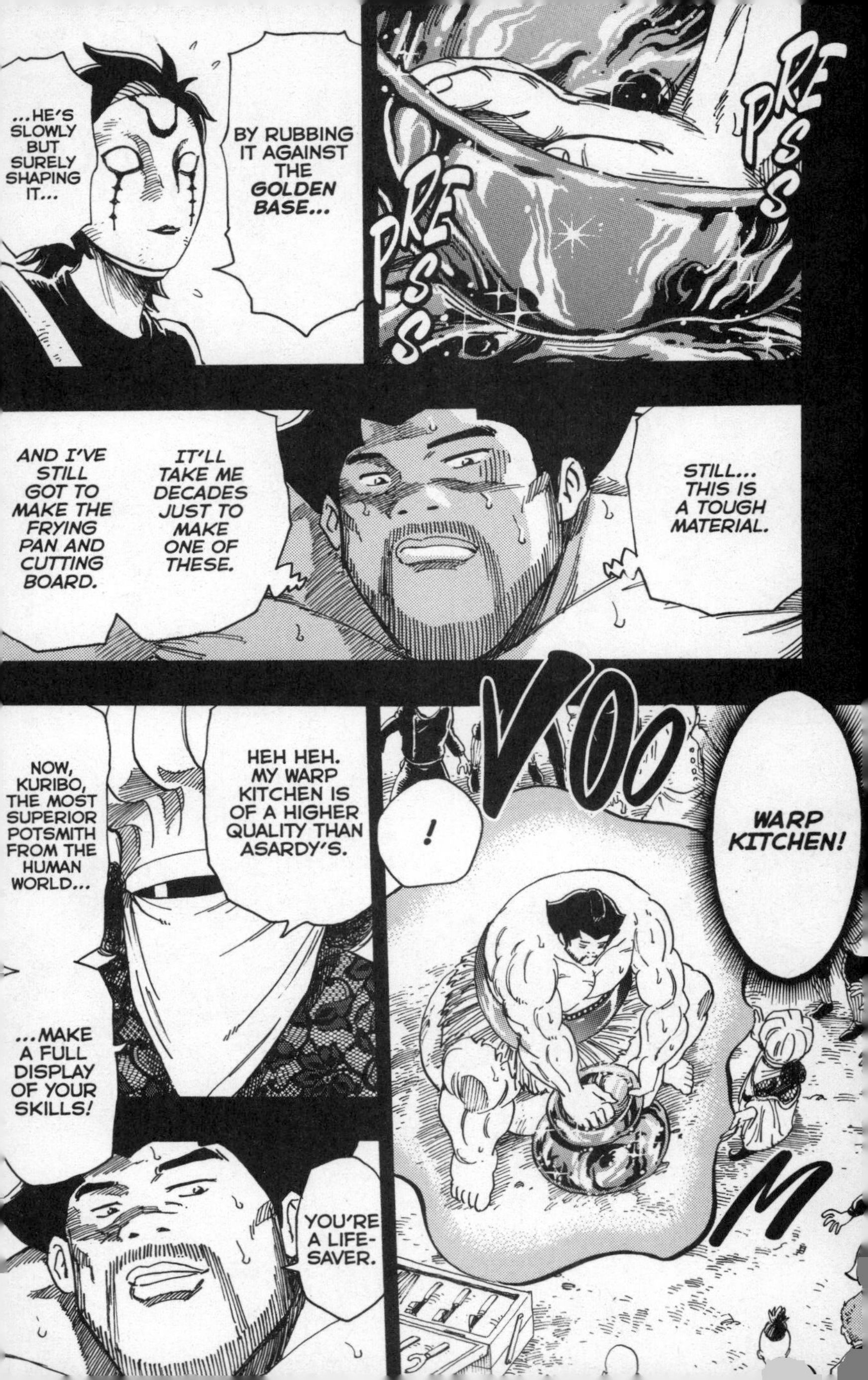
PRESS
PRESS
BY RUBBING IT AGAINST THE GOLDEN BASE...
...HE'S SLOWLY BUT SURELY SHAPING IT...
STILL... THIS IS A TOUGH MATERIAL.
IT'LL TAKE ME DECADES JUST TO MAKE ONE OF THESE.
AND I'VE STILL GOT TO MAKE THE FRYING PAN AND CUTTING BOARD.
WARP KITCHEN!
VOOM
!
HEH HEH. MY WARP KITCHEN IS OF A HIGHER QUALITY THAN ASARDY'S.
NOW, KURIBO, THE MOST SUPERIOR POTSMITH FROM THE HUMAN WORLD...
...MAKE A FULL DISPLAY OF YOUR SKILLS!
YOU'RE A LIFE-SAVER.

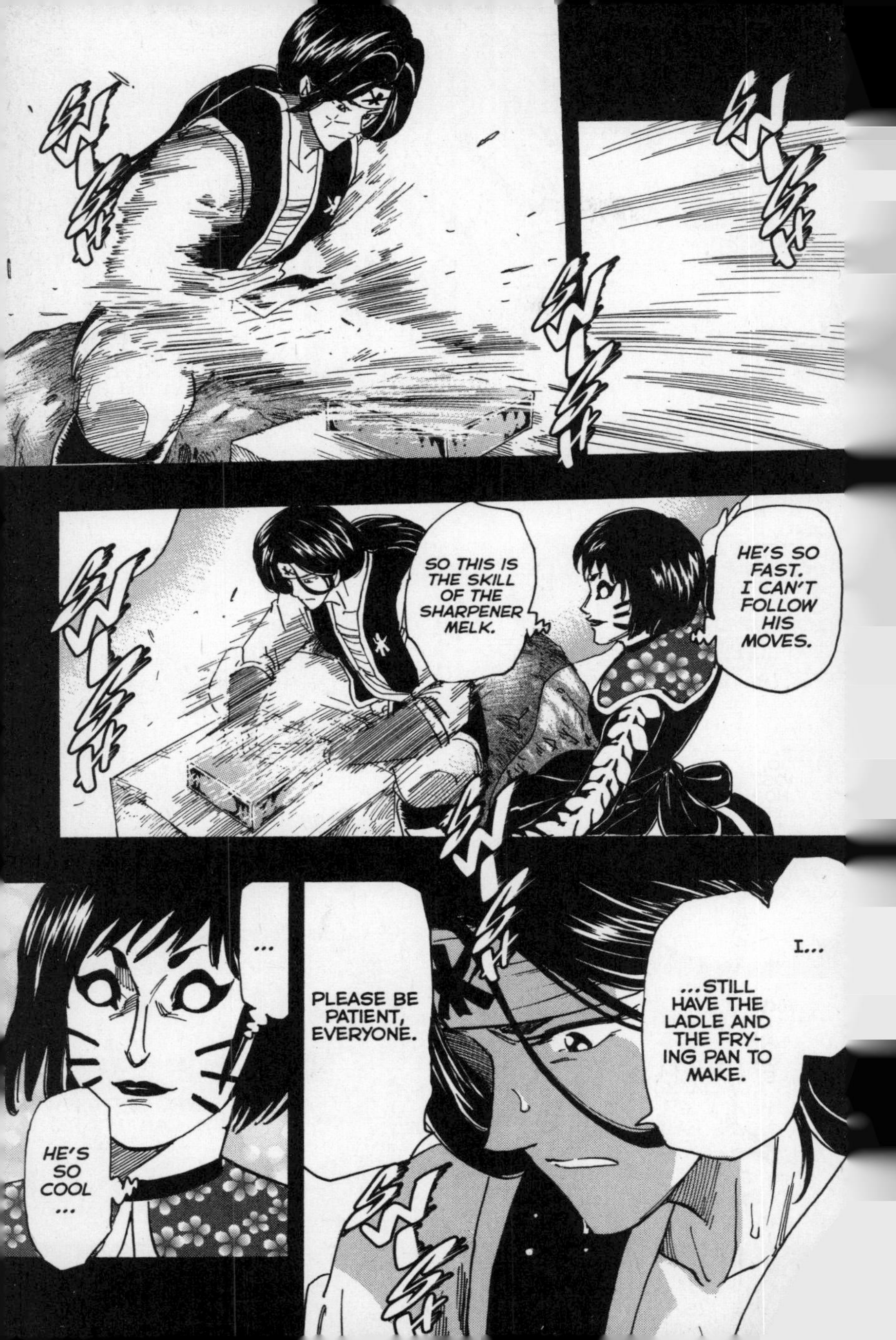
HE'S SO FAST. I CAN'T FOLLOW HIS MOVES.
SO THIS IS THE SKILL OF THE SHARPENER MELK.
I...
...STILL HAVE THE LADLE AND THE FRYING PAN TO MAKE.
PLEASE BE PATIENT, EVERYONE.
...
HE'S SO COOL...

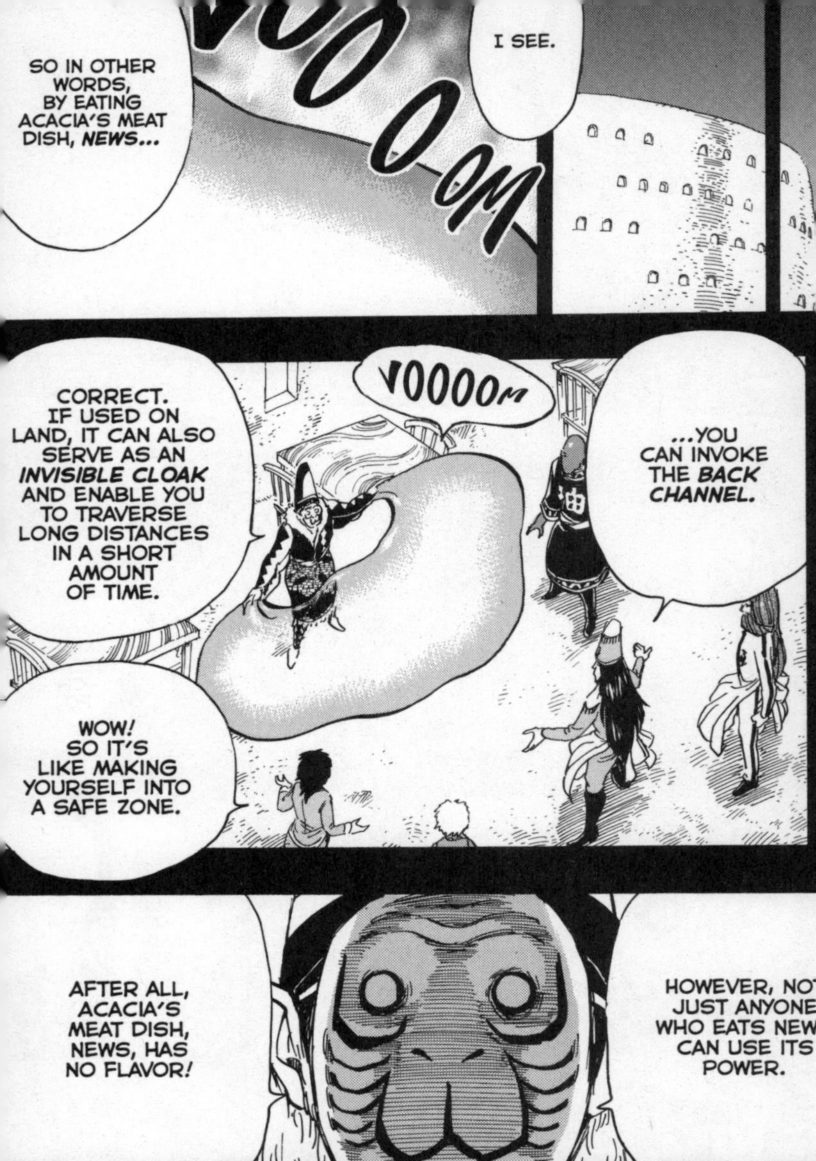
I SEE.
VOOOOM
SO IN OTHER WORDS, BY EATING ACACIA'S MEAT DISH, *NEWS*...
...YOU CAN INVOKE THE *BACK CHANNEL.*
VOOOOM
CORRECT. IF USED ON LAND, IT CAN ALSO SERVE AS AN *INVISIBLE CLOAK* AND ENABLE YOU TO TRAVERSE LONG DISTANCES IN A SHORT AMOUNT OF TIME.
WOW! SO IT'S LIKE MAKING YOURSELF INTO A SAFE ZONE.
HOWEVER, NOT JUST ANYONE WHO EATS NEW CAN USE ITS POWER.
AFTER ALL, ACACIA'S MEAT DISH, NEWS, HAS NO FLAVOR!

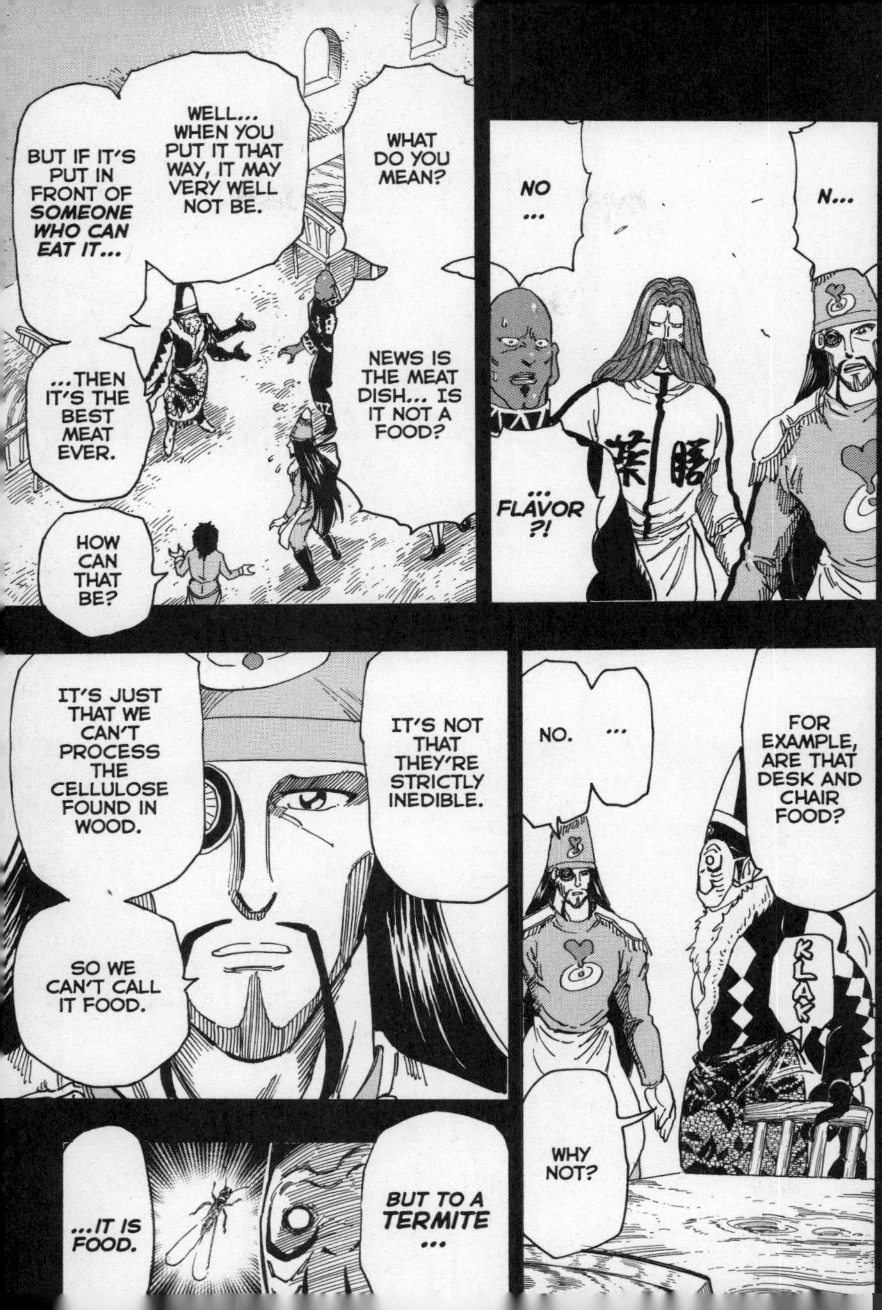
N...
NO ...
... FLAVOR ?!
WHAT DO YOU MEAN?
WELL... WHEN YOU PUT IT THAT WAY, IT MAY VERY WELL NOT BE.
BUT IF IT'S PUT IN FRONT OF SOMEONE WHO CAN EAT IT...
NEWS IS THE MEAT DISH... IS IT NOT A FOOD?
...THEN IT'S THE BEST MEAT EVER.
HOW CAN THAT BE?
FOR EXAMPLE, ARE THAT DESK AND CHAIR FOOD?
NO. ...
KLAK
WHY NOT?
IT'S NOT THAT THEY'RE STRICTLY INEDIBLE.
IT'S JUST THAT WE CAN'T PROCESS THE CELLULOSE FOUND IN WOOD.
SO WE CAN'T CALL IT FOOD.
BUT TO A TERMITE ...
...IT IS FOOD.

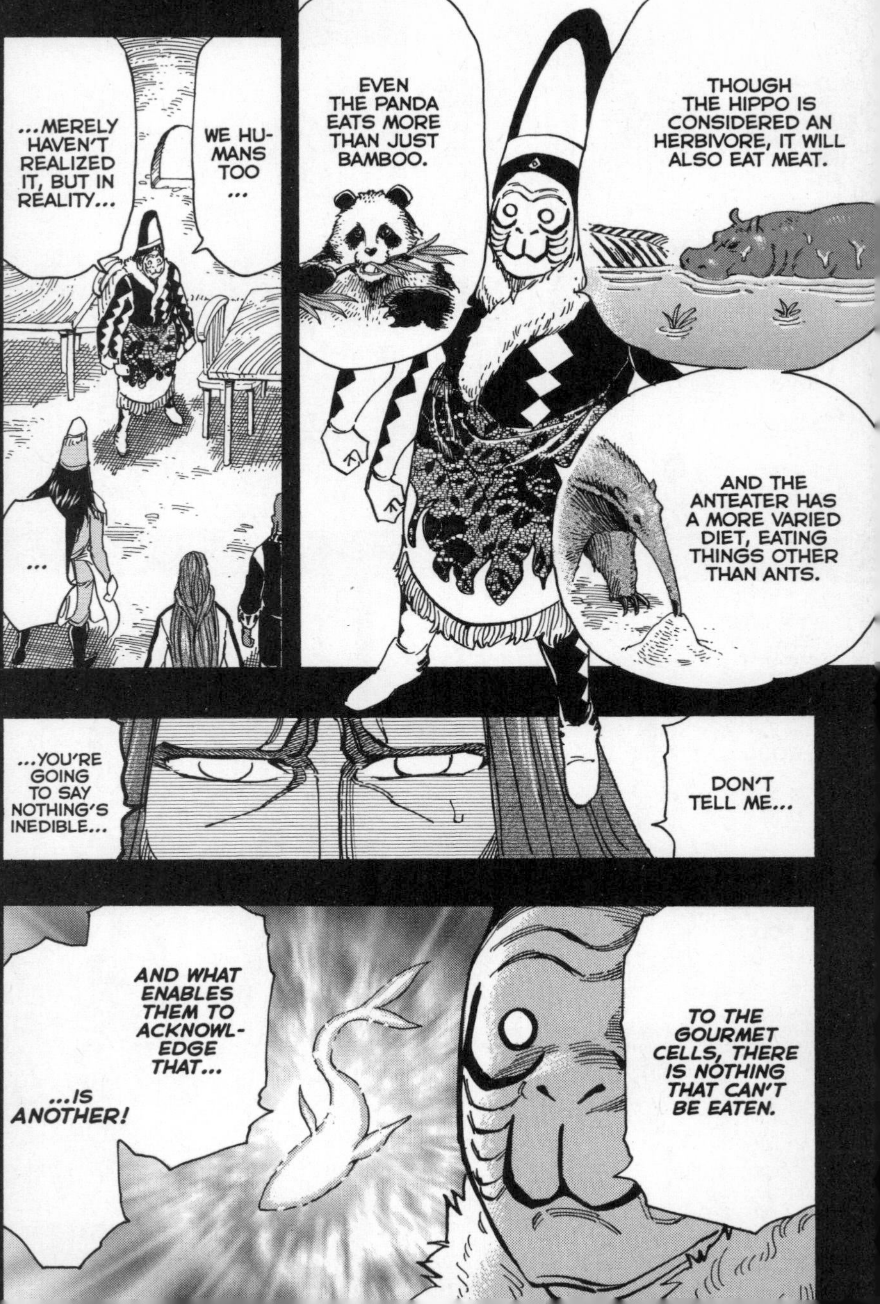
THOUGH THE HIPPO IS CONSIDERED AN HERBIVORE, IT WILL ALSO EAT MEAT.
EVEN THE PANDA EATS MORE THAN JUST BAMBOO.
AND THE ANTEATER HAS A MORE VARIED DIET, EATING THINGS OTHER THAN ANTS.
WE HU-MANS TOO ...
...MERELY HAVEN'T REALIZED IT, BUT IN REALITY...
...
DON'T TELL ME...
...YOU'RE GOING TO SAY NOTHING'S INEDIBLE...
TO THE GOURMET CELLS, THERE IS NOTHING THAT CAN'T BE EATEN.
AND WHAT ENABLES THEM TO ACKNOWL-EDGE THAT...
...IS ANOTHER!

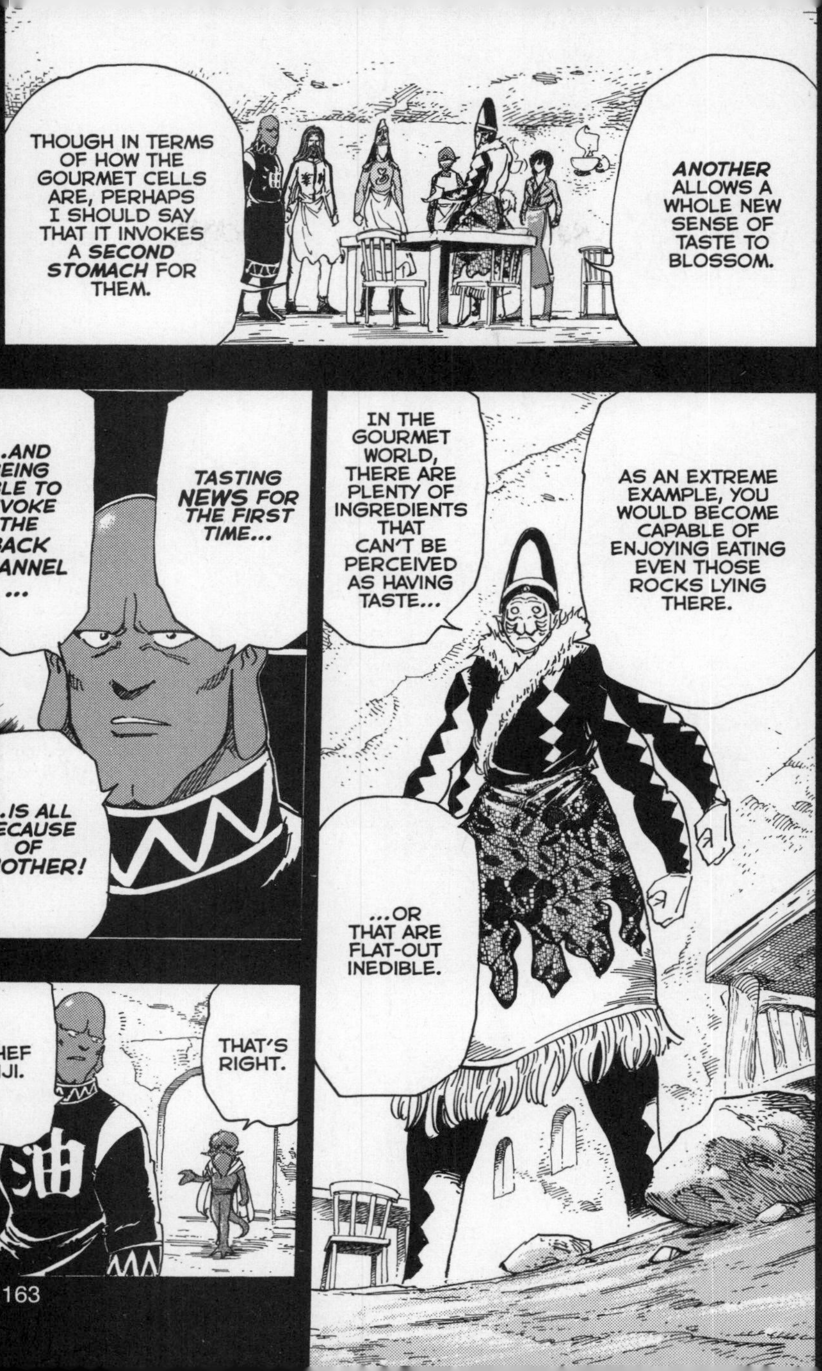

ANOTHER ALLOWS A WHOLE NEW SENSE OF TASTE TO BLOSSOM.
THOUGH IN TERMS OF HOW THE GOURMET CELLS ARE, PERHAPS I SHOULD SAY THAT IT INVOKES A *SECOND STOMACH* FOR THEM.
IN THE GOURMET WORLD, THERE ARE PLENTY OF INGREDIENTS THAT CAN'T BE PERCEIVED AS HAVING TASTE...
...OR THAT ARE FLAT-OUT INEDIBLE.
AS AN EXTREME EXAMPLE, YOU WOULD BECOME CAPABLE OF ENJOYING EATING EVEN THOSE ROCKS LYING THERE.
TASTING *NEWS* FOR THE FIRST TIME...
...AND BEING ABLE TO INVOKE THE *BACK CHANNEL*...
...IS ALL BECAUSE OF *ANOTHER!*
THAT'S RIGHT.
CHEF JIJI.

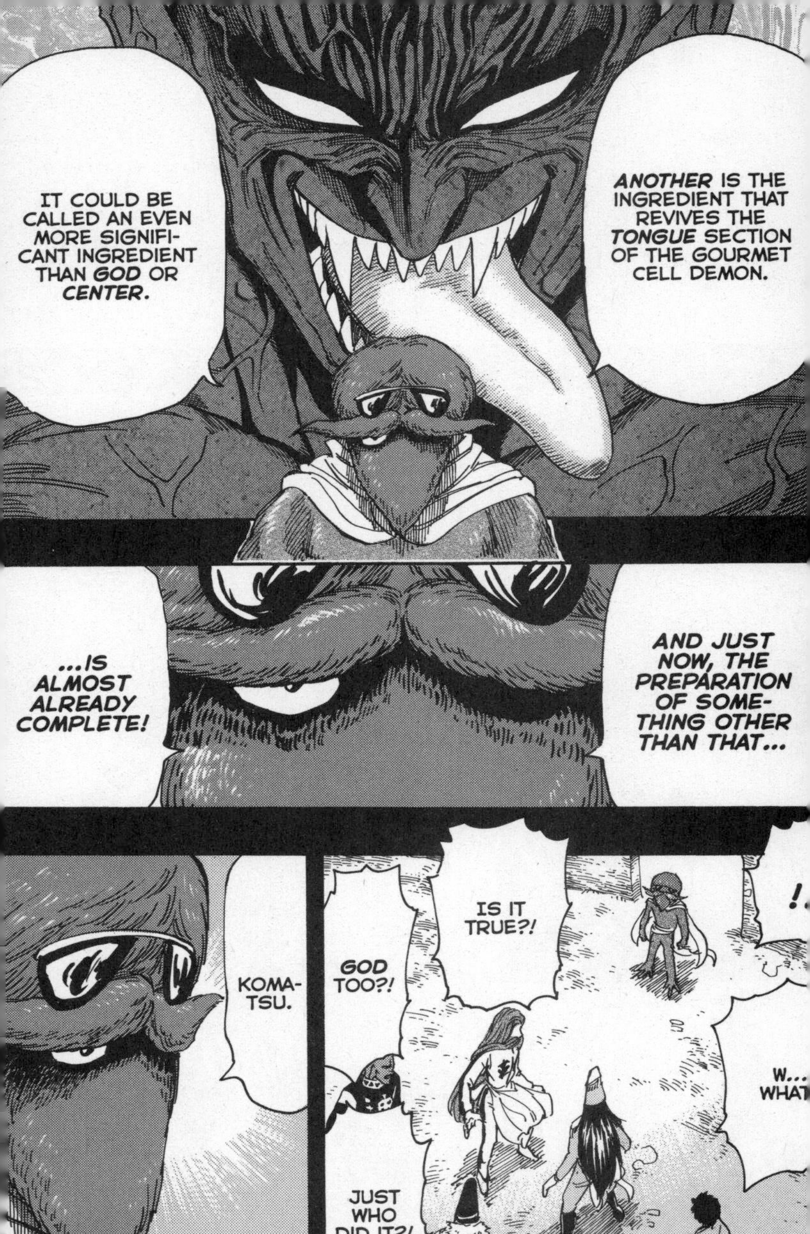
ANOTHER IS THE INGREDIENT THAT REVIVES THE TONGUE SECTION OF THE GOURMET CELL DEMON.
IT COULD BE CALLED AN EVEN MORE SIGNIFICANT INGREDIENT THAN GOD OR CENTER.
AND JUST NOW, THE PREPARATION OF SOMETHING OTHER THAN THAT...
...IS ALMOST ALREADY COMPLETE!
!
W... WHAT
IS IT TRUE?!
GOD TOO?!
JUST WHO DID IT?!
KOMATSU.

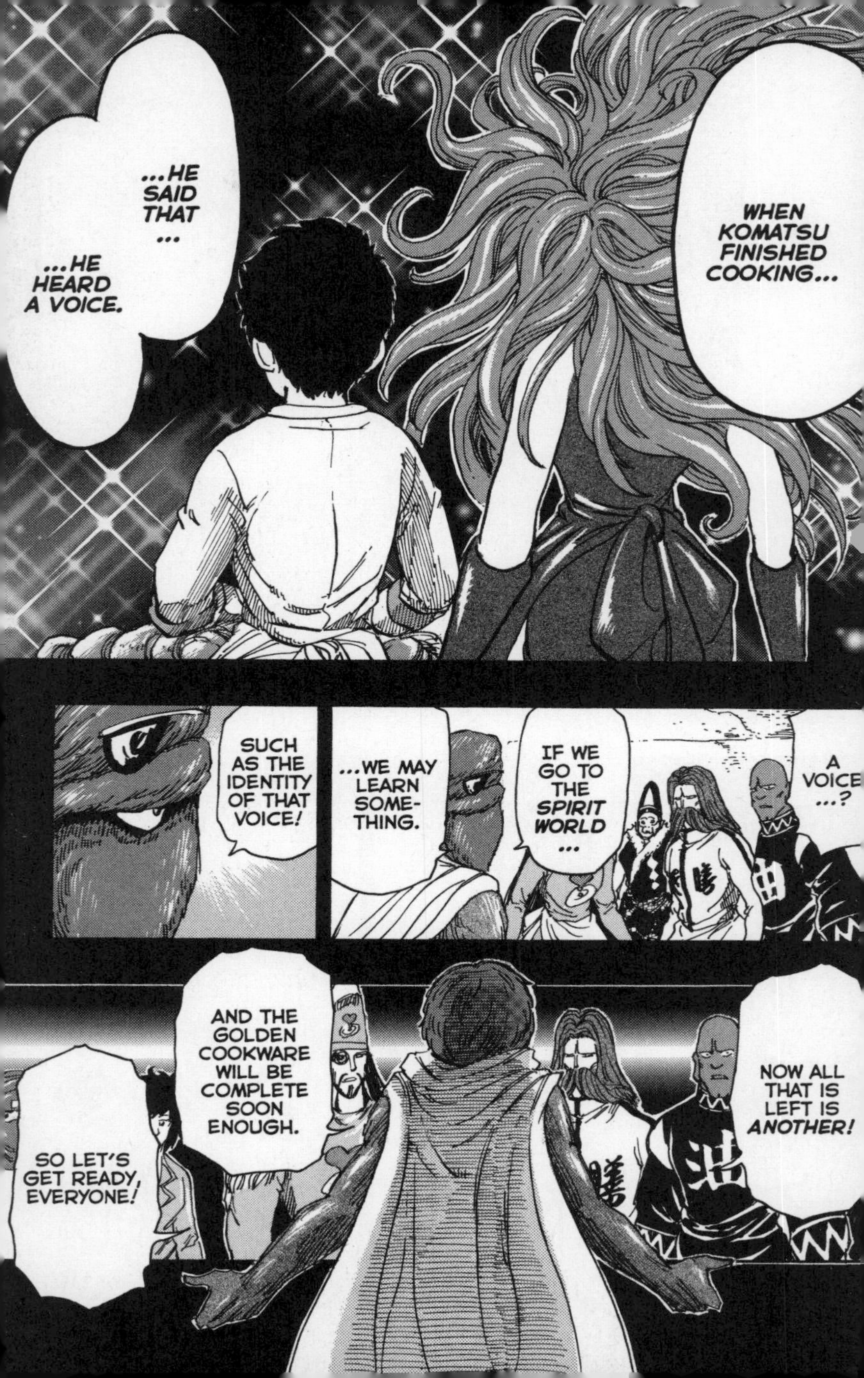
WHEN KOMATSU FINISHED COOKING...
...HE SAID THAT...
...HE HEARD A VOICE.
A VOICE...?
IF WE GO TO THE SPIRIT WORLD...
...WE MAY LEARN SOMETHING.
SUCH AS THE IDENTITY OF THAT VOICE!
NOW ALL THAT IS LEFT IS ANOTHER!
AND THE GOLDEN COOKWARE WILL BE COMPLETE SOON ENOUGH.
SO LET'S GET READY, EVERYONE!

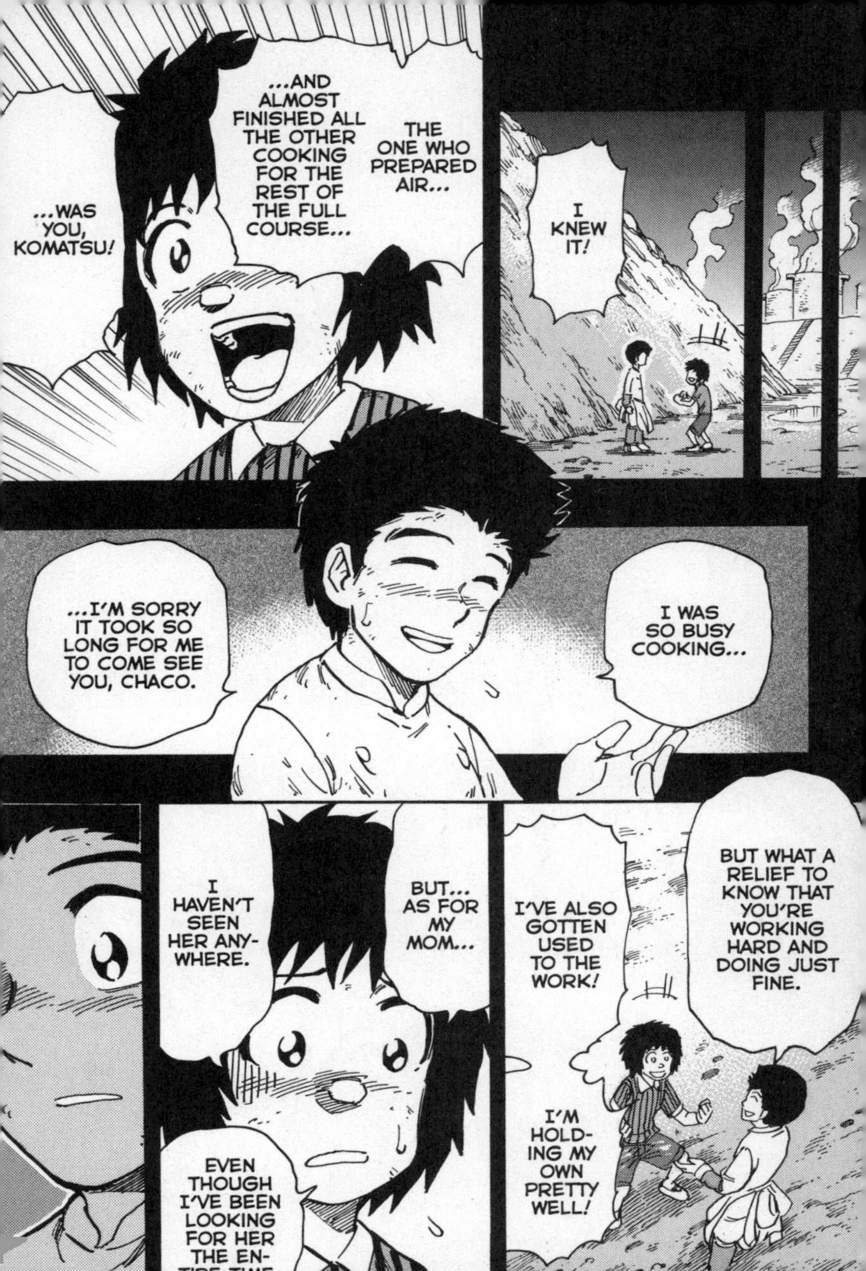
I KNEW IT!
THE ONE WHO PREPARED AIR...
...AND ALMOST FINISHED ALL THE OTHER COOKING FOR THE REST OF THE FULL COURSE...
...WAS YOU, KOMATSU!
I WAS SO BUSY COOKING...
...I'M SORRY IT TOOK SO LONG FOR ME TO COME SEE YOU, CHACO.
BUT WHAT A RELIEF TO KNOW THAT YOU'RE WORKING HARD AND DOING JUST FINE.
I'VE ALSO GOTTEN USED TO THE WORK!
I'M HOLD-ING MY OWN PRETTY WELL!
BUT... AS FOR MY MOM...
I HAVEN'T SEEN HER ANY-WHERE.
EVEN THOUGH I'VE BEEN LOOKING FOR HER THE EN-

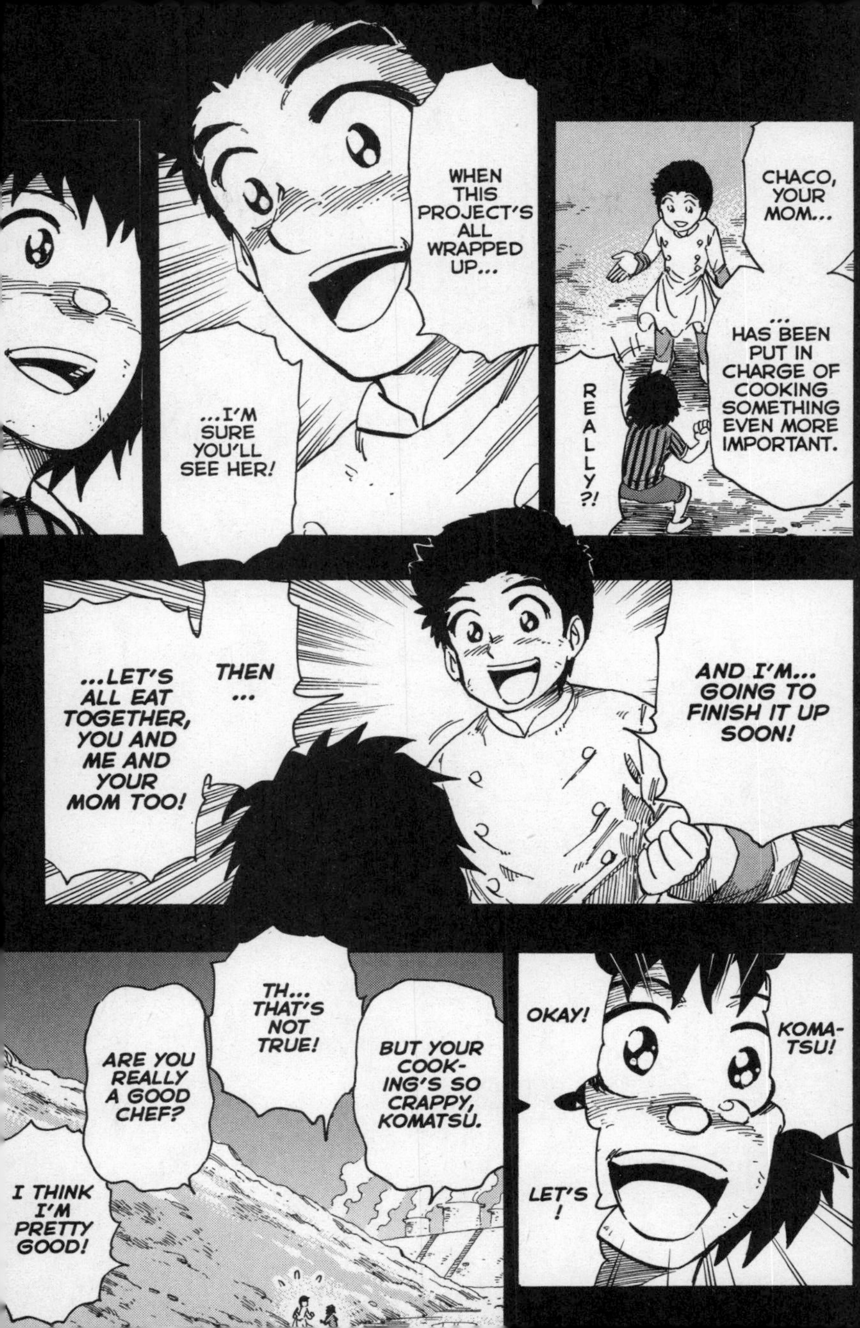
CHACO, YOUR MOM...
...HAS BEEN PUT IN CHARGE OF COOKING SOMETHING EVEN MORE IMPORTANT.
REALLY?!
WHEN THIS PROJECT'S ALL WRAPPED UP...
...I'M SURE YOU'LL SEE HER!
AND I'M... GOING TO FINISH IT UP SOON!
THEN...
...LET'S ALL EAT TOGETHER, YOU AND ME AND YOUR MOM TOO!
KOMA-TSU!
OKAY!
LET'S!
BUT YOUR COOK-ING'S SO CRAPPY, KOMATSU.
TH... THAT'S NOT TRUE!
ARE YOU REALLY A GOOD CHEF?
I THINK I'M PRETTY GOOD!

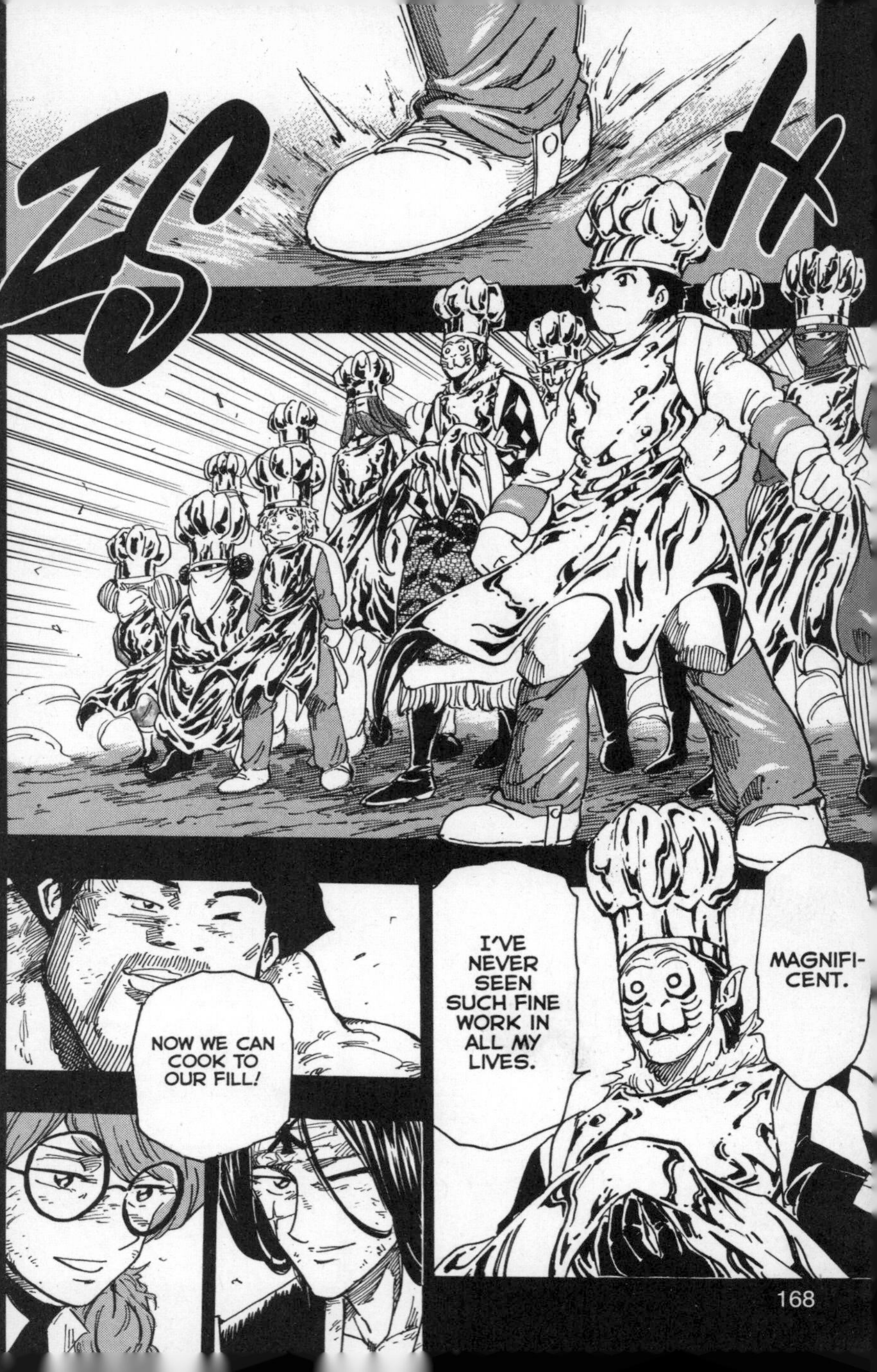
ZSH
MAGNIFI-CENT.
I'VE NEVER SEEN SUCH FINE WORK IN ALL MY LIVES.
NOW WE CAN COOK TO OUR FILL!

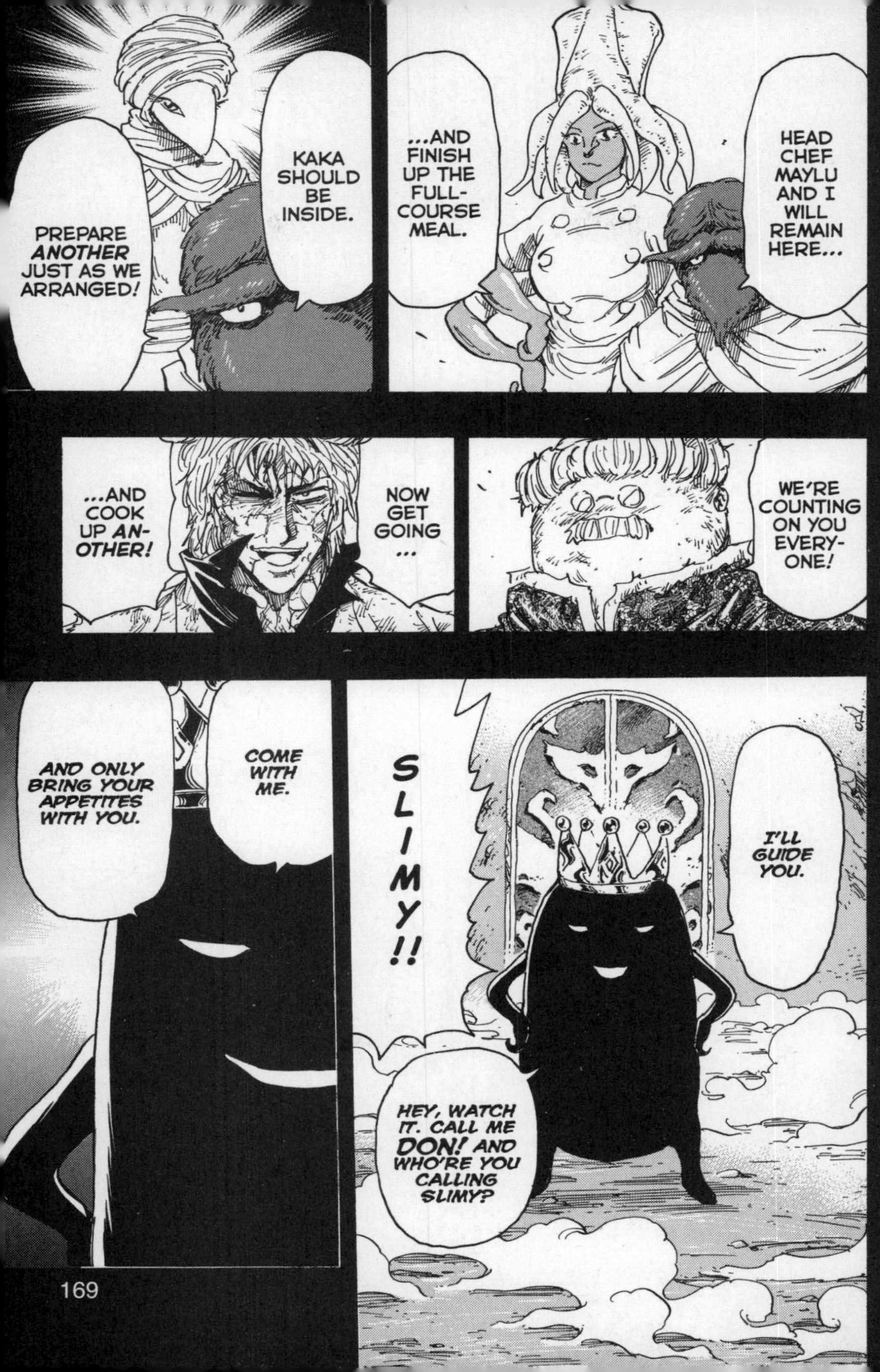
HEAD CHEF MAYLU AND I WILL REMAIN HERE...
...AND FINISH UP THE FULL-COURSE MEAL.
KAKA SHOULD BE INSIDE.
PREPARE ANOTHER JUST AS WE ARRANGED!
WE'RE COUNTING ON YOU EVERYONE!
NOW GET GOING...
...AND COOK UP ANOTHER!
I'LL GUIDE YOU.
SLIMY!!
HEY, WATCH IT. CALL ME DON! AND WHO'RE YOU CALLING SLIMY?
COME WITH ME.
AND ONLY BRING YOUR APPETITES WITH YOU.

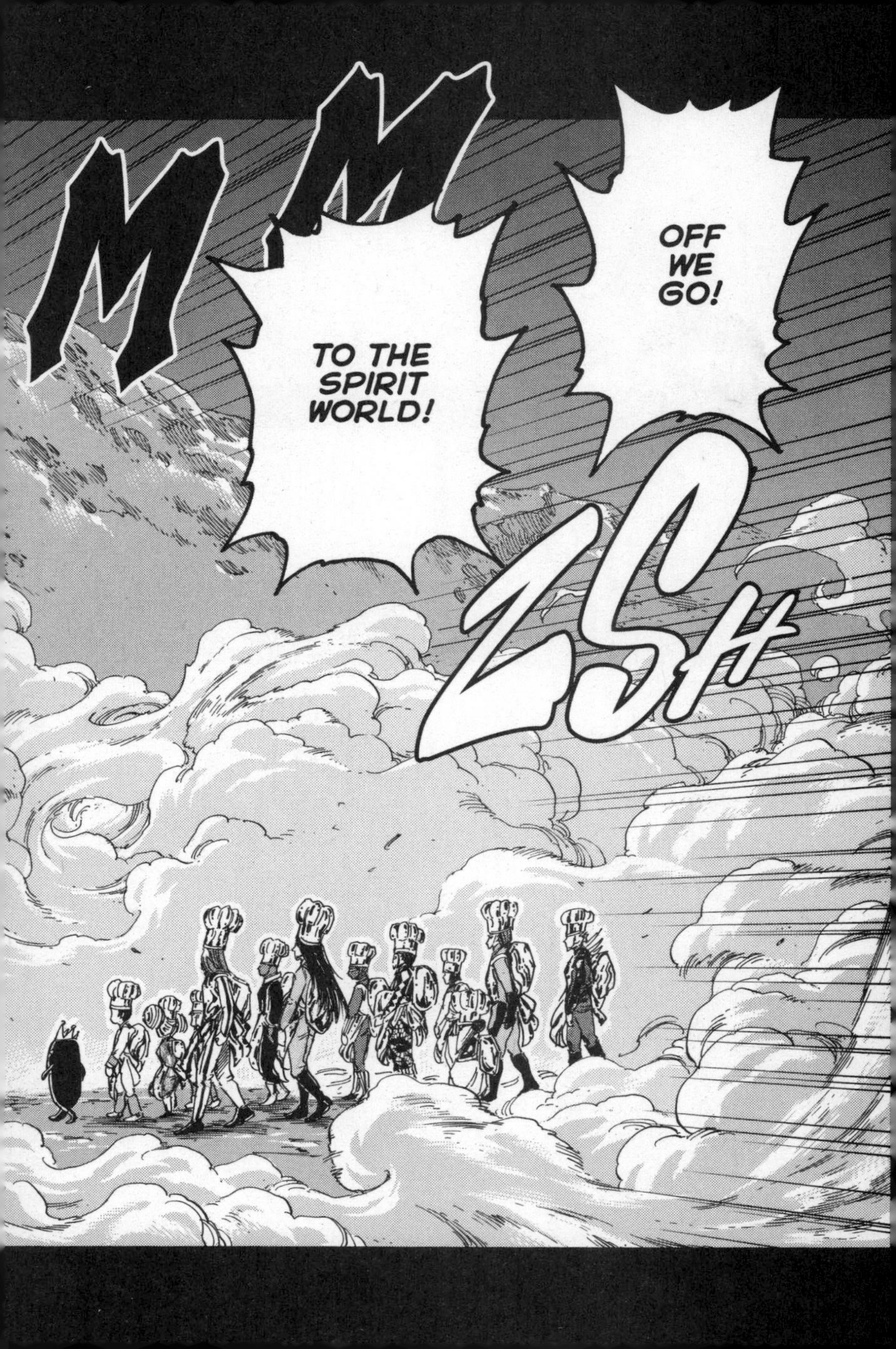
OFF WE GO!
TO THE SPIRIT WORLD!
MMM
ZSH

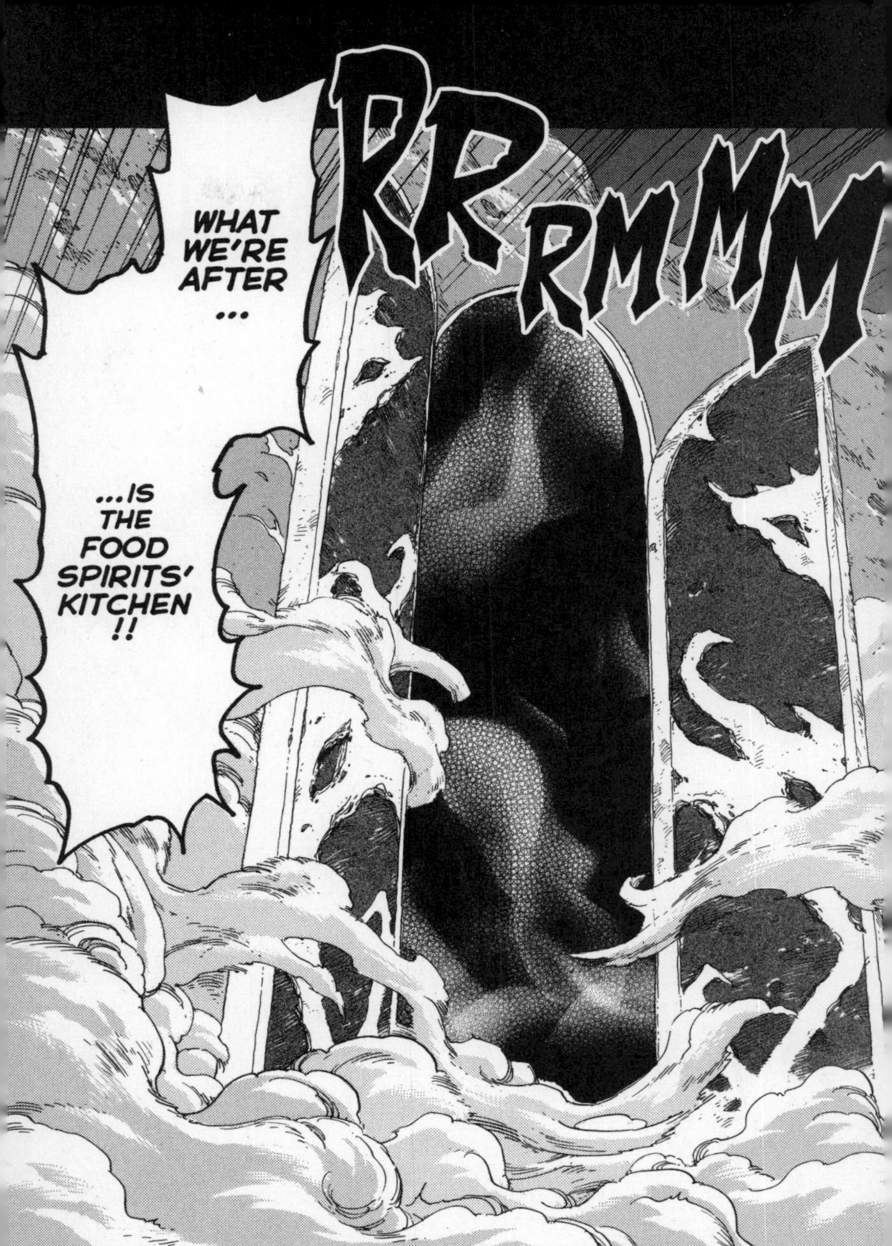
RRRMMM
WHAT WE'RE AFTER ...
...IS THE FOOD SPIRITS' KITCHEN !!

TORIKO

GOURMET CHECKLIST

Vol. 379

PAIR
(THE MONKEY KING'S BALLS)

CAPTURE LEVEL: 6,000
HABITAT: AREA 7
SIZE: 45 CM
HEIGHT: ---
WEIGHT: 1 TON
PRICE: NOT PRICED

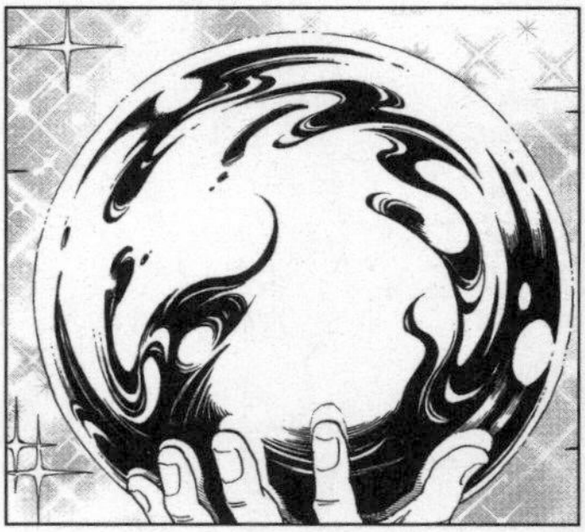

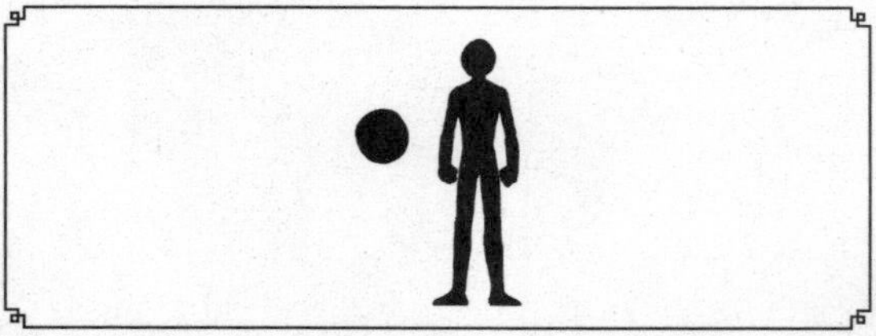

SCALE

THE FOOD TREASURE OF THE GOURMET WORLD'S AREA 7 AND THE SOUP DISH IN ACACIA'S FULL-COURSE MEAL. IT'S SO RICH IN NUTRIENTS THAT IT'S ABLE TO MAKE PLANTS AND ANIMALS GROW TO TREMENDOUS SIZES AND IS ALSO BLESSED WITH HEALING PROPERTIES THAT WILL REGENERATE ANY MISSING BODY PARTS. WHEN YOU DRINK A CERTAIN AMOUNT OF PAIR, ITS MYSTICAL FLAVOR WILL CAUSE YOUR BODY TO SWITCH TO THE OPPOSITE GENDER AND ENABLE YOU TO GAZE INTO THE BACK CHANNEL. THAT IS WHY THEY CALL THIS FOOD TREASURE THE DOUBLE-SIDED DROP. THE MORE THE MONKEY KING DANCES THE MONKEY DANCE, THE MORE DELICIOUS PAIR GROWS, AND ONLY BY DANCING IT TO COMPLETION IS IT POSSIBLE TO EVER CAPTURE IT. IT WOULD BE NO EXAGGERATION TO SAY THAT CAPTURING PAIR, WHICH ENTAILS FACING OFF AGAINST THE MONKEY KING, IS THE MOST DIFFICULT COURSE TO CAPTURE IN ACACIA'S FULL-COURSE MEAL.

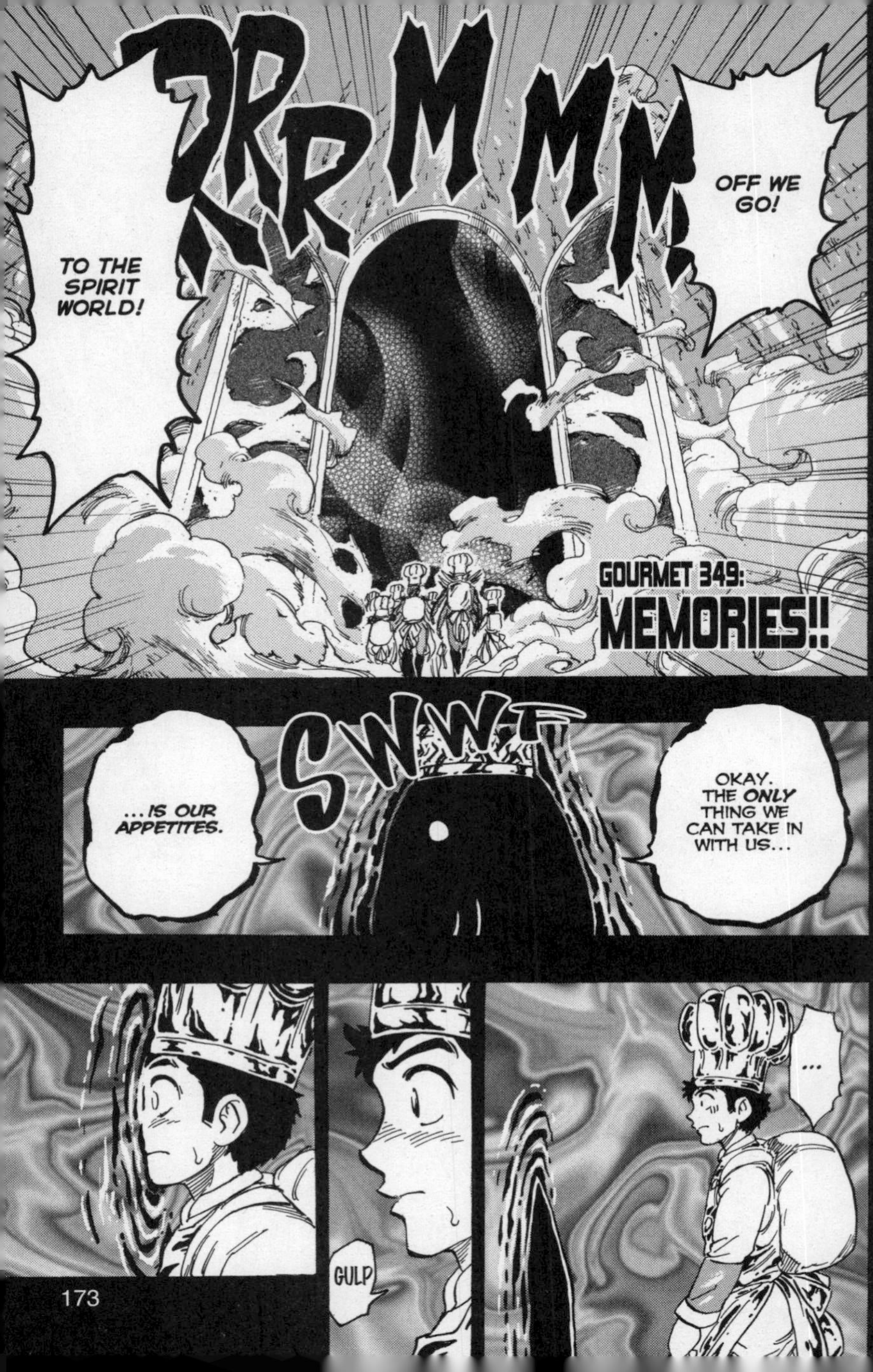
DRRMMM
OFF WE GO!
TO THE SPIRIT WORLD!
GOURMET 349: MEMORIES!!
SWWF
OKAY. THE *ONLY* THING WE CAN TAKE IN WITH US...
...IS OUR APPETITES.
...
GULP

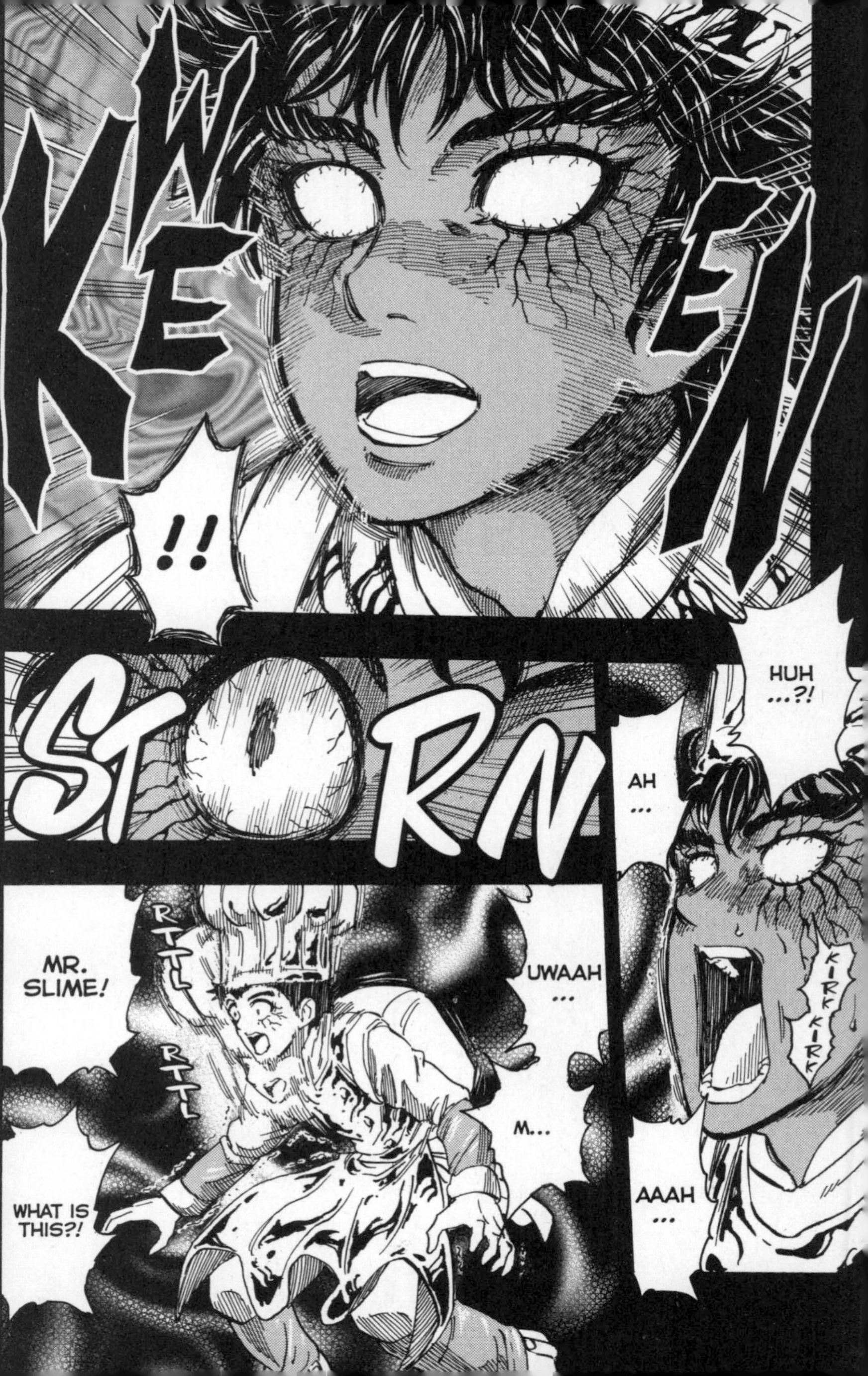
KWEEN
!!
HUH ...?!
AH ...
KIRK KIRK
AAAH ...
STORN
UWAAH ...
M...
RTTL
RTTL
MR. SLIME!
WHAT IS THIS?!

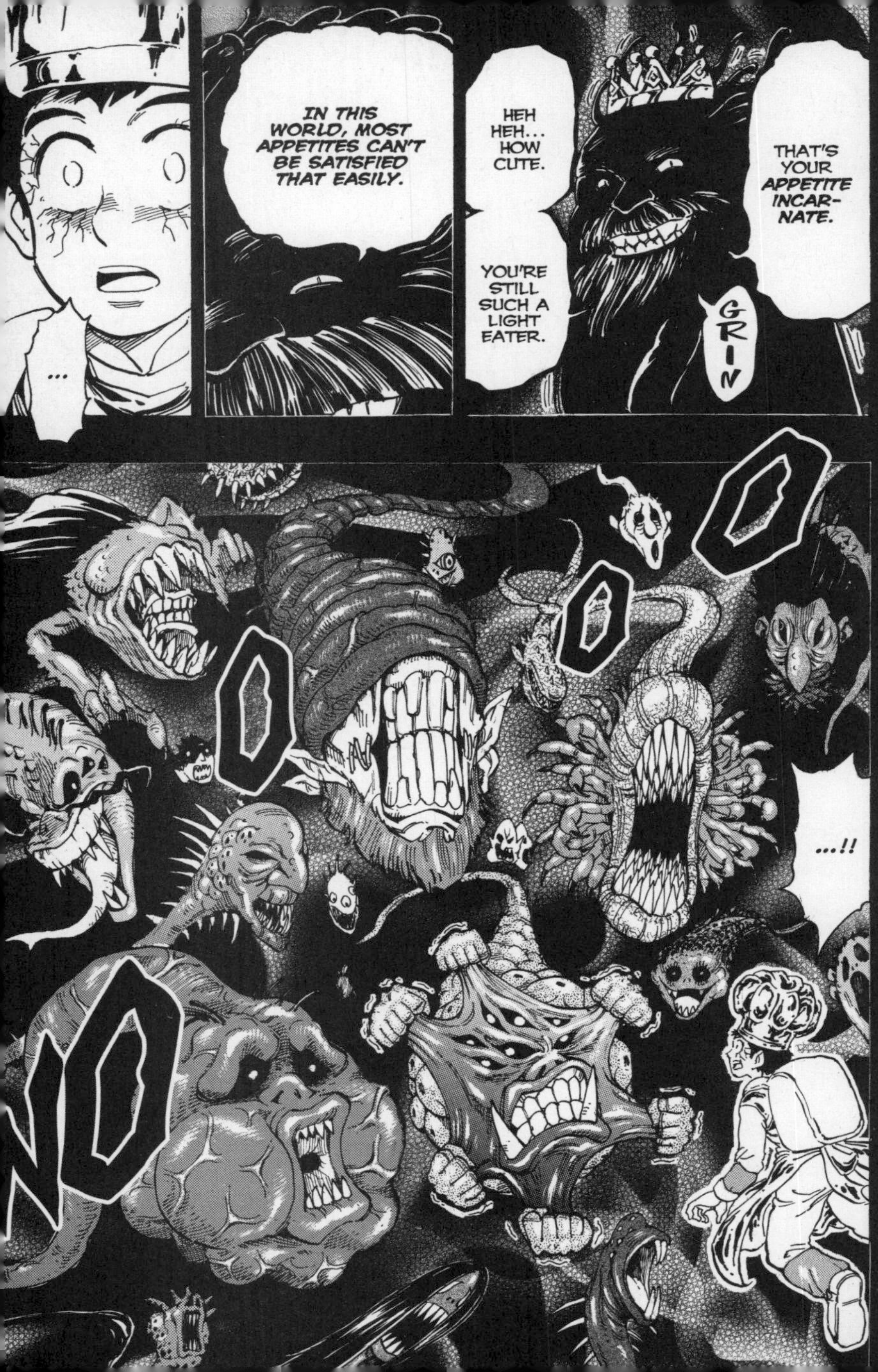
THAT'S YOUR APPETITE INCARNATE.
GRIN
HEH HEH... HOW CUTE.
YOU'RE STILL SUCH A LIGHT EATER.
IN THIS WORLD, MOST APPETITES CAN'T BE SATISFIED THAT EASILY.
...
...!!

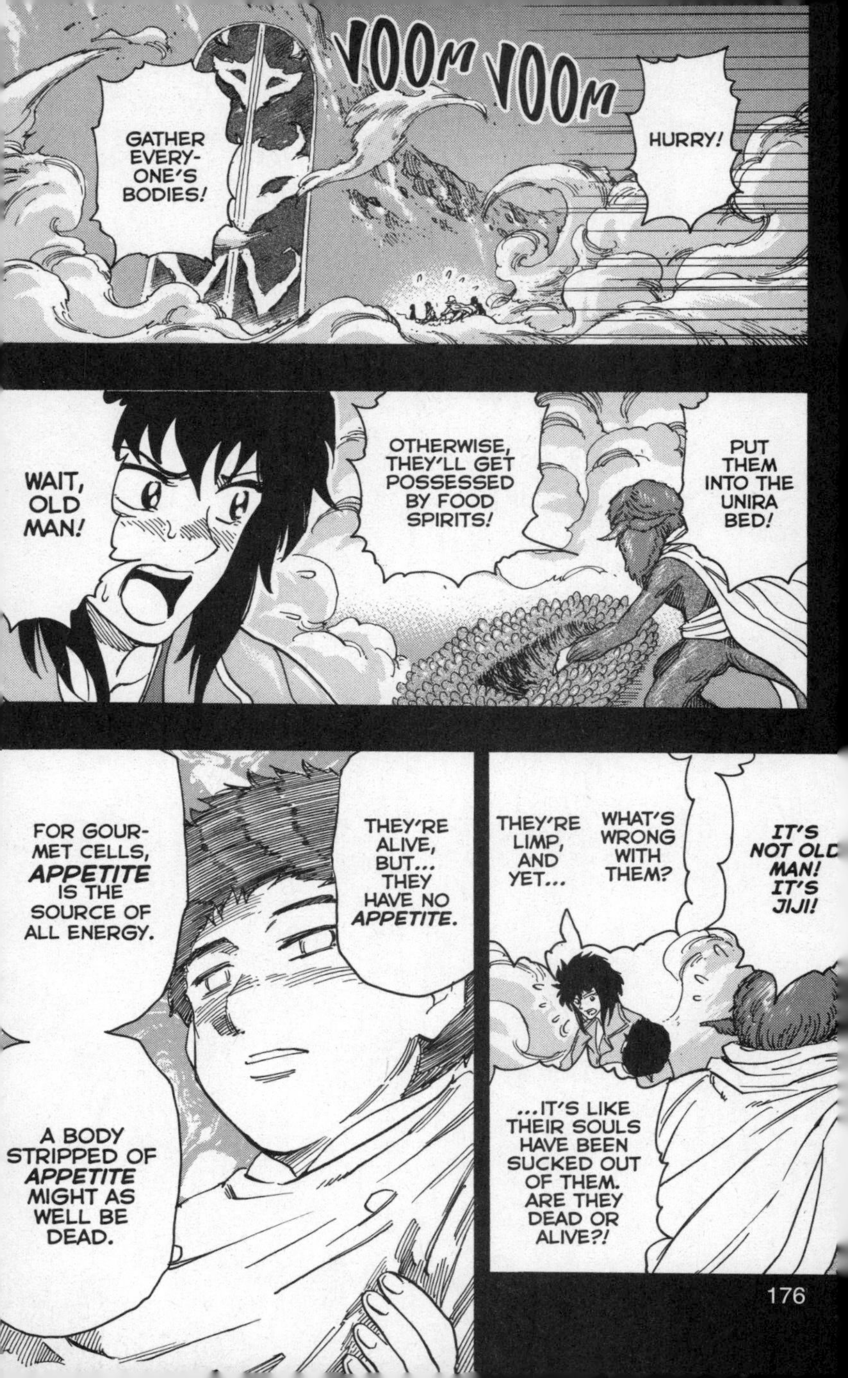

HURRY!
VOOM VOOM
GATHER EVERY-ONE'S BODIES!
PUT THEM INTO THE UNIRA BED!
OTHERWISE, THEY'LL GET POSSESSED BY FOOD SPIRITS!
WAIT, OLD MAN!
IT'S NOT OLD MAN! IT'S JIJI!
WHAT'S WRONG WITH THEM?
THEY'RE LIMP, AND YET...
...IT'S LIKE THEIR SOULS HAVE BEEN SUCKED OUT OF THEM. ARE THEY DEAD OR ALIVE?!
THEY'RE ALIVE, BUT... THEY HAVE NO APPETITE.
FOR GOUR-MET CELLS, APPETITE IS THE SOURCE OF ALL ENERGY.
A BODY STRIPPED OF APPETITE MIGHT AS WELL BE DEAD.

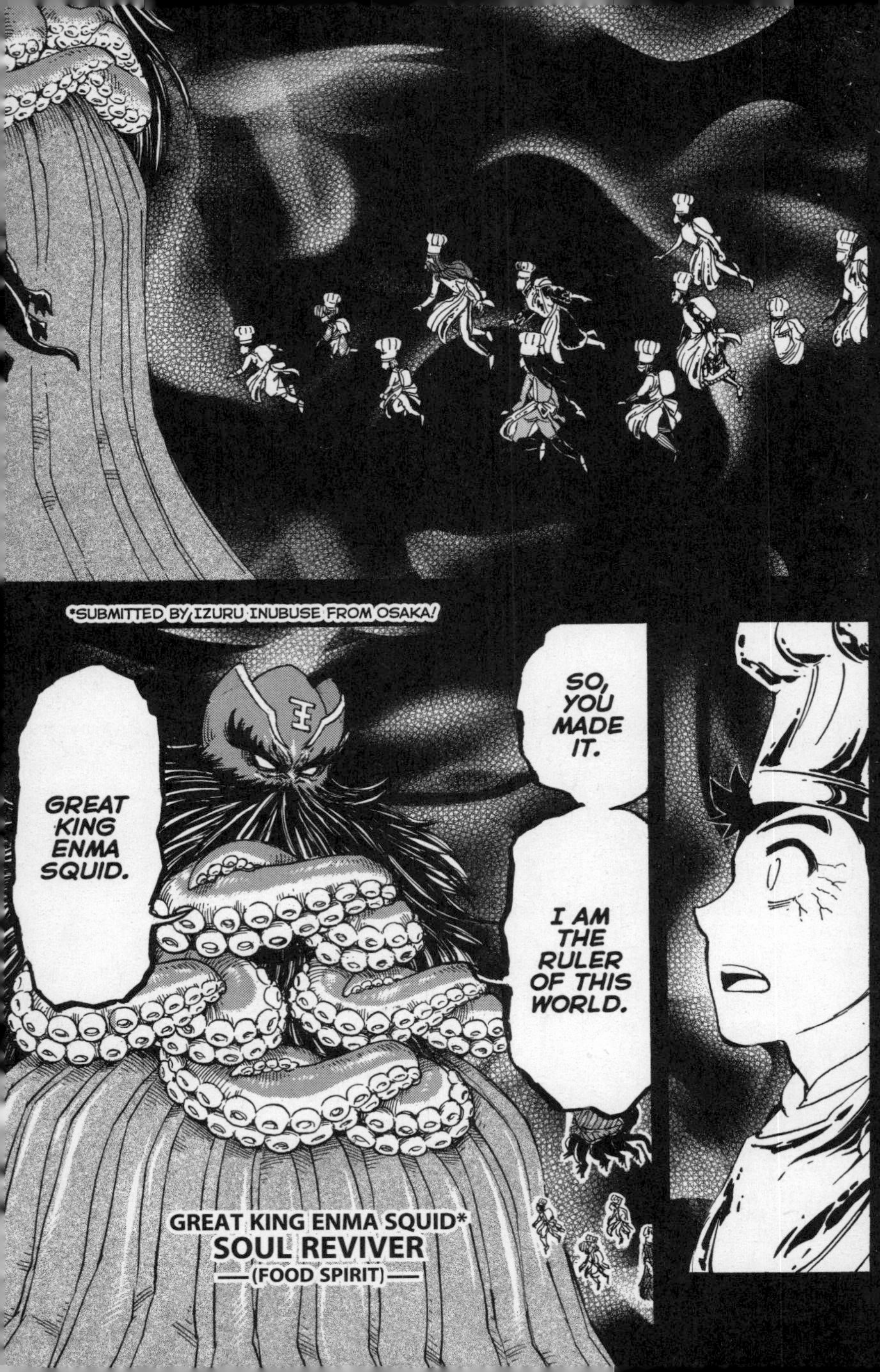
SO, YOU MADE IT.
I AM THE RULER OF THIS WORLD.
GREAT KING ENMA SQUID.
GREAT KING ENMA SQUID*
SOUL REVIVER
—(FOOD SPIRIT)—
*SUBMITTED BY IZURU INUBUSE FROM OSAKA!

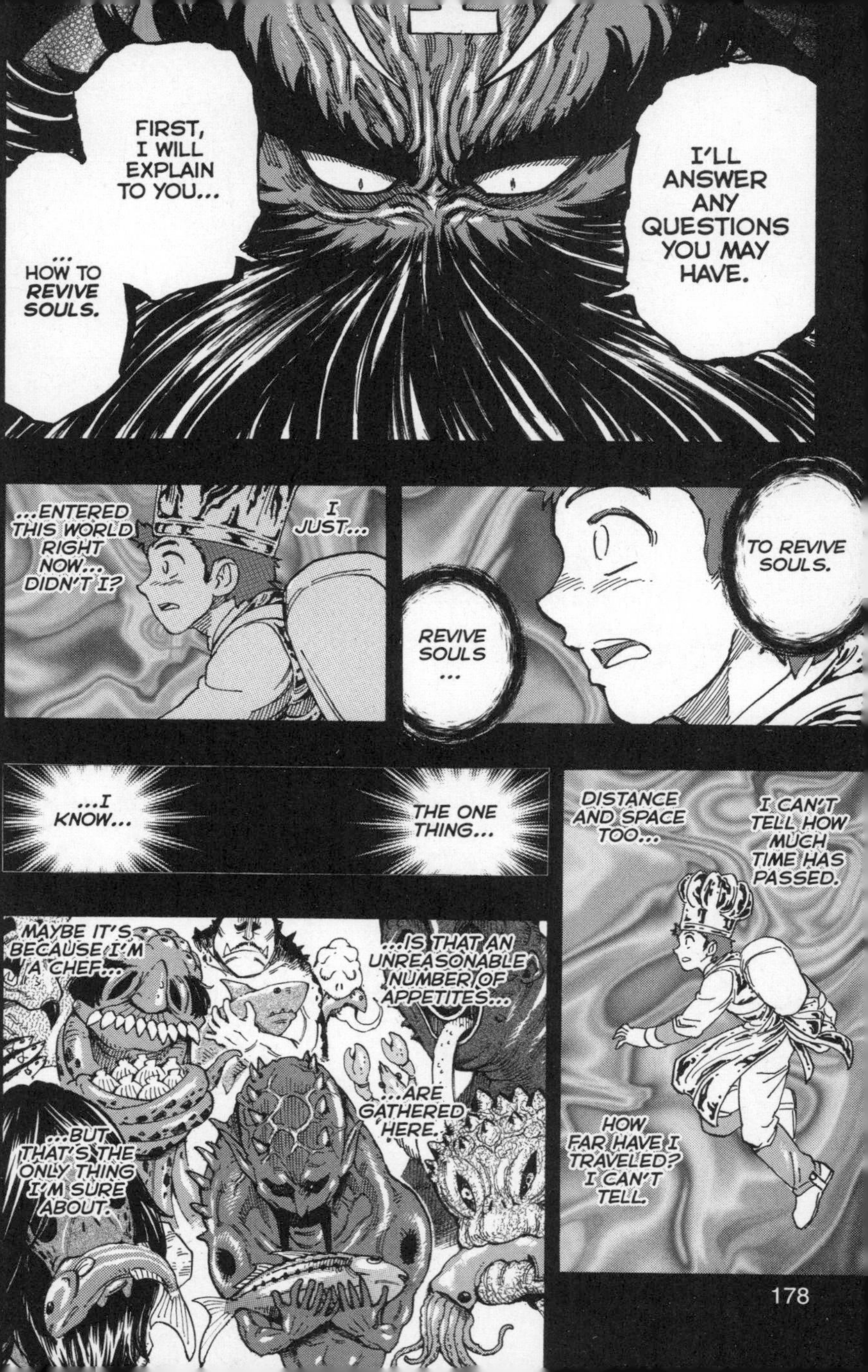

FIRST, I WILL EXPLAIN TO YOU...
...HOW TO REVIVE SOULS.
I'LL ANSWER ANY QUESTIONS YOU MAY HAVE.
TO REVIVE SOULS.
REVIVE SOULS...
I JUST...
...ENTERED THIS WORLD RIGHT NOW... DIDN'T I?
I CAN'T TELL HOW MUCH TIME HAS PASSED.
DISTANCE AND SPACE TOO...
HOW FAR HAVE I TRAVELED? I CAN'T TELL.
THE ONE THING...
...I KNOW...
...IS THAT AN UNREASONABLE NUMBER OF APPETITES...
...ARE GATHERED HERE.
MAYBE IT'S BECAUSE I'M A CHEF...
...BUT THAT'S THE ONLY THING I'M SURE ABOUT.

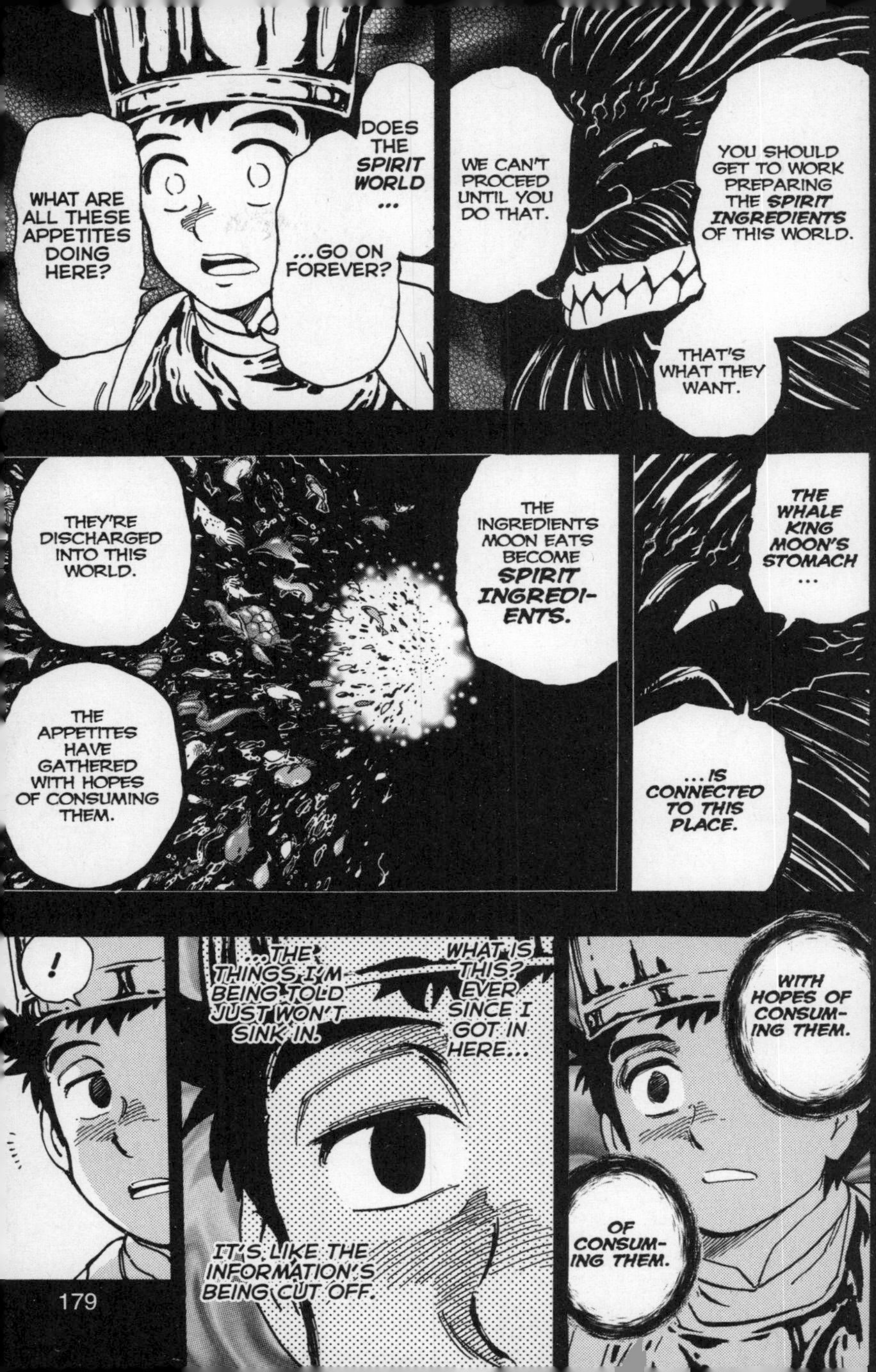
YOU SHOULD GET TO WORK PREPARING THE SPIRIT INGREDIENTS OF THIS WORLD.
WE CAN'T PROCEED UNTIL YOU DO THAT.
THAT'S WHAT THEY WANT.
DOES THE SPIRIT WORLD ...
...GO ON FOREVER?
WHAT ARE ALL THESE APPETITES DOING HERE?
THE WHALE KING MOON'S STOMACH ...
...IS CONNECTED TO THIS PLACE.
THE INGREDIENTS MOON EATS BECOME SPIRIT INGREDI-ENTS.
THEY'RE DISCHARGED INTO THIS WORLD.
THE APPETITES HAVE GATHERED WITH HOPES OF CONSUMING THEM.
WITH HOPES OF CONSUM-ING THEM.
OF CONSUM-ING THEM.
WHAT IS THIS? EVER SINCE I GOT IN HERE...
...THE THINGS I'M BEING TOLD JUST WON'T SINK IN.
IT'S LIKE THE INFORMATION'S BEING CUT OFF.
!

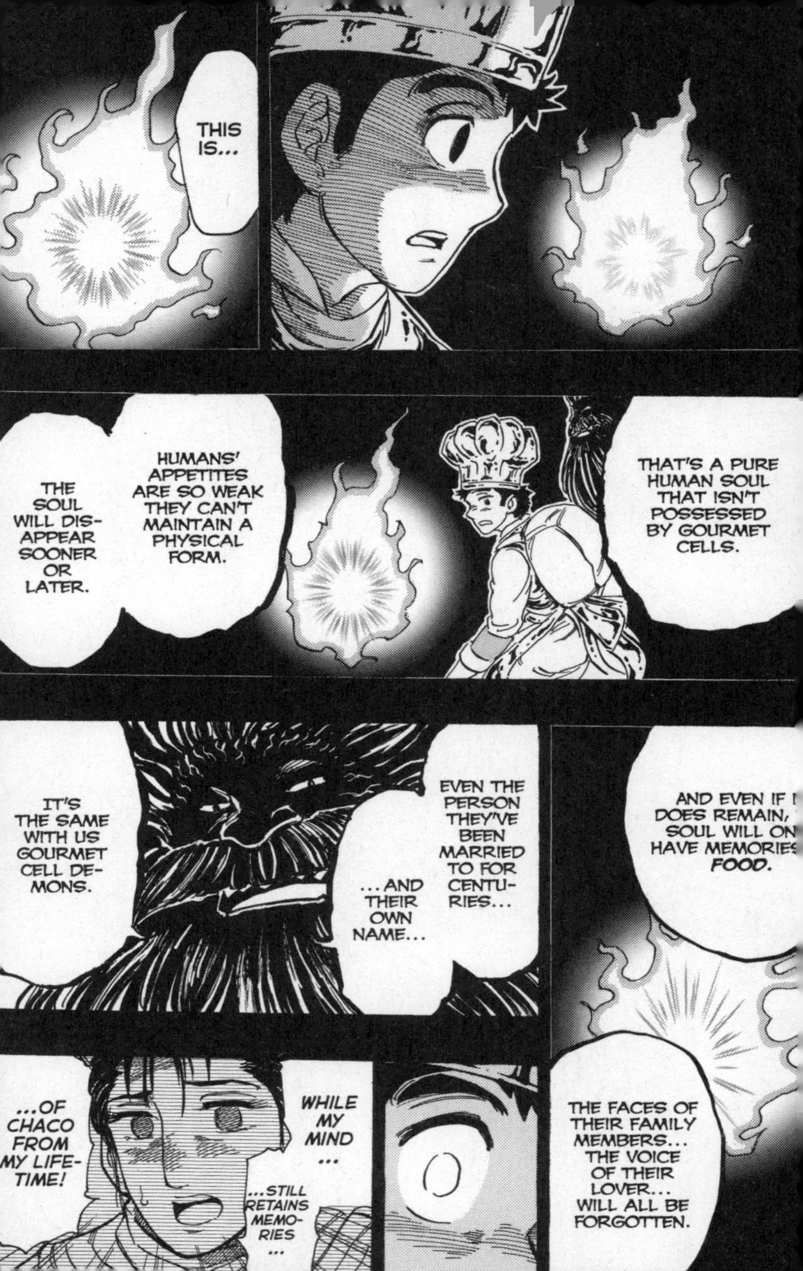
THIS IS...
THAT'S A PURE HUMAN SOUL THAT ISN'T POSSESSED BY GOURMET CELLS.
HUMANS' APPETITES ARE SO WEAK THEY CAN'T MAINTAIN A PHYSICAL FORM.
THE SOUL WILL DIS-APPEAR SOONER OR LATER.
AND EVEN IF DOES REMAIN, SOUL WILL ON HAVE MEMORIES FOOD.
THE FACES OF THEIR FAMILY MEMBERS... THE VOICE OF THEIR LOVER... WILL ALL BE FORGOTTEN.
EVEN THE PERSON THEY'VE BEEN MARRIED TO FOR CENTU-RIES...
...AND THEIR OWN NAME...
IT'S THE SAME WITH US GOURMET CELL DE-MONS.
WHILE MY MIND...
...STILL RETAINS MEMO-RIES...
...OF CHACO FROM MY LIFE-TIME!

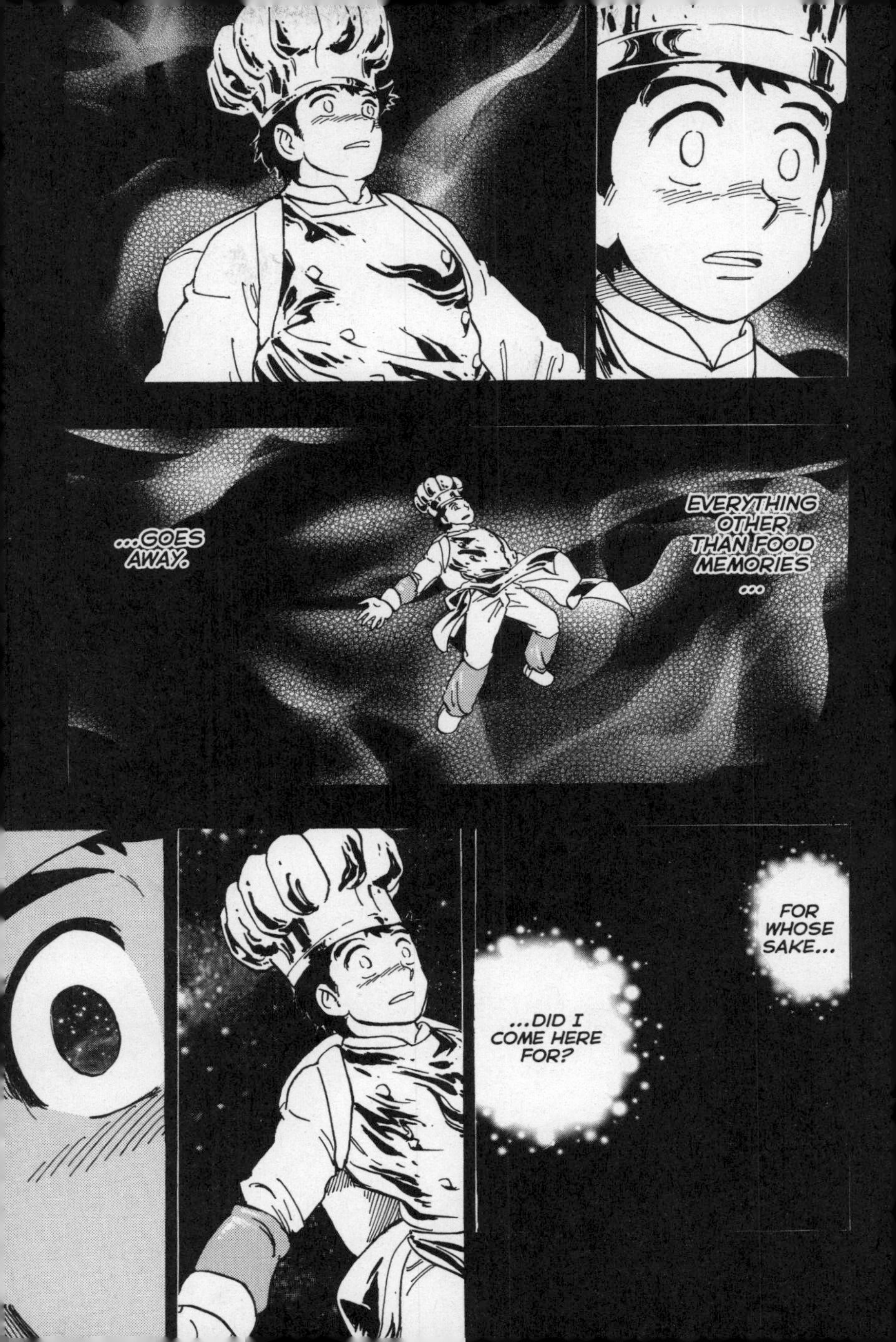
EVERYTHING OTHER THAN FOOD MEMORIES...
...GOES AWAY.
FOR WHOSE SAKE...
...DID I COME HERE FOR?

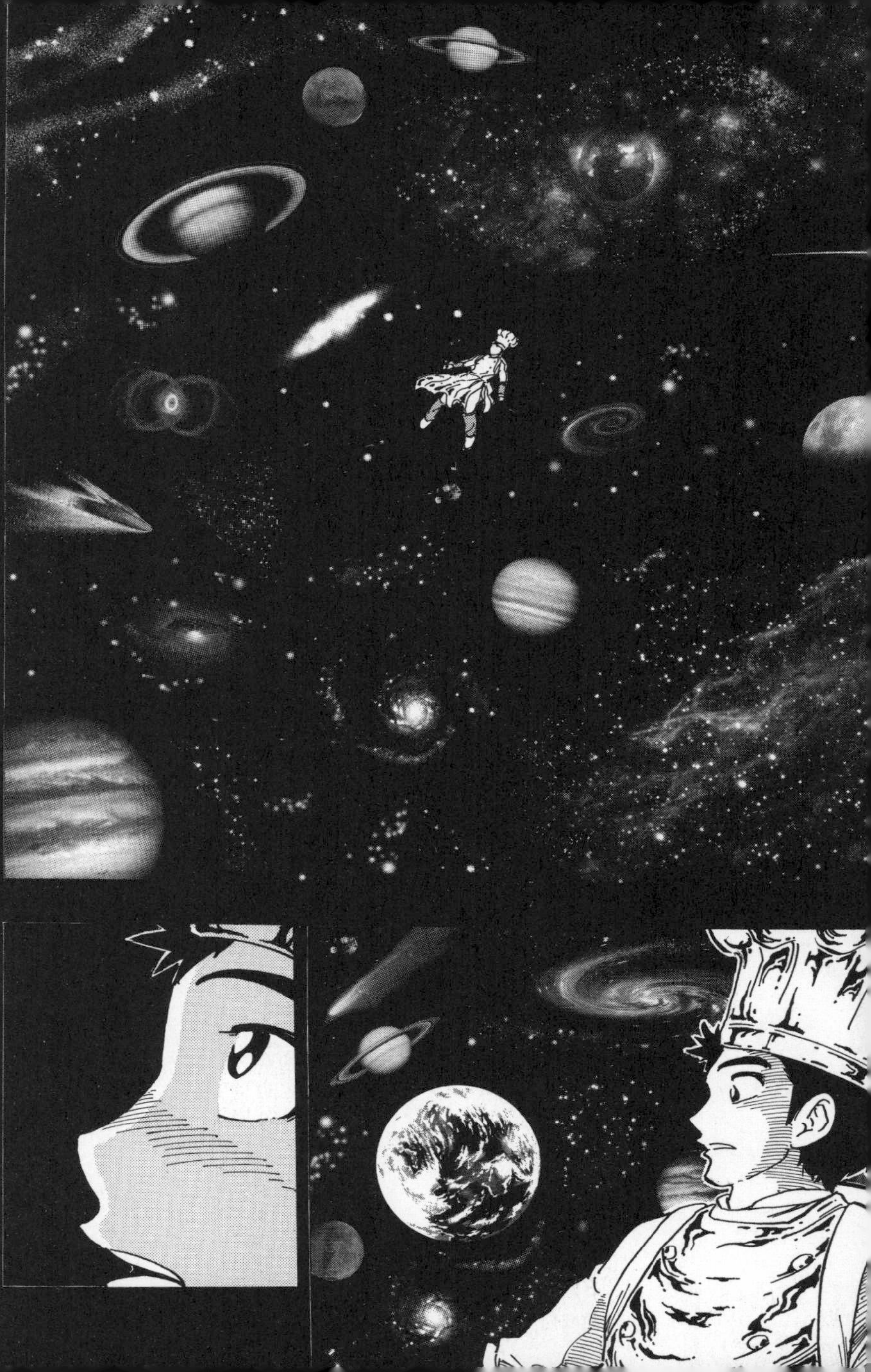

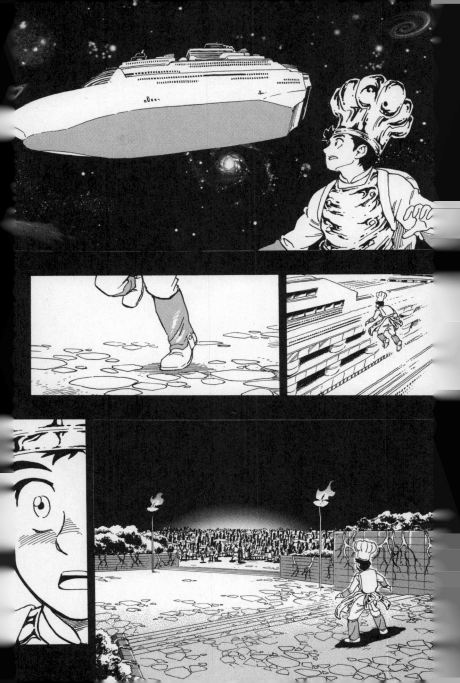

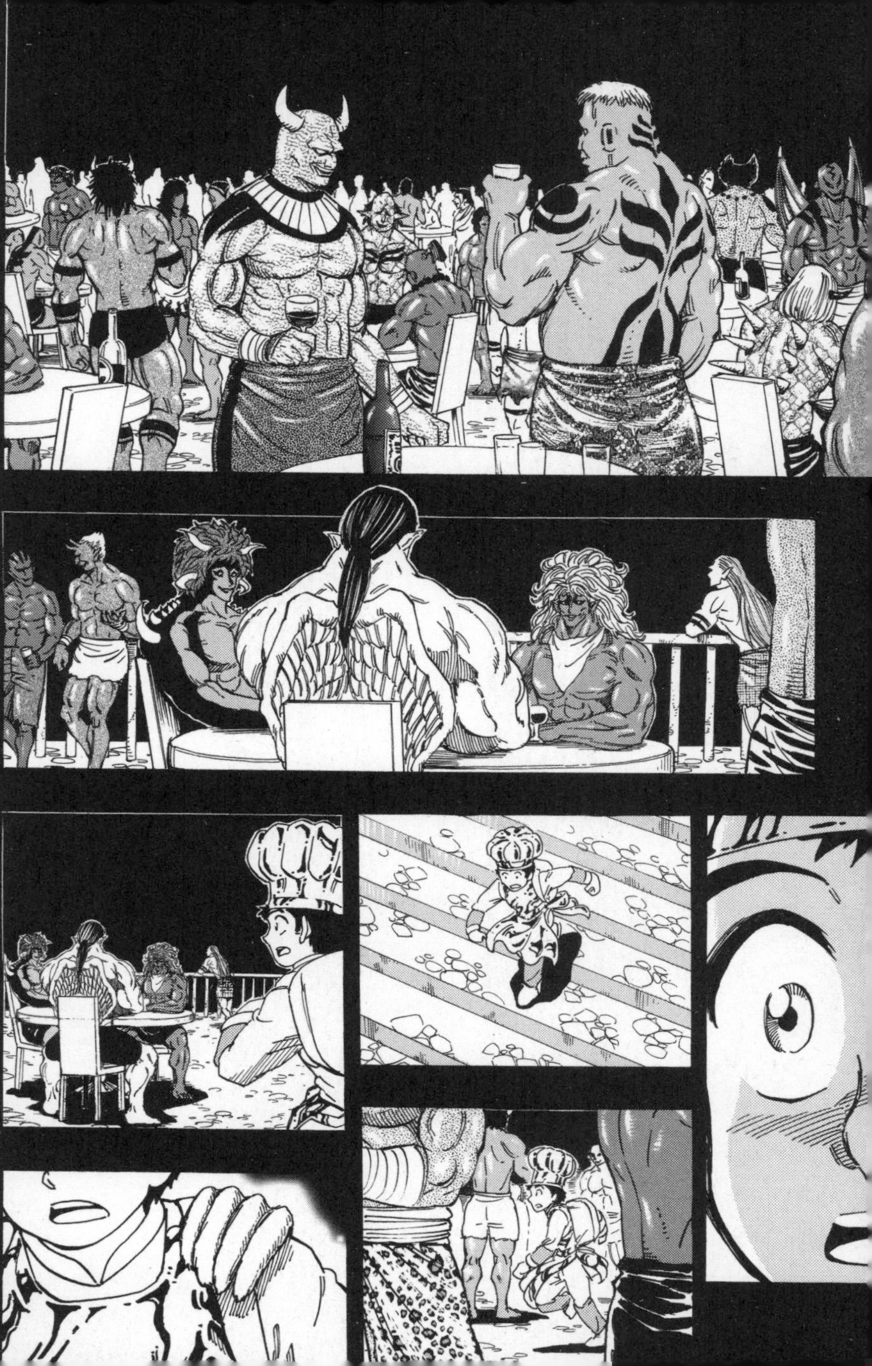

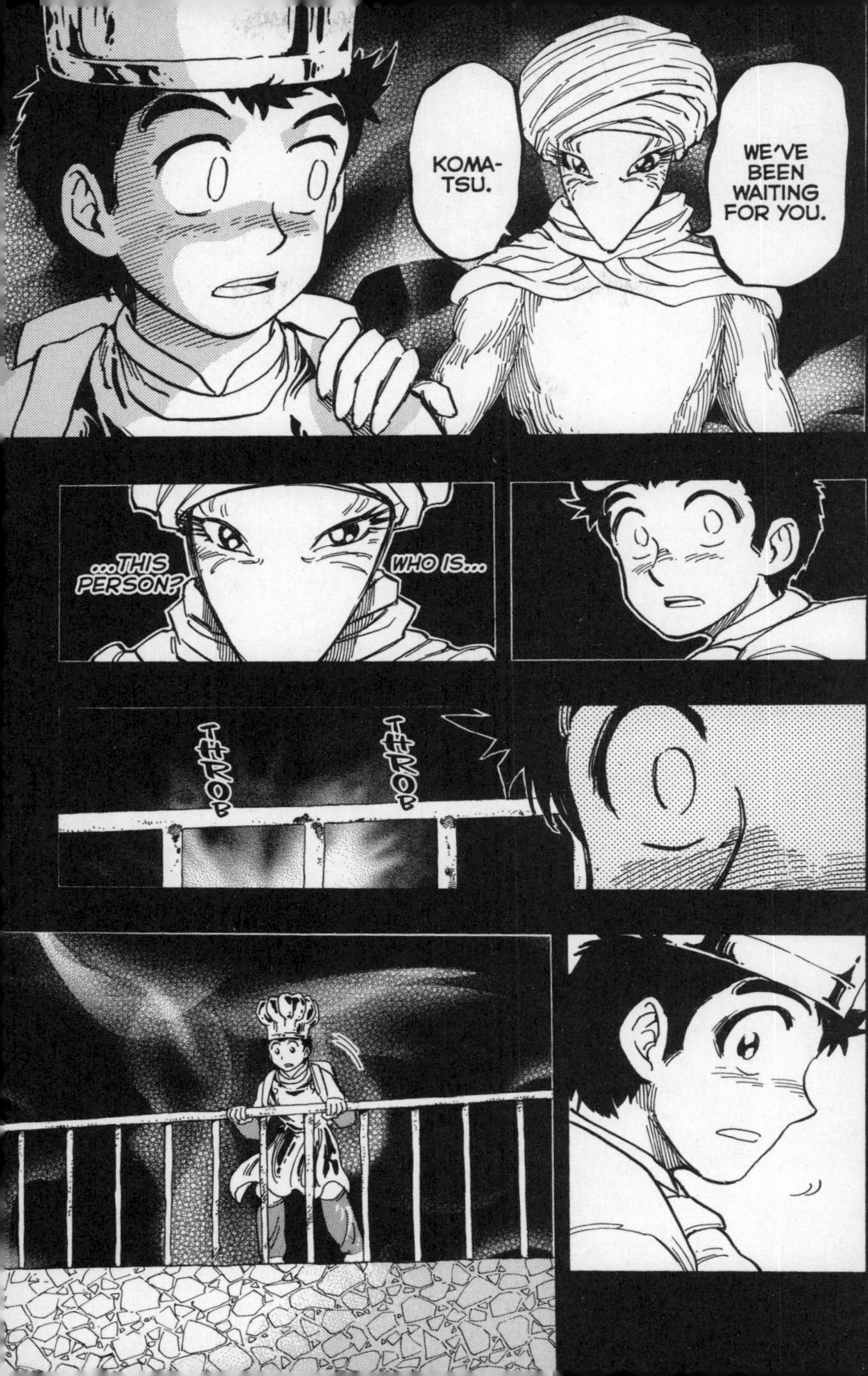
WE'VE BEEN WAITING FOR YOU.
KOMA-TSU.
WHO IS...
...THIS PERSON?
THROB
THROB

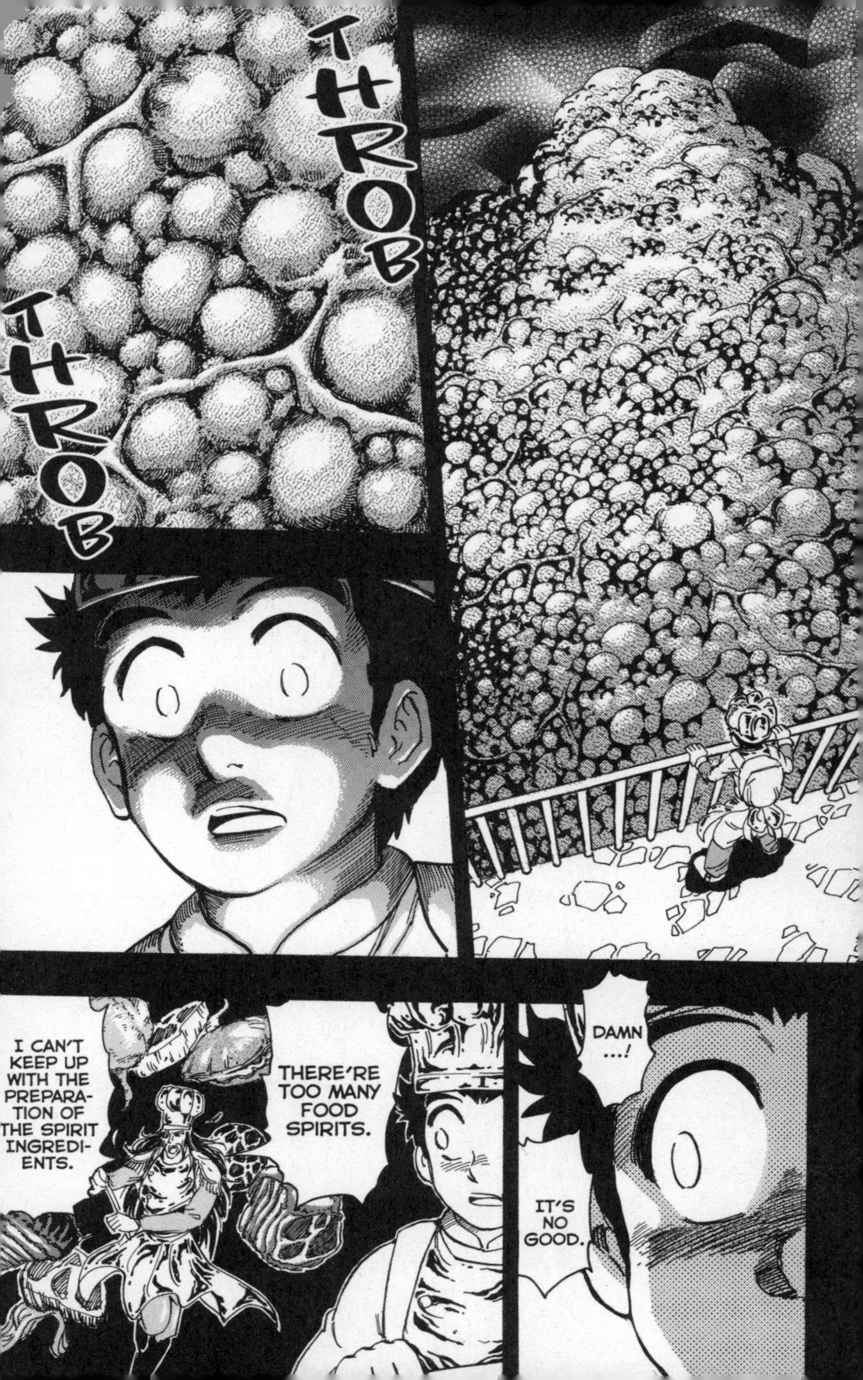
THROB
THROB
DAMN ...!
IT'S NO GOOD.
THERE'RE TOO MANY FOOD SPIRITS.
I CAN'T KEEP UP WITH THE PREPARATION OF THE SPIRIT INGREDIENTS.

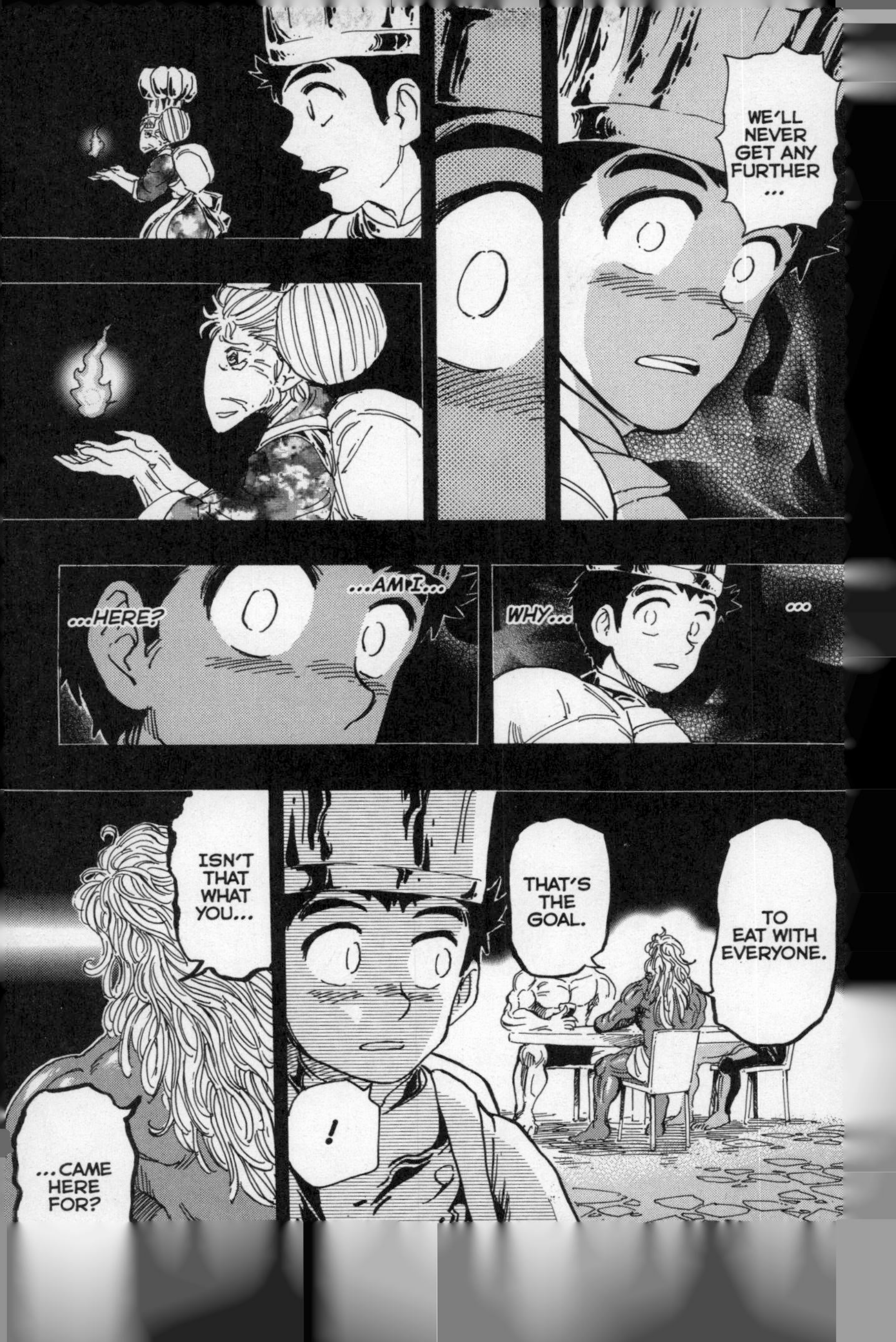
WE'LL NEVER GET ANY FURTHER ...
...
WHY...
...AM I...
...HERE?
TO EAT WITH EVERYONE.
THAT'S THE GOAL.
!
ISN'T THAT WHAT YOU...
...CAME HERE FOR?

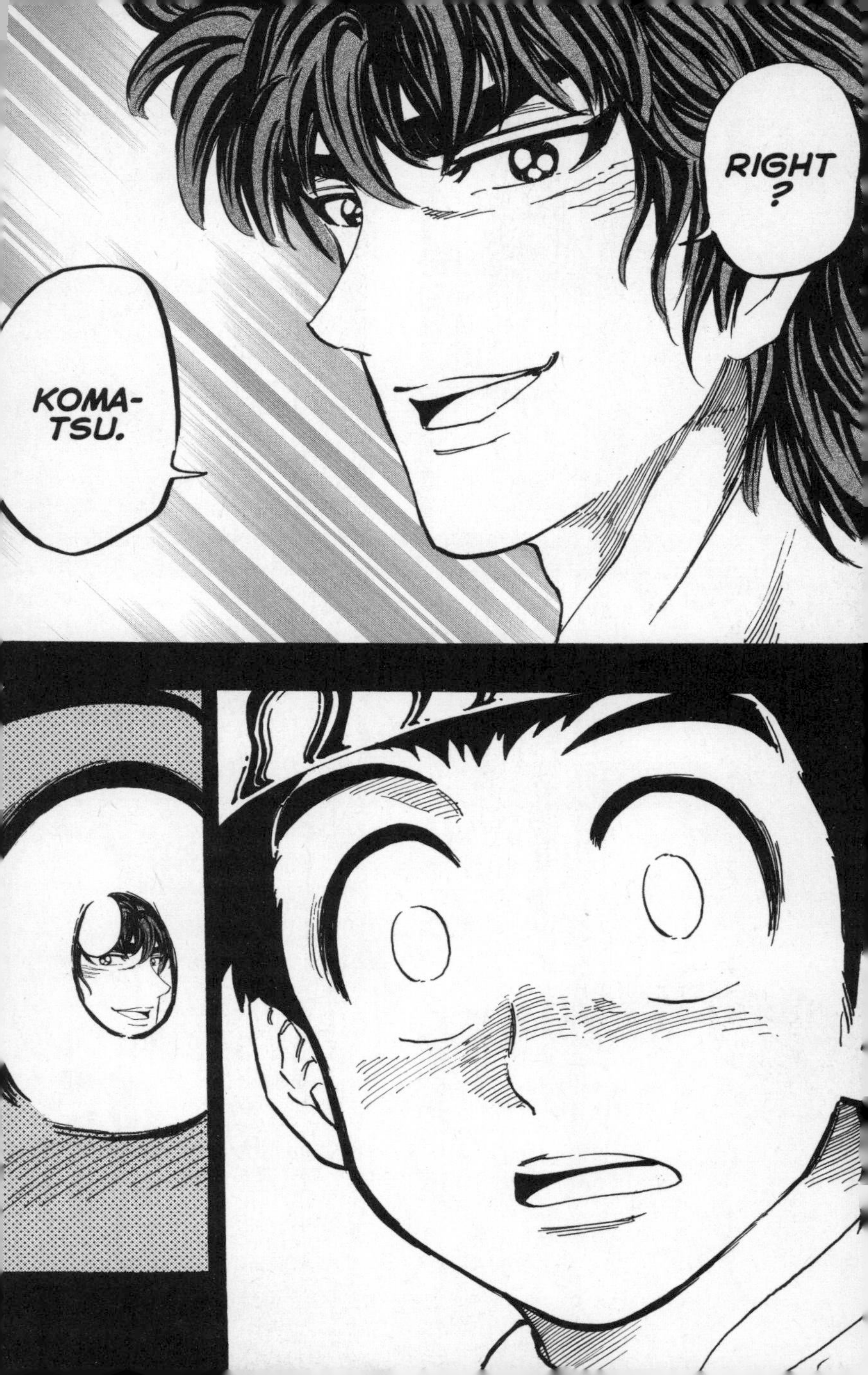
RIGHT?
KOMATSU.

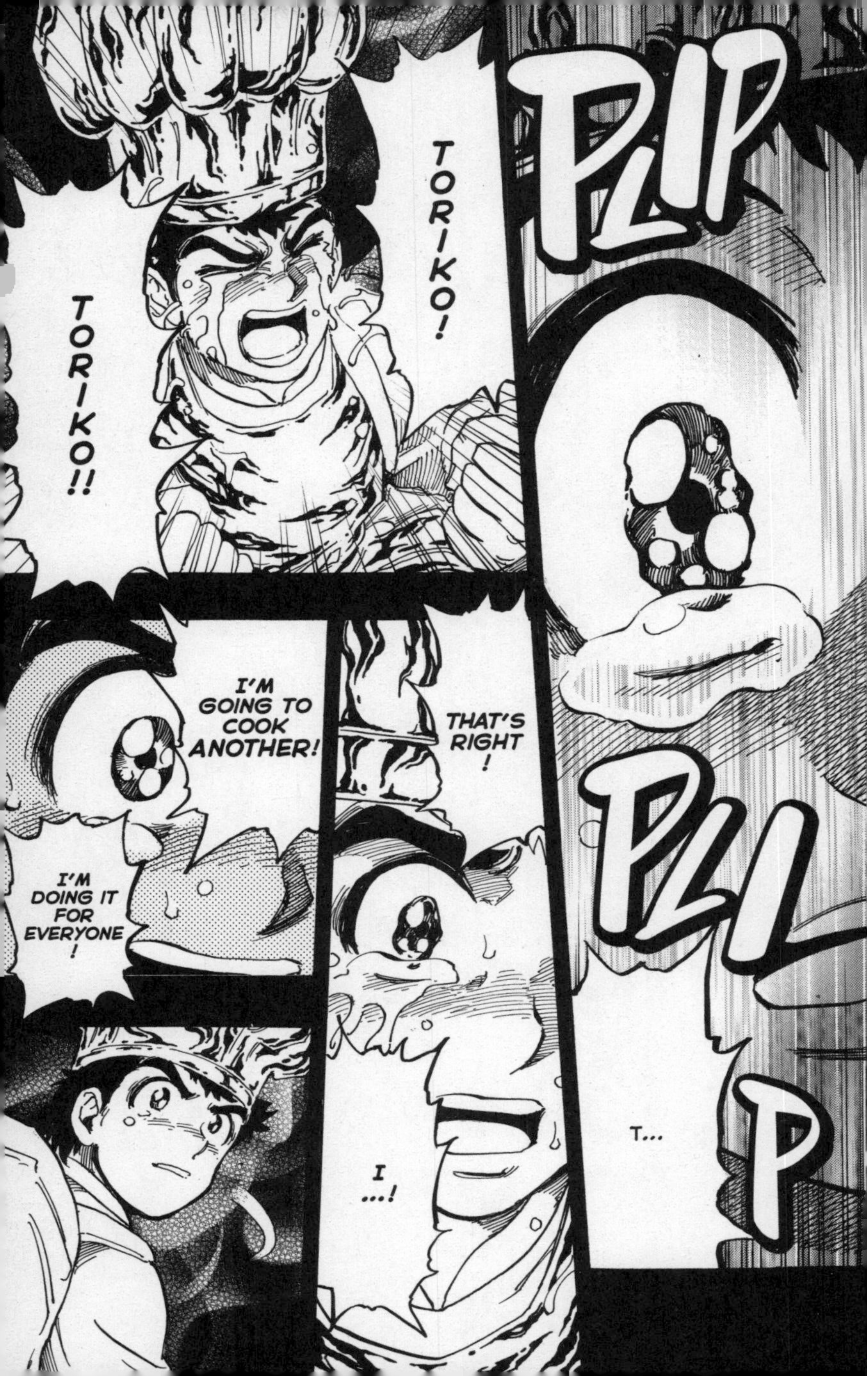
PLIP
PLIP
T...
TORIKO!
TORIKO!!
THAT'S RIGHT!
I...!
I'M GOING TO COOK ANOTHER!
I'M DOING IT FOR EVERYONE!

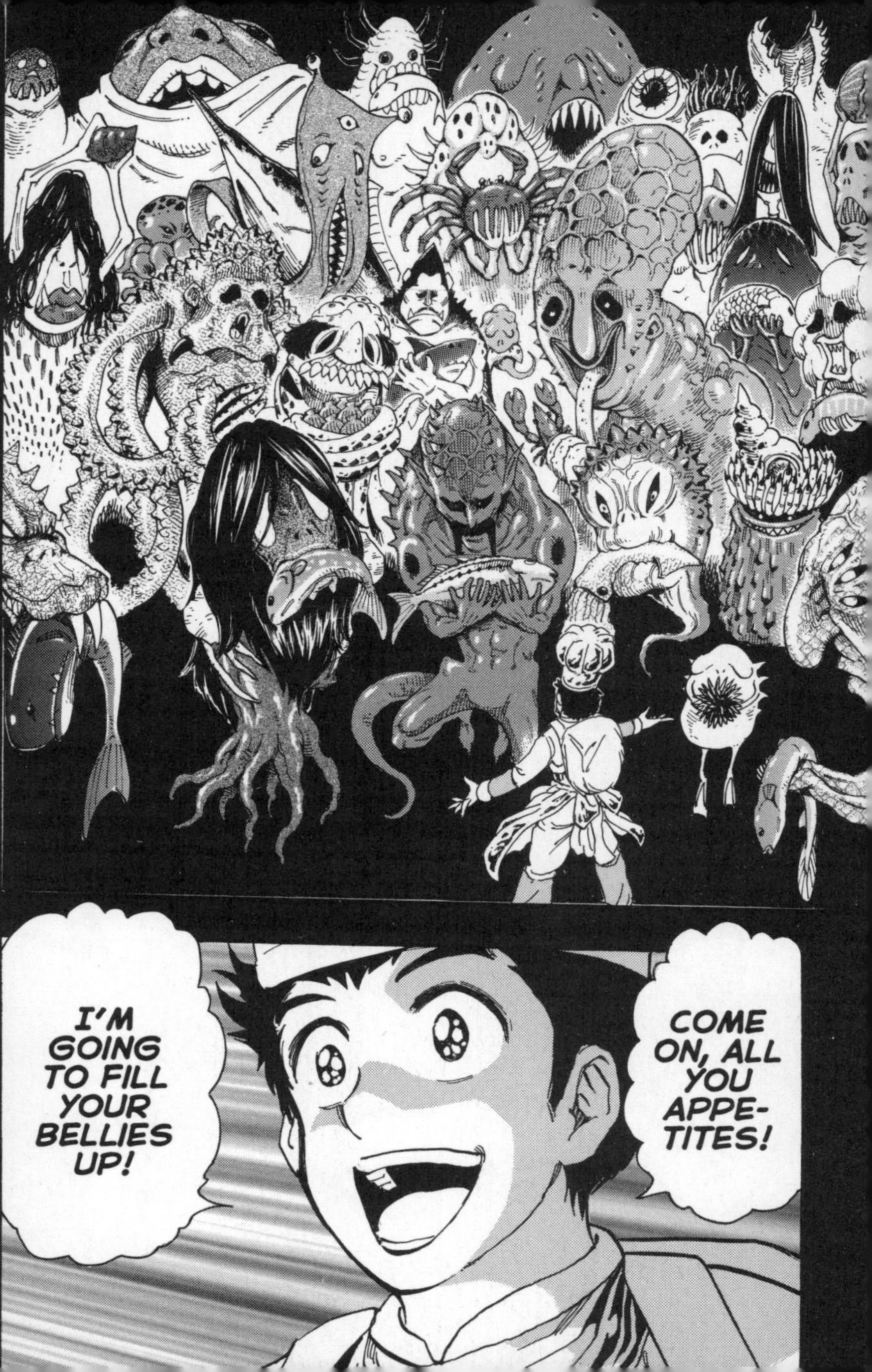
COME ON, ALL YOU APPE-TITES!
I'M GOING TO FILL YOUR BELLIES UP!

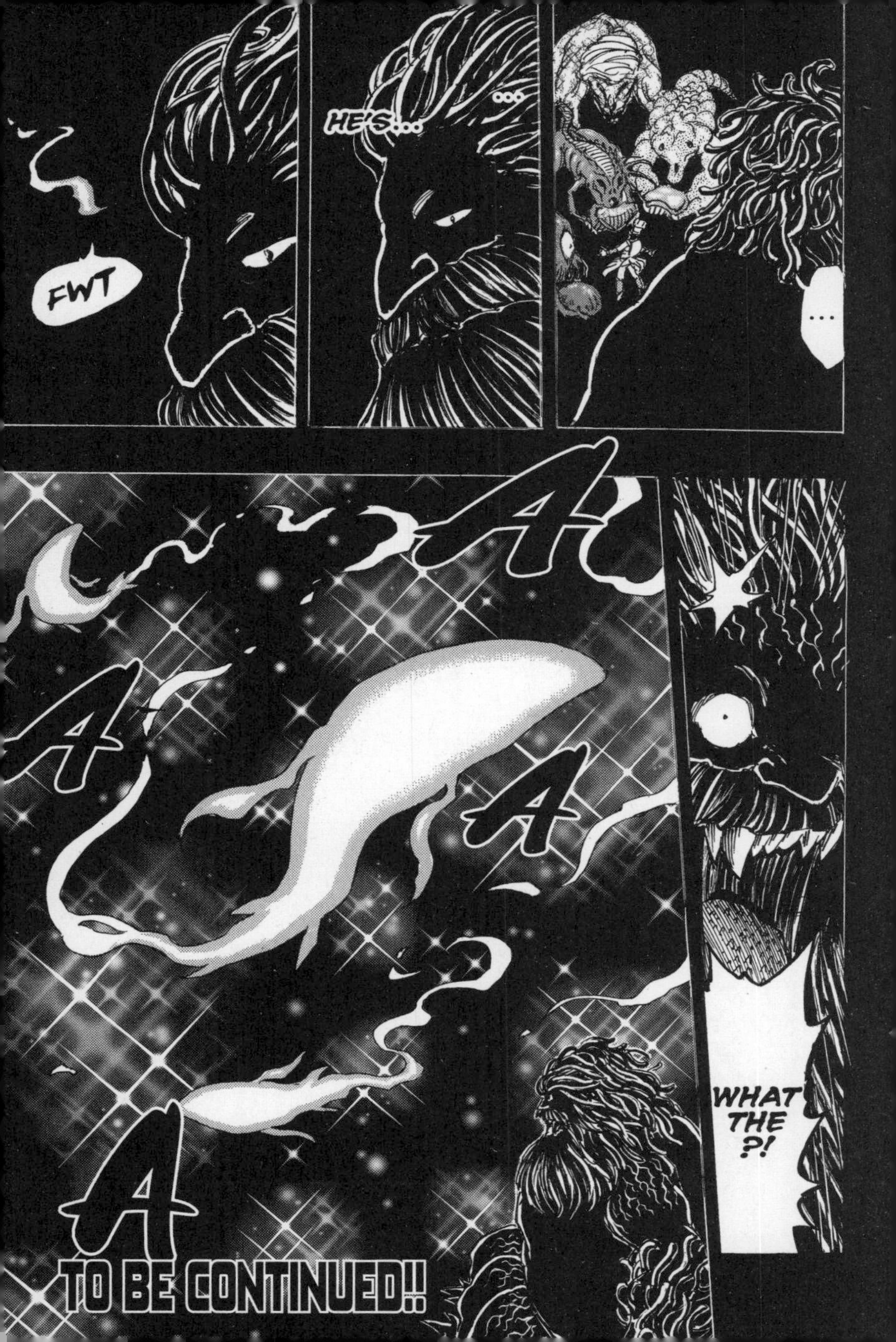
...
...
HE'S...
FWT
WHAT THE ?!
AAAAA
TO BE CONTINUED!!

TORIKO

GOURMET CHECKLIST

Vol. 380

FLYING NIMBUTT

(THE MONKEY KING'S POOP)

CAPTURE LEVEL: 1,500

HABITAT: AREA 7

SIZE: ---

HEIGHT: ---

WEIGHT: ---

PRICE: NOT EDIBLE

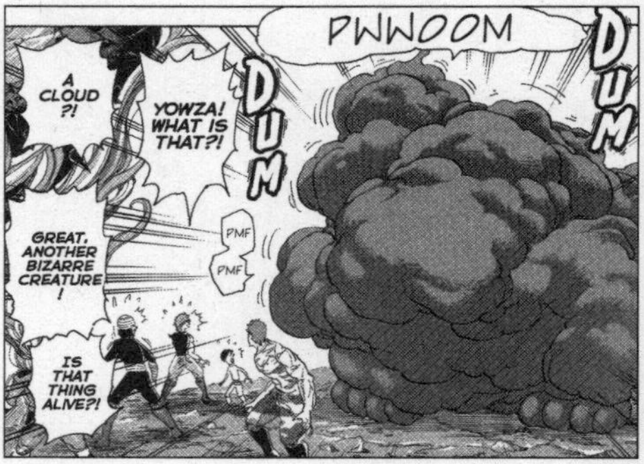
DUM
PWWOOM
DUM
YOWZA! WHAT IS THAT?!
A CLOUD ?!
PMF
PMF
GREAT, ANOTHER BIZARRE CREATURE!
IS THAT THING ALIVE?!

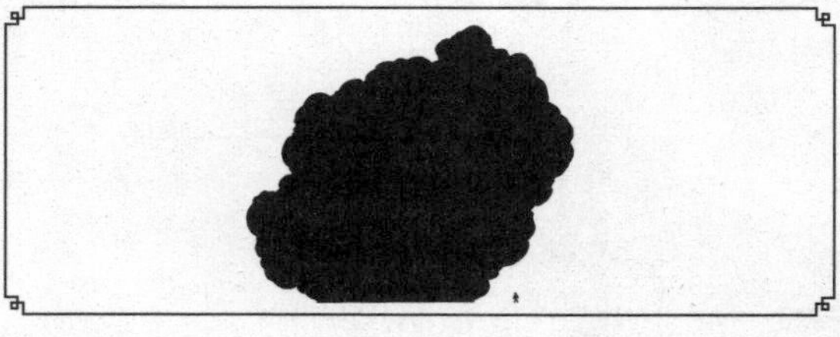

SCALE

A CAMPING MONSTER THAT CAN CARRY A LARGE AMOUNT OF PEOPLE TO SAFETY IN EVEN THE HARSHEST OF ENVIRONMENTS. IT'S A CLOUD-LIKE STOOL AND REALLY STINKY, BUT ALSO APPARENTLY INCREDIBLY FAST. SOME SAY THAT IT'S ACTUALLY THE MONKEY KING'S POOP.

CHARACTER PROFILE

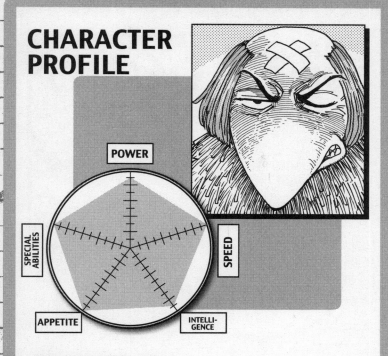

POWER

SPECIAL ABILITIES

SPEED

APPETITE

INTELLI-GENCE

CHICHI

AGE:	UNKNOWN	BIRTHDAY:	UNKNOWN
BLOOD TYPE:	UNKNOWN	SIGN:	UNKNOWN
HEIGHT:	165 CM	WEIGHT:	460 KG
EYESIGHT:	20/2	SHOE SIZE:	50 CM

SPECIAL MOVES: ● THE PREPARATION OF ACACIA'S FULL-COURSE MEAL

ONE OF THE FLAVOR HERMITS, WHO IS ALSO KNOWN AS THE BRONZE CHEF. ABOUT 500 YEARS AGO, CHICHI WAS IN "DROUGHT DORMANCY" FOR TENS OF THOUSANDS OF YEARS WHEN ICHIRYU WOKE HIM UP. EVER SINCE THEN, HE'S MISSED ICHIRYU. OF THE THREE CHEFS, HE'S ALSO THE BIGGEST PERV, BUT HIS ABILITIES AS A COOK ARE SAID TO BE THE GREATEST OF THE THREE CHEFS.

CHARACTER PROFILE

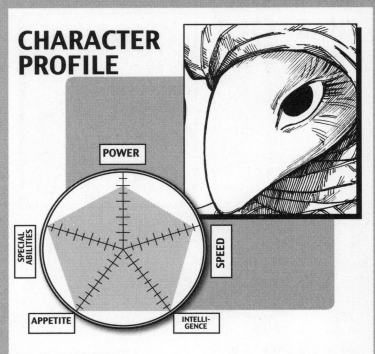

POWER
SPEED
INTELLI-GENCE
APPETITE
SPECIAL ABILITIES

KAKA

AGE:	UNKNOWN	**BIRTHDAY:**	UNKNOWN
BLOOD TYPE:	UNKNOWN	**SIGN:**	UNKNOWN
HEIGHT:	170 CM	**WEIGHT:**	380 KG
EYESIGHT:	20/1.65	**SHOE SIZE:**	47 CM

SPECIAL MOVES:
- THE PREPARATION OF ACACIA'S FULL-COURSE MEAL

ONE OF THE FLAVOR HERMITS, KAKA IS ALSO KNOWN AS THE SILVER CHEF. KAKA IS THE NITRO THAT TORIKO AND THE GANG WOKE FROM DROUGHT DORMANCY IN THE GOURMET PYRAMID. AS SLAVES OF THE BLUE NITRO, KAKA AND THE OTHERS WERE PUT IN CHARGE OF PREPARING ACACIA'S FULL-COURSE MEAL, BUT WHEN KAKA BETRAYED THEM, SHE WAS KILLED BY THE BLUE NITRO. HOWEVER, EVEN NOW HER SOUL DRIFTS THROUGH THE BACK CHANNEL.

CHARACTER PROFILE

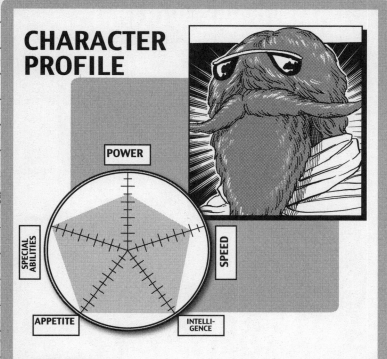

POWER

SPECIAL ABILITIES

SPEED

APPETITE

INTELLI-GENCE

JIJI

AGE: UNKNOWN		**BIRTHDAY:** UNKNOWN	
BLOOD TYPE: UNKNOWN		**SIGN:** UNKNOWN	
HEIGHT: 168 CM		**WEIGHT:** 350 KG	
EYESIGHT: 20/3		**SHOE SIZE:** 45 CM	

SPECIAL MOVES: ● THE PREPARATION OF ACACIA'S FULL-COURSE MEAL

THE GOLDEN CHEF. THE REASON WHY THE FLAVOR HERMITS BETRAYED THE BLUE NITRO WAS BECAUSE THEY LEARNED THAT THE BLUE NITRO'S GOAL WAS TO RESURRECT ACACIA'S GOURMET CELL DEMON, NEO. IN ORDER TO STOP THAT FROM HAPPENING, THEY ARE NOW INITIATING THE PREPARATION AND SKILLS NEEDED TO PREPARE ACACIA'S FULL-COURSE MEAL FOR TORIKO.

COMING NEXT VOLUME

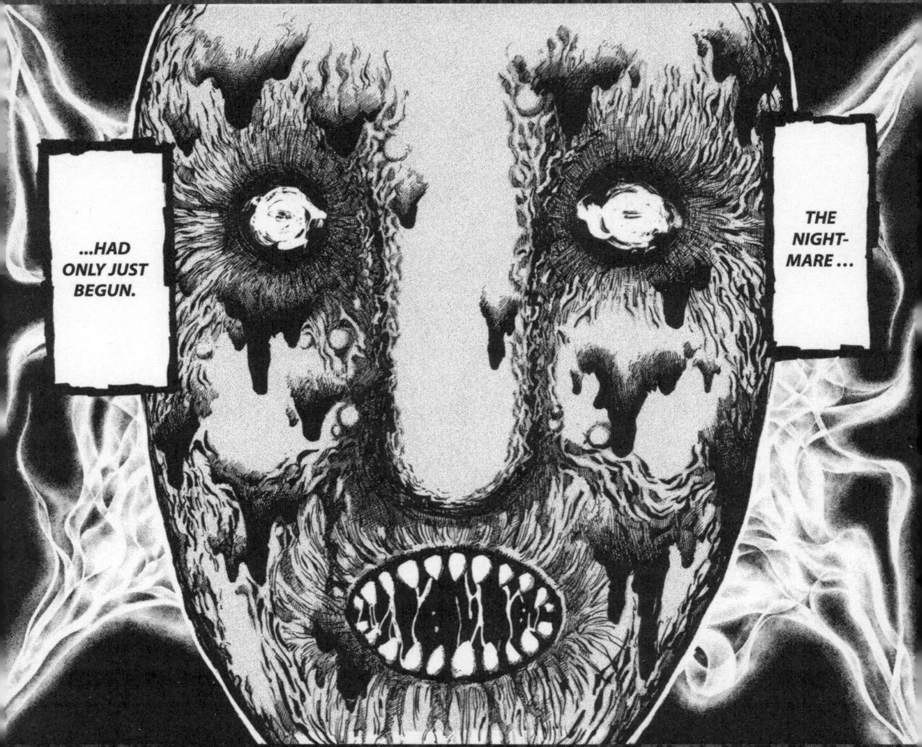
THE NIGHT-MARE ...
...HAD ONLY JUST BEGUN.

THE CREATURE KNOWN AS NEO!!

The Gourmet Eclipse is quickly approaching and time is of the essence. But the Back Channel is not a forgiving place. The darkness alone is enough to devour any unprepared soul—appetite and all! Will Komatsu be able to find Another and prepare it in time?! Meanwhile, the reemergence of God is at hand, and Toriko and Starjun gear up for the fight of their lives against the almighty Battle Wolf. But they are not alone! One of Neo's spawn is prepared to challenge them for a taste of the mysterious king of ingredients, God, too!!

AVAILABLE AUGUST 2017!

A SUPERNATURAL SAGA OF A 13-YEAR-OLD BY DAY, AND A LEADER OF A DEMON CLAN BY NIGHT

NURA: RISE OF THE YOKAI CLAN

STORY AND ART BY
HIROSHI SHIIBASHI

While the day belongs to humans, the night belongs to yokai, supernatural creatures that thrive on human fear. Caught between these worlds is Rikuo Nura. He's three-quarters human, but his grandfather is none other than Nurarihyon, the supreme commander of the Nura clan, a powerful yokai consortium. So, Rikuo is an ordinary teenager three quarters of the time, until his yokai blood awakens. Then Rikuo transforms into the future leader of the Nura clan, leading a hundred demons.

You're Reading in the Wrong Direction!!

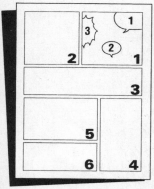

Whoops! Guess what? You're starting at the wrong end of the comic!

...It's true! In keeping with the original Japanese format, **Toriko** is meant to be read from right to left, starting in the upper-right corner.

Unlike English, which is read from left to right, Japanese is read from right to left, meaning that action, sound effects and word-balloon order are completely reversed... something which can make readers unfamiliar with Japanese feel pretty backwards themselves. For this reason, manga or Japanese comics published in the U.S. in English have sometimes been published "flopped"— that is, printed in exact reverse order, as though seen from the other side of a mirror.

By flopping pages, U.S. publishers can avoid confusing readers, but the compromise is not without its downside. For one thing, a character in a flopped manga series who once wore in the original Japanese version a T-shirt emblazoned with "M A Y" (as in "the merry month of") now wears one which reads "Y A M"! Additionally, many manga creators in Japan are themselves unhappy with the process, as some feel the mirror-imaging of their art skews their original intentions.

We are proud to bring you Mitsutoshi Shimabukuro's **Toriko** in the original unflopped format. For now, though, turn to the other side of the book and let the adventure begin...!

—Editor

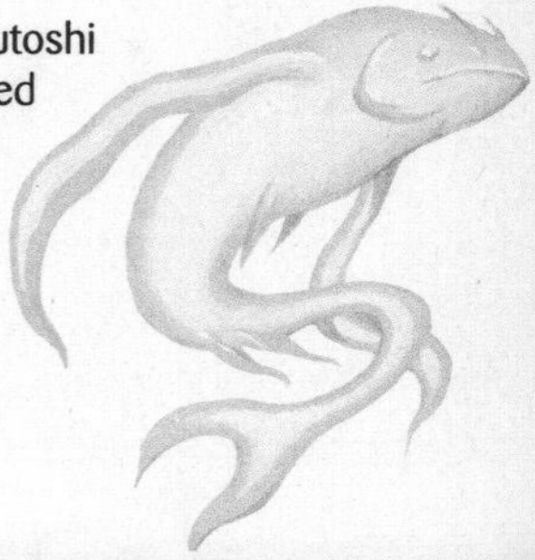